"San Francisco, San Mateo, Marin and Sonoma 2006" gives a snapshot of these coastal counties and their cities at a time of rapid change.

School Rankings, including the latest academic rankings (STAR test) for public schools, college placements by high school, SAT scores, a directory of private schools — they are all inside.

Community profiles. Home prices, rents. Descriptions of cities, towns and neighborhoods.

The perfect guide for parents or people shopping for homes or apartments or just interested in finding out more about their schools and their neighborhoods and communities.

Local weather. Directory of local colleges and universities.

Hospital services and medical care. Directory of hospitals.

Child Care. Directory of infant-care and day-care centers. Most popular names for local babies.

Places to visit, things to do.

Vital statistics. Population, income and education by town. Republicans and Democrats. Presidential votes. Crime, history, trivia and much more.

McCormack's Guides, edited by former newspaper reporters and editors, was established in 1984 and publishes the most popular general-interest guides to California counties. For a list of our other guides and an order form, see the last page. Or visit: www.mccormacks.com

Publisher and editor Don McCormack formed McCormack's Guides in 1984 to publish annual guides to California counties. A graduate of the University of California-Berkeley, McCormack joined the Contra Costa Times in 1969 and covered police, schools, politics, planning, courts and government. Later with the Richmond Independent and Berkeley Gazette, he worked as a reporter, then editor and columnist.

Maps illustrator Louis Liu attended Los Medanos College and the Academy of Art College in San Francisco, where he majored in illustration.

Many thanks to the people who write, edit, layout and help publish McCormack's Guides: Martina Bailey, Paul Fletcher, Mary Jennings, Meghan McCormack, John VanLandingham

DISCLAIMER

Although facts and statements in this book have been checked and rechecked, mistakes — typographical and otherwise — may have occurred. Census data, test scores and other information have been updated to the time of publication using cost-of-living figures, mathematical averaging and other tools, which by their nature must be considered estimates. This book was written to entertain and inform. The authors, the editors and the publisher shall have no liability or responsibility for damages or alleged damages arising out of information contained in the "San Francisco, San Mateo, Marin & Sonoma 2006" edition of McCormack's Guides.

Indexed   ISBN 1-929365-76-4

SAN FRANCISCO
SAN MATEO
MARIN
SONOMA 2006

Edited by Dc

3211 Elmquist Court, Martinez, CA 94553
Phone: (800) 222-3602 & Fax: (925) 228-7223
bookinfo@mccormacks.com • www.mccormacks.com

Contents

Chapter **1**   **San Francisco at a Glance**   **8**
Population, income, vital statistics, history,
baby names, trends, politics.

Chapter **2**   **San Francisco Neighborhoods**   **22**
Descriptions of neighborhoods. Home prices.

Chapter **3**   **San Mateo County at a Glance**   **59**
Population, income, vital statistics, history.
politics, trends, baby names.

Chapter **4**   **San Mateo City Profiles**   **73**
Descriptions of towns and cities. Home prices.

Chapter **5**   **Marin County at a Glance**   **129**
Population, income, vital statistics, history.

Chapter **6**   **Marin City Profiles**   **141**
Descriptions of towns and cities. Home prices.

Chapter **7**   **Sonoma County at a Glance**   **178**
Population, income, vital statistics, history.

Chapter **8**   **Sonoma City Profiles**   **189**
Descriptions of towns and cities. Home prices.

Chapter **9a**   **State School Rankings**   **220**
How local schools rank statewide.

Chapter **9b**   **State 1 to 10 Rankings**   **245**
How Cal. Dept. of Ed. ranks schools academically.

Chapter **10**   **How Public Schools Work**   **257**
SAT scores, college attendance rates by high
school. Directory of school districts.

Chapter **11**   **Private Schools**   **286**
What to expect. Directory of private schools.

Chapter **12** **Infant-Baby Care**   301
Directory of infant centers.

Chapter **13** **Day Care**   307
Directory of daycare centers.

Chapter **14** **Hospitals & Health Care**   327
Overview of local medical care, insurance.
Directory of Hospitals.

Chapter **15** **Fun & Games**   340
Museums, parks, hiking, outdoor sights,
arts, entertainment.

Chapter **16** **Newcomer's Guide**   346
Where to get a driver's license. Where to
register to vote. Grocery prices. Home prices.

Chapter **17** **Rental Housing**   353
Apartments, hotels, residency hotels, homes.

Chapter **18** **New Housing**   359
Developments in San Francisco, San Mateo,
Marin, Sonoma and other nearby counties.

Chapter **19** **Colleges & Job Training**   364
College directory. Job training. Jobless rate.

Chapter **20** **Commuting**   367
Driving miles, costs. Commuting tactics.
Carpooling, mass transit, alternate routes.

Chapter **21** **Weather**   373
How weather works. Rainfall. Temperatures.

Chapter **22** **Crime**   380
Homicides and crime rates by city. Putting
numbers into perspective.

On the Cover:
*Genencor, one of the
major employers of
Silicon Valley.*

Chapter 1

San Francisco at a Glance

ONE OF THE MOST BEAUTIFUL CITIES on the planet, San Francisco is located atop a peninsula and measures east to west and north to south roughly eight miles and covers 48 square miles, about twice the size of Manhattan. Residents, who number 799,263, call the place "The City."

To the west of San Francisco is the Pacific, to the east the Bay, on many a day filled with billowing sails, and to the north the Golden Gate, the entrance to San Francisco Bay. Hills run up and down San Francisco. Mt. Davidson, the highest ,rises to 927 feet. Delightful vistas. Golden sunrises and sunsets. In summer, the fog pours through the Golden Gate and cascades over the hills and into valleys — damp and cold (many hate it) but entrancing to behold.

You can walk San Francisco, from Bay to Pacific, in about two hours. Every year, in a race known as the Bay-To-Breakers, 50,000 people, many in zany costumes, run the east-west route, many in less than an hour, and the fastest in about 35 minutes.

To an extent that often surprises newcomers, San Francisco is an intimate city. Politicians often descend from old-line political families or move quickly from neighborhood leaders to city leaders. The electorate in important races numbers only about 200,000 and in minor races less than 25,000.

San Francisco is not the most populous city in Northern California. That honor goes to San Jose, 944,857 residents. But in history, tradition, allure and power to cast spells, it is, unmistakably, The City, one of the magic places of the world. In politics, social verve and leadership, San Francisco sets the tone for Northern California and often much of the state.

Commute

Compared to other counties, San Francisco has probably the best commute in the Bay Area. Eight miles, after all, is eight miles, and no bridges to cross.

The MUNI, as the local light rail-bus-trolley system is called, is widely used by the locals. San Francisco, along with Alameda, Contra Costa and San Mateo counties, is by BART, which in 2003 extended its line to San Francisco International Airport. Also by the former Southern Pacific, now called Caltrain. A commute rail, it starts in the downtown (near the baseball stadium) and runs down the Peninsula to Gilroy.

San Francisco Population vs. Other Counties

County	1990	2000	2005*
Alameda	1,279,182	1,443,741	1,507,500
Contra Costa	803,732	948,816	1,020,898
Marin	230,096	247,289	252,485
Napa	110,765	124,279	133,294
San Francisco	**723,959**	**776,733**	**799,263**
San Mateo	649,623	707,161	723,453
Santa Clara	1,497,577	1,682,585	1,759,585
Solano	340,421	394,542	421,657
Sonoma	388,222	458,614	478,440

Population by Age Groups in San Francisco

City or Area	Under 5	5-19	20-34	35-54	55+
San Francisco	31,633	95,711	236,472	241,522	171,395

Source: 1990 Census and 2000 Census. *California Dept. of Finance, Jan. 1, 2005.

Because it has a good system of buses and trains, San Francisco has shorted parking garages. Not completely. Shoppers will still find garages in the downtown. But in the neighborhoods, often it's hard to find street parking. Some people have taken to parking on sidewalks and lawns.

An earthquake in 1989 damaged freeways in the downtown. San Francisco, which has never liked freeways, tore down its damaged Embarcadero spur and other spurs and refused to rebuild several downtown access ramps. In compensation, it fielded more buses in the downtown and brought in a transit professional who seems to know his business.

Even if you have a car, you will often find it faster to take a bus or a train or BART or light rail. As for the cable cars, some residents find them useful but most of the passengers are tourists.

Housing

Although few open parcels remain in the City, San Francisco is still building, mainly in the downtown and south of Market Street and in Hayes Valley, north of Market.

On the south side, industrial buildings are being demolished to make way for apartments and condos and office and research buildings.

With Mission Bay and its bio-tech complexes, San Francisco is betting on the future. In 2005, Mission Bay landed the headquarters for stem-cell research, a state-sponsored project.

For the rest of the city, San Francisco runs to single homes and apartment complexes that in many neighborhoods rarely rise above five stories. Many

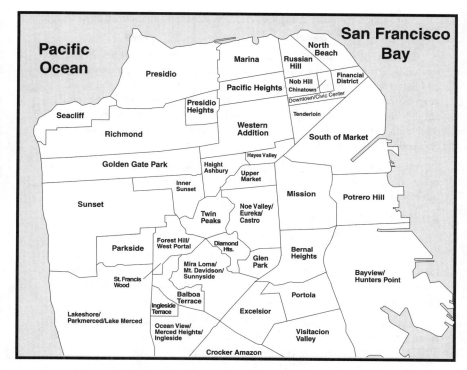

sections are carpeted with single homes; many change very little from year to year.

Rental units outnumber owner-occupied units 65 percent to 35, census figures show.

This ratio has created a large and powerful renter class. San Francisco has probably the toughest rent-control laws in California. And the renters are always trying to keep rents down and restrict the powers of landlords; endless arguments and part of the City's vocabulary.

Singles, Children and Moving Along

The median age of residents is 37. Males outnumber females 394,828 to 381,905.

Among California's 58 counties, San Francisco has the lowest percentage of children. The 2000 census put just 14 percent of the City under age 18. San Francisco has supported its schools by voting for bonds but education and the problems of school often excite only the parents.

School-age children number about 96,000 and about 30 percent of them attend private schools, a tradition in the City. In its early years, San Francisco attracted Irish and Italian immigrants and they built many parochial schools.

San Francisco runs a complex school system. See chapter on How Public Schools Work.

Because of this and other factors, some urban experts call San Francisco, especially for families, a transition town. People settle in when they are young and leave when they have children. Many exceptions of course and some neighborhoods are more family oriented than others. But even in the family neighborhoods, the old people might hold onto the house, the sons and daughters move to the suburbs. About three-fourths of the housing units have two bedrooms or less, city hall reports.

San Francisco is a singles' town. Census figures show that compared to other counties, San Francisco has a disproportionate number of people who have never married.

An Immigrant's City

San Francisco has always welcomed immigrants and newcomers.

The roster of recent mayors: Jordan (Irish), Agnos (Greek), Feinstein (Jewish), Moscone (Italian), Alioto (Italian), Willie Brown, African American, out of Texas — not one descended from the Puritans. The current mayor, Gavin Newsom, comes from an old San Francisco family.

The immigration continues. Over the last two decades, Asians, many of them Chinese, and Hispanics sharply increased their numbers in the City. In the 1990s, thousands of Russians settled in San Francisco.

The 2000 census counted 338,909 Caucasians, 239,565 Asians, 109,504 Hispanics, 67,076 African-Americans, 3,458 American Indians and 3,844 Native Hawaiians and other Pacific Islanders.

San Francisco and San Mateo

San Francisco owns much of San Mateo, the county to the immediate south. The city's holdings include the international airport and miles of watershed located on the west side of San Mateo County. Many people who live in San Mateo County work in San Francisco or the airport or the businesses surrounding the airport. If San Francisco is "The City," what is San Mateo. Many call it "the Peninsula," a name that takes on some parts of Northern Santa Clara County, notably Palo Alto.

San Francisco's Place in Northern California

Although the acknowledged cultural and social leader in Northern California, San Francisco in many ways is out of step with the region.

Politically, Northern California votes slightly left of middle. Among California's 58 counties, San Francisco, by a count made in the 1990s, had the lowest percentage of Republicans and (joined by Alameda County) almost invariably votes liberal Democratic: Not just Gore and Clinton but McGovern, Mondale, Dukakis, Kerry and had he made the ticket, Howard Dean, whom San Franciscans would have loved.

San Francisco

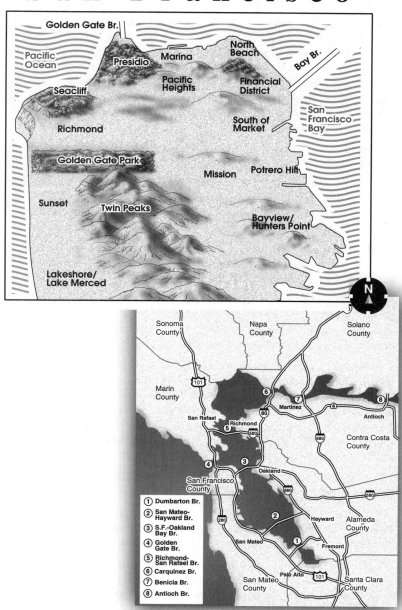

1. Dumbarton Br.
2. San Mateo-Hayward Br.
3. S.F.-Oakland Bay Br.
4. Golden Gate Br.
5. Richmond-San Rafael Br.
6. Carquinez Br.
7. Benicia Br.
8. Antioch Br.

Suburban communities these days take a much more enlightened view of homosexuals than they have in the past. But in terms of sexual live-and-let-live, San Francisco leads the way. It forgave Bill Clinton before Monica surfaced. San Francisco City College has a gay studies department. Prostitutes and body piercers have formed unions. Condoms can be obtained at the high schools. The board of supervisors has passed measures forbidding discrimination against transsexuals and providing funding for sex changes. Safe and sane bondage and whipping? Classes, with college credits, are available. The S&M folks describe themselves as ordinary people, and — outside of their sexual practices — many are just that. They work, shop, send their kids to schools and fret over the bills.

In 2000, supervisors decreed that it was against the law to discriminate against the short and the fat or anyone based on body shape.

One of the first things Gavin Newsom did upon taking over the Mayor's office in 2004 was to recognize gay marriages. For months, thousands of gay couples took their vows at city hall, then the state courts said, sorry, the city does not have the right set marriage policy.

In ignoring so many taboos, San Francisco perversely has taken some of the sizzle out of sex, made it bland, instead of shocking. Not everything goes; the city still locks up rapists and molesters.

The district attorney declared publicly that she will not seek the death penalty. Shortly after this announcement was made, a police officer was ambushed and shot dead and a suspect arrested. Although it upset many officers, the district attorney stuck to her ban on seeking the death penalty.

In crime, many of San Francisco's neighborhoods are as safe as a typical suburb. But some parts of the City are high in crime and this has pushed the San Francisco rate into an urban pattern. In 2004, San Francisco reported 88 homicides, many of them occurring in Bayview, a low-income section. The counts for previous years are 69, 68, 41, 66, 66, 58, 59, 84, and 99. In the first six months of 2005, homicides dropped but concerns about Bayview and nearby neighborhoods remain.

A light-rail line is being extended to Bayview, arriving in 2006. This may bring in more housing and revive the neighborhood.

Both the City and suburbs have their homeless and beggars. But San Francisco has them in greater numbers and year in and out, they top or come close to the top on polls that identify what bothers the residents.

Mayor Newsom installed a program — Care Not Cash — that diverted welfare funds that went directly to the homeless into structured care. Critics of the old system charged that the homeless spent the money on drugs and drink.

Education Level of Population Age 25 & Older

City or County	ND	HS	SC	AA	BA	Grad
Alameda County	7%	19%	22%	7%	21%	14%
Contra Costa County	8	20	24	8	23	12
Marin County	5	12	21	6	31	21
Napa County	10	21	26	8	17	9
Oakland	13	18	20	6	18	13
San Francisco	**8**	**14**	**17**	**6**	**29**	**16**
San Jose	11	18	21	8	21	11
Santa Clara County	9	16	20	7	24	16
San Mateo County	8	18	22	7	24	15
Solano County	10	25	29	9	15	6
Sonoma County	8	20	27	9	19	10

Source: 2000 Census. Figures are percent of population age 25 and older, rounded to the nearest whole number. Not shown are adults with less than a 9th grade education. **Key**: ND (high school, no diploma); HS (high school diploma or GED only, no college); SC (some college education); AA (associate degree); Bach. (bachelor's degree only); Grad (master's or higher degree).

Over the long run, the mayor thinks that more housing would greatly alleviate the problems of the homeless. Fed up, San Franciscans earlier had voted in laws that curtailed begging.

And not a few residents will tell you that San Francisco would not have half its problems with the homeless if other cities did their share.

Despite these Differences ...

Northern Californians continue to look to San Francisco for leadership, and in ways large and small the City exerts great influence on the region.

Former Mayor Brown for years was the speaker of the California Assembly. Dianne Feinstein, U.S. senator, is a former mayor of the City. Barbara Boxer, the other U.S. Senator, is from Marin County, on the other side of the Golden Gate, but in politics and temperament, very much in the San Francisco tradition: liberal and proud of it. San Francisco Congresswoman Nancy Pelosi is the House Democratic leader.

Only a few cities in the north have shown metropolitan energy — the will and imagination to attempt and manage big projects.

In the arts and amusements — museums, plays, exhibits, operas, symphonies, restaurants, saloons and more — San Francisco remains light years ahead of what the suburbs can muster.

In 2005, San Francisco opened its rebuilt De Young Museum in Golden Gate Park and later that year the Museum of the African Diaspora in the downtown.

In style, despite (or perhaps because of) its zanies, San Francisco is the only Northern California city that can be called cosmopolitan.

Average Household Income in San Francisco, Other Counties

County	1990	2000	*2005
Alameda	$68,000	$82,500	$84,200
Contra Costa	81,600	86,500	88,200
Marin	98,900	123,200	125,700
Napa	67,900	76,500	78,000
San Francisco	**67,300**	**84,000**	**85,700**
San Mateo	86,700	110,500	112,700
Santa Clara	83,600	114,600	116,900
Solano	64,700	66,800	68,100
Sonoma	65,600	75,900	77,400

Source: Association of Bay Area Governments, *"Projections 2002"*. Average income per household includes wages and salaries, dividends, interest, rent and transfer payments such as Social Security or public assistance. Based on 2000 Census data and Consumer Price Index. Income is stated in 2000 dollars. *Projections.

A Word About Government

San Francisco is the only city in California that is also a county. Instead of a city council, San Francisco elects an 11-member board of supervisors as its legislative body. Members serve four years. The mayor is elected directly to a four-year term and can veto legislation by the board. Because it is a charter city, San Francisco can amend its powers at the polls without seeking permission from the state. Almost every election features ballot amendments.

The school district, governed by an elected board, is an agency unto itself, separate from the city government.

San Francisco Before the Europeans

Before the Europeans, there were the Indians, called Costanoans by the Spanish and Ohlones by modern historians. The Indians fished for salmon in the Bay and ocean, gathered shellfish, ground acorns for meal and hunted deer, bear and other animals. Historians estimate that about 10,000 lived between San Francisco and Monterey. Their ways were the ways of their ancestors; very little changed apparently over several thousand years. They had no contact with the great outside world and when contact was made, it destroyed them.

Nothing about the days of the Dons (the Spanish and Mexican periods) makes sense unless it is realized that they came late and few in number. Fierce Indians and a hostile desert discouraged exploration north from Mexico and ship explorations of the coast were rare and hazardous. Sir Francis Drake supposedly set foot in Marin County in 1579.

The Spanish Arrive

Not until 1769, on the eve of the American Revolution, did the Spanish (Gaspar de Portola and Junipero Serra) discover the Bay. The mission, named after St. Francis of Assisi, and the Presidio followed. Lacking their own laborers (at the time of the Mexican-American War, fewer than 7,000 Spanish-Mexicans resided in California), the Spanish dragooned the Indians. They were

How Residents Make Their Money

City or Town	MAN-PRO	SERV	SAL-OFF	FARM	CON	MANU-TRANS
Alameda County	42	12	26	0	8	12
Contra Costa County	41	13	28	0	9	9
Marin County	53	12	25	0	6	5
Napa County	35	18	24	3	9	11
Oakland	39	16	25	0	7	12˙
San Francisco	**48**	**14**	**26**	**0**	**4**	**8**
San Jose	41	12	24	0	8	14
San Mateo County	43	14	27	0	8	9
Santa Clara County	49	11	23	0	7	11
Solano County	31	16	28	1	11	13
Sonoma County	35	15	27	2	10	11

Source: 2000 Census. Figures are percent, rounded off, of working civilians over age 16. **Key**: MAN-PRO (managers, professionals); SERV (service); SAL-OFF (sales people, office workers); FARM (farming, fishing, forestry); CONSTRUCTION (building, maintenance, mining), MANU-TRANS (manufacturing, distribution, transportation).

brought to the missions where they were trained as field hands and under the tutelage of the padres ushered into Catholicism. The policy, as it worked itself out over the next 75 years, killed almost all of the Indians, mainly by measles, smallpox and other diseases.

The Mexicans overthrew the Spanish in 1821.

The new leaders secularized the missions in the 1830s, weakening the little protection afforded Indians. Rancheros were carved out of the countryside for the original soldiers and their heirs.

The Yankees

Meanwhile, the United States had beaten the British and purchased the Midwest. Over the mountains came the Americans, first trappers, then merchants and farmers. When war came in 1846, the Americans didn't so much beat the Mexicans, although there were skirmishes, as overwhelmed them by numbers.

Two years later, while building a mill in the Sierra, James Marshall caught sight of shiny flakes in the water. The Gold Rush was on. Within a year, even though sailors abandoned ships for the gold fields as soon as they arrived, San Francisco's population jumped from 800 to more than 25,000, and the City became the financial and commercial heart for mining towns. Factories were built and thrived.

The Railroad

The continental railroad, built largely by the Chinese and the Irish, was finished in 1869, a great boost to the West Coast economy. Four years later, cable manufacturer Andrew S. Hallidie built a railroad of a different sort — the city's first cable car. His invention was the safest means of transportation over the city's many hills.

This was the era of fabulous fortunes and fabled men and women. Plagued by thieves and murderers (the section near Pacific Avenue and Kearney Street was known as the Barbary Coast), San Francisco formed a Vigilance Committee and hanged or banished the worst. Great mansions were erected on Nob Hill. Streets were laid out, parks planted, the arts encouraged, and vice, to a certain extent, ignored. San Francisco has always been sympathetic to flesh, the foundation of its modern sexual tolerance. San Francisco entered the 20th century confident of its future and boasting a population of 342,782.

The Great Quake

Six years later, on April 18, 1906 a great earthquake struck the City. Little damage was done initially but the quake destroyed the water mains, making it impossible to put out the fires that consumed the financial section and most of the downtown. The fire line was Van Ness Avenue. If you want to see Victorians, don't look east of Van Ness; look west.

About 700 people were killed, 300,000 lost their homes and the damage exceeded $500 million, in those days an enormous sum. But San Francisco came roaring back, part of its legend. The destroyed neighborhoods were rebuilt, the saved expanded.

In 1915, a new San Francisco showed itself off to the world by hosting the Panama-Pacific International Exposition, celebrating the opening of the Panama Canal. By 1930, the city's population had almost doubled to 634,394.

The 1930s also saw San Francisco shine. While other cities stagnated in the Depression, San Francisco (and its neighbors) built the region's two great public works: the Bay Bridge, 1936, and the Golden Gate Bridge, 1937.

After the War

World War II brought another population boom. Tens of thousands came to the City to build ships and work in the war industries. Thousands of GIs embarked for the Pacific through the port of San Francisco. In 1945, San Francisco served as host for the formation of the United Nations.

The postwar period is often portrayed as a period of stagnation. San Francisco's population, fattened to 827,000 by the war, shed over 200,000 residents by 1980. The new suburbs attracted the City's middle class, leaving behind a disproportionate number of the poor and the old.

Unfortunate decisions were made. Victorians were demolished to make way for ugly public housing. Neighborhoods were sacrificed to freeways, and the Embarcadero freeway commissioned, cutting off the Bay. The Embarcadero was to have run up to the Golden Gate Bridge but citizens revolted and stopped it well short of Fisherman's Wharf. The port, always the pride of the City, faded in the postwar years. Oakland and the oil wharves of Contra Costa County now handle most of the shipping to Northern California.

Presidential Voting in San Francisco

Year	Democrat	D-Votes	Republican	R-Votes
1948	Truman*	167,726	Dewey	160,135
1952	Stevenson	167,282	Eisenhower*	188,531
1956	Stevenson	161,766	Eisenhower*	173,648
1960	Kennedy*	197,734	Nixon	143,001
1964	Johnson*	230,758	Goldwater	92,994
1968	Humphrey	177,509	Nixon*	100,970
1972	McGovern	170,882	Nixon*	127,461
1976	Carter*	133,733	Ford	103,561
1980	Carter	133,184	Reagan*	80,967
1984	Mondale	193,278	Reagan*	90,219
1988	Dukakis	201,887	Bush*	72,503
1992	Clinton*	230,007	Bush	56,373
1996	Clinton*	188,858	Dole	39,974
2000	Gore	240,935	Bush*	51,367
2004	Kerry	**296,772**	Bush*	**54,355**

Source: Calif. Secretary of State. *Election winner nationally.

Hippies, Drugs and Cults

San Francisco celebrates the Hippie era but it made drug usage popular, not only here but throughout the country. Modern crime in the City owes much to drugs. Eccentrics have always been welcome in the City but in the 1970s the outlandish became the tragic. Jim Jones established his People's Temple on Geary Boulevard, cozied up to politicians and was on his way to fame and fortune before tripping over his own malevolence. The whole business ended sordidly in South America with the shooting death of a congressman and the suicide of hundreds, including Jones.

Months later, Dan White, a disgruntled ex-fireman and politician, climbed through a city hall window and gunned down Mayor George Moscone and Harvey Milk, the City's first openly-gay member of the board of supervisors. White's lawyer said his man had strained his nerves by eating many cupcakes, a tactic known in local lore as the "Twinkie Defense." The jury bought this and other arguments and let White off with voluntary manslaughter. That night, gays rioted in the downtown. After serving his term, White committed suicide.

The '80s— Highs and Lows

In the 1980s, the homeless began appearing in great numbers, particularly in the downtown and around city hall. San Francisco is a humane town and the City tried to do well by its unfortunates. But crime rose, appearances suffered and confidence eroded in the ability of government to solve problems.

The City closed out the 1980s on what promised to be a high note — a World Series showdown in October 1989 between the Giants and the A's — but just as the third game was to start, the Loma Prieta earthquake struck. The Bay

How They Voted
(San Francisco & Other Counties)

City or County	Bush	Kerry
Alameda County	130,911	422,585
Contra Costa County	150,608	257,254
Los Angeles	1,076,225	1,907,736
Marin County	34,378	99,070
Orange County	641,832	419,239
San Diego County	596,033	526,437
San Francisco	**54,355**	**296,772**
San Mateo County	83,315	197,922
Santa Clara County	209,094	386,100
Sacramento County	235,539	236,657
Solano County	62,301	85,096
Sonoma County	68,204	148,261

Source: Secretary of State, Dec., 2004.

Bridge collapsed in one spot and many structures in the Marina District were badly damaged.

If problems abounded, however, so did triumphs, although perhaps less appreciated.

The City joined Contra Costa and Alameda counties in constructing a rail rapid transit system called BART. Service started in 1972. The international airport was expanded several times to keep up with growing air traffic. Davies Symphony Hall was built. The downtown, not without opposition, underwent a building boom. It's a much different, livelier downtown than it was 30 years ago. And a much higher one; many skyscrapers.

After years of decline, the population in the 1980s began to rise, much of the increase coming from Asians and Hispanics. When people vote for a city with their feet, when they commit themselves to reside in that city, that's a strong vote of confidence. The Forty-Niners and Joe Montana and Steve Young, with their winning ways, put a lot of sparkle in the town.

The Nineties

One-term mayors start cropping up, the city's politics unsettled by its failure to find solutions to the homeless and other problems. For all the misery of the 1989 earthquake, many San Franciscans were glad it demolished the much despised freeway that had intruded into the beloved waterfront. The waterfront, with newly-cleared vistas to the Bay, is undergoing a renaissance. With the end of the Cold War, the Army gave up the Presidio, which has glorious views of the Golden Gate. George Lucas of Star Wars fame built a studio and digital facilities at the site.

2000-2003

The City started flush with money. Then came 2001 ... thud! Tourism down, air travel down, tax revenue down, employment down.

But amid the losses, some triumphs. In 2000, the City, next to its downtown, opened what many consider the prettiest ball park in the U.S.

In 2003, work began on the Bay Bridge, one of traffic lifelines to and from San Francisco. The job will take about five years and probably raise havoc with travel but it needed to be done; bridge was damaged in the 1989 earthquake.

With the BART extension to the airport in 2003, other stations were opened along the route at South San Francisco, San Bruno and Millbrae. This will help getting around the City and the Peninsula.

Leash laws were tightened, a big deal in San Francisco, long a friend the furry ones.

The city restored two vintage landmarks. The 104-year-old Ferry Building which withstood the 1906 earthquake, and the ensuing fire was completely renovated. Also restored, for $25 million, the 124-year-old Conservatory of Flowers in Golden Gate Park.

The City in 2003 opened a third trade show hall, the $187 million Moscone West.

In 2003, the University of California at San Francisco opened its first research building at Mission Bay, the giant project that is remaking the waterfront south of Market Street.

2004

Giants fold in finish, Forty-Niners free-fall and pick up velocity, court says "whoa" to gay marriage, Barry Bonds smacks 700th home run and the ball sells for $804,129. (But steroid questions dog the slugger.)

Local newspaper reviews all the good things that came out of the 1989 earthquake — museums, city hall and public buildings rebuilt (seismics), freeways demolished, vistas created, neighborhoods revived, residential construction stimulated. Ah yes! The earthquake! Nothing like it to put a little spring in the municipal step.

Peregrine falcons, almost wiped out by pesticides, take up residence in San Francisco high rises.

2005.

• One museum opened, another re-opened.

• Stem-cell headquarters headed for Mission Bay.

• Final touches being put on Bloomingdales to open in downtown in 2006.

• Giants swoon, Forty Niners hopeless. Can't have it all.

Chapter 2

San Francisco Neighborhoods

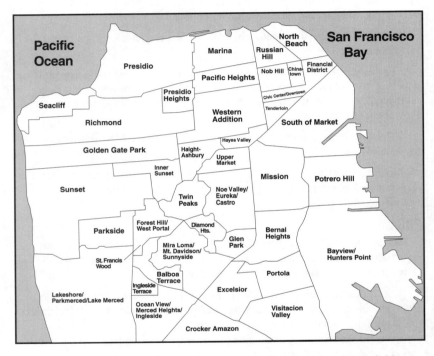

OTHER COUNTIES HAVE TOWNS and cities; San Francisco has neighborhoods. Within the borders of the City, residents identify location by Noe Valley, Sunset, Pacific Heights and over a dozen other neighborhoods.

Books and boosters sing the praises of neighborhood diversity and are fond of noting the different housing styles but sometimes the business is overdone.

Some neighborhoods are a hodgepodge of buildings. Old homes have been demolished, new ones erected. Many buildings have been divided into condos. San Francisco is famous for opposing change but change does come.

San Francisco has a distinct Chinatown but Chinese and Chinese-Americans are found in many other neighborhoods.

The Richmond and Sunset districts, divided by Golden Gate Park, are considered separate neighborhoods but in housing styles they are quite similar.

Twin Peaks and its environs includes about ten neighborhoods, including West Portal, St. Francis Woods, Balboa Terrace, Sherwood Forest, Forest Hill, Forest Knolls and Clarendon Heights. For the newcomer, these neighborhoods, with exceptions, may seem to blend into one another but beneath the surface the lines are defined by residential associations and real estate descriptions and obscure landmarks. Some people take offense if you put them in the "wrong" neighborhood.

Neighborhoods share important characteristics: the sections west of Twin Peaks are in the summer fog belt. If you don't like fog, you might confine your search to the east side of the City. In some places, a half mile or a few blocks makes a big difference in the weather. See chapter on weather.

In politics, the Sunset, the Richmond District, Parkside, West of Twin Peaks, the Pacific Heights, Sea Cliff, Chinatown and North Beach are considered conservative, which in the parlance of the outside world means moderate to liberal.

Western Addition, Bernal Heights, Haight-Ashbury, Potrero Hill, Eureka Valley, Bayview and the downtown are considered liberal, which means very liberal. Other neighborhoods fall between.

On some maps, "neighborhoods" disappear — folded into other neighborhoods. Hayes Valley is sometimes counted as part of the Western Addition, the Inner Sunset as part of the Sunset, Chinatown as part of North Beach.

All this granted, in many ways the neighborhoods are individualistic. San Francisco was built out from the downtown, from east to west and from north to south. The great majority of the housing was erected from 1850 to 1950. When it became timely to develop the outlying sections, developers built according to the styles and market values of their eras.

Pacific Heights and Haight-Ashbury have Victorian homes; these neighborhoods were developed in the latter half of the 1800s. The Sunset was built during the early 20th century, a time when Americans were switching from horses to cars. Many homes in the Sunset and Richmond districts have "one-car" garages, the garage typically placed under the living room (sometimes the garages are deep, allowing space to park a second car or to construct a "granny" unit).

The land near San Francisco State University was developed after World War II. Homes and apartments there tend to have a 1950s look.

San Francisco is ethnically diverse: People of all races are scattered around the City. But it also has its neighborhoods or pockets of ethnic groups: Blacks, Chinese, Hispanics, Japanese, Italians, Irish and various other nationalities, including Koreans, Samoans, Vietnamese and Russians.

The City also divides by age and sexual persuasion. Many students live next to San Francisco State University and the University of San Francisco. Many homosexuals favor Castro Street and environs but of late straights have been moving in. City planners tag much of San Francisco as "transitional," meaning it is always changing. The group that defines a neighborhood in one decade may not be around 20 years later or its members may be far fewer.

The state tally in 2005 showed 355,903 residential units: 62,953 single homes, 48,738 single attached, 243,652 apartments, 560 mobile homes.

A word about crime. It varies from neighborhood to neighborhood, and often from block to block. The poorer neighborhoods generally are higher in crime than the rich and middle-class sections. See chapter on crime.

In the late 1990s, homicides started to fall but in 2004 the south side of the city seemed to be drenched with violence and killings. Good sense demands wariness.

In 2004, homicides totaled 88. The counts for the preceding years are, 69, 63, 62, 41, 66, 66, 59, 84, 99, 91, 129, 117, 94, 101, 73, 92 and 103. A young police officer in 2004 was killed in an ambush; suspect arrested.

The police department increased patrols in troubled areas, seized more guns, installed surveillance cameras at hotspots, tightened up on parolees and took other actions. But in a few neighborhoods, crime remains a big problem.

Not everyone can afford their first pick in housing. Sometimes the choice comes down to a bigger, cheaper unit in a marginal or transitional neighborhood against a smaller, more expensive unit in a stable neighborhood. For a single person, the first might be quite acceptable. For a parent, the second might be preferable.

Because of the high rents and home prices, many people are sharing rentals.

Take your time. Ask questions. Drive the neighborhoods. Think about what you value, in safety, schools, commuting, closeness to parks and other amenities. Here is a capsule overview of many neighborhoods. Local Realtors and rental agents will usually have more detailed information. San Francisco has strict and complex rent-control laws that are always being amended. Also complex and about to be changed again, school assignment rules. If you have children, check out the school situation right away.

BAYVIEW, HUNTERS POINT

WORKING-CLASS neighborhood on southeast side of the City, near former Navy yard and Candlestick Park. A mix of single family houses, apartments, four-plexes, factories — but changing.

Crime and low school scores have depressed home prices and rents but other forces are taking the sting out these shortcomings.

Over the next five years, Hunters Point, a former Navy shipyard, should become a hot spot for new homes. After almost 30 years of cleanup and preparations, construction is underway or soon will be on 1,600 residential units, mostly townhouses.

San Francisco, built out years ago, rarely gets large tracts of new housing. The developer is bringing in modern designs, stores and commercial space. Some homes will be built on hills with sweeping views of the Bay. Another condo project, 500 units, is in planning.

MUNI is extending its light-rail line from the Giants' stadium down Third Street through Bayview and Hunter's Point and is adding some class to the stations by installing various works of art. The $550 million project will include 19 new stations and 5.4 miles of track. Projected date of completion, 2006.

At Hunter's Point, Pacific Gas and Electric operates two obsolete power plants, a source of pollution that worries some people. These plants are to be closed in 2007.

When you look at this extension, the new homes and the up-market units going in around Mission Bay and the Giants stadium you may have the makings of an upscale shift on the southeast side of the City. Keep in mind that San Francisco is small. Bayview-Hunters Point is only a few miles from Mission Bay, the new bio-tech center.

Bayview is a neighborhood that attracts newcomers because of its low-cost housing. Many residents own their homes. Third Street, running north and south, is the main commercial strip.

In the 1990s, Bayview built a new police station. There's a community center. Following an upsurge in violence in 2004, police stepped up patrols. Mayor and city hall are paying more attention to area.

New housing, priced for professionals, has been nibbling into the neighborhoods, particularly on the south side of Candlestick Park. Some homes have been built on hills with great views of the Bay. In the flatlands, the homes run to single-family detached, many old, many in need of fixing up. But a good number of the homes show a lot of care. Rising into the hills on the north side, the housing mixes old and new with views of the Bay.

Parks and playgrounds are scattered around neighborhood. Shoreline around Candlestick Park is part of state recreation area. Small trailer park here. Plans call for more commercial space, apartments and homes. Empty lots are being filled in.

Commute good. Right off Highway 101. Thousands of jobs at or near San Francisco International Airport, a 5-10 minute drive down Highway 101.

The Forty-Niners have the City's OK and a loan to rebuild the stadium at Candlestick Park and add a mall. This job has been on the board for years but, according to news reports, 2006 might be the year when definite plans and a schedule are revealed.

Candlestick, by the way, comes from the name given a rock formation, long gone, at the tip of Candlestick Point.

• Hunters Point, a former military base, is being decontaminated. Many of the businesses have been chased out until the job is done.

BERNAL HEIGHTS

ONE OF THE OLDER neighborhoods of the City. Located about three miles south of downtown. Good commute. Housing quaint and well-maintained. Considered slightly upscale in an artsy way. In 2005, newspaper reported that it was attracting more young families.

Many residents own homes, which helps neighborhood stability. Some homes have security doors but many do not.

Spread over several hills, centered on park that includes Bernal Hill, 440 feet high. Good views of Bay and hills to the west. Trees and small lawns and shrubs adorn the fronts of mostly single-family homes, many of which have been remodeled.

Victorians and Queen Annes lend to the charm. In spring, the red of the bottlebrush, the yellow of the daffodil and the orange of the poppy plus blues and purples from a variety other plants brighten the streets.

Protected by the hills, Bernal Heights escapes the fog and enjoys some of the nicest weather of the City. Close to downtown. Businesses along Cortland Avenue, Chavez Street.

Neighborhood activists came to life in 1980s and pressured city hall to make long overdue street improvements and pay more attention to planning. One resident called Bernal Heights a "village in the middle of San Francisco."

Other words used, "rural" and for developers, "impossible." Residents are very selective about what kind of housing will be built. For years they fought the construction of public housing on a parcel above Alemany Boulevard and managed to cut the number of apartments to 45 (from 120). Home Depot wants to open a store; residents opposed.

Two parochial schools and a public school.

At least four parks, several playgrounds. Indoor sports at the schools, the shows, movies, clubs, night life and cultural ornaments of the downtown a few minutes away. Delis, restaurants, a library, a community center.

Annual neighborhood garage sale is a big draw. Usually includes about 140 garages.

Home Price Sampler from Classified Ads

Bayview/Hunters Point
- 3BR/1BA, lrg. bckyrd., $615,000
- 3BR/2BA, townhome, $539,000

Bernal Heights
- 4BR/2BA, form. DR, $995,000
- 3BR/2BA, 1 car gar., $759,000

Diamond Heights
- 4BR/2BA, wide lot, $899,000
- 3BR/2BA, condo, $779,000

Eureka Valley
- 2BR/2BA, $585,000
- 2BR/1BA, views, $689,000

Excelsior
- 3BR/1BA, upgrades, $650,000
- 2BR/1BA, basement, $750,000

Financial District
- Condo, nr. waterfront, $489,000
- Condo, open flr. plan, $909,000

Forest Hill/West Portal
- 2BR/2BA, remod., $999,000
- 3BR/2BA, hrdwd. flrs., $699,000

Glen Park
- 4BR/3BA, views, $1.3 mil.
- 4BR/2.5BA, 2 story, $999,000

Golden Gate Heights
- 3BR/2BA, view, $899,000
- 4BR/2BA, $1.3 mil.

Haight-Ashbury
- Flat, $625,000
- 2BR/1BA, Victorian, $799,000

Ingleside Terrace
- 3BR/2BA, remod., $775,000
- 3BR/1BA, $699,000

Marina
- 3BR/2.5BA, 3 frplcs., $2 mil.
- Condo, Med. style, $1.4 mil.

Mission
- Condo, $409,000
- Condo, $535,000
- 3BR/2BA, parlor, $945,000

Nob Hill
- Flat, 2BR/1BA, $650,000
- Condo, den, $845,000

Noe Valley
- 2BR/2BA, quiet, $849,000
- 5BR/4BA, renov. Vict., $2.5 mil.

Outer Mission
- 2BR/1BA, upgrades, $699,000
- 4BR/2BA, near trans., $799,000

Pacific Heights
- Flat, 4BR/2BA, $980,000
- Condo, 2BR/2BA, $759,000
- Condo, 2BR/2BA, $835,000

Parkside
- 3BR/1BA, remod., $675,000
- Condo, 3BR/2BA, $649,000

Portola
- 2BR/1BA, garage, $625,000
- 5BR/3BA, custom, $980,000

Potrero Hill
- Loft, 2BR/2BA, $649,000
- 2BR/1BA, Med. style, $979,000

Presidio Heights
- Flat, 3BR/1BA, $535,000

Richmond
- 4BR/3BA, remod., $1.3 mil.
- Townhouse, $765,000
- Condo, $649,000

Russian Hill
- Loft, 1BR/1BA, $575,000
- Condo, 2BR/2BA, $1.5 mil.

St. Francis Wood
- 3BR/2BA, $1.6 mil.

SOMA
- Loft, 1BR/1.5BA, $649,000
- Condo, 2BR/2BA, $839,000

Sunset
- 3BR/2BA, $798,000
- 5BR/3BA, $900,000
- 2BR/1BA, $648,000

Twin Peaks
- 4BR/2BA, garage, $899,000
- Condo, 3BR/2BA, $849,000

Visitacion Valley
- Condo, 2BR/1BA, $445,000
- 5BR/3BA, $549,000

Western Addition
- Flat (1 flr.), 2BR/2BA, $500,000
- Condo, 2BR/2BA, $549,000

Top 30 Baby Names

San Francisco County

Boys		Girls	
William	57	Isabella	42
Joshua	51	Emily	41
Ryan	44	Olivia	33
Daniel	43	Sophia	33
Alexander	42	Ashley	32
Jonathan	41	Grace	31
John	40	Samantha	30
Nicholas	40	Jasmine	29
Ethan	39	Jessica	29
Benjamin	38	Sofia	28
Andrew	37	Chloe	27
Jack	37	Alexandra	26
Michael	37	Emma	25
Anthony	36	Katherine	25
David	36	Natalie	25
Aidan	35	Zoe	25
Jason	34	Elizabeth	24
Justin	32	Maya	24
Matthew	30	Anna	23
Christopher	29	Mia	23
Gabriel	29	Lily	22
Henry	29	Rachel	22
James	29	Sarah	22
Owen	29	Ava	21
Eric	28	Ella	21
Kevin	28	Lauren	21
Nathan	28	Tiffany	21
Jackson	27	Jennifer	20
Samuel	27	Michelle	20
Diego	25	Audrey	19

California

Boys		Girls	
Daniel	4157	Emily	3388
Anthony	3797	Ashley	2922
Andrew	3464	Samantha	2474
Jose	3379	Isabella	2435
Jacob	3327	Natalie	1942
Joshua	3292	Alyssa	1808
David	3246	Emma	1740
Angel	3232	Sophia	1715
Matthew	2853	Jessica	1700
Michael	2844	Jasmine	1666
Christopher	2754	Elizabeth	1595
Jonathan	2541	Madison	1572
Ryan	2511	Jennifer	1483
Alexander	2440	Kimberly	1460
Joseph	2430	Alexis	1434
Ethan	2356	Andrea	1374
Nathan	2302	Abigail	1314
Brandon	2208	Hannah	1310
Kevin	2133	Sarah	1304
Juan	2106	Vanessa	1299
Christian	2022	Mia	1270
Jesus	2012	Stephanie	1246
Nicholas	1999	Brianna	1221
Diego	1977	Michelle	1152
Luis	1957	Olivia	1149
Adrian	1824	Kayla	1147
Dylan	1757	Leslie	1137
Gabriel	1735	Grace	1127
Isaac	1722	Maria	1099
Carlos	1638	Victoria	1083

Source: California Department of Health Services, 2004 birth records. Number of children with the given name. Some names would move higher on the list if the state grouped essentially same names with slightly different spellings, for example, Sarah and Sara. But state computer goes by exact spellings.

Bernal Heights, which drew its name from one of the Spanish land grant families, got its start in the late 1800s when San Francisco began moving out from its downtown.

Douglas Mount, historian, reported that the first residents were mainly Irish immigrants, later followed by Italian and German and Hispanic immigrants. St. Anthony's Church opened in 1894.

Street cars spurred construction but many lots were empty when 1906 earthquake struck. Bernal Heights escaped almost unscathed and this impressed many. Over the next 10 years, development boomed. One study showed that about 65 percent of the neighborhood's 7,000 residential units were built before World War II and 28 percent in the 15 years just after the war. About 60 percent of the units are single homes; the rest duplexes and apartment complexes of three and four units.

Some streets, especially on the south side of Bernal Hill, fade almost into wide trails — seclusion to a comforting degree, but maneuvering a car or pickup must be challenging. A neighborhood group negotiated a deal with city officials concerning parking: no ticketing unless someone complains. Many residents were parking in front of their driveways, a ticketable offense.

Some hillside lots have been converted into community gardens. Several neighborhood groups stay in touch with the politicians and sound out opinions on issues.

In 1876, a Frenchman discovered what he thought was gold on Bernal Hill and set off a minor rush; turned out to be mica (fool's gold).

Bernal Heights is close to Mission Bay, the project that is remaking San Francisco's southern waterfront.

• In 2005, the library was being rebuilt.

CROCKER, AMAZON

BLUE COLLAR, middle-class neighborhood on southern border of City, near Highway 101 and Interstate 280. Many of the homes were built in the 1940s.

Stucco and wood homes. Many lawns and landscaping well-kept, an indication of social stability. Window bars and door grills on some streets.

Close to Cow Palace and McLaren Park, one of biggest in San Francisco. It has a golf course and a lake. Large playground, called Crocker-Amazon. Newspaper in 2004 reported that many people avoided McLaren Park on week days because of concerns about crime. Weekends different; many visitors.

No tourist attractions that call attention. Nothing chi-chi or artsy. Bedroom. Streets spill into Daly City neighborhoods and into Excelsior district.

Neighborhood took name from Crocker Land Company, the developer, and from Amazon Avenue.

Many of the jobs in this area are oriented more toward San Francisco Airport (SFO) and its environs than downtown San Francisco. Buses to BART station or directly to downtown.

If you are looking to buy in San Francisco and can't afford the prices close to downtown, Crocker-Amazon is a good place to look. Its prices will be cheaper.

With the opening in 2003 of BART all the way to the airport, Crocker-Amazon residents have an easier time getting to SFO jobs.

EUREKA VALLEY, UPPER MARKET, THE CASTRO

ABOUT TWO MILES southwest of downtown. Noted for its large gay population and interest in rights of gays but now attracting some straights, including young families.

Many shops, restaurants, delis, bars along Castro Street. Movie house, famous for showing classic movies. Bookstores. Hilly. Pretty. Many Victorians. Many artists perform concerts at the Castro Theatre. If any felt like performing Bach, the venue could accommodate them with its pipe organ.

Residents want to discourage stores that attract tourists but this neighborhood will always attract visitors.

Much care lavished on neighborhood and homes. About 73 percent of residents are renters.

Free and easy style. No apologies here for sexual orientation. A neighborhood that will charm and shock granny. For some gays, almost a holy place, and according to polls, the most popular spot for gay tourists in the country. Here's where a lot of actions were started that led to more freedom, less persecution of gays.

San Francisco is still a leader in social progress. In 2002 a LGBT (lesbian, gay, bisexual and transgender) community center opened at the corner of Octavia and Market Streets. Brings segments of the community under one roof.

On the somber side, the Castro intentionally calls attention to AIDS and the deaths it has caused. In 1994, Harvey Milk Institute opened on Church Street, an academy devoted to gay and lesbian studies. Milk, a gay and a county supervisor, was assassinated.

Neighboring Noe Valley is considered by some as part of the Eureka Valley-Castro district.

Buses and light rail to downtown. Within walking distance (if you like to walk) of many of the cultural offerings of the City. East of Twin Peaks, which means some protection from the fog.

Short bus ride (30-40 blocks) to the Giants' stadium and to the jobs at Mission Bay.

According to news stories, young families like the neighborhood because it has been fixed up. Other forces at work: changing attitudes toward gays. In many other parts of the City and in many suburbs in the Bay Area and urban-suburban California, they are no longer considered social pariahs. For this reason, some gays are moving to other neighborhoods or the suburbs. Or simply not moving into the Castro.

Like many cities, San Francisco is always changing, new groups replacing old and sometimes old replacing new.

• Many communities would pay a bounty to land a Trader Joe's, the fresh-food purveyor. In the Castro, after a year of trying, a bid to open a Trader's was withdrawn. People objected to the traffic the store would generate.

• San Francisco is getting into wi-fi. The Castro is one of the first benefi-ciaries: thanks to a Silicon Valley firm the neighborhood was "wired" for free.

EXCELSIOR, PORTOLA DISTRICT

WORKING-MIDDLE CLASS. For orientation, key on McLaren Park. Excelsior borders the park on the east, Portola District on the north.

Favored in past by Italians, now home to other immigrants and newcomers. Homes, about 55 years and older, are usually single-family, stucco and wood frame construction built over one- and two-car garages. Some apartments along with duplexes and four-plexes.

Appearances range from dilapidated and in need of paint and remodeling to near-mint condition. You'll find in these neighborhoods many nice, well-cared-for homes. Many in-law units, portions of homes that have been remodeled as rental units. These neighborhoods attract buyers who can't afford downtown prices but want to live in the City.

In reputation, Portola District and Excelsior come across as transition neighborhoods. They have fewer homicides than the Mission District and Bayview.

Shops along Mission Street. Large malls with discount stores just over the border in Daly City. A half-hour bus ride to downtown. Near Highway 101 and Interstate 280. BART station (trains to downtown). Good commute to downtown or to job centers of San Mateo County. McLaren, which has a golf course, is one of the largest parks in the city.

Balboa High School, which serves the southern sections, was threatened with closure in 1991 but parents, alumni and students rallied to its survival and persuaded the school board to keep it open. Both neighborhoods are close to City College of San Francisco — many classes and activities.

When Interstate 280-Highway 101 interchange was overhauled for earthquake repairs, Caltrans tried to eliminate the freeway ramps serving the Portola District. Residents and merchants fought back. Ramps reopened in 1996.

In 2005, the Excelsior district threw a celebration in memory of one of its favorite sons, Jerry Garcia of the Grateful Dead.

The Excelsior library is being remodeled.

FOREST HILL,
W. PORTAL, ST. FRANCIS WOOD

ALTHOUGH FOREST HILL-WEST PORTAL border and are sometimes included in Twin Peaks, its prices and architectural style are so different that it makes sense to break it out as a separate neighborhood.

Mix of two-story houses with gables and Tudor styling and single-story homes built over the garages. Trees line the streets. Well-kept lawns. Some older homes have been remodeled inside and converted into apartments or condos. Most homes owner-occupied.

West Portal is one of the nicest shopping blocks in the City: a mix of restaurants, salons, coffee, antique, flower shops.

St. Francis Wood, built in the 1910s, carries the tag "ritzy." Fountains and gateways. Tall pines and eucalyptuses shade the streets. Utility lines buried. Mix of housing styles, many favoring a mixed Spanish revival (terra-cotta roofs) but parts of the neighborhood seem to step out of New England.

Impressive homes, large, well kept, many remodeled. Streets laid out in part by Frederick Law Olmstead, who also designed Central Park in New York. One of the best neighborhoods in the City.

Active homeowner associations. Kind of neighborhoods that pay attention to quality, planning and conditions that might breed crime. Low in crime (but take precautions).

Open to ocean fog. A short drive to the Pacific. You can smell the salt air. Close to Stern Grove. Summer concerts. Also close to zoo, three golf courses. Some homes have views of the Pacific; many don't. Starting from the Pacific, the terrain rises slowly, then jumps when it reaches Twin Peaks. St. Francis Wood is built over the lower hills.

Buses and streetcars to the downtown. West Portal refers to the western opening in the streetcar tunnel to the downtown. These neighborhoods and several others on the west side came to life when the tunnel was opened in 1917.

Shopping at Stonestown Galleria (Nordstrom, Macys). Large discount stores to the south, in Daly City. Close to San Francisco State University, which through its extension program, offers many classes for the public.

HAIGHT-ASHBURY

WHEN THE 1906 EARTHQUAKE destroyed much of old San Francisco, the Haight and its quaint buildings were spared. During the 1960s, the Haight became the home of the flower children — hippies and would-be hippies who came to San Francisco and the little neighborhood around the intersection of Haight and Ashbury streets searching for excitement and freedom. Many Victorians and lofts became communes for writers, musicians, dancers and other artists.

Today, the flower children are gone and the Victorians have been gentrified into boutiques and offices, or duplexes and triplexes. Expensive. Many young people and artists share the rent in the older homes.

The Haight, because of fame, attracts wandering young who see it as a shrine to yesteryear. Residents are trying to stop the opening of new saloons and lower the crime and mischief and make the neighborhood more kid friendly.

Next to Golden Gate Park, a cornucopia of museums, flora, activities. The park's panhandle defines the northern border. On-street parking is in short supply.

Just to the south of the Haight, the terrain rises into hills with some of the loveliest views of the city and the Pacific. Winding streets. Wooded. Some streets open to fog, some protected. These are upscale neighborhoods: Parnassus, Ashbury Heights, Corona Heights, Clarendon Heights.

Also in the Haight, two other large parks, Buena Vista and Corona Heights. The Pacific is within a half-hour walk.

Book, art, music, clothing stores. Bike and in-line skate rentals. Groceries. Many San Francisco neighborhoods have their restaurant rows; so does this neighborhood. The Haight's has a reputation for being pleasant, diverse and interesting.

Buses and streetcars. About five miles from the downtown, which is long in San Francisco, but a hop-and-a-skip for the rest of the world. Visitor traffic often congests the arterial streets.

The Haight attracts a fair number of students. The giant UC Medical Center, a teaching hospital, and the University of San Francisco are close by, and San Francisco State University is within a 15-minute bus ride. Major renovations to be made to UC facilities, about $500 million worth.

HAYES VALLEY

A SMALL NEIGHBORHOOD that died and now is emerging from its grave. Named after landowner.

Located in the downtown between Larkin Street on the east, Webster on the west, Fulton on the north and Fell on the south.

Years ago, a well-known neighborhood, mentioned frequently in local histories, Hayes Valley declined when a Highway 101 spur (called the Central Freeway) was run through it and shattered its coherence. Many of the stores went empty, crime became a problem.

Then that great urban renewer, the 1989 earthquake, weakened and forced the dismantling of part of the freeway and a new Hayes emerged: artsy, small shops, diverse.

In 1997, San Francisco voters by a slim margin said that they wanted to keep and rebuild what remained of the Central Freeway, one of the main access roads to people living in the Richmond and Sunset districts. But in 1998, another vote was held: tear it down.

In the end, it was demolished. Traffic now exits on Octavia Boulevard, which was turned into a major thoroughfare and lined with trees.

About 5,000 housing units are in the works for what is called the Octavia-Market corridor. Some people are warning that the additional traffic may overload the streets and make parking scarcer. But the project has its supporters, who think that it will benefit the neighborhood. The next few years will tell the story.

Hayes Valley is located just west of Davies Symphony Hall, the opera house, the main library and the Asian Museum. All these cultural ornaments are working to push this neighborhood up the scale.

UC Berkeley used to have an extension campus in Hayes Valley. UC wants to raze the place, now empty, and turn the land to apartments. Some residents are saying, save the campus (and its murals) and sell it to a private college.

LAKESHORE

THE LAST NEIGHBORHOOD in the City to be developed. Located on the Pacific on the southern border. Includes San Francisco State University, Lake Merced, two golf courses, a shore park and the only "suburban" shopping plaza in the City, Stonestown. Two other golf courses located nearby.

Also Parkmerced complex, short and tall (12-story) apartment buildings. Built in the late 1940s for elderly, it now houses all ages.

Just below Sloat Boulevard, the northern boundary, are middle-class homes built just after World War II. Small tracts, condos and single homes, very nice, tucked here and there. Dominant type of housing in the district is the apartment. Middle-class neighborhood.

East of Junipero Serra Boulevard the terrain rises into hills and to middle- and upper middle-class housing. This is another San Francisco situation where if you drive three or four blocks in any direction the housing changes. Moving north, the homes improve.

San Francisco State University has dorms but for much of its housing the university has been purchasing apartment buildings in Parkmerced. In 2005, the university bought an apartment complex in another area. The 670 units will be used to housing students, faculty and staff.

For information about housing, students should contact the university housing office at (415) 338-1067 or see housing@sfsu.edu.

Foggy and sometimes cold in the summer, balmy in the winter.

By San Francisco standards, a long way to the downtown. But freeways and Junipero Serra Boulevard are close by. BART station nearby in Daly City. Also, buses go directly to the downtown.

For amusements, the zoo, the golf courses, the lake, the Pacific (gorgeous sunsets), beaches, Stern Grove (concerts), Golden Gate Park close by. The Pacific a strong presence. Trap and skeet range. Golden Gate National Recreation Area extends along the coast. Lot of greenery. Harding Park golf course recently got a $15 million renovation.

The water needed to keep fairways green had been drained from Lake Merced. In 2002, three golf courses agreed to replenish the lake by using recycled water instead of tapping area wells. More shopping, including large discount stores, over the border in Daly City.

MISSION

LARGE, VIBRANT NEIGHBORHOOD with an ethnic mix that can be described as United Nations. Having escaped the 1906 fires, the Mission has a fair number of Victorians. Also many apartments.

Duboce-Division streets mark the north border, Potrero Avenue the east, Chavez (formerly Army) Street the south. At least some Realtors mark the western border as Guerrero Street but this line excludes Mission Dolores and its namesake park and Mission High School. Some people probably would place the west border at Dolores Street.

Site of the first Spanish settlements in San Francisco. Mission Dolores, built in 1791, still stands and is popular with tourists. About 5,000 Indians are buried in the churchyard. The Mission District, however, is not touristy. Too many working people for that. But it has a reputation for being colorful, exuberant and cosmopolitan, and at the same time friendly. Parts of Mission are moving upscale, especially on the west side, Valencia and Guerrero streets.

Realtors say that you have to take the Mission block by block and they're right. Within two or three blocks, conditions can change dramatically. When rents shot up in the late 1990s, rent control dampened increases somewhat and allowed many low- and low-middle income residents to stay in the Mission.

Small shops, groceries, lively restaurants, cheap food. Culturally adventurous.

People crowd the shops along Mission and Dolores streets. Murals decorate walls. The Mission has over a dozen churches that provide social outlets and services, such as child care, and recreational opportunities. Some churches are striking or historically famous. Several private schools.

Crime a problem in some sections despite efforts down through the years to improve matters. Many blocks enjoy peace and many residents go about their business without getting into trouble. Cops have beefed up presence, placed some officers on bicycles, opened a new station. New library. New skate park coming to or recently opened at Potrero Del Sol Park.

Commute great. Buses. BART runs through Mission. A short hop to downtown, to Giants stadium at China Basin and to Mission Bay, big development now swinging into high gear. Mission District is protected from fog and cold winds of the Pacific by Twin Peaks, the range of hills to the west.

NOB HILL, RUSSIAN HILL

A NEIGHBORHOOD whose name has entered the language as a metaphor for great riches. If you live on "Nob Hill" you have arrived.

The hill once was home to the Bonanza kings (mining) and the Big Four — Leland Stanford, Charles Crocker, Mark Hopkins (for whom the hotel was named) and Collis Huntington — builders of the transcontinental railroad. Great views of Bay and Golden Gate.

Many of the great homes were destroyed in the fire that followed the 1906 earthquake. Or they were dynamited to stop the fire's spread. Among the survivors, the home of James Flood, a Bonanza king; it was later converted into the Pacific Union Club.

Modern Nob Hill: Several hotels surrounding a small park. Grace Cathedral, the largest Episcopal Church in the City and a pleasing presence, interested in the larger community. Concerts and other events are presented at the cathedral. Just off the hill, high-rise apartment and condo buildings, which make this section one of the most populated of the City.

Many tourists. Restricted parking. Great commute. Walk down the hill and you're in the financial district, or in the other direction, Fisherman's Wharf. Chinatown and North Beach a short walk. Cable cars cross paths on California and Powell streets.

Russian Hill, located just north of Nob Hill, also has great views. More of a residential neighborhood, it lacks — and doesn't want — the glitz and popularity of Nob Hill. Couple of restaurants. Little else in the way of businesses. High-rise apartments and three-story flats. Here's where Lombard Street squiggles its way down a hill. Lombard residents want the City to close the street to traffic. City is trying to discourage traffic but the street remains open.

Many nice homes, some oddly shaped to fit contours of hills.

Some of the steepest streets in the City and one of its most desirable locations. Close to everything. Small. In this area, a stroll of a few blocks will take you into another neighborhood.

NOE VALLEY, GLEN PARK

ANOTHER CHOICE NEIGHBORHOOD, Noe (no-ee) Valley nestles on east slope of Twin Peaks and is bordered on the south by Diamond Heights and on the north by hills. You can reach it by driving west on 24th street.

About 30 years ago, it was a working-class neighborhood with fading Victorians, many of them subdivided into apartments.

Since then the homes have been generally and nicely refurbished, greatly adding to the beauty of the neighborhood, and many of the apartments folded up into flats or condos — the pluses and minuses of gentrification.

Small stores — meat, fish, produce — some saloons and highly rated neighborhood restaurants. Bookstores and coffee houses. Sidewalk benches. Library. Window boxes filled with brightly colored flowers adorn many of the homes and the yards are landscaped with mature trees and shrubs. The smell of eucalyptus trees graces the air in some sections.

Residents are famous or, depending on your point of view, notorious for fighting stores and projects they dislike. When restaurant odors displeased residents, they lobbied to close the eateries.

In the streets near the Mission District, door grills suggest crime may be a problem. Noe Valley is sometimes included in Eureka-Castro District.

Easy commute. BART station at 24th Street. Buses to downtown. Some Noe streets narrow traffic to one way. If you're energetic, you can walk to downtown or peddle a bike. About 25 blocks to city hall.

Glen Park is a small, hilly neighborhood south of Noe Valley, just east of Diamond Heights. Homes old but well tended. Lawns and shrubs also show much care.

Glen Park blends into Diamond Heights and Twin Peaks, upper-income neighborhoods with great views of the Bay. Highway 280 defines the east side of Glen Park and kind of buffers it from the Mission District. Playground and recreation center in Glen Canyon Park, in the hills.

Small shopping section on Bosworth, near a BART station.

The hills to the west of Noe Valley block out much of the fog but on many days cool air drifts into Noe.

NORTH BEACH, CHINATOWN

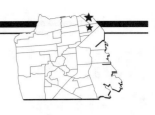

NOT TOO LONG AGO, it was almost impossible to say North Beach without adding Italian. Many Italians settled in the neighborhood; the restaurants, bakeries and delicatessens and shops strongly reflected Italy.

The Italian presence is still strong but — an old San Francisco story — it's being shared by other immigrant groups, mainly Asian. Chinatown is still favored by the Chinese but many of the descendents of the first immigrants have moved to the suburbs or other parts of San Francisco.

North Beach's glittery strip of Broadway, for years the domain of topless clubs, has taken on a more diverse look. The night life is still active but most of the strip joints are gone, replaced by cafes. No chain stores allowed; that's the local law. Public housing was demolished and replaced by a complex of 341 apartments.

Kids play in the streets or in mini parks with basketball courts. Chinese men and women rise early, gather in groups and, in tai-chi slow-motion ballet, exercise their bodies. Women walk to morning Mass at Saints Peter and Paul. Men chat at Washington Square. Fisherman's Wharf and Pier 39, the little restaurant-amusement plaza, are part of North Beach. Old St. Mary's Church, in 2005, celebrated its 150th year.

When the Embarcadero Freeway was torn down (earthquake damage), it opened views to the Bay and awakened San Francisco to the possibilities of the stretch that goes from the Bay Bridge to Fisherman's Wharf.

Since then, the City has planted palms, widened the sidewalks into a promenade, added antique street cars and built a plaza in front of the Ferry Building, a landmark. Recently the Ferry Building was reopened as sort of restaurant-shop emporium with offices for the port authority.

Muni purchased old buses from other states and from Italy and routed them from the downtown to Fisherman's Wharf, traveling the Embarcadero. Nicely done and well received.

Big-time recreation complex is supposed to be built on the Embarcadero. Some residents are cool to this project, fearing the Embarcadero will be yuppiefied out of its maritime history. But the City says it is working to preserve some older buildings.

More hotels are going up in the downtown. Also more apartment buildings. The destruction of Bayshore freeway has rejuvenated this part of San Francisco.

In many ways, these are great neighborhoods, full of restaurants, interesting people, bookstores, places to visit. Here's where the Beat Generation got its start. The city has named a street in honor of local bookstore owner and poet, Lawrence Ferlinghetti.

Parking's a problem but you can walk to work. Housing a mix: apartments with bay windows overlook busy streets. At Telegraph Hill, the streets and the prices ascend rapidly. Great views of Bay and East Bay hills.

City is prodding Chinatown to vote in an improvement district and tax itself to improve services. One problem: much of land is owned not by individuals but by family associations with many members and it is unclear how the vote could be counted.

OCEAN VIEW, INGLESIDE

MIDDLE-CLASS NEIGHBORHOODS in southwest section. Homes generally single-family, many built between 1900 and 1940. Wood and stucco, zero lot lines. Gentle and steep hills.

Close to Pacific. Good views of San Bruno Mountain and Mt. Davidson. Also nearby, San Francisco State University, Lake Merced, Stonestown Shopping Center, and to east, City College.

Ocean View and Ingleside are sometimes bundled with another neighborhood called Merced Heights. The three are called informally OMI.

Safety grates cover some doors and windows. Citizen groups are working to divert the young people into safer pursuits. Police squad assigned to neighborhood and thanks to a variety of efforts crime has decreased.

Goverment center opened in 2005. Houses representatives of city departments and bring services closer to residents.

Recreation center at Ocean View Park.

This is a neighborhood that almost demands to be driven for its merits to come through. Some of the older homes command great views. As you move north, homes and appearances improve markedly and some streets stand out. Some blocks mix homes in need of repair and attention with homes that have been well kept.

Unusual street design. Urbano Drive, an oval, traces what used to be Ingleside Racetrack.

Fog belt. Often cold in summer, balmy in winter.

One of the longer hauls to the downtown, but buses and BART available, Interstate 280 close by. BART station in nearby Daly City.

PACIFIC HEIGHTS, MARINA, PRESIDIO HEIGHTS

PACIFIC HEIGHTS, the most prestigious neighborhood in the City, is situated on hills overlooking the Bay and Golden Gate, glorious views, and is home to corporate execs, civic officials, lawyers and, if there is such a group, ordinary people with money. Many of the homes are large and grand and pleasingly designed in an old-fashioned way.

Presidio Heights is a small enclave of elegant homes. It borders the Presidio, the former Army base being transformed in parts into business and digital-media parks.

The Marina District, which has the most housing, is located on flat land at base of Pacific Heights but some streets ascend into low but steep hills with tall apartment-condo buildings. Marina, built on filled land, took a bad hit in the 1989 quake: homes and apartments destroyed. Repairs have been made.

Level of care in all these neighborhoods is high. Lombard Street runs to typical big-city commercial, restaurants, fast-food places, stores. For the upscale and fashionable, try Union Street or Chestnut. Victorians on Union have been converted into stores. Restaurants, bookstores, boutiques, shops. Nice to stroll. Between Pacific Heights and the Marina is a small, pleasant section called Cow Hollow.

About three miles to downtown. Buses. Controlled parking; residents get stickers. No bars on windows but many alarm systems. Home and condo prices vary in these neighborhoods but some homes go for millions, a few for tens of millions. Higher the elevation, generally the higher the rent or price.

Views of Golden Gate. Close to pleasures and restaurants of downtown. Marinas. Jogging, strolling, sunbathing along the shore. Swimming in Aquatic Park. Fishing. Windsurfing. Skulling. Palace of Fine Arts, which has a lagoon that in 2005 was being restored. Fort Mason, on the shore, has exhibits, plays. Miles of trails with lovely views. Improvements are being made along the shore to nourish wildlife. Several private schools. Fog shoots through Golden Gate, adds beauty, allure to the views.

Tourist country. People walk and drive through neighborhoods. Some concern that Presidio as a park-business will attract too many people. Quaint is nice but the supermarkets are small and the parking scarce.

POTRERO HILL

ONE OF THE CLASSIC neighborhoods of San Francisco. Compact, hidden, great views of downtown. Many nice homes, a mix of Victorians and single homes, carefully and lovingly restored. In its past, Potrero Hill has housed several immigrant groups and is now favored by artists and professionals.

Generally located between Interstate 280 and Highway 101. Chavez Street (formerly Army) defines the south border, 15th Street the north. Hilly, which accounts for much of the neighborhood's allure. From its heights, Potrero has a view of downtown spread east to west, tall, wide and imposing, and bright. The afternoon sun seems to light up the high-rise offices.

Some homes have views of the Bay and San Francisco to the south. Some look down on the Mission District. Homes on east side are shoehorned onto lots and served by winding streets.

Sheltered by the hills from the fog. Warmer than other neighborhoods. Library. Small stores. Three parks. Recreation center.

Easy access to freeways but many people take the bus to work. Or Caltrain. Station near Interstate 280; end of line near Giants ball park.

Mission Bay and Giants stadium are located 10 to 15 blocks northeast of Potrero Hill. Homes, offices, a medical complex are also included in the Mission Bay development. All this has made this section a hot housing market.

Much of the land directly east of Potrero Hill, now industrial-office-warehouse, may be converted into housing.

Residents are a vocal group and fight to preserve quality of neighborhood.

UC San Francisco wanted to build a 17-story tower next door at its Mission Bay campus.

A political power, John Burton, who lives next to the proposed skyscraper, did not like the idea. Result: lower building.

PRESIDIO

FORMER MILITARY BASE, now a park, 1,480 acres. Possibly the oldest "neighborhood" in San Francisco. Located east and west of the Golden Gate Bridge. One of the choicest spots in the City and probably in the world. Its hills look out over the Golden Gate.

In 2005, the City turned out to welcome the Letterman Digital Arts Center, the new headquarters for LucasFilm of Star Wars fame, and to rub shoulders with George Lucas.

The center, built on the site of Letterman Hospital, consists of four buildings, each four stories. Three will be occupied by 1,500 Lucas employees; the fourth, leased to another firm or firms. The site was landscaped to include a lagoon and a stream and planted with a great variety of shrubs and trees.

Besides supplying jobs, the center boosts San Francisco as an entertainment leader, a sort of Hollywood north.

Settled first by the Spanish who built the fort (Presidio). Later taken over by the U.S. Army and for 140 years or so used as a military base. Thousands of soldiers were stationed at the Presidio and treated at its hospitals.

When the Soviet Union went belly up and the Cold War collapsed, the Pentagon gave up the Presidio to the Golden Gate National Recreational Area. Left intact were 550 homes and barracks that were later turned to use as rentals (about 1,200 units). Golf course and renovated pool and gym open to public. Many of the more dilapidated buildings have been demolished and dozens of private firms or organizations have moved into the remaining structures.

Along the shore, the park, to the west, ties in with another large park, which includes the Palace of the Legion of Honor (a lovely art museum) and a golf course. Under the Golden Gate Bridge is Fort Point, one of the oldest forts in the west, nicely restored. Politicians, environmentalists and local officials are trying to secure federal money to restore and improve the Presidio, which is supposed to make itself self sufficient (and seems to doing so).

Pacific and Presidio Heights border the Presidio, lovely neighborhoods but few houses. Most of the nearby housing will be found in the Richmond District. So pleasant an assignment was the Presidio that at its closing, the commanding general said, "It is said that an officer has three wishes: to be a general, to go to the Presidio and to go to heaven."

RICHMOND, SEACLIFF

THE NEIGHBORHOOD NORTH of Golden Gate Park. Middle class, considered a step-up address for first- and second-generation Americans. First residents included Russians, refugees from the Revolution. Russian church with onion domes on Geary Boulevard.

One of the biggest residential sections of the City. Homes, for the most part, built between 1900 and 1940, a mix of styles, the most popular probably the single home, zero lot line with the living room over the (small) garage. Some quite striking stuff, Mediterranean style, on bluffs overlooking the Pacific in section called Seacliff where homes command million-dollar prices.

Streets clean. Homes generally well-kept. Much remodeling, especially in the streets near the ocean. Apartment-condo complexes near ocean, just removed from the Great Highway. Graffiti scarce. Gates on many doorways but reputation is low in crime, conservative (by San Francisco standards), middle class but moving up the scale. Neighborhood has own police station.

Golden Gate Park is a plus, all sorts of activities, and on occasion, probably a minus: traffic, visitors taking up parking, homeless sometimes sleeping in bushes. Lincoln Park, with the renovated Palace of the Legion of Honor and a golf course, is located on the north.

Also on the north, the Presidio, miles of park, trails and vistas of the Golden Gate. Short walk to the Pacific and long beaches open to the public. Richmond also encompasses the University of San Francisco. Books and basketball. Lovely church and dome.

Fog belt. In summer, it can get cold and windy and this turns off some people. Clear winters. Other drawback: congestion along Geary. Hard to find street parking. Seacliff residents have stopped large tour buses from driving through their neighborhood but it still draws many visitors. Price of beauty.

Geary Boulevard is a straight shot to downtown. Buses. Many restaurants, some first class, and shops along Geary and Clement. A few Irish saloons. Meryvns department store on Geary. Kaiser Hospital on east border of neighborhood.

On the ocean, you can see the ruins of the Sutro Baths, in its day the largest bath house in the world. The owner, Adolf Sutro, built a rail line from the baths to the downtown, opening the sand dunes to development.

SO. OF MARKET, CHINA BASIN, MISSION BAY

ONE OF THE HOT SPOTS for housing and office and high-tech and bio-tech jobs. Many new apartments and condos. A little orientation.

• SOMA. South of Market Street, the main boulevard in downtown San Francisco. SOMA is sometimes used to describe the entire area we are talking about but often it is broken down into small neighborhoods. These include:

• China Basin. On the Bay, south of Giants Stadium.

• Rincon Hill, about Second and Brannan streets, just south of the Bay Bridge.

• South Beach, on the Embarcadero, south of Rincon Hill, and just north of Giants Stadium.

• Mission Bay. Just east of China Basin, between Interstate 280 and approximately Third Street and Channel Street.

Built out decades ago, San Francisco about 30 years ago started to tear down the old and dilapidated to make way for the new. Much of the decrepit, along with thriving businesses, was located South of Market and for decades the neighborhood, with its many saloons and flophouses, was considered the town's skid row. It was also — and to a diminishing extent still is — a place where people with little money could survive.

The Moscone Convention Center gave the neighborhood its first shove up the scale and by and by artists and young professionals came to appreciate the neighborhood's proximity to the downtown. Some buildings were converted to apartments or work-lofts. Dance clubs were opened. The Museum of Modern Art was later opened across from the Moscone. SOMA took on some sizzle and began building new housing.

Mission Bay, located about 1.5 miles south of the Moscone Center, was an industrial zone with rail yards. About 1980, developers and others pushed for a plan to bulldoze just about the entire sector and convert it into a bio-tech-residential neighborhood.

The plan was thrown into the grinder of public opinion and hearings and market conditions blew cold and nothing seemed to be moving but in the 1990s, as if popping out of a cake, Mission Bay showed up. The University of California, San Francisco (medical research) committed itself to moving many of its facilities from west side of town to Mission Bay, and this gave the project credibility. UCSF has about 21,000 employees and is a major force in town.

In 2003, the first building of the UC complex opened, Genentech Hall followed shortly by another building. At least 1,600 apartment units have been built at Mission Bay, which covers 303 acres. Plans call for 6,000 apartments and condos and office towers. Recent addition: public art in the plaza, Richard Serra's "Ballast." Weathered steel, two plates about 50 feet high, five inches thick, 160 tons total. "Like blades stuck in the ground," said architect.

Several years ago Californians voted to fund their own stem cell research and passed a tax that will raise billions. Up and down the state, cities competed to win the headquarters for this research, the grandly named, California Institute for Regenerative Medicine. In 2005, the winner was announced: Mission Bay.

In 1989, an earthquake damaged the Embarcadero Freeway, a short stub of highway that ran north of the Bay Bridge. At one time, state engineers and the cement-freeway crowd wanted to run this highway all the way around to the Golden Gate Bridge. The job had enough political muscle to get started but then City residents revolted and stopped it in its tracks.

When the 1989 earthquake did its work, the City had the choice rebuilding the freeway or tearing it down. No brainer. Down it came, and to the surprise of many this revived the Embarcadero, the shore road that runs from Fisherman's Wharf down to Giants Stadium. Within a few years, with the help of some improvements — foremost the rebuilding of the Ferry Building into shopping-culinary pavilion — the Embarcadero turned itself into a pretty and popular promenade.

In the 1990s, the Giants opened their stadium just south of the bridge, further elevating the neighborhood and bringing in more housing. The stadium is located at the end of the Caltrain line that brings in riders from the Peninsula.

The city ran a light-rail line down to the stadium. This rail line is being extended down to Mission Bay and beyond, all the way to Hunters Point-Bayview, one of the poorest neighborhoods of the City, and near Candlestick Park, where the Forty Niners play.

In 2005, the politicians and developers worked out a deal to build on or near Rincon Hill 2,200 condos in five towers, at least one going up 55 stories. In exchange, the developers agreed to put up money to subsidize rents and housing around SOMA and in other parts of the City.

OK ... one job here, one there, the unexpected (the earthquake damage) ... in the end, everything came together in the revival of a big section of San Francisco, and the work continues. Recently opened or soon to open near the stadium: two supermarkets and a private gym-exercise place.

More buses have been added to the SOMA routes. From Mission Bay, it's a long walk to downtown San Francisco. From other the neighborhoods, it's a short jog or bike ride.

SOMA is sheltered by the hills from the worst of the ocean fogs.

Many young professionals, college grads, business people, researchers, doctors. If you are searching for the right mate, of whatever persuasion, but monied and promising, this should be a good place to connect.

Lots to do. Short cab or bus ride to opera house, symphony hall, main library, Asian Museum, MOMA, etc. Plays, movies, bookstores. Loads of restaurants. Not too many parks but more are planned.

Lovely vistas, pleasant walks. Ride your bike, line skate or stroll one of the prettiest promenades on the West Coast.

Close to the best of San Francisco shopping, including Bloomingdales to open in 2006. Almost unheard of for San Francisco, which hates discount stores, there's a Costco on the east side of SOMA.

New housing, which may not sound like a big deal. But most of San Fran housing is old and employs designs popular decades ago. The new stuff comes with modern wiring, double-paned windows, often larger closets, open kitchens, and so on.

Drawbacks

At peak hours, the traffic on some streets is not even Stop-and-Go. It's Stop-and-Stew. But if they can reconfigure the streets this might improve.

For most people, no subsidies. Housing priced at market rates, which can be high.

Skid Row has shrunk in size. Hasn't gone away but for the most part it's located east of SOMA.

When the Giants play, traffic increases. But according to news reports, residents seem to take the games in stride.

The future: you don't need a crystal ball to predict that SOMA and elements are going to become more popular.

• Opened in 2005: Museum of African Diaspora.

• On the way in 2007, the Contemporary Jewish Museum.

• When the noise and incidents got excessive at a China Basin night club and residents complained, the City and authorities issued warnings and then shut the place down for two months. San Francisco tolerates what many other cities would suppress but it has its limits.

• Just below Mission Bay along Third Street is a small neighborhood called Dogpatch. Protected by a marsh, many of its buildings survived the earthquake of 1906 and in recent years have been fixed up.

SUNSET

ONE OF THE LARGEST NEIGHBORHOODS of San Francisco. Will appear on some maps as Taraval. Sunset district borders but stands aloof from Golden Gate Park, the zoo and the Pacific. They attract visitors and tourists; the Sunset generally doesn't. Middle class but moving upmarket. Crime low. Homes generally well-maintained. Streets clean. Graffiti rare.

Population about 70,000 but some people place Forest Hills, St. Francis Wood and Parkside in the Sunset and put the population close to 100,000. The Sunset is defined alternately as a district including neighborhoods and as a neighborhood.

Glorious sunsets, balmy winters, mild summers — when the fog lifts. In the summer, it often doesn't; many days cold, damp and dim. If you are buying or renting in the Sunset, think about the weather. Many love it, many hate it.

Commute, good. By MUNI, about 30 to 45 minutes to downtown San Francisco. Shorter if you drive. BART station at Daly City.

A neighborhood traditionally favored by immigrants and first-generation Americans on their way up and, usually, out (to the suburbs). Considered a good address, and with home values rising, attracting more professionals. The district started to develop in the early 1900s, when streetcar lines were extended and the downtown ran out of building space. In the 1930s and early 1940s, contractor Henry Doelger built thousands of homes on the sand dunes of the Sunset and set the architectural look of the district.

At that time, builders were wrestling with a new problem: what to do with the car. The horse, noble but stinky, had been shunted into the stable, separate from the house. The horseless carriage, now being mass produced, could be brought into the house, but where. Doelger stuck it under the living room. The typical Sunset home is a two-story affair: garage on the ground floor, stairs to the second floor, living room with picture window looking out to street, kitchen to rear of living room, and off the hallway, two bedrooms and one bathroom. In many homes, a third bedroom and a second bathroom were added. Lots 25 feet wide. No front yard or just a patch of grass. Small rear yard. Pinched views, if any, of the Pacific. Stucco relieved by decorative balconies, tile and other knickknacks. Many homes are large enough for extended families or in-law units, a selling plus.

Doelger priced his homes at $5,000 each, which in the Depression was a lot of money but not an overwhelming amount, and as much as anything this defined the social character of the Sunset. It was built for people ascending into the middle class. The Sunset is sometimes criticized for being bland — the White Cliffs of Doelger — but had it added views, rooms and more yard space, it would have priced itself beyond its intended market. Doelger's homes, many remodeled, now sell for well over $500,000.

First came the Irish and the Germans, immigrants or their children. As the initial wave grew old and the kids moved to the suburbs, many of the homes came on the market, to be purchased by Chinese immigrants or their children moving out of Chinatown. But the Sunset still retains quite a mix. Ten or 20 or 30 years from now ... who knows ... the Sunset will probably catch the Hispanic middle class moving out of the Mission District.

Fearing their children would lose their religion in public schools, the Irish and Italians in San Francisco and elsewhere built their own schools. Four Catholic elementary schools, two high schools were built in or near the Sunset. They serve as a sort of alternate school system and accept many non-Catholics.

On pleasant evenings, people jog or stroll to the ocean. Miles of beach. Besides playgrounds and Golden Gate Park, there's a community center, a seniors center, social clubs, and Stern Grove, which offers popular Sunday concerts. Also the city zoo, municipal golf course and several libraries. Restaurants, coffee bars, and shops many and diverse: Irish pubs, Chinese diners, kosher markets. Most are concentrated on a few streets, among them Judah, Noriega, Taraval and Portal.

Increasingly, a good neighborhood for dining out. Stonestown Mall, which includes a Macys and Nordstrom, is located just south of the Sunset. Many people shop at large discount malls in Daly City and Colma, a short drive down Highway 1.

See the shore for apartments and drive around Judah Street for homes built around the turn of the century. Inner Sunset, which includes the giant University of California Medical Center, a teaching-research institute, is sometimes broken out as a separate neighborhood. Hilly. Older homes, more in tune with the nearby Haight.

Many students and UC personnel live in the Sunset and Richmond districts. The students attend the University of California, the University of San Francisco, San Francisco State University and San Francisco City College, all located within a drive or bus ride of one to four miles.

TENDERLOIN

DEPRESSED NEIGHBORHOOD that seems to be constantly changing. Meets housing needs of poor and elderly. Bordered by shopping district and major hotels. Crime hot spot. Attracts many tourists.

By day, full of business people, conventioneers, tourists and government workers. At night, along the western edge, frequented by people going to opera or symphony. Exhibit hall. Large library opened in 1996 — a nice plus for San Francisco and neighborhood. Asian Art Museum. Elementary school opened in 1998.

Boundaries described as Market on the south, Post on the north, Van Ness on the west, Powell on the east. Population about 24,000.

Porno theaters and adult bookstores. Pimps, prostitutes, druggies, winos, homeless. Not everywhere. A lot of businesses try to run legit, keep up appearances and avoid trouble. The cops, who patrol on foot, or authorities crack down on the places that have many problems.

Home to immigrants and people of modest means. Also several thousand children. Community and charitable groups have built or secured or will soon secure apartments for about 4,500 low-income residents. St. Boniface Church, recently renovated. There's even a few small gated complexes of regular homes.

In 2000, the city opened a shelter for young adults, 18 to 24, many of them runaways or homeless. They can stay up to four months in the shelter and receive job training.

San Franciscans have never sorted out their feelings about the homeless and for this reason, the city has found it difficult to come with a consistent program for housing and caring for them. So the appearances of the Tenderloin wax and wane according to the moods of the citizens.

The City is trying a new approach, Care Not Cash (see chapter one) and voters passed a measure restricting panhandling.

The Tenderloin is also being influenced by what's happened south of Market and near Market Street — new hotels, more office buildings.

Within walking distance of downtown. Buses and BART trains to other destinations. Good place to save commuting costs. But take care.

TREASURE ISLAND

A NEIGHBORHOOD San Francisco lost and then got back in 1997. Located mid-Bay, Treasure Island was built from fill for the 1939 World's Fair and is connected to Yerba Buena Island, 150 acres, a rocky hill that serves as the middle anchor for the Bay Bridge.

San Francisco owned Treasure Island until the Navy took it over in 1942. With the end of the Cold War, Treasure Island was decommissioned and given back to the City.

The location is choice, the views delightful, the possibilities, seemingly, endless. On the downside, because the island has sunk about four feet since it was built and might need extensive earthquake reinforcing, its infrastructure costs may limit anything large and grand.

For the present, there are about 1,000 apartments on the island, a good portion of them rented out. About 200 units were built for the homeless. Small marina.

Every year or so, someone used to advance a scheme for What To Do with Treasure Island.

The ideas keep bubbling up but have firmed somewhat around 2,800 housing units, a ferry slip, hotels, a conference center and shops. About 200 acres of the 400-acre island would be left in open space. At least two parks, one facing San Francisco, the other the East Bay. Playing fields in the middle of the island. Nature park-wetlands at the north end.

As for what will be built ... the City does not have a developer panting to get to work on the island. Until a firm comes forward and submits a plan, the ideas will stay at the conceptional stage.

Movie and television studios rent some of the facilities. A good deal of "Nash Bridges," featuring Don Johnson, was filmed in an old hangar-sound stage. The old administration buildings hosted high-school proms.

TWIN PEAKS, MT. DAVIDSON, DIAMOND HTS.

IN THE MIDDLE of San Francisco several hills rise to about 900 feet and run north-south for about two miles. Views great. You can see the Pacific and Golden Gate and, if faced east, the Bay. Golden Gate Park is within a mile. Market Street, which leads to downtown, is at the base of the eastern slopes.

Tie the package together and you come up with some of the most desirable neighborhoods in the City. Many of these tracts were developed just before and after World War II, and the general housing looks modern compared to the Victorian neighborhoods. Tudors, Spanish styles with terra-cotta roofs, mostly single homes but some townhouses, American substantial, American flimsy, the posh and the plain can be found in these neighborhoods

In describing San Francisco, Realtors and writers frequently use the term "West of Twin Peaks." This is the fog line. The hills block the fog from the downtown neighborhoods or impede its progress. If you live on the west side, if you can see the Pacific, you will often be socked in by the summer fog.

Crime low but residents wary. Homes have alarms, not barred windows. Lot of tender loving care into homes and lawns and appearances. Mature trees on some streets. Hedges and flower gardens.

Mt. Davidson, 927 feet, topped by a cross, is popular with Easter worshippers. A park, wooded, protects the top from further development but blocks some views. Atheists and others want cross down. In a complicated deal in 1997, it was sold to Armenian group as memorial for Armenians massacred by Turks. This way cross went to private hands; no conflict between church-state.

On top of Mt. Sutro, to the north, is planted a tall (977 feet) TV transmission tower, hated by many but a fascinating sight when fog rolls in. Looks like a sailing ship emerging from a cottony sea.

For its views, Twin Peaks was placed on the 49-mile scenic drive, which means some tourist traffic. Parking restricted on some streets. The twin peaks, which the Spanish explorers called Los Pechos de la Choca, or the Breasts of the Indian Maiden, rise to 904 and 913 feet. If shopping for a home or apartment, map is a must. Streets curl all over the place.

VISITACION VALLEY

BEDROOM NEIGHBORHOOD on southern border, east of McLaren Park. About 16,000 residents. Named by Franciscans in 1777 when they sighted the valley on the Feast of the Visitation. Also called "Vis Valley."

Historically, a transitional neighborhood for immigrants or people on the way up from some of the poorer sections and it still seems to be following that path. In recent years, Vis Valley has attracted many Asian and Pacific-Island immigrants.

Younger working-class people are buying older rental homes, remodeling and occupying them. Single homes, row on row. Stucco. Living room over the garage, a common pattern in San Francisco. Zero side yards. Near the county line, off Geneva Street, you'll find townhouses and apartments. Neighborhood that requires map. Many streets deadend at McLaren Park or Highway 101.

In 2005, more housing was added, about 100 apartments.

Visitacion Valley had two public housing projects: Sunnydale and Geneva Towers. The latter, a complex of 20-story buildings, became notorious for crime. In 1998, it was dynamited and replaced with apartment complexes. A police substation has been opened in Sunnydale project, in a community center. In some areas, the crime problems remain.

Shopping done at small stores, many family owned. Views from some locations.

In 2005, work began on a two-year project to spruce up the neighborhood by planting flowers and shrubs in median strips and gardens in empty lots, installing benches and street lights, and redesigning traffic lanes to make the streets safer. The hope is to attract more businesses, elevate the morale of residents and reduce crime.

Buses to downtown. You can pick up BART a few miles east, on Geneva. A short drive on Highway 101. Also a short drive to the airport, one of the biggest employers on the Peninsula. Candlestick Park, home field of the Forty Niners, is located just east of Highway 101.

Cow Palace, which hosts sporting and recreational events, is just across the border in Daly City.

McLaren Park, which has a golf course, is one of the biggest in the City. Vis Valley has added a skate park for the kids.

WESTERN ADDITION
Fillmore

LOCATED JUST WEST of city hall in the downtown. Sometimes called the "Fillmore." A mixed neighborhood where the poor blend with the middle class and well-to-do. On some streets, concerns about crime. In 2005, patrols were stepped up and in a few places surveillance cameras installed.

Home to the 5-acre Japanese Cultural and Trade Center which includes a consulate, hotel, restaurant, two Japanese-language theaters and three Buddhist temples. Neighborhood also takes in Cathedral Hill and St. Mary's, the last hurrah for grand churches in San Francisco. Organ employed for concerts.

Large Kaiser hospital, renovated and expanded (offices, replacement outpatient clinic, parking).

Before World War II, about 5,300 Japanese lived in the neighborhood. When they were interned, thousands of newcomers, hired to work in the shipyards and war industries, moved in, and the housing units multiplied. After the war, many Japanese returned and an effort was made to provide the neighborhood with decent housing.

The Western Addition borders the fire line of the 1906 earthquake. East of the line homes were destroyed, west saved. The district salvaged a great store of Victorians. In a misguided effort that supposedly lost more housing than it produced, many Victorians were demolished and replaced by projects. Over the last 25 years, the remaining Victorians, which had faded with neglect, made a comeback. Many have been restored. Remodelings are common.

Fillmore Center, 1,113 apartments over five blocks (Steiner and Turk streets). Homes and apartments on the northern border of the district glide into Pacific Heights, the most prestigious neighborhood in the City.

Public housing on Buchanan and Eddy Streets demolished and the 193 apartments of Plaza East built in its place. Rent is pegged to a percentage of a resident's income. Some concern that the poor are being driven out of neighborhood but it is also argued that the Western Addition was overdue for a change. City is trying to make the Fillmore into a jazz district.

Commute a nothing. Walk to downtown, opera, Davies Symphony Hall, San Francisco's largest library. Catholic school was to be closed; instead it will stay open and be renovated. Summer fog often makes its way down to Western Addition. In 2005, the whole neighborhood was fixed for wi-fi.

Chapter **3**

San Mateo County at a Glance

BORDERED BY THE PACIFIC on the west and the bay on the east, San Mateo is a county of 723,453 residents, the great majority of whom owe their livelihoods to the county's neighbors.

On the northern border sits San Francisco, owner of the most valuable piece of real estate in San Mateo County: San Francisco International Airport. The airport recently opened an international terminal. In 2003, BART (commute rail) extended its line to the airport and opened stations at South San Francisco, San Bruno and Millbrae.

San Francisco stores its water supply in San Mateo and to assure its purity has placed thousands of acres in watershed.

On the southern border sits Santa Clara County, home of Stanford University and the original Silicon Valley. Short of space, Silicon Valley has spread into San Mateo County and opened giant office and research complexes. Among the biggest, Sun and Oracle.

In the lexicon of the locals, San Mateo makes up much of what is called "The Peninsula."

Hills and mountains run down the spine of San Mateo County, with the happy result that thousands of residents enjoy vistas of waters and rising and setting suns. Some of the tallest waves in the world crash against its 55 miles of Pacific coast.

The county's cities and neighborhoods, with few exceptions, are low in crime. Many of its schools score among the highest in the state but some are struggling.

San Mateo County encompasses 440 square miles, about one-third the size of Santa Clara County, and about 10 times the size of San Francisco. From north to south, the county runs about 40 miles, and from east to west, at the widest point, about 15 miles. The highest point, elevation about 2,600 feet, is a place called Long Ridge, on the south side of the county, in the coastal mountains. Running up the center of the county is the San Andreas Fault. Yes, this is earthquake country. The whole Bay Area is earthquake country.

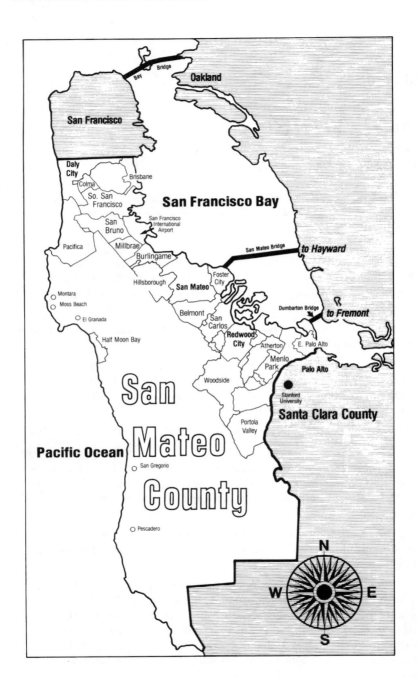

San Mateo County Population

City or Area	1990	2000	2005*
Atherton	7,163	7,194	7,256
Belmont	24,127	25,123	25,470
Brisbane	2,952	3,597	3,724
Broadmoor	3,739	4,026	NA
Burlingame	26,801	28,158	28,280
Colma	1,103	1,191	1,567
Daly City	92,311	103,621	104,661
East Palo Alto	23,451	29,506	32,202
El Granada	4,426	5,726	NA
Emerald Lake Hills	3,328	3,899	NA
Foster City	28,176	28,803	29,876
Half Moon Bay	8,886	11,842	12,688
Highlands	2,644	4,210	NA
Hillsborough	10,667	10,825	10,983
Menlo Park	28,040	30,785	30,648
Millbrae	20,412	20,718	20,708
Montara	2,552	2,950	NA
Moss Beach	3,002	1,953	NA
North Fair Oaks	13,912	15,440	NA
Pacifica	37,670	38,390	38,678
Portola Valley	4,194	4,462	4,538
Redwood City	66,072	75,402	75,986
San Bruno	38,961	40,165	42,215
San Carlos	26,167	27,718	28,190
San Mateo	85,486	92,482	94,212
South San Francisco	54,312	60,552	61,661
West Menlo Park	3,959	3,629	NA
Woodside	5,035	5,352	5,496
Countywide	649,623	707,161	723,453

Source: 1990 Census, 2000 & 2005 Census. *Every year the California Dept. of Finance puts out an estimate of populations for legal cities. Unincorporated towns, signified by NA, usually have to wait for the census, every 10 years, for population updates.

The 1989 earthquake gave the county a rousing jolt. Windows broke, chimneys toppled, water and gas lines ruptured and thousands, possibly millions, of glasses and jars fell and broke. No one was killed in the county.

Should you worry about the Next One? Some do. Many don't. But you should read the literature on earthquakes and get prepared. The beginning of your telephone book is a good place to start.

In its informal 2005 tally, the state numbered the county's residential units at 266,842 of which 152,932 were single homes, 22,880 single attached, 87,459 apartments or hotel rooms and 3,571 mobile homes. To state this a different way, single homes make up 66 percent of the housing stock and apartments-hotel rooms 33 percent. To comfort and shelter travelers, hotels have sprung up in the cities around the airport.

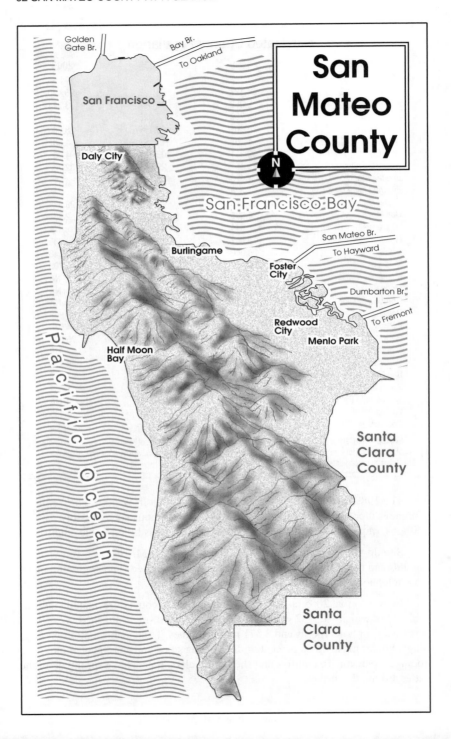

San Mateo County Average Household Income

City	1990	2000	*2005
Atherton	$279,600	$355,800	$360,200
Belmont	89,000	107,500	116,400
Brisbane	63,700	73,100	77,100
Burlingame	78,900	100,300	101,700
Colma	55,900	57,000	57,800
Daly City	67,800	84,500	86,400
East Palo Alto	52,200	48,300	57,700
Foster City	103,200	124,000	132,700
Half Moon Bay	90,100	112,800	125,100
Hillsborough	268,900	345,900	349,700
Menlo Park	102,200	122,500	132,300
Millbrae	80,900	102,600	106,000
Pacifica	75,700	94,300	96,100
Portola Valley	191,700	248,800	252,700
Redwood City	74,800	96,400	101,300
San Bruno	70,100	88,000	89,000
San Carlos	96,400	115,900	126,800
San Mateo	80,100	102,300	104,300
South San Francisco	66,300	83,500	85,900
Woodside	263,200	329,100	345,200
Remainder	113,000	124,500	130,600
Countywide	86,700	110,500	112,700

Source: Association of Bay Area Governments, *"Projections 2002"* Average income per household includes wages and salaries, dividends, interest, rent and transfer payments such as Social Security or public assistance. Based on 2000 Census data, income is stated in 2000 dollars. *Projections.

In the 1990s, the county built about 10,000 housing units, about half single homes.

Median age of San Mateo County residents is 37. Children and teens under 18 make up 23 percent of the county. People over age 55 years, 21 percent. Demographically, this translates into a mature county, not that many children, many gray heads, many empty nesters.

For decades, the county had one phone area code (415). In 1998, it was switched to 650. Part of Brisbane and about half of Daly City retain 415. If you are calling either Daly City or Brisbane and bomb with 415, try 650.

Because of its location and beauty, San Mateo County is considered one of the most desirable addresses in the state. In 2001, on median income for joint tax returns, San Mateo placed third among the 58 counties of the state, $84,760. Marin was first with $101,660, Santa Clara second with $89,475. Many homes in San Mateo, even the plain three-bedroom tract jobs, 50 years old, sell for over $600,000. Throughout the late 1990s and into 2000, home prices and rents soared. In 2002, 2003 and 2004, rents slipped and then stabilized but home prices, buttressed by low interest rates, kept on rising.

How San Mateo Earns its Money

City or Town	MAN-PRO	SERV	SAL-OFF	FARM	CON	MANU-TRANS
Atherton	70%	6%	19%	0%	2%	3%
Belmont	54	7	27	0	6	6
Brisbane	47	12	23	0	9	9
Burlingame	52	11	27	0	6	5
Colma	19	19	35	1	10	17
Daly City	29	17	35	0	7	12
East Palo Alto	18	32	23	0	12	15
El Granada	46	14	22	2	9	8
Foster City	62	6	25	0	4	4
Half Moon Bay	43	15	23	4	9	7
Hillsborough	72	4	21	0	1	2
Menlo Park	63	9	19	0	4	5
Millbrae	41	12	31	0	8	8
Montara	50	8	23	1	11	8
Moss Beach	53	7	27	1	5	8
Pacifica	39	13	29	0	10	9
Portola	72	5	19	0	2	2
Redwood City	42	15	24	0	9	9
San Bruno	32	16	32	0	9	10
San Carlos	56	8	26	0	6	5
San Mateo	43	14	28	0	7	8
South San Francisco	30	15	32	0	10	13
Woodside	69	8	17	0	3	2
San Mateo County	43	14	27	0	8	9

Source: 2000 Census. Figures are percent, rounded off, of working civilians over age 16. **Key**: MAN-PRO (managers, professionals); SERV (service); SAL-OFF (sales people, office workers); FARM (farming, fishing, forestry); CONSTRUCTION (building, maintenance, mining), MANU-TRANS (manufacturing, distribution, transportation).

All this suggests a region of great wealth but the reality is more complex. Many San Mateo residents, especially those who have been here a while, are "wealthy" on paper — the equity in their homes. The great majority of these people, however, work in ordinary, middle to upper-middle jobs: office workers, baggage handlers, trucking and delivery, aircraft mechanics, computer technicians, teachers, and so on.

A fair number of people are poor or have low incomes. The county, since its inception, has served as home to immigrants and first-generation Americans. This tradition continues, the latest arrivals including Hispanics, Asians and Filipinos.

For a long time, the three counties — San Mateo, Santa Clara and San Francisco — provided housing that met the needs or desires of the rich, the poor and the middle class. Nowadays, all three find it increasingly difficult to house the low-income and many of the middle class.

Weather

For most towns, the average rainfall is less than 20 inches. But it can reach 50 inches in the mountains. Temperatures rarely fall below freezing, rarely rise above 90. Humidity rarely bothers anyone. Rarely does thunder rumble or lightning strike.

San Mateo claims to have the mildest climate in the Bay Region. The coastal hills and mountains shelter the Bay cities, where most people reside, from the cold fogs and winds of the Pacific. Yet enough cooling breezes come down the Bay or over hills to take the edge off the summer heat.

Commuting-Travel

Two freeways traverse the county north and south. Two bridges connect San Mateo with the East Bay. BART (commute rail) runs trains to Daly City and Colma and now South San Francisco, San Bruno, Millbrae and SFO.

Caltrain runs commuter trains from Gilroy in Santa Clara County through San Mateo up to San Francisco. In 2004, Caltrain introduced bullet service, cutting travel time to San Francisco for many commuters by up to 45 minutes. See chapter on commuting.

SamTrans buses carry passengers to downtown San Francisco and throughout the neighborhoods of San Mateo County.

No urban county in California enjoys an easy commute. In the Bay Area, San Mateo does it better than almost all.

City and County

There are two San Mateos, a point of confusion. San Mateo, the city, is the second-most populous city in San Mateo, the county.

The county government legislates generally for all who do not reside within a city. County supervisors represent districts but they are elected countywide.

In some instances, the county government performs services that in other states are provided by cities. The county provides medical care for the poor, even if they live in a city.

Nine out every ten residents reside in 20 cities. Besides the City of San Mateo, they are: Atherton, Belmont, Brisbane, Burlingame, Colma, Daly City, East Palo Alto, Foster City, Half Moon Bay, Hillsborough, Menlo Park, Millbrae, Pacifica, Portola Valley, Redwood City, San Bruno, San Carlos, South San Francisco and Woodside.

In the 1990s, the county increased its population by about 58,000. Most of the new comers settled in the City of San Mateo, Daly City, Redwood City and East Palo Alto.

Top 30 Baby Names

San Mateo County

Boys		Girls	
Daniel	68	Sophia	63
Ryan	61	Emily	59
Matthew	59	Ashley	57
Alexander	58	Samantha	46
Joshua	55	Isabella	44
Nicholas	55	Julia	38
Andrew	53	Emma	36
Anthony	53	Jessica	32
Jonathan	53	Katherine	32
William	52	Elizabeth	31
Ethan	51	Lauren	30
David	49	Olivia	29
Jose	48	Ava	28
Christopher	46	Ella	28
Dylan	43	Mia	28
Justin	43	Stephanie	28
Nathan	42	Jennifer	27
Jacob	41	Natalie	27
Zachary	41	Sofia	27
Jack	40	Maya	26
Joseph	40	Alyssa	24
Angel	39	Sydney	24
John	38	Jasmine	23
Aidan	36	Megan	23
Kevin	34	Abigail	22
Michael	34	Kaitlyn	22
Diego	33	Nicole	22
Benjamin	32	Sarah	22
Brandon	31	Hannah	21
Brian	31	Michelle	21

California

Boys		Girls	
Daniel	4157	Emily	3388
Anthony	3797	Ashley	2922
Andrew	3464	Samantha	2474
Jose	3379	Isabella	2435
Jacob	3327	Natalie	1942
Joshua	3292	Alyssa	1808
David	3246	Emma	1740
Angel	3232	Sophia	1715
Matthew	2853	Jessica	1700
Michael	2844	Jasmine	1666
Christopher	2754	Elizabeth	1595
Jonathan	2541	Madison	1572
Ryan	2511	Jennifer	1483
Alexander	2440	Kimberly	1460
Joseph	2430	Alexis	1434
Ethan	2356	Andrea	1374
Nathan	2302	Abigail	1314
Brandon	2208	Hannah	1310
Kevin	2133	Sarah	1304
Juan	2106	Vanessa	1299
Christian	2022	Mia	1270
Jesus	2012	Stephanie	1246
Nicholas	1999	Brianna	1221
Diego	1977	Michelle	1152
Luis	1957	Olivia	1149
Adrian	1824	Kayla	1147
Dylan	1757	Leslie	1137
Gabriel	1735	Grace	1127
Isaac	1722	Maria	1099
Carlos	1638	Victoria	1083

Source: California Department of Health Services, 2004 birth records. Number of children with the given name. Some names would move higher on the list if the state grouped essentially same names with slightly different spellings, for example, Sarah and Sara. But state computer goes by exact spellings.

City councils, directly elected by local residents, run the city governments. All use city managers. The council sets policy; the manager executes it. Often the reality is that the managers and other administrators, being trained in the business, exert a great deal of influence on policy.

Many cities now are turning inward, trying to "redevelop" (a legal term dealing with tax structuring and building incentives) their old neighborhoods, especially the downtowns. New BART stations could strengthen downtowns.

Of the remaining government entities, school boards, which are directly elected and not tied to municipal governments, are probably the most important. Some are confined to one city, some cover several cities. The boards hire and fire superintendents and help set policy for schools.

The Past — The Indians

The Indians arrived maybe 20,000 years ago. They spoke the Costanoan dialect and gathered in small tribes that went by such names as Iamsin, Salson, Puyson, Shiwam. Stocky and copper-skinned with beards and mustaches — so the Spanish described them.

The Indians lived on a gruel made of local edibles and gathered buckeye nuts, acorns, blackberries and huckleberries. Fish were netted, oysters and clams scooped up. Snares, spears and bows and arrows were used to trap or kill deer, rabbits, squirrels, pheasants, quail and other small game.

The Indians lived by streams, had no written language, kept pretty much to themselves and were utterly unprepared for what followed.

The Spanish

Although they had claimed California since the 1500s, the Spanish rarely ventured north from Mexico. Not until 1769 did Gaspar de Portola lead the first expedition to explore what is now San Mateo County and to discover San Francisco Bay. For more than 200 years Europeans had sailed the coast of California without finding the Golden Gate. In 1776, Colonel Juan Bautista de Anza, on his way to San Francisco with the first settlers, camped about mid-peninsula near a stream he named after Saint Matthew, "San Mateo."

Spanish policy was to take the Indians to the San Francisco mission and indoctrinate them in the tenets of the church. Unfortunately, the padres could not know that the Indians had no immunity to European diseases.

Many died. Some fled. Some rebelled. A few turned outlaw. Pomponio was the most famous. He raided settlements, killed other Indians and at least one soldier before he was betrayed by a woman. He escaped, was caught again and went to the wall. A creek and later a state beach were named in his memory.

When the Spanish arrived, historians estimate that about 1,500 Indians lived in or near the county.

Within 100 years, after many Indians were taken from interior villages and brought to San Mateo, only eight Indians were reported living on the Peninsula.

The Yankee Invasion

In the 1770s, the United States won its independence from England and looked to the west to expand. In 1803, Thomas Jefferson purchased the Midwest from Napoleon and dispatched Lewis and Clark to explore the region and beyond. Other Americans followed, notably John Fremont. Clearly, the U.S. had designs on the West. And so did the Russians, who opened a trading

San Mateo County Voter Registration

City	Democrat	Republican	*NP
Atherton	1,402	2,603	831
Belmont	6,871	3,804	2,924
Brisbane	1,214	353	487
Burlingame	7,076	4,509	3,032
Colma	320	80	138
Daly City	21,011	6,322	9,630
East Palo Alto	5,152	917	1,628
Foster City	6,464	4,396	3,504
Half Moon Bay	2,885	1,869	1,309
Hillsborough	2,042	3,457	1,300
Menlo Park	8,415	5,343	3,555
Millbrae	5,149	3,022	2,084
Pacifica	11,731	4,030	4,539
Portola Valley	1,339	1,297	571
Redwood City	15,922	9,929	6,596
San Bruno	10,205	3,801	3,675
San Carlos	8,070	5,605	3,290
San Mateo	22,019	12,201	8,697
South San Francisco	15,074	4,522	5,396
Woodside	1,308	1,656	718
Unincorporated area	15,746	8,165	6,613
Countywide	169,415	87,881	70,517

Source: County registrars of voters, 2000. **Key**: Demo. (Democrat), Repub. (Republican), *Non-partisan (Declined to state any political party preference). Note: voter registration peaks at presidential elections, then falls off, often sharply, and changes from election to election. These figures are from the presidential election.

post in what is now Sonoma County, and the English, who were pushing into the Northwest.

Meanwhile, hostile Indians along the Mexican border closed the overland route to the Bay Region. Few settlers followed the Hispanic pioneers — called the Californios — and the Napoleonic Wars sapped the energy of Spain and all but halted its colonizing efforts. This left California sparsely populated — less than 7,000 Hispanics in the whole state on the eve of the Mexican-American War.

Lacking workers, the Hispanic pioneers fell into the only economy that could support them: cattle ranching. Great herds roamed California.

Until 1821, Mexico remained a colony of Spain, which emerged greatly weakened from the Napoleonic wars. The Californios, ignored for decades, were in effect governing themselves. When Mexico declared her independence, she tried to secure the affection of the Californios by awarding large grants of land to the descendents of the original settlers.

Hardly had the ink dried on the grants when the Yankee invasion came, and in the war of 1848, California went to the U.S. American courts were

VOTE **Presidential Voting in San Mateo County**

Year	Democrat	D-Votes	Republican	R-Votes
1948	Truman*	34,215	Dewey	48,909
1952	Stevenson	50,802	Eisenhower*	87,780
1956	Stevenson	63,637	Eisenhower*	100,049
1960	Kennedy*	97,154	Nixon	104,570
1964	Johnson*	140,978	Goldwater	77,916
1968	Humphrey	106,519	Nixon*	98,654
1972	McGovern	109,745	Nixon*	135,377
1976	Carter*	102,896	Ford	117,338
1980	Carter	87,335	Reagan*	116,491
1984	Mondale	122,268	Reagan*	135,185
1988	Dukakis	135,002	Bush*	102,709
1992	Clinton*	138,261	Bush	68,414
1996	Clinton*	152,284	Dole	73,496
2000	Gore	166,757	Bush*	80,296
2004	Kerry	197,922	Bush*	83,315

Source: Calif. Secretary of State. *Election winner nationally.

obliged to uphold the grants but enforcement was slow, few grants were properly surveyed and lawyers' fees were exorbitant. One lawyer took over 5,000 acres, including a good deal of Belmont.

Within a few decades the rancheros had been replaced by Yankees who turned to farming and subdividing.

San Mateo became a county in 1856. In 1863, the last spike was driven for a rail line between San Jose and San Francisco, which should have opened San Mateo to rapid development. But local service was sacrificed to express runs. Millionaires, meanwhile, tired of the fog of San Francisco, built estates up and down the peninsula and took land off of the market.

The county finished the century with 12,000 residents. Retrospectively, San Mateo County was going to be settled sooner or later. What was needed was good transportation and enough people to spur housing demand.

The 20th Century

The 20th century provided both, in the form of the streetcar, roads, the automobile and four wars that brought millions to the West Coast. Gradually, towns and industries spread down the Bay shore. Some highlights:

- The great earthquake of 1906. It did little damage to San Mateo County, destroyed San Francisco and persuaded many that perhaps San Mateo County was safer. Within four years the county's population doubled.

- Hetch Hetchy. To secure its water supply, San Francisco between 1910 and 1934 dammed the Hetch Hetchy Valley in the Sierra and channeled the flow into Crystal Springs Reservoir in San Mateo.

Good for the City, good for San Mateo County. Almost all San Mateo communities now tap into the delicious Sierra water. San Francisco owns the system, sells the water and uses the money. The aging system is replacing and upgrading its pipes and facilities.

Hetch Hetchy was beautiful, the rival of Yosemite and even today someone is always saying, let's blow up the dam and turn Hetch Hetchy back to nature. Don't hold your breath. To protect Crystal Springs, San Francisco purchased 23,000 acres in the hills and mountains surrounding the reservoir. Central San Mateo looks like one big forest — great for hiking (some areas are off limits).

- The airport. San Francisco had thought about building its big one where Treasure Island stands but rational minds won out and in 1926 the City took an option on a couple of hundred acres of marsh off San Bruno.

As with many new ventures, the airport had its bad days. When Lindbergh, piloting a plane with 32 passengers, got stuck in the mud in 1929, some said let's give up the site. By 1940, however, the airport was handling 18,000 flights and 130,000 passengers a year. During World War II, the military took over and expanded the facility.

After the war, SFO just kept growing and serving more people and creating more business along the shore. Today, the airport, which recently built an international terminal, is the mainstay of the county's economy and recently has been handling about 28 million passengers annually.

The airport has added flight paths and angered many residents up and down the Peninsula. If buying or renting, take the time to listen for plane noise.

The airport or government agencies have put up money to "sound proof" thousands of homes. In 2000, the airport elevated the approach heights of some planes, from 4,000 feet to 5,000 feet. Information about flight paths can be obtained from local city halls or the airport.

- Bridges. The car and the new roads led naturally to bridges across the Bay. The Dumbarton, 1.2 miles, was built in 1927, the first Bay crossing and has since been rebuilt. San Mateo Bridge came next, 1929. For a while it was billed as the longest bridge in the world, 8 miles. In 2003, a second bridge, built along side the first, opened, to the delight of of motorists.

- Prohibition. It raised hell with law enforcement but is recalled as one of the most colorful eras in San Mateo history. The county's coast, often shrouded in fog, made it a favorite for smugglers. The forested interior hid stills. The law was full of loopholes, police departments were understaffed, politicians willing to wink at violations. But some escapades did raise eyebrows.

Bootleggers one night seized the lighthouse at Pigeon Point and used the light to guide their ships in. In Pescadero, they took over the town. A local group dug up a $20,000 cache of liquor buried on the beach. Incensed, the

Education Level of Population Age 25 & Older

City or Town	ND	HS	SC	AA	BA	Grad
Atherton	2%	5%	11%	4%	36%	40%
Belmont	4	14	41	7	31	21
Brisbane	7	17	27	6	23	17
Burlingame	4	15	22	8	30	18
Colma	9	31	24	6	10	3
Daly City	9	21	24	8	23	7
East Palo Alto	21	18	15	4	7	4
El Granada	3	14	19	8	32	19
Foster City	3	11	18	8	36	24
Half Moon Bay	10	15	21	6	22	13
Hillsborough	3	8	15	4	34	36
Menlo Park	6	10	13	4	31	31
Millbrae	8	24	22	8	23	11
Montara	5	13	28	5	28	19
Moss Beach	1	12	2	4	42	21
Pacifica	5	21	27	9	24	10
Portola Valley	1	5	9	7	36	41
Redwood City	8	18	23	7	21	14
San Bruno	10	22	28	8	18	8
San Carlos	4	16	21	9	30	20
San Mateo	7	18	22	7	26	13
South San Francisco	11	24	22	8	9	6
Woodside	2	8	15	7	31	37
San Mateo County	8	18	22	7	24	15

Source: 2000 Census. Figures are percent of population age 25 and older, rounded to the nearest whole number. Not shown are adults with less than a 9th grade education. **Key**: ND (high school, no diploma); HS (high school diploma or GED only, no college); SC (some college education); AA (associate degree); Bach. (bachelor's degree only); Grad (master's or higher degree).

bootleggers invaded Pescadero, applied some muscle and got their booze back.

Gambling flourished. One gambler founded Daly City's first newspaper and led the fight for incorporation. Reforms came slowly, then accelerated after World War II when the county began its suburban phase.

World War II and the Years After

- World War II. County turned into a military camp. Installations were built at many points, including Half Moon Bay and Coyote Point. Cow Palace, built in Thirties, was turned into a motor pool and barracks. To the later shame of the county, residents of Japanese ancestry were rounded up and taken to internment camps.

Cheap housing was built along the shore. Many workers migrated in for the jobs. They stayed after the war. Many soldiers, sailors came back.

- The great boom. The figures just about tell the story. On the eve of World War II, San Mateo County had 111,782 residents. By 1950, it had 235,000; ten years later, 445,000; and by 1970, about 556,000.

  This was the era when homes seemed to march over the countryside, so strong was the demand. Daly City and South San Francisco provide the best examples of the immediate postwar boom.

  You can trace the prosperity of the nation and the county through the housing. The Forties boxes gave way to expanded homes with two-car garages in the Fifties and Sixties. The Seventies and Eighties saw the rise of the townhouse and condo and the estate home on small lots.

  Also, the ascendancy of the hotel. Tourism, thanks to the airport, is one of the county's major industries. In the 1970s, land became scarce and cities more selective in their housing. The 1980 census counted 587,329 residents, the 1990 census 649,628, the 2000 census, 707,161.

  The Association of Bay Area Governments predicts that by the year 2010, San Mateo County will have 772,300 residents — a distinct possibility but anti- or slow-growth movements are popular in many cities.

- The new immigration. Changes in immigration law opened the door in the late 1970s and 1980s to many immigrants from Mexico and Central America, and from the Philippines and Asian and Southeast Asian countries. In the last decade, almost all these groups doubled their numbers in the county. How is everyone getting along? No doubt there is friction and instances where cultures clash. There is the problem of educating children who speak one language and teachers who, for the most part, speak another.

  San Mateo and California in general have learned some lessons in ethnic harmony. The county has a tradition of absorbing immigrants — Irish, Italians, Japanese, Portuguese. San Mateo County is part of the real world and has real-world problems. But compared to many other counties, the county does remarkably well in pursuing peace, tranquillity and happiness.

  The 2000 census counted 353,355 Caucasians, 154,708 people of Hispanic descent, 141,684 of Asian or Pacific Islander heritage, 24,840 African-Americans, 3,140 American Indians and 9,403 Native Hawaiians or other Pacific Islanders.

- San Mateo economy is heavily dependent on San Francisco International Airport. Following Sept. 11, 2001 airlines cut their staffs and operations. The hotels and restaurants and many high-tech firms also suffered. Going into 2006, the airport and tourism are making a comeback. The county is home to many bio-tech firms, a thriving sector.

Chapter

San Mateo City Profiles

SOME GUIDELINES TO BUYING homes or renting in San Mateo County: Views generally cost more. High academic scores and low crime cost more. Old and small and no views or cramped views cost less. Flatland and next to Highway 101, with some exceptions, cost less.

Short commutes, in many instances, cost less. Daly City, one of the "affordable" cities of the county, has its own BART station and one of the shortest drives to downtown San Francisco.

The housing sampler and home price sales for 2005, from DataQuick, will give you a good idea of up-to-date-prices.

Check out the noise from planes landing and taking off at San Francisco International Airport. Many residents are used to it; some are irritated by it. Some communities have received money to "sound proof" or suppress noise in some homes.

The airport wants to add or extend runways. There's an argument for expansion: the growing population of the Bay Region, the introduction of larger airliners, safety. But for the present, the airport has given up on the fight and neighborhood foes are proclaiming victory. Time will tell.

Chambers of commerce will often provide information packets. Send $15 to cover the cost of mailing.

Your best bet is to drive the neighborhoods and talk to local Realtors. Happy hunting!

ATHERTON

Daly City • SFO

Redwood City

★ Atherton

ONE OF THE MOST PRESTIGIOUS addresses in the Bay Area. Pretty, leafy (many trees), many large homes and a few mansions. Trees and tall hedges hide the homes along the arterial streets. Population 7,256.

No stores and none allowed. No sidewalks, no street lamps and when the city installed street reflectors the size of coasters, residents complained. Atherton raises most of its revenues through the property tax, fees and state subventions and a parcel tax that was renewed in 2005 — $750 a year for the majority of homeowners.

Located in south county, a short drive from Palo Alto and Stanford. The town starts in the flatlands then moves west up the hills, until it reaches Highway 280.

Although it's adding homes here and there, Atherton is essentially built out. The 1990 census counted 7,163 residents; the 2000 census, 7,194.

Nonetheless, there's a good deal of building, in the form of remodelings and expansions, going on in the town. Atherton limits home sizes to 8,000 square feet above ground. Many homeowners are digging out large basements to get more space.

Median age of residents is 45. Children and teens under 18 make up 24 percent of town; people over 55 years, 33 percent. Lots of grannies and grandpas. A town where the kiddies will get to know each other. The 2000 census counted only 371 under the age of five. One of the wealthiest communities in the Bay Area, according to census. More cars, 5,680, than adults, 5,500, reported 2000 census. When Google went public and created instant millionaires this set off a bidding war, local newspapers reported,for the few Atherton homes on the market.

Named after Faxon Atherton, rich hide-and-tallow trader from Chile who bought over 600 acres and built the first south-county mansion. Son George married Gertrude Franklin who, as Gertrude Atherton, became a famous novelist.

Other estates followed, at least one from a Bonanza king (Flood), and over the years they were broken into large lots for modestly luxurious homes, many of ranch design. Influenced by Hillsborough, wishing to protect property values and privacy, Atherton incorporated in 1923 and adopted tough zoning codes. Residents shop in Menlo Park, Redwood City, Palo Alto.

The state in 2005 tallied 2,532 residential units — 2,493 or 98 percent single homes, 32 single-family attached, 7 multiple units and no mobile homes. Luxury homes in the flats, luxury homes in hills. Lot sizes are one-acre minimum. Many are larger. In some years, only about three or four homes are added to the housing stock. Much of the construction consists of tearing down an old home and replacing with a larger one, with modern wiring and devices.

Bay view from hills. Good commute to Stanford, Silicon Valley. Long haul to San Francisco. But if one freeway is jammed, there's another to try. Caltrain to City or to Silicon Valley but in 2005, to the anger of local residents, the Atherton station was closed. Not enough Atherton riders and we're short of money, said the train authorities. For train commuters, try Redwood City or San Mateo stations. Dumbarton Bridge close by.

One park but probably plenty to do. Homes are little rec centers: tennis courts, pools. Private clubs, including a large country club that specializes in horses and trains the kids in equestrian events. Private high school-college (Menlo).

School rankings among tops in state — no surprise. Kids attend schools in Menlo Park and Las Lomitas elementary districts. In the 1990s, voters in both elementary districts passed bonds to renovate the schools and equip them for high tech and passed parcel taxes to maintain the quality of instructional programs and increase the pay of teachers.

Teens usually attend Menlo-Atherton High in Sequoia Union High district. In school rankings, Menlo-Atherton lands in 60th to 70th percentile. The school draws students from demographically diverse towns and neighborhoods and this affects scores. But Menlo-Atherton, through its prep program, graduates many students into the top colleges. Bonds were passed in 1996, 2001 and 2004 to renovate all the schools in the Sequoia district and equip them for high tech uses. In 2002, Menlo-Atherton High completed work on new track and field facilities. Several private schools in town. About half the kids attend private schools, census revealed.

Crime rate low. City has own police department. Zero homicides between 2003 and 1997, one in 1996. Caretaker killed. Suspect arrested. This was Atherton's first homicide in 49 years. See crime chapter.

Cops respond to every call. One woman called the cops when she found a discarded 7-11 cup in her driveway. She wanted the cops to send it to the FBI lab so the litterbug could be identified. Cops took the cup and let it go at that. On other occasions, the cops have supplied ear plugs when residents complained about construction noise, picked up newspapers for vacationing residents and rounded up two miniature horses that slipped out of a corral. Many residents leave extra keys with the cops in case they need to get into a home to check something. While this stuff raises smiles, it also pleases residents and reflects community values (zero tolerance for crime).

BELMONT

A CITY BUILT for the most part on hills overlooking the Bay. Many homes have views. Name translates into "Beautiful Mountain." Population 25,470. Median age of residents is 39.

Kids under 18 account for 19 percent of inhabitants; over 55 years, 23 percent. Mature town, many singles, empty nesters.

Built out. Much of Belmont's energies go into polishing and improving what it has and upgrading or replacing its infrastructure, particularly roads and sewers.

Elementary school rankings high. In 1997 residents passed $12 million bond to upgrade schools and to open another elementary school in Redwood Shores (a nearby neighborhood in Redwood City). Redwood Shores is home to the giant Oracle complex and other software firms. In 2001 and 2002, the elementary district lost a vote on a tax to raise money for programs and teacher salaries but in 2004 the third try was successful.

Crime rate very low. Zero homicides in 2004, one in 2003, zero between 2002 and 1999. In previous years one, zero, zero, three, zero, zero, zero, zero, zero, one, one, zero, one.

After years of steep increases, home prices are still up there. Modest three-bedroom homes going for over $700,000. If the home has a view, it might command another $200,000. Over the 1990s, Belmont increased its housing stock by about 550 units (census) but in some years this amounted to fewer than two dozen homes. Meanwhile, the number of high-tech jobs exploded. High demand, low supply, high prices. The dot-com crash mauled the job market but, thanks to low-interest rates, home prices increased. The high prices encouraged many residents to remodel or tear down the old, the small and the plain and replace it with the large, the modern and the stylish. This said, Belmont has many modest homes that were built in the 1950s and 1960s following the tract designs of those decades. But they get a lot of tender care. Many trees and shrubs. Decks plentiful to catch the views. Evening barbecues popular.

Belmont rises from flats to steep hills. Sage and chaparral grow on the steeper hillsides. Town very picky about building in the hills.

Stores, coffee shops, restaurants in a small downtown, which the city is constantly sprucing up. Large supermarket. New city hall, converted from an office building. A swanky deli, Safeway and both a Peet's and a Starbucks meet commuters by the Caltrain station. Residents shop at small plaza in hills — Lunardi's market, restaurants, etc. New library under construction; to open in 2006.

In 1864, William Chapman Ralston, one of the Silver kings and a founder of the Bank of California, purchased a large ranch at Belmont and using the palatial ranch house as a core, built an opulent mansion. The rooms numbered over 80, the banquet hall was mirrored, the gym had a Turkish bath, the stable was paneled with mahogany inlaid with mother-of-pearl. Among visitors to the mansion were Ulysses Grant, Admiral David Farragut, Bret Harte and Mark Twain. Ralston built housing for servants and other workers, and all this, plus the arrival of the railroad, got Belmont started residentially. A speculator, Ralston made some bad bets. In 1875, his body was found in the Bay, a suspected suicide. The mansion passed through several owners and, restored, it graces Notre Dame University.

Over the next 75 years the town grew slowly, adding residents to cultivate fields of chrysanthemums and during World War II to work in electronic industries. By 1950, Belmont had about 5,500 people living in 1,700 homes and apartments. Then the postwar boom began.

In the 1950s, Belmont built about 2,800 residential units, in the 1960s, about 3,200, and the following decade, 2,200. The population soared to 16,000 by 1960, then to 23,500 by 1970 and to 24,500 by 1980. Then Belmont ran out of land. The 1990 census actually showed a decrease in population, to about 24,127. The state in 2005 counted 10,745 residential units, of which 6,290 were single detached homes, 609 single attached homes, 4,121 multiples.

Elementary academic rankings up there, among top 20 percent compared to other California schools. Day care at public schools. Kids move up to schools in Sequoia High School District, where much more demographic mixing takes place. Scores range from middling to high. Most graduates attend Carlmont High in Belmont. Six private schools in town. In 2001 and 2004, the Sequoia district passed bonds to renovate its schools.

Good commute. Ralston Avenue on one end connects to Highway 101 and on other, with a short dogleg, to I-280. Ralston also ties into Highway 92, which runs to Half Moon Bay and San Mateo Bridge. Caltrain station near Highway 101. City in 1999 built two underpasses to take traffic under railroad and to freeway and in 2005 opened an overpass — all time savers.

Sixteen parks-playgrounds, including one around lake, another at Bay. Sports park (baseball and soccer fields, rec. building with meeting hall). Five tot lots around town. Ice skating rink. On Sunday summer afternoons, free concerts delight visitors at Twin Pines Park. Notre Dame University stages plays and presents lectures and events open to public. If buying near the shore, check out the noise from San Carlos airport. Chamber of commerce (650) 595-8696.

BRISBANE

MORE A HAMLET than a town. For about a half century Brisbane added few new homes but after a long fight, a developer won permission to erect about 600 homes and apartments in the hills on the north side. Population 3,724.

The rest of Brisbane's housing is concentrated in a small area on the east slopes of San Bruno Mountain (elevation 1,315 feet). Many residents see themselves as guardians of the mountain, which is why the developer had a helluva time getting anything approved. In the 1990s, Brisbane increased its population by 645.

Median age of residents is 40. Kids under 18 account for 18 percent of town; over 55 years, 18 percent. Translation: mature town, few kids, many singles and empty nesters. Town promoter supposedly came from Brisbane, Australia.

Located a short distance from San Francisco International, Brisbane has benefitted from the office-hotel boom generated by the airport. The city has an office park down on the Bay that includes the national headquarters for Hitachi America. Among new arrivals, on the waterfront, an eight-story hotel with 210 rooms. In the works, on a former landfill, 541 acres, that has been cleaned up, a retail-commercial center with auto dealerships, a convention center, restaurants and movies.

Sheltered by the mountain, Brisbane often enjoys sunny weather while its neighbors shiver in the coastal fog and winds.

Much of Brisbane's housing was built before World War II. Small lots. Some flat tops. With the hills steep and most homes spread over two or more stories, you do a lot of climbing. The views are sweeping and the town backs up to a large county park. Park and small shopping center at entrance to city. Skate park. Usual sports, activities. Town has a rec center and a community pool.

The state in 2005 tallied 1,900 residential units — 1,060 single family, 260 single-attached, 537 multiples, 43 mobile homes.

Crocker Industrial Park was annexed in the 1980s. Land set aside for industry dwarfs residential land. Residential section is buffered from business-industrial-warehouse. Offices and marina east of Interstate 101. Quarry to west of the city. The business section generates taxes that help pay for municipal services.

San Mateo County Single-Family Home Prices

City	Sales	Lowest	Median	Highest	Average
Atherton	8	$1,165,000	$1,805,500	$4,400,000	$2,224,500
Belmont	98	224,000	885,000	1,900,000	965,995
Brisbane	9	490,000	715,500	1,700,000	821,000
Burlingame	123	273,000	1,550,000	5,688,000	1,804,298
Daly City	240	30,000	746,000	4,513,000	754,294
El Granada	10	400,000	722,500	1,125,000	752,700
Half Moon Bay	63	80,000	839,000	2,300,000	919,421
La Honda	6	64,000	524,750	670,000	478,917
Menlo Park	75	108,500	1,075,000	4,100,000	1,183,486
Millbrae	54	650,000	937,000	1,800,000	1,032,750
Montara	10	250,000	769,500	2,200,000	875,800
Moss Beach	6	152,000	827,500	1,795,000	923,667
Pacifica	122	110,000	700,000	1,310,000	711,805
Portola Valley	13	350,000	1,520,000	3,000,000	1,458,077
Redwood City	292	75,000	860,000	6,550,000	939,231
San Bruno	139	166,000	750,000	1,250,000	741,304
San Carlos	99	623,000	960,000	2,730,000	1,066,942
San Mateo	382	333,000	862,500	2,925,000	930,229
South San Francisco	156	150,000	740,000	1,425,000	757,052

Source: DataQuick Information Systems, LaJolla: Single-family residence sales from May 1, 2005 through July 31, 2005. Median means halfway. In 100 homes, the 50th is the median.

Served by Brisbane Elementary District, enrollment about 610, two elementary schools and a middle school. In 1999, the district, by one vote, passed a parcel tax to teach the kids art and music and improve their reading. The tax was renewed in 2005 — $96 annually per parcel. An $11 million renovation bond passed comfortably in 2003. Older children move up to schools in the Jefferson High School District. Terra Nova High seems to be the most popular choice but the kids have the option, space available, to choose any school in the district.

Zero homicides between 2003 and 1996, one in 1995, zero in 1994. Overall crime rate is low. There are only two roads into the major part of town; no through traffic. Access and familiarity conspire against intruders.

Good commute. San Francisco is right over the border, the international airport is about five miles to the south. Many jobs, firms in this part of San Mateo County. Highway 101 close by. Train station and BART station in nearby South San Francisco. Train goes north to downtown San Francisco and south to Silicon Valley and San Jose. Buses.

Fees were raised to overhaul the town's sewer and water system.

Yours is not to reason why; yours is to dial and guess why the-powers-that-be divided Brisbane into two area codes, 415 and the new 650. If the first fails, try the other. Chamber of commerce (415) 467-7283.

BURLINGAME

A BAY-TO-HILLS TOWN that has many businesses yet is known primarily as a bedroom community, peaceful and well-to-do. Many hill homes have views of Bay. Added about 1,400 residents in the 1990s but just about built out.

Population 28,280. Located just south of San Francisco International Airport. Good commute. Median age of residents is 38. Under 18 years, 19 percent. Over 55 years, 24 percent. Mature and getting more so.

Loaded with trees, about 11,000 in total, many of them towering.

Slumbered through the 19th century and woke up with a bang, literally, when the 1906 earthquake leveled San Francisco. Eyes turned south and the virtues of Burlingame were discovered. Within a year the population had blossomed from 200 to 1,000. Burlingame incorporated as a legal city in 1908. Named after Anson Burlingame, ambassador to China, who once owned 1,200 acres nearby (but never lived in the town).

Two Burlingames: residential and office-hotel-business. Located near airport, having flat land, some recovered from the Bay, Burlingame has attracted many businesses. Airport Boulevard shines with sleek hotels, about 4,000 rooms, and office buildings. Ten hotels in the town. City Hall estimates that about 26,000 people work in town.

Moving west from the water, you encounter modest and small homes and apartments, well-kept, traffic congestion (price of progress) and two shopping sections: Broadway and the bigger, more popular, ritzier Burlingame Avenue (shops, restaurants, bookstores, sidewalk cafes).

Then the town ascends to the hills and home prices rise with elevation. Great views of Bay and of planes taking off. Home buyers should ask neighbors about noise; better happy than irritated.

Streets lined with eucalyptuses, magnolias, sycamores. Wood shingle roofs, rock gardens, many shrubs. Good-looking neighborhoods. Designs favor ranch style. Council in 1994 voted to restrict size of new homes — no "monsters." Level of care is unusually high, not only because residents are wielding rake, hoe and paint brush but because the city has pumped millions into the infrastructure, down to and including repairs to sidewalks. Burlingame, as a government entity, is rich. Hotel tax alone sometimes yields over $13 million annually. When you add in the tax revenue from auto dealers and other businesses, Burlingame covers over half the town's expenses from business sources. This has its downside. When the economy went south after 2001, tax revenue plunged and civic improvements had to be delayed.

Crime rate low. Zero homicides between 2004 and 1998. In previous years, one, zero, zero, zero, one, two, three, zero, zero, zero, zero, four, zero. In 2002, robbers held up bank and shot manager dead. Suspects arrested.

Fifteen parks and playgrounds. Trails along the Bay. Tennis and basketball courts. Baseball fields. Fishing pier. Bird sanctuary. Recreational center. Movies. Library renovated and expanded; holds 250,000 volumes. The booklet of offerings from the city recreation department runs to about 75 pages and includes many activities for kiddies, including tumbling, play school, dance, arts and crafts. For older children and teens, there's acting, softball and basketball; for adults, computer classes and aerobics, volleyball, tennis, foreign languages, music; for the elderly, excursions and classes — and much more. A drive of about 15 minutes will bring you to the Pacific. Restaurants, small shops, galleries, cafes, delis in the downtown. Every once in while a news article surfaces about this or that city wanting to improve its downtown. Occasionally, Burlingame's downtown will be cited as something to be imitated.

School rankings high, 70th to 90th percentile, on statewide comparison. Voters have passed bonds to renovate elementary schools and add classrooms and labs and a parcel tax to improve instructional programs. After several tries, voters in 2001 approved a bond to renovate all the schools in the high-school district including Burlingame and Mills High. Compared to many other cities, Burlingame supports its schools very well. Parents and school supporters also raise money through donations and fundraisers. Burlingame is divided between the attendance zones of Burlingame High and Mills High (in Millbrae). In 2005, city and school district combined to open a pre-school for children with special needs. Four private-parochial schools, including Mercy High, which is housed in one of the loveliest mansions on the Peninsula.

The 2005 census showed 12,947 residential units — 6,156 single homes, 423 single-family attached, 6,368 multiples. Town has no mobile homes.

Highway 101 runs through flatlands, Interstate 280 along western border. In 2005, Caltrain, which runs passenger trains to San Francisco and Silicon Valley, closed one of its two Burlingame stations and directed riders to the other station. Some grumbling but the closed station was serving fewer than 200 riders a day. SamTrans buses serve the street routes. BART station in Millbrae. Free downtown trolley. Chamber of commerce (650) 344-1735.

• For as long as anyone can remember giant eucalyptus trees along El Camino Real impressed and charmed motorists and residents. Alas, the trees are at the end of their natural lives and are being replaced by elms.

• Cities along El Camino Real are talking to each other about sprucing up El Camino Real throughout the county and making it into a Grand Boulevard.

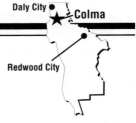

COLMA

SMALLEST AND LEAST POPULATED, by the living, city in San Mateo County. The state in 2005 counted 1,567 residents. Median age of residents is 37. Children and teens under 18 make up 25 percent of town; people over 55 years, 23 percent.

Famous for its cemeteries. Colma is where San Francisco and other towns bury their dead — so far over 1.5 million in number. Catholic, Chinese, Jewish, Greek, Serbian, Japanese, Italian and pet cemeteries — all located within hilly Colma. William Randolph Hearst and Wyatt Earp are buried here, the latter, a Protestant, in the Jewish cemetery. His wife was Jewish. Also buried: Tina Turner's dog, in Tina's fur coat, and a Hell's Angel leader with his Harley.

In 2003, the BART line, which has a station in Colma, was extended to San Francisco International Airport. The Colma station with its parking lot, 1,400 spaces, eases the commute for local residents. In 2004, Colma built 68 apartments near the BART station and for the first time in decades substantially increased its population — by 21 percent or 286 people.

For a while Colma was known as Sand Hill or Schoolhouse Station, then Lawndale. Some credit current name to the fog and a lad who got off the train and exclaimed, "Gee, it's cold, ma!" When San Francisco went through its periodic reforms, sin moved just over the border to Colma and Daly City. Gambling and dog racing flourished, elections were rigged, prize fights were staged. In 1909, in Colma, Jack Johnson knocked out Stanley Ketchel. Booze flowed in Prohibition days. Gradually, Colma cleaned up its act, but after much argument Colma in 1990s said OK to a 43-table poker parlor that has become a big tax source for the city. Revenues from the parlor and two shopping malls has been used to spruce up streets, build a rec center and provide free cable to all the town's living residents.

Colma took up cemeteries when San Francisco outlawed burials within its borders. Local businesses tied in with cemeteries: stone cutters, florists. Golf course. Seniors center. Museum. Commercial zone has auto dealerships. Large shopping malls located in Daly City, next to Colma city hall.

About 456 residential units — 216 single homes, 66 single-family attached, 168 apartments, 6 mobiles (2005 state count).

Zero homicides between 1998 and 2003. In previous years one, zero, zero, zero. See crime chapter. Chamber of commerce (650) 755-3900.

DALY CITY

SAN MATEO COUNTY'S most populous city, 104,661 residents. Plain-Jane reputation but many charms. Pacific or Bay views from many streets. Median age of residents is 35. Kids under 18 account for 22 percent of inhabitants; over 55 years, 21 percent.

Served by several elementary districts and one high school district that covers other towns. Compared against other California public schools, Jefferson, the largest elementary district, scores generally in the 50th to 70th percentile. Bonds have been passed to renovate almost all the schools.

Three homicides in 2004, zero in 2003, two in 2002, five in 2001, one in 2000, seven in 1999. In previous years six, four, zero, three, one, seven, two, four, five, three, zero, six and four, reports the FBI.

One of the best commutes in the Bay Area. Daly City borders San Francisco, the job center for many of its residents, and is close to San Francisco Airport and the bio-tech firms in South San Francisco.

The town is served by two freeways (Highway 101 and Interstate 280), several parkways (Guadalupe Canyon and Skyline Boulevard), SamTrans buses to downtown San Francisco and other parts of San Mateo County, and by BART. BART has one station in town and one just outside of town. Both are short drives by bus or car or even walks for many Daly City residents.

In 2003, BART was extended to the airport; some airport workers and residents will find this helpful. The Daly City BART station has revived its neighborhood. It has shops and restaurants, a movie house with 20 screens and new housing. BART is trying to get other towns to do something similar with their stations. CalTrain station in adjoining town; line goes to downtown San Francisco.

A city of hills and dales, Daly City almost spans the peninsula, with the massive San Bruno Mountain protruding into its middle. Homes open to the Pacific winds will catch the cold summer fogs. Daly City in July can be jacket weather. Homes sheltered behind hills will escape the fog or get less of it.

In some spots, Daly City has its rundown homes. But overall there is much here that pleases: homes and yards well maintained, paint applied, inviting neighborhoods.

Old, established cities usually do very well by recreation and Daly City is no exception. Soccer, baseball, basketball, over 260 youth sports teams, exercise and enrichment classes, golf courses, community centers and more. Thirteen parks, two swimming pools, movie theaters, large state park on the beach. San Francisco and all its delights are within a short drive or train or bus ride.

Daly City got much of its housing right after World War II when the county government, lax in planning controls, politically ruled much of the farm land in North San Mateo County.

During the Depression, home construction had been negligible. After the War, millions of veterans were guaranteed home loans — the G.I. Bill. An enormous housing boom was about to begin, and few people realized this.

Henry Doelger, and not too far behind him, the Gellert brothers, Carl and Fred, were exceptions. They had made fortunes building homes in the Sunset District of San Francisco, they knew the political game, they knew their market.

Doelger purchased 1,350 acres on the west side, just over the San Francisco border, and over the next 20 years or so built the Westlake subdivision. The Gellerts purchased 1,000 acres south of Westlake and built and built. Others came after.

In many instances Doelger and the Gellerts and others followed the typical Sunset design: one-car garage inside the house, living room with large picture window directly above the garage, kitchen to the rear of the living room, two bedrooms, one bath (the remodelings and additions would come later). One tree out front. A typical price then: $16,000.

As each section was built, it was annexed to Daly City, which supplied the municipal services: police, fire, recreation, road maintenance, etc.

Many were the complaints, especially from the city residents, who were picking up the costs of these services, but for a long while the developers had a free hand. They built monotonously: row upon row of homes, almost all rectangular boxes and, except for a little gingerbread often indistinguishable from one another, often all the same distance from the street.

Malvina Reynolds wrote a song deriding the little houses on the hillside. Some called Doelger's streets, The White Cliffs of Doelger. To this day, Daly City suffers from its looks. It is a city of plain housing, and some home buyers probably cross it off their list because of its plainness.

But there is another perspective: Doelger and his colleagues built to a market discipline. If they didn't, the homes would not have sold. They may be small and plain but they have features that translate into homeowner appeal.

Many homes, back yards and streets command spectacular views of the Bay and the Pacific. One neighborhood directly overlooks the Pacific.

The result: many neighborhoods have retained the affection of their owners. You can see it in the level of care bestowed on yards and homes.

The state in 2005 counted 31,682 housing units: 16,104 single detached homes, 4,507 single attached, 10,429 multiples, 642 mobile homes.

As the postwar prosperity caught on, home sizes increased. For the larger units, often laid out row upon row, take a look at the southern portion of the city, along Callan Drive. Another spot: the neighborhood surrounding Seton Medical Center (the city's largest employer). For new, modern housing, with great views, drive to the top of Crocker Avenue.

For the older, often cheaper housing, look around the BART station and nearby streets. Daly City has been around for a while, as the street names attest. Cavour, Bismark, Moltke and Garibaldi celebrate statesmen and generals of pre-World War I.

Daly City has always been a congenial address for newcomers, including immigrants. John Daly, who gave the city its name, hailed from Boston and made it to the West as a boy by crossing the Isthmus of Panama. The latest arrivals are Filipinos and people of Asian descent. Schools and the city are making efforts to help everyone get along. Annual Gateway Festival celebrates all cultures. There's also a Festa Italiana.

Although close to downtown San Francisco and its shops, Daly City has come a long way in its shopping choices and the city goes out of its way to promote and nourish small businesses. The Westlake neighborhood recently spruced up its shopping section. Restaurants and stores are plentiful. The town has a large mall, Serramonte, and neighboring Colma for years has been adding large stores. For residents in the north part of town, San Francisco's Stonestown Mall is a drive of five minutes.

Daly City is talking up office and business opportunities. Chamber of commerce (650) 755-3900.

Some neighborhoods may get noise from planes from San Francisco International. City hall has information.

Some homes with lovely views of the ocean fell into the ocean when rain and waves eroded the bluffs. Ask questions.

Daly City surrounds a small island of unincorporated land, called Broadmoor. Some of its street names delineate its age: Midway, MacArthur, Nimitz. Rare for an unincorporated village, Broadmoor has its own police department.

EAST PALO ALTO

SMALL TOWN, population 32,202, in the south county that offers a great commute and, because of social problems, some of the lowest home prices in Silicon Valley. Crime has dropped, home prices are rising. School scores low but many students transfer to the highest-scoring schools in the region.

After hitting a record 39 homicides in 1992, the number dropped to three in 1993, seven in 1994, six in 1995, and one in 1996. In 1997, homicides rose to 16 but dropped again to seven in 1998. In 1999, the city posted one homicide and in 2000 and 2001, six and seven in 2002, nine in 2003 and seven in 2004. Sheriff's substation in town puts more cops on the streets. Crime still a worry but the community is safer.

Median age of residents is 26. Kids under 18 account for 35 percent of town; over 55 years, 10 percent. Family town; loads of kids.

In 2000, voters approved a $10 million bond to rewire and renovate all public schools. Bill Gates of Microsoft put up $2.2 million to convert an existing school into a charter school run by the Aspire program. These types of schools give parents and administrators more flexibility in designing curriculum and programs.

Waterfront location, on the Bay. Close to Silicon Valley and the Dumbarton Bridge. Buses. Train station (to Silicon Valley and San Francisco) nearby. In 1994, Sun Microsystems opened a research complex just over the northern border of the town. East Palo Alto is protected by hills from coastal fogs. Breezes from the Bay. Balmy. Golf course on southern border. Parks, wetlands, trails, new community pool. Annual Collard Greens Festival.

Regional mall less than 2 miles away. World-renowned university, Stanford, loaded with cultural activities, also less than 2 miles off. Foreign movies, coffee houses, bookstores, art galleries — all within 5-10 minutes. Shopping center (Home Depot, Office Depot and fast-food restaurants) was recently opened near the freeway. Another addition: near Highway 101, a hotel-office building. Opened in 2003 after years of arguing, a giant furniture store (IKEA). All these businesses pump a lot of sales tax revenue into the city's coffers. In 2005, East Palo Alto opened a Four Seasons Hotel, 200 rooms, prices from $340 a night to $2,050. Newspapers and civic leaders hip-hip-hurrayed — 300 jobs with 30 percent going to the locals, and more tax revenues. Also noted: the hotel and other stores had turned around Whiskey Gulch, a run-down neighborhood. The hotel and the revival are a plus for the town but perhaps more so for Palo Alto and upscale Silicon Valley. The hotel is on the Stanford side of Highway 101 and draws its market from Stanford, Palo Alto and Silicon Valley. With housing supply short, Silicon Valley especially near the freeway, has been infiltrating East Palo Alto for a decade and, newspapers report, pushing up rents and home prices.

Rural to 1940, East Palo Alto took off after World War II when thousands of poor people were recruited from the South to work in war industries. The 1940s saw the construction of 900 residential units, the 1950s, the boom era, 2,700 units, followed in the 1960s by 1,600 units, then 900 units, and in the 1980s, 500 units. In the last decade, almost nothing (300 units) was built but in 2000 new homes in small developments, some gated, sprouted on the east side, near the freeway. The housing styles tell the story: the flattop roofs of the forties and fifties give way to the slopes of the sixties and seventies, the single garages blossom into two-car spaces, the two-bedroom homes grow into three. The latest homes are often two-story.

Until residents voted the town into cityhood in 1983, East Palo Alto was unincorporated and governed by the county. The 1980s saw an influx of immigrants. East Palo Alto today is one of the most diverse towns on peninsula. In historical perspective, people came because whatever its problems, it's better than the place they left.

Six of the 11 public schools in the town score below the 30th percentile. Most schools are in the Ravenwood district. In 1996, voters passed a $6 million bond to renovate all schools in the district. In 2004, they voted to tax themselves $98 per parcel for five years for programs and to recruit and train new teachers. Newcomer classes for non-English speaking. Stanford University, businesses, civic groups have "adopted" schools, try to help with programs and upgrade their computer-electronics capabilities. To head off legal difficulties over accusations of segregation, Palo Alto and Menlo Park schools — scores in the top 10 percent in state — and other school districts agreed years ago to accept minority transfers from East Palo Alto. Many parents like this arrangement but some Ravenswood school officials say the "brain drain" brings down the local scores. Under study, a plan to start another school run by Stanford and the Ravenswood district.

All of this raises a big point about East Palo Alto. It's not uniformly depressed. Many of its residents live below the poverty line but many live above. About 11 percent of the residents, or 2,227 people, are college graduates, the 2000 census reported. On some blocks, many homes are in need of paint, repairs and a lawnmower. On others, quite the opposite. The trade-off: when it comes to home prices, the market recognizes the problems, which is why you can buy many three-bedroom homes for much less than what's charged in Palo Alto or Menlo Park. Residences total 7,756 — single homes 3,946, single attached 376, multiples 3,275, mobile homes 159 (2005 state figures). Chamber of commerce (650) 482-9711.

FOSTER CITY

LOCATED HALFWAY DOWN THE PENINSULA, this city of 29,876 residents has done perhaps the best job of any town in the Bay Region of mixing housing with water. Median age of residents is 38. Under 18 years, 21 percent. Over 55 years, 22 percent. Many singles and empty nesters.

Drawn from the Bay, the water meanders throughout Foster City and here and there collects into lagoons. Many homes and apartments oriented toward the water. On summer evenings, residents take to their rear patios and decks where they dine and watch the ducks paddle by.

If they feel like exercising, residents may break out the canoe or small sailboat (Motor boats and jet skis are forbidden). Or head over to the Bay, which is fringed with a trail-promenade that extends up to Coyote Point in Burlingame. The trail is popular with walkers, runners, skaters and cyclists.

Served by two districts. San Mateo-Foster City district covers grades kindergarten through eighth and includes the City of San Mateo. At eighth grade, students move up to schools of San Mateo Union High District, which extends north to San Bruno. Most of the Foster City kids attend San Mateo and Hillsdale High schools. After spending several years in portable buildings, students at San Mateo in 2005 took over a new campus. The old buildings had been deemed earthquake unsafe.

At the elementary level, Foster City schools score generally in the 70th to 90th percentile, among the tops in the state. The two high schools land generally in the 70th and 80th percentiles. The elementary district in 1997 won voter approval of a $79 million bond. Money was used to add classrooms, renovate and rewire buildings, and construct a district theater. In 2003, voters approved a parcel tax for teacher recruiting and program retention. In 2000, after several tries, voters approved a bond measure to renovate every high school in the San Mateo Union High School District.

For the high schools, school starts in mid August.

The elementary district has designated about nine of its as magnets, schools that teach the basic curriculum and then specialize in different pro-grams — gifted, Montessori, science, music, high tech, etc.

Because of magnets and the district's choice policies, many children attendance schools outside their neighborhoods. Some schools may be over subscribed. Lotteries are sometimes held to decide admissions to some schools.

Home Price Sampler from Classified Ads

Atherton
- 4BR/5BA, $2.5 mil.
- 5BR/4BA, $9.9 mil.

Belmont
- 3BR/2BA, $839,950
- 4BR/2BA, $1 mil.

Brisbane
- 3BR/2BA, $665,000
- 4BR/3BA, $1.5 mil.

Burlingame
- Condo, 2BR/2BA, $795,000
- 3BR/3BA, $989,000
- 4BR/4BA, $2.4 mil.

Daly City
- Townhouse, 1BR/1BA, $375,000
- 2BR/1BA, $560,000
- 4BR/2BA, $648,000

Foster City
- Loft, 1BR/1BA, $467,000
- 3BR/2BA, $630,870

Half Moon Bay
- 3BR/1BA, $699,000
- 4BR/2.5BA, $1.3 mil.

Hillsborough
- 4BR/3.5BA, $2.5 mil.
- 5BR/4BA, $4.7 mil.

Menlo Park
- Cottage, 2BR/1BA, $649,950
- 3BR/1.5BA, $1.5 mil.
- 6BR/5.5BA, $4.4 mil.

Millbrae
- 3BR/1BA, $699,000
- 3BR/2BA, $1.4 mil.

Pacifica
- Condo, 2BR/2BA, $480,000
- 3BR/2BA, $699,950

Portola Valley
- 2BR/2BA, $1.3 mil.
- 5BR/3BA, $2.9 mil.

Redwood City
- 2BR/1BA, $700,000
- 3BR/2BA, $930,000
- 4BR/3.5BA, $1.5 mil.

Redwood Shores
(Redwood City Neighborhood)
- Condo, 2BR/2BA, $575,000
- 3BR/2BA, $659,900
- 5BR/3BA, $1.5 mil.

San Bruno
- 1BR/1BA, $337,500
- 3BR/2BA, $729,000

San Carlos
- 3BR/1.5BA, $819,999
- 3BR/2BA, $864,000
- 4BR/3.5BA, $2.7 mil.

San Mateo
- 1BR/1BA, $399,950
- Loft, 1BR/1BA, $440,000
- 3BR/1BA, $585,000
- 3BR/2.5BA, $828,000

South San Francisco
- 3BR/1.5BA, $688,000
- 3BR/2BA, $725,000
- 3BR/3BA, $799,000

Woodside
- 4BR/4BA, $2.2 mil.
- 6BR/6BA, $8 mil.

Application deadlines are important. Parents should check with the school district straight off to get information. Or do search under the San Mateo-Foster City Elementary School District.

The same applies to the high school. The district offers choices among its schools.

At the elementary schools, ask about the calendar. Some schools run on year-round schedules.

Zero homicides between 1997 and 2004, one in 1996, one in 1995, zero in 1994. For previous years, homicides numbered one, one, two, one, one, zero,

zero. In 2005, a 33-year old man, stopped by cops because of suspicions about his car's registration, apparently attempted to escape by swimming across a lagoon. He drowned.

Foster City is situated about a dozen miles south of San Francisco International Airport, the major employment center of San Mateo County. Many residents work for the airlines, reports the chamber of commerce. For them, the commute is a hop-and-a-skip up Highway 101.

Foster City has a done a good job of attracting businesses (about 600), many of them in bio-tech. It's the headquarters city for Visa. About a dozen or so office complexes have been built nearby at the intersection of Highways 101 and 92. Many local jobs mean a short commute for Foster City residents.

For those who head for San Francisco, 21 miles to the north, or to the Silicon Valley cities to the south, the commute probably falls into the category of "not bad."

SamTrans runs express buses to downtown San Francisco. Caltrain can be picked up in nearby San Mateo.

Highways 101 and 280 serve the freeway drivers. For people working in the East Bay, Foster City borders the Hayward-San Mateo Bridge, which opened another span in 2003. This is speeding the commute to and from the East Bay.

In appearance, Foster City is clean and well-maintained. New. Almost all the homes were built in the last 40 years. Graffiti zero. Utility lines buried. Waterways and lagoons add charm.

Recreation plentiful. About 20 parks scattered around city. Pooper-scooper laws. Fishing pier extends into Bay. Large library with children's room and computers. Nine-hole golf course with driving range.

City rec department runs sports and activities for toddlers, children and teens, and for adults and the elderly. Usual kids sports: soccer, baseball, etc. Summer camps. Other activities in adjoining cities. Summer swimming in lagoons. Boating, wind surfing. Thoroughbred racing at Bay Meadows, just over city limits. Big ticket shopping at Hillsdale Mall in San Mateo. Half-hour to ocean. On Fourth of July, people take to boats to watch fireworks at Ryan Park. New civic center. Park for dogs; allows them to run off-leash. Supposedly, one of the best dog parks in Bay Area. Synthetic turf. Rover won't track mud into the house.

No more than a reclaimed island 30 years ago, used for growing hay, Foster City owes its existence to Jack Foster, a rags-to-riches orphan. He purchased the island, devised an imaginative financing scheme, laid out the streets, brought in seemingly endless loads of fill, built bridges, carved out lagoons, installed sewers and utility lines, and constructed homes and apartments — just your basic job of building a city from scratch. Foster City has 223 acres of waterways, 13 miles of shoreline and 12 residential islands.

It is a master-planned city, which may sound unexceptional but most Bay Area cities are not "master planned."

The typical city started off with some zoning and a basic plan for the downtown, which usually was oriented to the train station. As the population and the city grew, streets and parks and schools were added, often haphazardly. When the freeways came, stores moved to the access ramps, weakening but rarely killing the downtowns and pulling traffic flows this way and that.

Children of the late 20th century, master-planned communities are oriented toward the freeway and are designed in grand scope. Before anything is built, the arterials are laid out, the park and school sites identified, the neighborhood shopping plazas spotted, the office and business zones delineated (near the freeway).

The clever people who thought all this up even built in neighborhoods. Foster City has nine, each anchored by a park or parks. Many streets have nautical names, some dashing and heroic — Corsair Lane and Farragut Boulevard — some not, as in Cod Street and Gull Boulevard. Nina, Pinta and Santa Maria Lanes are located near one another. For those who take a pessimistic view of life ... sorry no Titanic Street or Lusitania Boulevard.

The result: well, it's not San Francisco. It's not a jumble of styles and custom homes. It's not eccentric. But to use a worn-out suburban word: it's nice. And it's efficient. The hassles are fewer. The city has its laws. And the homeowner associations, many in number, have theirs.

For about 10 years, the Foster family or a developer ran the city as a company town but it was only a matter of time before residents, generally professionals, decided they wanted to do the governing. Foster City incorporated in 1971, and in 2001 celebrated its 30th year as a city.

Foster City has some custom homes, built on the water. It also has many apartments. The state in 2005 counted 12,478 residential units, of which 4,809 were single detached homes, 2,464 single attached, 5,198 apartments or condos, 7 mobiles.

Planes approaching San Francisco International glide down just east of Foster City, over the Bay. Very little noise but check it out for yourself. Some residents are concerned about noise from San Carlos Airport.

Marina Lagoon, which borders Foster City on the east, is outside city limits and open to motorboats. Another place to check out noise.

Chamber of commerce (650) 573-7600.

• In 2005, city council passed ordinance that forbids new comers from bringing in dogs that have been labeled "dangerous." Dangerous dogs already in the city may be allowed to stay if muzzled. Check with city hall.

HALF MOON BAY

Daly City ● SFO

Half Moon Bay

Redwood City

SMALL TOWN ON THE PACIFIC. In parts quaint. Forever arguing about growth and voting on this or that measure to control it. Continues to grow but slowly. Population in 1993 broke the 10,000 mark and now stands at 12,688. Median age of residents is 39. Children and teens under 18 make up 22 percent of town; people over 55 years, 20 percent.

Half Moon Bay wants to shape its growth to provide local jobs and boost the town's economy without greatly increasing the population. In 2001, Ritz-Carlton opened a luxury hotel on the ocean, 261 rooms, a spa, two golf courses.

One of the oldest communities in the county. For a long time a farm town that owed its livelihood to the cultivation of strawflowers, artichokes, cabbages and sprouts. Farming still counts in Half Moon Bay but not as much as it used to.

Mixed housing. Apartments down near shore. Older homes east of Highway 1. To south of town country club estates with fairway homes. Quite pretty, quite expensive. Some upper-middling housing near Frenchman's Creek Road. Downtown these days is looking like something out of Marin: delis, fine restaurants, boutiques, bookstores, streets that invite strolling.

Residences in 2005 numbered 4,438 — single homes 2,782, single attached 536, multiples 693, mobile homes 427. In the 1990s, Half Moon Bay erected about 300 housing units.

Town is built on flat land; few, if any, view homes. Ocean is within a few blocks of any home. State beach runs along the shore. Hills look down on the city. Fog country. Often socked in during the summer, clear in the winter.

Commute not as bad as might be thought. San Francisco, along Route 1, is a long drive but nearby Route 92, one of the few east-west arterials in the county, takes you over the ridge and down to 280 and 101, the roads to Silicon Valley, San Francisco, the Hayward-San Mateo Bridge. On weekends and summer days, roads are often congested with tourists.

Route 92 has been improved: curves straightened, shoulders widened for cyclists, uphill and turnout lanes added.

Chamber of commerce estimates the rush-hour commute to San Francisco as 47 minutes, to City of San Mateo 24 minutes, to Palo Alto 35 minutes, to Silicon Valley 53 minutes.

Private airfield north of city. If you have bucks, fly to work.

After years of protests and legal actions, work was started on condo-hotel-conference center to north of town on the coast. In 1996, someone torched it and burned it to the ground. Rebuilt, it opened in 1997. This will give you some idea of intensity of feeling about development not only in Half Moon Bay but along the whole San Mateo coast.

Crime rate low. Zero homicides between 2004 and 1998, one in 1997, and zero in 1996, 1995 and 1994.

Cabrillo Unified School District. Academic rankings, with few exceptions, come in well above the 50th percentile, an indication of strong parental and community interest. Hatch Elementary is educating the kids in English and Spanish. Voters in 1996 passed a $35 million bond to renovate elementary schools and libraries, build a middle school, expand the high school and upgrade science and computer labs. But they have turned down several ballots for a parcel tax to improve programs.

Lots of outdoorsy things to do: salmon and rock fishing, whale watching, surfing (it's cold, wear wet suit), horseback riding, golfing. Up the road is the village of Princeton with its restaurants, marina and fishing boats. You can buy fish right from the boats.

When many in the Bay Area feel like hollowing out a gourd, cutting holes out of it and lighting it up with a candle, they head down Highway 92 to Half Moon Bay. Before Halloween, the annual pumpkin festival can draw up to 250,000 people. Even on non-festival October days, the pumpkin patches take on a carnival atmosphere to lure jack o' lantern-hunting motorists. Prize to the biggest pumpkin; in 2005 the champ weighed 1,229 pounds and measured at its widest 10 feet-10 inches. It and its competitors were driven to Half Moon Bay on flatbed trucks.

Other more sedate festivals are also celebrated, including Heritage Festival (ethnic diversity). Tourism drives large portion of local economy (restaurants, bed and breakfast places, shops). Business people are trying to boost coast as place to visit. Homes in old section have been restored. Walking tours.

Some of the tallest waves in the world break on "The Mavericks" just north of Pillar Point. "So heavy, so radical," murmured a local surfer. And so deadly, killing a world-class surfer in 1994. Lots of tsk-tsking in the press but the death only made the place more attractive to surfers.

Chamber of commerce (650) 726-8380.

HILLSBOROUGH

RENOWNED FOR ITS WEALTH, this San Mateo town of 10,983 residents in many ways lives up to its reputation but it does not overwhelm.

The mansions are there, gorgeous creatures, but many of the homes can be described as upper-middle-class comfortable, ranchers, Tudors, Mediterraneans, and at least one A-frame, large and elegant.

A town for tycoons and heirs of tycoons ... yes. But also a town for doctors and lawyers and Silicon Valley strivers and the ordinary rich. An ethnically diverse city that in recent years has welcomed many Asians and Asian-Americans.

The trees are tall and full and numerous, pines, redwoods, eucalyptuses. The lawns are tended with loving care, putting-green quality. The landscaping is lush and imaginative and often pressed into the service of privacy. Much of Hillsborough hides behind tall hedges. No noisy leaf blowers on Saturdays. Town law. Disturbs peace of weekends. Just about built out. Added about 200 residents in the 1990s.

The town's three schools are among the highest scoring in California and several years ago, Crocker Middle School, was named by the Swedish Academy of Sciences as one of the four best on the planet. A schools foundation and a parents club raise about $700,000 a year for the three schools. The parents club asks parents to contribute a certain amount for each child, in effect a parental tax (similar "taxes" can be found in many high-income communities.) Parents also volunteer time for the schools. Annual Concours d'Elegance (car show) raises money for schools. Hillsborough residents impose a parcel tax upon themselves to pay for school programs.

Teenagers usually attend San Mateo High or Burlingame High, scores generally in the 80th and 90th percentiles. In 2000, a bond was passed to renovate these schools. San Mateo High, for earthquake safety, was rebuilt, the job finished in 2005. About 20 percent of the students, Hillsborough school district reports, attend private high schools.

One of the lowest crime rates in California but not immune to violence. In 2004, two men killed a woman while robbing her home. She suffocated after her face was taped and her hands tied. As we go to press, no suspects arrested. Zero homicides from 1999-2002, one in 1998 and zero from 1984-1997. In 1998, a local woman was kidnapped and murdered. Suspect convicted in 2002.

Compared to what others endure, commute not bad. Highway 280 runs along the top of Hillsborough, about 21 miles to the Bay Bridge. Adjoining Burlingame has a train depot; trains and buses to downtown San Francisco. San Francisco International can be reached within 10-15 minutes by driving nearby Highway 101. BART station at Millbrae.

The City of Hillsborough doesn't have a recreation department. Town and school district combine to run sports programs for the kids, and the school grounds serve as playing fields. One park. Some homes have tennis courts and pools; many have recreation or family rooms. One golf course, the venerable Burlingame, a second just outside city limits, to the west. The College of San Mateo (many programs and rec classes) is located on the southern border. Miles of hiking trails can be found at Crystal Springs Reservoir, just west of Highway 280.

In 1892, the scions of the mining and railroad pioneers and other tycoons — the Crockers, the Tobins, the Spreckels, the Pullmans — formed the Burlingame Country Club following the Chevy Chase model: large course with opulent clubhouse, surrounded by country estates. Hillsborough was meant to be a country retreat, an alternative to the foggy winds and bustle of The City. Residents whacked the ball, chased the fox and galloped their polo ponies.

When the 1906 earthquake struck, many of the great mansions of the City were lost, and with the competition cleared, Hillsborough's reputation ascended as THE town of the wealthy. Hillsborough incorporated as a city in 1910 and passed zoning laws forbidding almost all businesses.

The laws remain in force. Hillsborough businesses number only about a half dozen, including the golf course, a racquet club, and several private schools or day-care centers, city officials report. Residents do most of their shopping at neighboring Burlingame. For municipal chores, mainly fire protection and police, residents pay an annual parcel tax in addition to the property tax. Local group has raised funds to fix up street islands, and groom the roads, school grounds and park.

Up until 1940s, Hillsborough luxuriated in semi-isolation, its residences numbering fewer than 400. After the war, a great boom swept over San Mateo County. Hillsborough added 1,100 homes in the 1950s, 725 in the 1970s, about 350 in the 1980s. In the boom, Hillsborough built mainly for the well-to-do, not the super wealthy. The low-slung rancher, popular in the 1950s, can be found in many parts of the city. In the last decade housing starts fell to 150.

Residences in 2005 numbered 3,866— single homes 3,846, single attached 11, multiples 9, and no mobile homes. Median age of residents is 46. Kids under 18 account for 25 percent of inhabitants; over 55 years, 33 percent. Many a head is gray in this town.

LA HONDA

VILLAGE, UNINCORPORATED, located in valley southwest of Portola Valley. Used to be logging camp and bootleggers' hideout.

Famous in hippie legend for being the home of Ken Kesey ("One Flew Over the Cuckoo's Nest") when he and his Merry Pranksters, at the start of the LSD age, threw wild parties at the Kesey cabin, then boarded a Day-Glo bus and took off on miscellaneous adventures. Kesey, who died in 2001, sold the house in 1997, asking price $239,000. Buyers supposedly were a mild couple from Stanford who wanted a quiet place to write.

In the Twenties, the well-to-do built summer homes that in the Sixties became all-year homes. In the Seventies, others discovered the charms of La Honda and built mansions, which inevitably sparked row over what kind of housing should be allowed and how much.

Argument has been resolved in favor of larger lots and fewer houses. Development would have been limited in any event as the water supply — a stream feeding into reservoirs — does not bubble to excess. The town council has the ear of the board of supervisors and greatly influences matters.

Surrounded by state parks. Protected by mountains from fog. PTA runs activities for the kiddies, soccer, etc. Annual street fair.

La Honda-Pescadero Unified School District. One elementary school, K-5, enrollment about 80. Older children attend schools in Pescadero. In 2005, voters approved a parcel tax to retain teachers, increase salaries, improve library services and through quality programs make the kids smarter.

Some homes were damaged by landslides caused by the winter rains of 1997-1998. In 2005, one slide moved again and tore up the main street to a subdivision. Efforts being made to stabilize the slide.

Local winery grows pinot noir grapes. It wants to expand. Residents wary; pressing county to make sure that expansion will not harm stream (water supply).

Long commute. When you buy country, you really get, in this case, country.

MENLO PARK

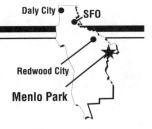

Daly City ● ● SFO

Redwood City
Menlo Park

PALO ALTO GOES HAND-IN-GLOVE WITH STANFORD but if the university could be said to have a second city, it would be this town on its northern border.

Menlo Park, population 30,648, provides housing for the Stanford community, draws businesses associated with the university and has benefited greatly from the wealth and ideas that the university has generated. Both cities share Sand Hill Road, the boulevard of venture capitalists (battered after the high-tech meltdown but supposedly is showing vigor).

Menlo Park also suffers some of the "town-gown" strains of university life. For years it fought Stanford over a development on Sand Hill Road — apartments, stores, road extension — that probably will add more traffic to some Menlo Park streets. Stanford won.

School scores are high, crime generally low, incomes substantial but Menlo Park doesn't fit neatly into the description "upper-middle-class suburb." East of Highway 101 it has a low-income neighborhood, called Belle Haven, that has inserted some diversity into Menlo Park life and given the town the opportunity to work through problems found in bigger cities.

Median age of residents is 37. Under 18 years, 22 percent. Over 55 years, 24 percent.

Served by Las Lomitas, Menlo Park and Ravenswood Elementary School districts. Many kids then move up to Menlo-Atherton High, which is in the Sequoia District. In 2001 and 2004, the Sequoia district passed bonds to renovate its schools. Las Lomitas passed a $12 million bond to modernize its two schools and build a gym at La Entrada Middle School. Voters also renewed a parcel tax to pay for smaller classes, for instruction in art, music and science, and for higher salaries. Ravenwood has also passed bonds and a parcel tax — overall, good support for schools. In 2005, the Menlo-Atherton Foundation donated $1.5 million to local schools — lot of money.

Scores in the Las Lomitas and Menlo Park districts are among the highest in the state. Scores in Ravenswood District range from low to middling to high.

School rankings are greatly influenced by parental education, family background and other forces that the California Dept. of Education has lumped under the name, "socioeconomics." Ravenswood district serves the low-income part of Menlo Park, and East Palo Alto, also low income. Their socioeconomics differ sharply from most of Menlo Park. Years ago school districts bordering Ravenswood agreed to accept transfers to promote integration. The policy has its pluses but it may also be draining some of the best students out of the Ravenswood district — an accusation that occasionally surfaces. About eight private schools. In 2001, a charter high school opened in East Palo Alto.

Three homicides in 2004. Zero homicides from 2003 to 2000, one in 1999, zero in 1998 and one in 1997. Counts for the previous years are one, one, five, two, one, four, one, one, one, one. New police station in Belle Haven. Also community center. Swimming pool. School district and city have built a library at one of the schools. City, through redevelopment (a tax targeting plan), and other groups are laying in improvements to the neighborhood, says city manager.

Compared to other cities, the commute is good. Interstate 280 borders the west side of the city, Highway 101 splits the city near the waterfront. Dumbarton Bridge feeds into Menlo Park, quick access to the East Bay. Caltrain up the Peninsula to San Francisco or down to Silicon Valley and San Jose. SamTrans buses. About 15-20 miles to three airports: San Francisco, San Jose, Oakland.

The fly in the punchbowl: internal traffic. El Camino Real, the main north-south boulevard, easily congests, which twangs the nerves.

Sunset Magazine is headquartered in Menlo Park, and from the town's looks, the magazine has many avid local readers. Many homes have been imaginatively landscaped.

Movies, two city swimming pools, two gyms. About a dozen parks in or near the city. Soccer and gymnastics are among the most popular sports for kids. Many activities for kids and adults. Boys and girls club. Little theater. Dance academy. Many clubs. Annual soapbox derby. In 2001, voters approved a $38 million bond to renovate parks and recreational facilities.

Named after the hometown of pioneering Irishmen, Menlo Park sprang to life in the 1860s when a railroad was run up the Peninsula, a station established in what is now the downtown, and large estates carved out of the countryside. When Stanford University was built, some of the faculty found homes in Menlo Park and in 1927 the village was incorporated as a legal city with a population of about 2,200. Over the next 10 or so years the number of residents increased by about 1,000 and then came the great postwar boom. By 1950 the population had jumped to 13,587 and by 1960 stood at 26,597.

Short of land, growth fizzled to almost nothing, then revived slightly. Menlo Park has 12,724 residential units, of which 6,849 are single detached homes, 930 single attached, 4,940 apartments or condos and 5 mobile homes (2005 state figures). Although Menlo Park has its opulent homes, mostly located near a golf course in the hills, it is a city that was built for blue collars and the middle class. These days, however, prices have gone through the stratosphere. Modest three-bedroom homes are selling for over $600,000.

Many of the homes have been remodeled. Tall trees envelop many streets and homes. In the fall, parts of Menlo Park could step straight out of a New England picture book.

Unlike many suburbs, Menlo Park has a historic center, near the train station and city hall. Restaurants, coffee shops and boutiques — an interesting mix. The British Bankers Club (a bar) on one side of the street, yoga instruction on the other side. Old movie house specializes in art films. When the town's long-time bookstore, Kepler's was forced to close because of web and chain-store competition, the town rallied round and Kepler's was reopened. Trader Joe's in Menlo Park, Whole Foods in Palo Alto. Like many cities, Menlo Park is mixing apartment with retail in its downtown. Another plaza, complete with restaurant and luxury condos was completed in 2002 alongside the tracks of the downtown train station.

Menlo Park has a fair number of large businesses or institutions. Besides Sunset, they include the U.S. Geological Survey, a Veterans Hospital, the Stanford Research Institute, Raychem and Addison-Wesley (educational printers). In 1994, Sun Microsystems opened a giant research complex near the Bay.

Besides yielding tax revenue to fund amenities, these businesses enrich the town and its society because they bring in people with different ideas and viewpoints. Employees also patronize the local stores.

St. Patrick's Seminary, just west of Highway 101, carved up 88 acres for 145 homes. Seminary remains.

Then there is Stanford and Palo Alto and all they offer: libraries, art shows, more movies, restaurants, the Stanford Shopping Center — a cornucopia of activities and cultural ornaments. Chamber of commerce (650) 325-2818.

MILLBRAE

HILLS TO BAY TOWN. Pretty. Well-cared-for. Middle class plus. Great views from hills. Located immediately west and above San Francisco International Airport. Built out. Millbrae has 20,708 inhabitants, about the same number the town had 20 years ago.

Millbrae has built a multi-storied transit hub for Caltrain, BART and SamTrans. In 2003, BART extended its line from Colma to Millbrae to San Francisco International Airport. The arrival of BART is encouraging development near the station and along El Camino Real, the main road (besides Highway 101). The new buildings tend to be larger and denser (more units) than the ones they replace and the buildings retained are moving to modern designs and giving El Camino Real a livelier look. City plans to build a large luxury hotel in the downtown. In 2004, Caltrain began bullet-train service to downtown San Francisco. From Milbrae to the downtown it's straight-through; no stops. In planning, a bike trail from Millbrae BART station to Colma station.

Darius Mills, rich landowner who built mansion, guided early development. Not much happened during most of its pioneer days. High prices discouraged subdividers. After World War I, homes started to cluster about the roadhouse stations along the main thoroughfare through the Peninsula.

Small subdivision in 1921. Big subdivision in 1927, called Highlands, aimed at upper end of market. After struggling with poor services for years and fighting annexation attempts, Millbrae incorporated as a city in 1948 and built its parks and municipal structure.

A lot of home building came after World War II. By 1954, Millbrae had 10,000 residents, by 1970 about 21,000. Population dipped in the 1970s, rose slightly in the 1980 and a little more in the 1990s. Like the rest of the county, Millbrae is becoming more diverse.

Median age of residents is 42. Children and teens under 18 make up 21 percent of town; people over 55 years, 31 percent. A retiring place.

Hills keep fog away, a point of pride in Millbrae.

Ten parks, one PAR course. Green Hills Country Club sits in the middle of town. Many activities for seniors, teenagers and kids. Annual arts and wine festival draws about 100,000. Western side borders Crystal Springs Reservoir, pretty. Skateboard park. Trails for hiking. Shoreline trail. Shops and restaurants in the downtown, which has been fixed up with planters and brick crosswalks.

Pubs, coffee houses, restaurants, shops, Trader Joe's. Big hotels on waterfront, if you want to try their cuisine. New library opened in 2004.

Of Millbrae's 8,122 residential units, single homes account for 5,319, single-family attached 269, multiples 2,523, mobile homes 11 (2005 state figures). Higher the elevation, higher the price.

Many two-story homes in the hills. Decks for viewing. Much landscaping and care. Arguments about views cut off by second-story additions. Near Highway 101 the homes are smaller, more modest but still well-kept. Apartments also near the freeway.

In 2000, slides damaged several homes in the hills and woke residents to the need for putting money into hillside stabilization and keeping culverts and drains unclogged to carry away water that triggered some of those slides.

Crime rate low. One homicide in each 2004, 2003 and 2002, zero from 1994-2001. In 1998, Millbrae officer Dave Chetcuti was shot to death on Highway 101 while coming to the assistance of another officer. Suspect, with a history of mental illness, was captured.

Saturday, May 11, 2005, about 7 a.m. According to statements to police. Man and woman, a couple, were waiting at bus stop to go to work. Two men, ages 19 and 20, and woman, 18, who had been partying, ask couple to buy them alcohol. Reply: No. Words. Men punch man, who pulls pocket knife. Men go to their car and return with Club, iron-bar security device. Fight. Bus woman hit over head with club. Man stabs 20-year-old. Trio take off in car, 20-year-old behind wheel. He drives a short distance and dies. No charges against bus man. Court dates for alleged attackers. Senseless, says cop.

Compared to other schools in the state, Millbrae elementary scores land in the 70th to 90th percentile. Taylor Middle School was renovated and opened a technology center. Day care at many of the public schools.

Many teens attend Mills High School, which frequently scores in the top 10 percent among state high schools.

In 2000, voters passed a bond to renovate all schools, including Mills, in the San Mateo Union High School District.

Sitting next to the airport, served by two freeways, and with buses, Caltrain and BART, Millbrae has to be considered an excellent commute. New underpass near BART station allows motorists to avoid hangups caused by trains.

More freeway improvements are planned but motorists will sometimes find the traffic irritating. Millbrae and many Peninsula towns were built when trains were kings and life revolved around the train station. The design of these old downtowns, even with improvements, clogs traffic and hangs it up at the signals. The left-turn lanes fill quickly and back up vehicles on the adjoining lanes.

Noise complaints near airport. Many homeowners have received money to buffer homes against plane noise. SFO cites reports that it is in compliance with federal noise standards but what a government agency deems acceptable might be otherwise to a person who has to put up with the noise. Chamber of commerce (650) 697-7324.

•Transit hub. BART and Caltrain run parallel and don't come together except at Milbrae station. BART goes all the way to downtown San Francisco; Caltrain stops at the edge of the downtown San Francisco, next to Giant Stadium and light-rail line. Transferring at Milbrae will ease the commute of some San Francisco travelers.

Daly City ● ⎫ SFO

MONTARA, MOSS BEACH

COASTAL VILLAGES SOUTH OF PACIFICA. Unincorporated, which means they are governed by board of supervisors, sitting in Redwood City, but through the Midcoast Community Council residents make their concerns known. Although talked of as separate hamlets, the two are close together, have connecting streets and common interests: protecting the shore against development. Seton Medical Center in Moss Beach.

Pretty. Rustic. Artsy look. Many pine trees. State beach in Montara, Fitzgerald Marine Reserve in Moss Beach. Lighthouse at Point Montara. Restaurants, stores. Half Moon Bay Airport, private, extends into Moss Beach. If buying or renting, check with neighbors about noise. Homes east and west of Highway 1. Many down on the ocean. Many residents along the coast want to limit development but these neighborhoods seemingly are always adding custom homes, if only one or two at a time.

Montara population 2,950, of whom 19 percent are over 55 years and 25 percent under 18 years. Kids under 5 number 191. Moss Beach has 1,953 residents — 17 percent over 55, about 24 percent under 18. Kids under five years: 94. (Census 2000). Median age of residents in both hamlets is 41 — getting up there.

Every ten years or so, Highway 1 gets washed out at Devil's Slide, an area north of Montara. The slide was patched up again in 1995 but a permanent fixing was not done because conservationists oppose widening the road, believing this will encourage development. In 1996, San Mateo County voters approved building a tunnel underneath the slide. But no money was available to build the job and for years it seemed to be wandering among the lost souls of highway funding. Then to almost universal shock, the feds came through and work started in 2005. Completion about 2011. The old road will be turned into hiking and biking path.

Kids attend El Granada Elementary, then move up to Cunha Intermediate and Half Moon Bay High. All are part of the Cabrillo Unified School District.

In this neck of the woods, gotta love that fog. Plentiful in summer. Many homes go in for large picture windows pointed toward the Pacific. Montara is trying to improve its water system, old and leaky.

• Mom not home. Son, 17, no key, wants in. Tries chimney. Makes it down to damper. Yells. Firefighters sledge hammer him free. Hugs from mom. "You could have been killed! " Happened in 2005 in Moss Beach.

PACIFICA

ON THE PACIFIC. Great views of the ocean. Warm in the winter. Often cold and foggy in the summer. On the map, Pacifica looks like it has loads of land for housing but a great deal has been locked up in parks and watershed. Remainder is often hilly (expensive for building). Population 38,678.

Many arguments over development but homes are going up — slowly. In the 1990s, the town added about 750 residential units, a little over half of them single homes.

In the storms of early 1998, some homes fell into the Pacific, one of the perils of building close to the shore. Pacifica has built a sea wall to slow beach erosion.

Median age of residents is 38. Kids under 18 account for 23 percent of inhabitants; over 55 years, 19 percent. Rounded town, not too many old or young.

After World War II, the housing boom spread out to and down the coast, engulfing old villages: Rockaway Beach, Vallemar, Sharp Park, Edgemar, Pacifica Manor, Linda Mar. Services and schools lagged behind development, planning was haphazard. Naturally, the residents became discontented and incorporated the villages in 1957 into city of Pacifica and took over their own planning and governing.

Pacifica started the 1960s with about 21,000 residents and in that decade added about 16,000 people. It began the 1970s with about 36,000 residents and over the next 20 years added only 1,700 people.

This will give you the flavor of the town's tracts. Much of the housing was built between 1950 and 1970 and aimed at the middle class. Very little jumps up the scale but many homes have great views of the Pacific and some homes are custom designed. Some streets in the old neighborhoods come across as a sort of artists' colony. Residential units in 2005 totaled 14,377, of which 10,358 were single homes, 786 single-family attached, 3,135 multiples, 98 mobiles. Much of Pacifica is built on mesas, divided by deep ravines. The neighborhoods are separate and distinct. Step out the door and over the fence and you'll usually find yourself among sage and chaparral. Apartments and small shops near the water, off Highway 1, the main drag.

Fishing pier that sticks out far enough into Pacific to catch salmon. Beach promenade, public golf course, beach park, 14 parks, 12 playgrounds, two public swimming pools, two libraries, tennis, bowling, riding and hiking trails, archery and shooting range, restaurants, hotels. Safeway, Rite-Aid, Ross store. Community center — arts and crafts, bocce, day care, seniors activities. Great hills for skateboards. New skateboard park. Arts center, home to 40 artists, and a performing arts center. Little theater, including kid productions. One of only two cities in county (San Bruno the other) that allows fireworks on the Fourth of July, as long as they are "safe and sane," a fire marshal rating. Helps raise funds for schools, sports and other community activities.

Commute is not bad. San Francisco and Interstate 280 are a few miles up the road. Sharp Park Road also leads to I-280 and down to Highway 101. Highway 1 goes from freeway to four-lane road. Although traffic moves, Pacifica would like Highway 1 improved but many don't want to turn it into a freeway, which would spur development. Recently the road was widened.

Crime rate low. One homicide each in 2004, 2003, zero in 2002 and 2001, one in 2000, zero in 1999. The counts for previous years: one, zero, zero, one, one, two, zero, one, zero. New police station.

Served by Pacifica Elementary District and Jefferson Union High School District. Elementary rankings range from about the 50s to the 90s. Oceana High and Terra Nova High are in Pacifica. Scores in the 60th to 80th percentile. Voters in 1995 approved raising taxes and spending $30 million on improving high schools. In 1997, Pacifica, which used to be called Laguna Salada, passed a $30 million bond to make improvements.

Skyline Community College just over the border. Big plus. Community colleges offer many activities, classes. In 2001, the college district passed a $207 million bond to renovate its campuses. Closed elementary has been converted into Sanchez Art School (private). Many artists in Pacifica.

Pacifica celebrates itself with Fog Fest. Event draws about 50,000 and includes Fog Dance, Fog Jog. Fog pattern: Generally absent in winter. Sunny and mild. Present in summer, cold and overcast often to late afternoon when sun burns through. Some days fog disappears. People tolerate, hate, love it. One bonus: no need for air conditioners.

A bedroom town. Largest employers are the school district and the city government. Residents would like to keep small-town feeling and protect beach and country but they also want enough business to generate taxes for amenities and basic services and repairs, such as filling potholes. Voters in 1993 and 2002 rejected proposals to build on a quarry near the Pacific.

Some noise from planes taking off from San Francisco International, which may put up money for sound insulation. Chamber of commerce (650) 355-4122.

PORTOLA VALLEY

Daly City · SFO

Redwood City

Portola Valley

AS THE SANTA CRUZ MOUNTAINS move south down the Peninsula, some flatten into small hills and plateaus. The Bay hills rise to the east, the mountains to the west, and in between sit Portola Valley, Woodside and the Crystal Springs Reservoir.

Portola Valley, population 4,538, is a pretty town, high income, a prestige address. Great deal of attention paid to schools. In 1998, voters approved a $17 million bond to renovate schools and wire them for high tech. The money also paid for 10 more classrooms, a music room and a language lab. In 2001, voters agreed to extra $6 million to finish the job. Residents also tax themselves to keep up the quality of instructional programs and in 2004 renewed this tax.

Big lots, tall trees, big homes, a few small vineyards. Woodsy hills mixed with open space. Majestic oaks. Quail flit across the road. Library, town hall.

Miles of trails in the hills. Playing fields at the town hall and at several other places. City has rec person that coordinates activities. Golf courses, shopping in Palo Alto and other cities. Some small shops in town, including market for food and sundries. Old roadhouse, the Alpine Inn, nothing fancy but mildly famous in the region.

Every once in a while a mansion will come on the market for $10 million or $15 million or more. Most homes, however, fall into the category of large suburban and go for $2 million plus. Many homes are content to nestle in the trees but some command great views of countryside and Bay.

Horse country. Corrals and ranches. Stop signs that say "Whoa." Equestrian center. Annual Equestrian Festival (hunter/jumper competitions) draws about 500 horses and riders from around the world.

Town was named after Spanish explorer and boosted by Andrew Hallidie, inventor of cable car, who bought property in valley and donated land for school and post office.

A long commute to San Francisco. One freeway, the pleasant I-280. A short commute to Silicon Valley, Palo Alto and Stanford.

Portola Valley, by reputation, is popular with Silicon Valley and Stanford types. The Stanford Linear Accelerator sits just over the city border, and Stanford owns much of the adjoining land.

Another single-home town — 1,806 residential units, of which 83 percent or 1,498 are single homes, 33 single-family attached, 275 multiple and no mobile homes (2005 state count).

Town incorporated in 1964 to slow growth and stop encroachment from neighbors. Has done just that. Portola Valley started the 1980s with 3,939 people and finished with 4,194, an increase of 255 — peanuts by California standards. The 2000 census counted 4,462 residents. In some years, Portola Valley adds fewer than six homes.

Many residents probably can be found in their rocking chairs: 36 percent are over age 55, about 23 percent under age 18. Kids under 5 number 223. Median age of all residents is 48. These figures do not include Ladera, an unincorporated subdivision off Alpine Road, near Interstate 280. It's considered part of Portola Valley but is actually outside city limits.

Elementary school rankings among highest in the state, not just in the 90s but the high 90s. Instruction includes art, music, physical education, science. Corte Madera was one of nine Bay Area schools awarded the national Blue Ribbon distinction. Middle school offers Spanish and French, and computers.

Through a private foundation, residents have raised several million to buy equipment, upgrade classes and improve the curriculum. In one benefit auction for the schools, parents raised $1,050,000.

Portola kids attend Woodside High, scores in the 60th and 70th percentiles. The high school, which draws kids from diverse social and ethnic groups, introduces some of the complexities of the larger world. The Sequoia district, which includes Woodside High, passed a bond in 2001 to renovate all its schools.

Private school, Woodside Priory.

Since 1997, the town has imposed a 2 percent tax on utility rates to buy open space.

FBI doesn't track crime stats but Portola Valley almost never makes the news. Thieves would have a hard time finding the place. Zero homicides in 2003, 2002, 2001, 2000. See chapter on crime.

One big reason for the pretty hills, ridges and valleys: Portola Valley sits astride the San Andreas Fault and takes quiet pride in location. And hints this is why it favors open space.

PRINCETON, EL GRANADA

VILLAGES, JUST ABOVE HALF MOON BAY. Marina at Princeton, which is sheltered by the curve of the Bay. Jumping-off spot for rock cod, crab and salmon fishing. Whale excursions. Nice restaurants. Bed-and-breakfast places. Small airport to the north. You can buy fish from the dock when the boats come in.

Touchy about development but homes are being built all the time, just not that many. The new ones tend to be custom designed and, if possible, oriented toward the ocean or the setting sun. New arrivals: hotel and more retail shops.

Residents make their feelings known through an elected "council" that advises the county government on growth and other problems.

El Granada lies east of Highway 1. Secluded (somewhat) subdivision. Homes rise into hills. Nice views of Pacific. A few streets need paving.

Behind the hills, the terrain rises higher and turns into miles of rugged countryside.

For all practical purposes, these two places should be considered part of Half Moon Bay. People shop in town, send kids to local schools. Every once in a while residents talk about annexing Princeton to Half Moon Bay. For schools information, see Half Moon Bay. Many students attend El Granada Elementary.

Population of El Granada and Princeton: 5,724. Median age of residents is 38. Under 18 years, 27 percent. Over 55 years, 15 percent. The 2000 census counted 2,097 residential units, of which 81 percent were owner-occupied.

Small airport near Princeton. Check out noise.

Fog in summer, cold, wet and blustery. But what turns some people off, pleases others. Weather is a key factor in living near coast. If you can, check it out before you move in.

Another consideration: the commute. Highway 92 will take you over the crest and down to Interstate 280 and Highway 101. Compared to many commutes in the Bay Area, this one falls into the category of endurable.

REDWOOD CITY

SUBURBAN TOWN that has managed to capture a good deal of high-tech in its newest neighborhood, Redwood Shores. Headquarters city for Oracle and for other software firms. Population 75,986.

In 2001, the city opened the first buildings of Pacific Shores, which is to include 1.5 million square feet of offices, an amphitheater, a restaurant and a fitness center. More housing is also going into Redwood Shores but there's some argument over how much.

Children attend the Redwood Elementary District, enrollment about 8,800, and move up to the schools of the Sequoia Union High School District.

Redwood Shores is in the Belmont Elementary District. In 1997, this district opened Sandpiper Elementary to serve Redwood Shores. Redwood City chipped in for a community center and playing fields at the school.

In 2005, Redwood Shores passed a neighborhood tax to buy land and build and improve school facilites — just for Redwood Shores.

Local schools have become more diverse and this is influencing how schools are run.

Redwood City is the third-most populous city in San Mateo. County seat. Many government buildings in downtown. Only city in San Mateo County with a port. It handles cement and recycled steel.

Redwood City is one of the few municipalities in the county that has built a fair amount of new housing in the last 25 years. The city added about 11,000 residents in 1980s and another 9,400 in the 1990s. Growth, however, appears to have slowed. According to the state's annual guess at city populations, Redwood City added only 600 residents between 2000 and 2005.

Median age of residents is 35. Children and teens under 18 make up 24 percent of town; people over 55 years, 18 percent. Rounded demographics.

Although Redwood City got its start about the Civil War, when it milled the redwoods cut in the mountains, it didn't boom until after World War II. The city started the 1940s with about 2,900 housing units, built 3,500 units in that decade, 6,500 in the 1950s, and 5,100 units in the 1960s. Timing is important because the prewar and immediate postwar housing favored the two-bedroom home. In the 1950s and 1960s, as prosperity took hold, the three-bedroom home came on strong.

About 60 percent of Redwood City's housing predates 1970 — many two- and three-bedroom homes and by the standards of Silicon Valley, affordable. Before prices took off in the mid 1990s, Redwood City was a move-up town for families from San Francisco.

Just south of Redwood City is an unincorporated neighborhood called Fair Oaks, which for a long time provided low -income housing.

When homes and rents are "affordable," people at the low end, including minorities, can buy in. The local economy, booming with jobs, welcomed them. Many of these children attend the schools of the Redwood district.

About five or so years ago, however, the tide changed, somewhat. Home prices rose so high that many middle class people were priced out of neighborhoods that were considered middle class. Some of these people turned then to Fair Oaks and other low-income sections, bought the homes and fixed them up.

Nothing stays still, or predictable, in Silicon Valley.

About the 1970s, homes expanded again, often to four bedrooms. Closets grew bigger, windows brought in more light, lots got smaller.

In 1959, Redwood City annexed over 4,000 acres and later drew up plans for a neighborhood that was called Redwood Shores. Development sputtered through the Sixties, got rolling slowly in the Seventies and blossomed in the 1980s. In this section, east of Highway 101, along the Bay shore, you'll find a mix of sleek office buildings, apartments, condos and single homes, a fair number of the last ascending into four bedrooms. Many of the homes back up to lagoons that are flushed by waters from the Bay. You'll also find a more modern and more congenial street and park system.

On the Redwood City streets built just after World War II, the driveway leads directly to the street, no matter that some streets are now arterials. In Redwood Shores, the residential streets are buffered from the arterial thoroughfares and have lower speed limits — which is not to say they are kid proof but they're safer.

In the late 20th century, planners discovered the linear park and the trail, as in hiking and jogging. Redwood Shores has them and seems more friendly to easy activity than the other sections of town (but the city does very well in parks and rec).

For the future, the city has in the works something on the bay called Marina Shores Village — office and condominium towers, about 2,000 apartments and townhouses, retail stores, a park and a marina. This project has been around a few years and seen many changes. Something will be built but at this stage more massaging has to be done. Much of the area's remaining land will be converted into a wildlife preserve.

The state in 2005 counted 29,200 housing units, of which 13,552 were single-family detached, 3,656 single attached, 11,159 multiples and 833 mobiles.

School scores often follow demographics. As Redwood City evolved into a mixed community, the school district restructured its programs to meet the different needs of the children. Redwood City Elementary has changed all of its schools into "magnet" institutions, offering enriched programs to draw the kids out of their neighborhoods and into a better ethnic mix. The theory is that middle-class kids will attend schools in the poorer neighborhoods if the schools offer something special: extra math, or science, etc. The program is voluntary. If parents want the local neighborhood school, the choice is honored. One school, North Star Academy, accepts students scoring in the top 15 percent of the district. It has the highest scores.

Sequoia High School District serves Redwood City and also draws students from Atherton, Woodside, East Palo Alto, Portola Valley and Belmont. The upper-income towns have very high elementary scores. The low-income communities often have low to middling schools.

When you look at the overall scores for the high schools, they land generally in the 50th to 80th percentile. Within their general program, the schools run college-prep programs, and graduate students into the UCs and other top universities. Students are permitted to transfer within high schools, space permitting.

Since 1996, the Sequoia district has passed three bonds, the latest in 2004, to renovate all schools and add facilities. Historic Carrington Hall was overhauled to stage performances by students and nonprofit organizations. The high-school district has spent almost $5 million to install state-of-art technology in the schools.

The Redwood elementary district, in 2002, passed a $22 million bond for renovation and disability repairs. In the late 1990s, it modernized almost all its schools and passed a $40 million bond to build a multipurpose room or library at each school, and more classrooms and technology centers. After-school care available at many public elementary schools. This district has tried several times to get its voters to approve an increase in the tax that supports programs. No luck.

Belmont elementary school district, serving Redwood Shores, won voter approval in 2004 for a tax to pay for salaries and extracurricular programs.

At almost all the schools parents are chipping in to make up some of the funding. Many of the schools run active fundraising campaigns.

Garfield Elementary, in the Fair Oaks neighborhood, receives extra money to reduce class sizes, expand teaching year from 180 to 210 days and encourage parent involvement. Garfield in 1994 was turned into a charter school, which gives it more control over its affairs.

Three unincorporated neighborhoods, Selby, Emerald Lake, Fair Oaks, located just outside city limits, add to housing choices.

Emerald Lake has 3,328 residents, 19 percent of whom are over age 55, about 23 percent under 18, the 1990 census reported. Homes here run to upscale and command great views of the Bay. Emerald Lake neighborhood pulled out of Redwood Elementary District and annexed to Woodside elementary district, one of highest scoring in state.

Old cities (Redwood City incorporated in 1868) often do unusually well in recreational and cultural activities because they have had so much time to pile up the parks and goodies.

Redwood City counts about nine parks, eight playgrounds, a movie complex, 20 public tennis courts, miniature golf, a roller-skating rink, an ice-skating rink, two municipal swimming pools, three libraries, a musem, several marinas and a yacht club.

Recreation-community center (gym, fitness rooms). Cañada Community College on city border; many classes, activities. Farmers' market, community theater, Sunflower Festival. University of California has opened a branch campus of its extension program.

Courts, jail, county and city buildings and about 2,000 government employees, plus lawyers and others, anchor the downtown economy. Through redevelopment (a taxing mechanism), the community has worked to keep the downtown a vibrant part of the town's life.

In recent years, a great deal has been overhauled or rebuilt and a large shopping complex with a Barnes and Noble bookstore, a jumbo supermarket and restaurants added. New city hall. Kaiser Medical Centeris rebuilding its downtown medical facility. In 2002, a 206-unit apartment complex was built near the Caltrain tracks. Homes by transportation, example of "smart planning." Old police station turned into an art center-gallery. Old-fashioned street lamps. Brick sidewalks. Whole Foods.

Civic leaders want to build more housing in and near the downtown.

One homicide in 2004, two homicides in 2003, one each in 2002, 2001 and 2000. In previous years four, two, one, three, six, four, three, three, one, two, zero, zero, three, three, four. Sheriff's office has opened a substation in Fair Oaks.

San Carlos has small airport near the freeway. Some Redwood Shores folks have complained about plane noise.

In the hills, disputes arise over views and sunlight. City passed an ordinance to control building of additions and second stories.

Redwood City is about 12 miles south of San Francisco Airport, the largest employer in San Mateo County, and about 10 miles north of Palo Alto, the intellectual center of Silicon Valley. About five miles to the north and three miles to the south, two bridges (the Hayward and the Dumbarton) tie Redwood City to the East Bay. Highway 101 serves the shore neighborhoods, Interstate 280, the hill sections. Caltrain feeds commute trains into downtown San Francisco and San Jose, with stops along the way. Throw in SamTrans buses and many local jobs and the commute enters the realm of "not that bad."

Chamber of commerce (650) 364-1722.

• Under construction in the downtown, another movie complex built atop stores and a parking garage. To open in 2006.

• Looking up. Ferrari dealership opened in 2005. Owner says that never mind the dotcom bust, there's heaps of money in Silicon Valley.

• Library to be build in Redwood Shores.

• Passion and the English. In 2005, a private group ran a soccer camp staffed by British coaches. The promotional literature suggested that because the Brits were most passionate about the game, they should be able to give excellent advice.

• For over a hundred years, salt was extracted from Bay ponds off of Redwood City and other communities. The state and the feds have purchased these ponds and are restoring them to wetlands, ideal for geese and ducks and other wildlife.

• New charter high school called Summit Prep. Enrollment about 200. Scores among the tops in the county. Charter schools draw a lot of their funding from the state.

SAN BRUNO

BEDROOM TOWN LOCATED JUST WEST of San Francisco International Airport. Rises from the flats to the hills. Great views. In 2003, opened a BART station near its giant mall, Tanforan, which was renovated and reopened in 2005. Among additions: a movie house with 20 screens.

San Bruno added 3,544 residents in the 1980s and about 2,700 in the 1990s. Population 42,215.

San Bruno for years has been just about built out. However, with the closure of one of the Bay Area's last military bases, about 20 acres went on the market for homes, restaurants and hotels. In 2001, Skyline College, located in the hills, sold 22 acres of excess land for $34 million. The City Council rezoned the property for single-family homes.

Skyline used some its profits to buy an adjoining school that was being closed and turn its classrooms to college use. The school district put its profits into building a replacement school with state-of-the art technology. It opened in 2002.

The city's name was probably inspired by Bruno Heceta, Spanish explorer who sought to honor his patron saint. In its initial years, San Bruno was situated near a toll road and a railroad junction and popular with duck hunters and all this, in a small way, encouraged the building of homes.

The town in 1914 incorporated as a legal city with a population of 1,000. Most of housing was built after World War II, and styles will remind you of Fifties and Sixties. Town is aging gracefully. Older, cheaper homes will generally be found near El Camino Real. Generally, lot of care, attention; pleasant looking burg. Median age of residents is 36. Kids under 18 account for 23 percent of inhabitants; over 55 years, 20 percent. Just about as many old as young.

San Bruno in 2005 counted 15,776 residential units, of which 9,127 were single homes, 566 single-family attached, 6,061 multiples, 22 mobiles. One condo-apartment complex, called Shelter Creek, has about 1,300 units.

Many Bayside cities stop at Interstate 280. San Bruno extends well on the other side of this freeway. From some western streets, you can see the Pacific, but most views are confined to the Bay. San Francisco city jail is hidden in hills. Also in hills, a shooting range where cops practice.

Weather is a little tricky. Coast mountains are not that high near San Bruno, which allows the fog to move all the way to the Bay. If driving Highway 101 on a late summer afternoon, look west toward the San Bruno ridgeline. The fog will be cresting the ridge and spilling down into the lowlands, but the farther it advances, the more it falls prey to the sun. Pattern changes from neighborhood to neighborhood. Those west of Interstate 280 might get a good amount of fog. If shopping for a home, talk to neighbors about weather.

One library, 15 parks including major county park, Junipero Serra. Nearby is Crystal Springs Reservoir, pretty and nice for hiking. Annual festival draws about 50,000. Municipal dog run, a place where Rover and pals can exercise and take care of business. Skyline Community College is a big plus, day and evening classes. San Bruno has a large poker parlor, Artichoke Joe's.

Shopping at Tanforan, Bayhill, Towne Center plazas, main sources of sales tax revenue for San Bruno. Tanforan is remembered for what it used to be: a race track and place where local Japanese, at start of World War II, were gathered before being shipped to internment camps. Tanforan will retain its Sears, Penneys and Target and a giant bookstore and a restaurant. New police headquarters to be located at the BART station, also at Tanforan.

The Tanforan section is bordered by Interstate 380, which connects Highway 101 and Interstate 280. The Caltrain station is located about seven blocks from Tanforan. With all this transit support and with the overhaul of the mall, this area along El Camino Real seems to be reviving. Golden Gate National Cemetery, about 125,000 graves, is located in the northern section of San Bruno. Also situated in the city: the Federal Archives and Records Center, favorite haunt of researchers.

One homicide in 2004 and 2003, five in 2002, zero in 2001, one in 1999 and in previous years, zero, zero, zero, two, zero, zero, zero, one, one, zero, one, zero, two, four. In 2002, the bodies of four murder victims were found in a San Bruno apartment. Suspects arrested.

San Bruno schools generally score well above the 50 percentile (statewide comparisons). Capuchino High scores in the 50th and 60th percentile. In 2000, the elementary district annexed Portola Elementary from another district.

San Bruno district in 1998 passed a $30 million bond to renovate the elementary schools. In 2000, after several tries, the high school district passed a bond to renovate all its schools. Space permitting, the high-school district allows students to transfer to school of choice.

Good commute. Two freeways, Skyline Boulevard, Caltrain, SamTrans buses. And, now, BART. If you miss a plane from this town, you're beyond help. Ask neighbors about plane noise. Money may be available for sound insulation for homes. Airport officials say noise is within state limits.

A town with a little bing, bang, boom. Fireworks allowed at the Fourth of July. Chamber of commerce (650) 588-0180.

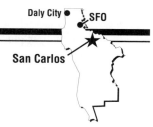

SAN CARLOS

LOCATED MID PENINSULA. Bay town that rises to hills and is divided by a large ravine that is broken up by several small ravines. This has created many sites to position homes that command views of the Bay. Population 28,190.

Peaceful. Bedroom community that has picked up some Silicon Valley-type industries. Small airport east of the freeway, on the Bay, away from homes. In 1998, the Hiller Aviation Museum was opened at the airport, 40 aircraft, including a 1912 biplane and an 1883 hang glider.

Several attempts were made around the turn of the century to get San Carlos going as a suburb but the town did not jell until about World War I.

Subdivision in 1924 aimed for upper end of market, and San Carlos has remained an upper-middle town. Incorporated as city in 1925, hit by suburban housing after war. Between 1950 and 1960, the city increased its population by 50 percent to 21,370, then gradually filled in. Added 1,457 residents in 1980 and 1,551 in the 1990s.

Median age of residents is 40. Kids under 18 account for 23 percent of town; over 55 years, 24 percent. Rounded town, old and young about equal.

Residential units number 11,911, of which 8,256 are single homes, 609 single attached, 3,030 multiples, 16 mobiles (2005 state figures). Just about built out.

San Carlos, to a large extent, built west from its train station. Near the station, the land is flat and contains pre-World War II homes and many apartment complexes. Moving west, the homes become newer, 1950s and 1960s designs, and as you move more west and further into the hills, 1970s and 1980s designs show up. At the top, the newest homes and duplexes, on Crestview Drive.

Many of the homes have been remodeled and upgraded. Many are positioned on their lots to command views. San Carlos residents spend a lot of time in their back yards and on their decks.

Despite the building, San Carlos somehow seems to have a lot of open space. Many of the hillsides are too steep for home construction. Large parks or preserves border the town on the west side.

Crime low. One homicide in 2004, zero from 1994-2003, one each in 1993, 1992, 1991 and 1990, zero in 1989, 1988, 1987, two in 1986, zero in 1985.

School rankings high, mostly 80s and 90s. Day care at all elementary schools. Educational foundation and Chickens Ball raise money for schools. Older kids move up to Carlmont (Belmont) or Sequoia (Redwood City) High schools, part of Sequoia District. This district in 1996 won voter approval of a $45 million bond, the money used to renovate and rewire all schools in the district. In 2001 and 2004, voters passed two more renovation bonds for the Sequoia district.

San Carlos Elementary District in 1997 won approval of a $21 million bond to improve all schools and renovate a closed school so it could be reopened. In 2003, voters approved a parcel tax to maintain elementary instructional quality and electives. And in 2005, they passed yet another bond for more renovations and additional classrooms.

In sum, good support of schools.

Elementary district in 1994 opened a charter school. New attempt to give teachers more flexibility on how school is run and to get parents more involved in education.

Local lad who made good: baseball star Barry Bonds.

Library, seniors center, dog run, 13 parks, 4 playgrounds, museum. New library opened in 1999. The children's section was expanded. Also in 1999, San Carlos opened a youth center, which includes a gym, computer room, crafts area and game room.

Downtown spruced up: remodelings, new facades, signs. One of the largest supermarkets in the county. Restaurants, stores and coffee houses along El Camino Real and Laurel Street, in the downtown. Nice little downtown, which seems to have held its own against shopping malls. Trader Joe's.

The usual two freeways to San Francisco but San Carlos looks more toward Silicon Valley than the City. Caltrain to San Francisco, Silicon Valley; shuttle buses to Caltrain station. SamTrans (buses). Not far from airport or bridges to East Bay.

In recent years San Carlos has built railroad underpasses or overpasses and improved freeway exits and approaches along Brittan Avenue. This has helped internal traffic. Highway 101 has been widened.

Land near Highway 101 to be developed: offices, retail, luxury hotels. The commercial area is located east of El Camino Real, the town's main drag.

Chamber of commerce (650) 593-1068.

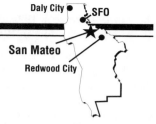

SAN MATEO

MIDDLE-CLASS, WELL-KEPT CITY that rises from Bay to hills that offer great views. On clear days, you can see Mt. Diablo, at the edge of the Sacramento Delta. In and near its downtown, San Mateo has built office and high-tech complexes.

Second-most populous city in the county, 94,212 people. Middle class but changing. Like many Peninsula cities, it is becoming ethnically diverse from an influx of immigrants and first-, second- and third-generation Americans. Median age of residents is 38. Under 18 years, 20 percent. Over 55 years, 24 percent. Growing a little gray.

Academic rankings generally well above the 50th percentile, compared to other California schools. San Mateo shares elementary schools with Foster City. The city's three high schools, on state rankings, usually land in the 70s, 80s, 90s.

In 2000, the San Mateo Union High School District passed a $138 million bond to renovate its high schools. San Mateo High, earthquake unsafe, was rebuilt, the work completed in 2005.

Residents approved a bond to renovate elementary schools and build new facilities, and a parcel tax to lower elementary class sizes and improve programs. Foundation raises money for schools.

The school district has installed Spanish immersion and "magnet" programs to meet the diverse academic needs of the children.

Parents have choice of sending kids to neighborhood school or to "magnets" which have enriched programs. Magnet schools mix the kids ethnically by offering programs to attract them out of their neighborhood schools. If you are new to town, call the school district right away and get the enrollment information. Some schools fill early. Deadlines are important. See web sites for San Mateo-Foster City Elementary School District and for San Mateo Union High School District. The high-school district assigns by neighborhood but space permitting allows transfers.

Like almost all California schools, San Mateo's now pay more attention to helping the kids to respect cultural differences.

Four homicides in 2004, one in 2003, zero in 2002, one in 2001, zero in 2000, 1999, three in 1998, two in 1997, one in 1996, six in 1995, one in 1994, three in 1993, three in 1992, one in 1991, one in 1990, zero in 1989, three in 1988, one in 1987, four in 1986, and two in 1985, reports FBI.

Good commute. San Mateo is crisscrossed by Highway 101 and Highway 92. The latter runs west to Interstate 280 and Half Moon Bay, and east to the San Mateo Bridge and the East Bay. The San Mateo bridge recently opened another span; it makes coming and going to Alameda County much easier. Caltrain to San Jose or San Francisco, with stops along the way. SamTrans buses carry riders all over the county and to San Francisco and new the BART station at Millbrae. Transit center at Third Avenue and Main Street.

New in 2004: bullet train, one stop (Milbrae) to downtown San Francisco. South bound bullet stops at Palo, Mountain View and San Jose. San Mateo station is at Hillsdale Boulevard and El Camino Real.

San Mateo is always fixing something up or filling in a lot or tearing something down and replacing it with something bigger or grander. Most of the work takes place near the freeway or in the downtown.

San Mateo had a race track with practice track for about 50 years. But attendance at horse racing fell off. The practice track in 1998 was torn up and replaced by homes, apartments, shops, offices, large Barnes and Noble bookstore. Most of the office space went to Franklin Templeton Investments, the mutual fund company.

The next to go: the race track itself. Tentative plans call for offices covering 1 million square feet and 1,500 residential units.

Recreation plentiful. 24 parks, 22 of them with play areas for children, performing arts center, marina, softball, bocce, soccer, baseball, football, ice skating rink. Farmers market. Bike paths. Municipal golf course. Senior and activity centers. YMCA (gym, pool). In 2003, a movie complex, 12-screens, opened in downtown. New library scheduled to open in 2005. The city is also renovating its two branch libraries. San Mateo's central park, designed when the town was small, is a charmer. In those days, they planted shade trees to cool picnicker and strollers. Walking tours of historic buildings.

Thoroughbred racing at Bay Meadows, while it is still open, wildlife center, Bay beach, windsurfing and swimming at Coyote Point. Crystal Springs Reservoir, miles of open space and trails, just west of the city. Garden Center, run by volunteers; classes on how to grow things.

City requires residents or business owners to scrub off or paint over graffiti within a few days of detection. Streets clean, parks maintained, lawns mowed, shrubs trimmed. San Mateo employs a code enforcement person to make sure people don't create eyesores.

The state in 2005 counted 39,072 housing units, of which 17,725 were singles, 3,492 single attached, 17,810 multiples and 45 mobile homes.

When you drive San Mateo streets, you see housing that is fairly new and of modern design, especially the townhouses, but the dominant styles, led by the two- and three-bedroom home, come out of the 25 years after World War II.

With few exceptions, the homes are well maintained and many have been remodeled.

In north San Mateo, between railroad tracks and Highway 101, the neighborhood has gone transitional, offering housing that meets needs of low-income residents.

Hillsdale Center — Macys, Nordstrom, Mervyns, Sears.

Fashion Island, a shopping mall east of Highway 101, was demolished and replaced by 20 acres of office buildings, apartments and such stores as Toys "R" Us, Home Depot and Target.

Two hospitals, Mills and San Mateo County General.

The whole area around the intersection of Highway 101-Highway 92 has been transformed into an office-research center. Many of the firms are located in Foster City.

Speakers club attracts some top names to San Mateo Performing Arts Center, which also stages an annual "Nutcracker."

To sum up, an old-new suburb that's loading up on high-tech and office jobs. This means short commute for many residents. New businesses will help revive downtown and give residents more shopping choices.

Chamber of commerce (650) 341-5679.

• About 2,000 elderly live in the downtown, which has several seniors' complexes, a hospital, a park, shops, hospital.

• Trader Joe's and Whole Foods.

SO. SAN FRANCISCO

HILL AND DALE TOWN. Also known as South City. One of key cities for biotech. Population 61,661. In 2003, opened a BART station.

Famous or notorious for its large white "South San Francisco, The Industrial City" blazoned across a hillside and visible from Highway 101. Letters are 60 feet high and made of cement.

Another sign graces the waterfront, "South San Francisco, Birthplace of Biotechnology."

For about 20 years now, South San Francisco has been one of the hot spots of construction on the Peninsula. Close to San Francisco International Airport. Several large hotels near the freeway.

South City is the headquarters of Genentech and over 50 other biotech firms. The waterfront is filled gleaming research and office buildings and the new hotels. South City is home to a See's chocolate factory, about 600 employees.

In 2003, the BART line was extended to San Francisco Airport and stations opened at South San Francisco, San Bruno and Millbrae. The South City station is located a few miles west of the waterfront. Whether this station proves helpful to the biotech employees remains to be seen but it has prompted some housing construction in its vicinity (Mission Boulevard near Grand Avenue). This neighborhood also has a Costco.

Taxes from hotels and businesses fund about half the city's budget. South San Francisco has over 45,000 jobs. This translates into a short commute for many residents.

Served by South San Francisco Unified School District. In comparisons with other schools in the state, many of the schools are hitting the 70th and 80th percentiles. In 1997, voters approved a $40 million bond to improve all schools in the district.

Three Catholic schools. Skyline Community College located about three miles to the south.

In the 1850s, as the Spanish land grants were broken up, a cattle baron purchased 1,500 acres at Point San Bruno. For the next 30 years, large herds were pastured here before being driven to the San Francisco stockyards.

About 1890, the baron died and his land went on the market. At that time, the big butchers — Swift, Armour, Cudahy, Morris — were looking for a spot to set up their West Coast operations. They purchased the 1,500 acres, added 2,000 and went into business as the Western Meat Company. In similar ventures, Augustus Swift had established and named South Omaha and South Chicago. And so ... South San Francisco. Absolutely no imagination!

Western Meat also set up a land company to build homes that workers could purchase and to attract other industries to Point San Bruno. Within 10 years or so, the cluster of homes jelled as a community and in 1908, the town was incorporated as the City of South San Francisco. Four of the five members of the first city council were employed by Western Meat.

In the beginning, South City had Irish, French, Italian and Chinese neighborhoods. Italian tradition is recalled annually in Italian-American games: bocce, track and more wrapped up with a dinner-dance. In recent years, other ethnic groups, have settled in South San Francisco.

In 1926, the City of San Francisco purchased for a municipal airport 1,100 acres just south of South City. Came World War II, the U.S military took over the airport, pumped in millions worth of improvements and started the airport down the road of what it is today: a gigantic and perpetual work in progress that underpins the economy of the region, jobs by the tens of thousands and supporting firms that also generate jobs by tens, etc. Stockyards closed in 1957.

 South City started 1940 with 1,300 housing units. In that decade, it almost tripled its housing, adding about 2,900 units. In the 1950s, the city exploded, building about 5,800 units and in the 1960s and 1970s, about 3,500 units each decade. In the 1980s, home construction dropped to about 1,700 units and in 1990s, the South City built about 1,400 units. In the last decade, the city increased its population by 6,000.

In housing styles, the city is easily described. The prewar housing can be found in and adjoining the downtown, which straddles Grand Street. A little farther out, the 1950s homes show themselves, then the 1960s and 1970s housing.

West of Interstate 280, the Westborough neighborhood is almost entirely devoted to townhouses and just to the south is another single-home neighbor-hood, circa 1960s to 1980s.

For the modern, Terrabay, master-planned development of townhouses and single homes on the slopes of San Bruno Mountain, some infilling along Chestnut Avenue and the units coming around the BART station. Construction continues near Terrabay, in the Mandalay development, with a tall condo tower (16 stories).

Residential units in 2005 totaled 20,544. Single homes accounted for 12,001 units, single-family attached 2,524, apartments and condos 5,610, mobile homes 409.

Median age of residents is 36. Children and teens under 18 make up 24 percent of town; people over 55 years, 21 percent. Rounded town.

Summing up, housing across the spectrum, modest to mildly upscale, with a lot in the middle. Many of the homes have been remodeled and improved. Larger homes are generally newer homes (but just about nothing opulent and some old housing near the downtown really shows its age).

The downtown has an intimate quality that planners and more Americans are starting to appreciate. For decades, suburbs have been treating residential and business as oil and water — never the twain shall mix.

There's a lot to be said for this approach. For one thing, it shelters kids playing on the streets from the traffic going to and from stores. But it also takes away some of the friendliness of our towns. The idea of an evening stroll to the local restaurant or deli or stopping for a beer at the saloon and chatting with friends or neighbors— in many countries this is common; in American suburbs it's rare. South City has this ambiance, especially in its downtown, which the city has played up with ornamental street lights, angled parking, brick cross walks, shrubs and trees. The section has several green grocers, delis, restaurants and a grand city hall with a library.

During Prohibition, South City ran wide open. One of the largest illegal distilleries was not only a member of the chamber of commerce, it was run by the chamber, wrote the late Alan Hynding in his history of San Mateo, "From Frontier To Suburb."

Occasional complaints about airport noise. The feds have put up several million to soundproof homes.

The new South City is better symbolized by the Oyster Point Marina Business Park — sleek, modern, futuristic, cool — than the dirty white lettering on the hillside.

The old lettering, however, has reached almost cult status — so desperate, so blatant, so tacky, so human. In 1996, a state commission voted to give it historical status.

Foggy in many neighborhoods. In July it's not uncommon to see people bundled in hooded sweatshirts. Coastal hills drop in elevation, allowing the fog to penetrate to the Bay.

Crime rate fairly low. One homicide in 2004, two in 2003, one each from 2002 to 1999, zero in 1998 and 1997, two in 1996, one in 1995, two in 1994 and 1993, one in 1992, three in 1991, one in 1990, two in 1989, two in 1988, one in 1987, four in 1986, three in 1985.

About 16 neighborhood parks. San Bruno state park on north side. Marina and waterfront park. Trails. Typical kid and adult sports, many sponsored by city hall. Most popular: baseball and soccer. Community pool. Community gym. Forty-Niner games are 5 minutes up the road, Giants games in downtown San Francisco. Delights of San Francisco close at hand. Golf course. If you want to swim in the Bay, lap lanes have been set up off Oyster Point. Marina. Windsurfing.

Great commute if you work in San Francisco or at the airport. BART station also at Daly City and Colma. So-so commute if you have to slog to Silicon Valley but there is an alternative: Caltrain, which runs commute trains to San Jose and Silicon Valley and north to downtown San Francisco. Station in South San Francisco. Chamber of commerce (650) 588-1911.

• How bio-tech can you get? South City named one of its streets "DNA Way."

WOODSIDE

PRESTIGIOUS TOWN LOCATED above Atherton and Redwood City, next to Portola Valley. Secluded for the most part. Quaint. Stable. In the 1980s, its population dropped by about 250 residents. In the 1990s, it added about 300 residents. Population, 5,496.

Median age of residents is 44. Kids and teens under 18 make up 23 percent of the town, over 55 years, 29 percent.

Horses, an estimated 2,000, may outnumber children, about 1,000.

Attuned more to Silicon Valley and Stanford than San Francisco. Stanford Linear Accelerator stops just short of the city limits.

Named after Woodside Store, which became center of logging activity. In 1993, the local historical association reopened the store as a museum.

Woodsy. Trees all over the place, some fairly big redwoods, second growth, and town is planting more.

After redwoods were logged, the rich in the early 1900s built estates in the Woodside hills. Gradually the town caught on as nice place to talk to the trees, relax, lead good life.

Horsey: corrals, pastures, stables, trails. Tennis courts. Deer-crossing signs. Town backs up against game refuge. Some residents dabble in vineyards. In 2004, the town opened another park with playing fields, paths and a playground.

Although some demurely gorgeous mansions hide behind walls of shrubs, a lot of the homes are modest. Valued for the location, for the company of cultivated neighbors, including Nobel winners and movie-media stars.

Cañada Community College, located in Woodside just east of Interstate 280, adds to cultural life. Annual art fair.

Low crime. Zero homicides in 2003 and 2002. In 1993, the city recorded its first homicide in six years, a man who lived out of town and who had been shot and left on the side of the road, newspaper reported. Crooks would have hard time finding Woodside — a deterrent since many crimes are crimes of opportunity. Patrolled by sheriff's deputies.

Library, post office, fire station. Game refuge and large park with trails on the north. Other large parks on the south. Residents have purchased other lands and placed them in wildlife preserves. Filoli, famous estate, open for tours.

A short drive to Silicon Valley, via Interstate 280. A long drive on same road to San Francisco. Highway 84 winds and twists through the town and ends at the Pacific.

Single-home burg. Of Woodside's 2,088 residences, 2,026 or 97 percent are single homes. The rest are single-family attached, 28; multiples, 33; mobile homes, 1 (2005 state figures). Very little construction, maybe a dozen or two dozen homes a year, and in some years, fewer.

Some grumbling about "e-money" and "Silicon Implants," references to Silicon Valley millionaires tearing down small, old homes and replacing them with giant jobs. Damn parvenus ... but then again, this is California. We've never had old money.

In Silicon money, Woodside is bit of the lore. Supposedly some of the biggest deals were cobbled together in Woodside restaurants and bars.

Elementary school rankings land in the top two percent of state. Yes, it is a one-school district with an enrollment of about 450.

Voters in 1993 renewed a parcel tax to support education programs. School foundation in some years raises over $700,000 for school programs or about $1,700 for each student. Voters in 1998 rejected a bond that would have renovated schools and added classrooms, mainly because they thought a two-story building would be ugly. The measure was retooled and it passed in 1999 — $5.2 million to upgrade buildings and replaced portables with a one-story structure. In 2005, another bond was passed to upgrade the schools with modern wiring and technology. In 2001, voters extended a parcel tax to raise the pay of the local teachers so they wouldn't leave for districts that paid more.

Some homes outside of Woodside are included in Woodside school district. Homebuyers should check to find out what district they are in. Older kids attend Woodside High, where they mix with a more diverse group. Scores in the 60th and 70th percentiles. Woodside High is in Woodside and in the Sequoia district, which in 2001 and 2004 passed bonds to renovate all its schools. See Redwood City profile.

McCormack's GUIDES

$15.95

How California Schools Work

A PRACTICAL
GUIDE FOR
PARENTS

FROM THE EDITORS OF McCormack's Guides

www.mccormacks.com
1-800-222-3602

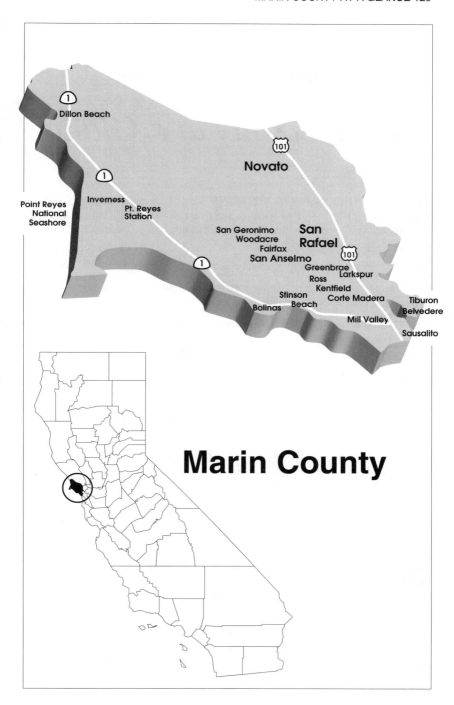

Chapter 5

Marin County at a Glance

RIDGED BY HILLS AND MOUNTAINS, Marin County is bordered on the west by the Pacific and on the east by San Francisco Bay. Its southern tip anchors one of the most famous bridges in the world, the Golden Gate.

The county is famed for its views, its money and its style — the good life, the adventuresome life, with a social conscience that sometimes misfires.

Marin bumper sticker: "Don't postpone joy." Marin doesn't. It is — and its inhabitants would nod agreement — a happy place.

The county closed 2005 with a visit from Prince Charles and Camilla, who came to support one of the prince's passions: organic farming. By all accounts, the royals charmed the birkenstocks off the locals and even Camilla — the oft-maligned second banana — was conceded to be pleasant and friendly and well ... OK, or a notch above.

Marin runs roughly 31 miles top to bottom along the Highway 101 corridor, 35 miles east to west, and is dominated near the middle by its single mountain, Tamalpais, elevation 2,571 feet, beloved by residents and visitors.

West of Tamalpais, in summer, the winds blow, the fogs swirl, the cold nips. East of Tamalpais, with the exception of a few days of bluster and rain (or a few weeks in nasty years), the weather is balmy from January through December. And the air clean, thanks to the winds, the lack of "smoke" industries and to smog restraints on cars.

Marin residents love the west: the Pacific, the waves, the views, the seals, the fish, the flora, the fauna. Aside from a few hardy souls, however, they live east of Mount Tamalpais. Mountain and hills shelter the east from cold fogs of summer. In land, Marin covers 520 square miles, about 11 times the size of San Francisco, but it's among the smallest counties in the state, third from bottom.

Marin had been turning itself into a media-software center. Lucasfilm (Star Wars, etc.) was based in Marin and the Mill Valley Film Festival is winning international attention. Several movie and television personalities live in the county. But, short of commercial space and unwilling to give up vistas and open space in exchange for the dollar, Marin remains essentially a bed-

It's the Experience!℠

HIGHLY EXPERIENCED RELOCATION AGENTS
TWO GENERATIONS OF REAL ESTATE SERVICE & KNOWLEDGE

THE MAXIMUM REAL ESTATE HAS TO OFFER

The Real Estate Leaders

Kathy & Mary Kay Yamamoto

mkyamamoto@remax.net / www.marinhomesmarykay.com

RE/MAX of Central Marin

(800) 570-REMAX

Service - The key to our success is our high standard of quality personal service.

Integrity - We are committed to maintaining our trustworthy reputation.

Expert Representation - We will guide you through the process of selecting the area and home that is best for you, assist you in obtaining any specific information that you need, negotiate your purchase, assist you with inspections and financing, and do all that is necessary to ensure a smooth transaction and transition.

Results - Our extensive knowledge of the market and over **40** years of combined experience in Marin and Sonoma Counties representing buyers & sellers gets you the results you need.

Marin County Population

City or Area	1990	2000	2005*
Belvedere	2,147	2,125	2,132
Bolinas	1,098	1,246	NA
Corte Madera	8,272	9,100	9,378
Fairfax	6,931	7,319	7,309
Inverness	1,422	1,421	NA
Kentfield	6,030	6,351	NA
Larkspur	11,070	12,014	12,014
Lucas Valley-Marinwood	5,982	6,357	NA
Mill Valley	13,038	13,600	13,686
Novato	47,585	47,630	50,586
Ross	2,123	2,329	2,349
San Anselmo	11,743	12,378	12,385
San Rafael	48,404	56,063	57,224
Santa Venetia	3,362	4,298	NA
Sausalito	7,152	7,330	7,374
Tiburon	7,532	8,666	8,772
Woodacre	1,478	1,393	NA
Countywide	230,096	247,289	252,485

Source: 1990 Census and 2000 Census. *California Dept. of Finance, 2005. NA (Not available)

room county. (In 2005, Lucasfilm moved many of its operations to San Francisco.)

What You See Now Is What You'll See Next Time

Marin is one of the slowest-growing urban counties in California. It started 1950 with 85,610 people, jumped to 146,820 within a decade, an increase of 72 percent, then to 208,250 in 1970, another 42 percent. Then slam went the door.

The population in the 1970s rose by 7 percent to 222,568 and in the 1980s by 3 percent. Marin started the 1990s with 230,096 residents and finished, according to the census, with 247,289, residents, an increase of about 17,000 or 7 percent. In 2005, the state estimated the population at 252,485.

The median age of residents is 41. Children and teens under 18 make up 20 percent of the county. Demographic translation: many singles and empty nesters, fair but not overwhelming number of kids. (Family counties come in over 30 percent).

In the 1990s, the county erected 5,500 residential units (state guess). Of these, about 56 percent or 3,095 units were single-detached homes, 7 percent single attached and 37 percent or 2,038 units apartments or condos.

Where did new residential units go up? Two cities accounted for 56 percent of the total. San Rafael increased its housing stock by 1,731 units and Novato by 1,351. A little less than 25 percent, 1,251 units, were built in unincorporated towns or neighborhoods or on single lots scattered around the county.

Marin County Voter Registration

City	Demo.	Repub.	NP
Belvedere	504	700	272
Corte Madera	3,067	1,282	1,177
Fairfax	3,114	530	1,010
Larkspur	4,097	2,046	1,504
Mill Valley	5,512	1,684	1,838
Novato	12,565	8,066	5,028
Ross	657	616	292
San Anselmo	4,833	1,261	1,573
San Rafael	14,556	6,938	5,534
Sausalito	2,503	1,063	1,287
Tiburon	2,592	1,832	1,258
Unincorporated	21,531	9,414	7,817
Countywide	75,531	35,432	28,589

Source: Marin County Registrar of Voters, California Secretary of State's Office, 2004.   Key: Demo (Democrat), Repub. (Republican), NP (Declined to state).

Presidential Voting in Marin County

Year	Democrat	D-Votes	Republican	R-Votes
1948	Truman*	12,540	Dewey	18,747
1952	Stevenson	14,236	Eisenhower*	29,574
1956	Stevenson	17,301	Eisenhower*	33,792
1960	Kennedy*	27,888	Nixon	37,620
1964	Johnson*	46,462	Goldwater	28,682
1968	Humphrey	36,278	Nixon*	41,422
1972	McGovern	47,414	Nixon*	54,123
1976	Carter*	43,590	Ford	53,425
1980	Carter	39,231	Reagan*	53,425
1984	Mondale	57,533	Reagan*	56,887
1988	Dukakis	69,394	Bush*	46,885
1992	Clinton*	71,605	Bush	28,144
1996	Clinton*	67,406	Dole	32,714
2000	Gore	78,192	Bush*	34,536
2004	Kerry	73,946	Bush*	26,141

Source: California Secretary of State's office. *Election winner.

The remainder, about 1,200 units, were erected in the county's remaining nine cities: Belvedere, Corte Madera, Fairfax, Larkspur, Mill Valley, Ross, San Anselmo, Sausalito and Tiburon.

To give you the flavor of the pace of construction: in the 1990s, according to state figures, Larkspur built 340 units, Ross 17, and Mill Valley 126.

If you want to buy a home in Marin, chances are good that you will wind up in the resale market.

In the latter half the 1990s and in 2000, the housing market was blistering and Realtors were imploring people to sell, sell, sell! The number of homes coming to market fell far short of the demand. By 2001, home prices seemed to be softening but then interest rates were lowered, home sales elevated and so did the prices, way up there. Modest homes, three bedrooms, often sell for over $800,000. Will the prices hold up? Who knows?

In 2005, the state counted in Marin 107,482 residential units, of which 65,278 were single homes, 8,593 single attached, 31,480 apartments or condos, 2,131 mobiles.

Among California's 58 counties, Marin is first in money. In a recent count (2002), Marin placed first in median income, joint returns, $92,481. Next came Santa Clara, $82,150, then San Mateo, $81,259.

Marin Style

"Only in Marin" pigeonholes the county for outsiders who think Marin has attracted an unusually large number of goofs. Marin residents, or some portion of them, are always searching, searching, for the right therapist or therapy, the special restaurant, the elusive diet, the skilled plastic surgeon — for the anyone and the anything that will enable them to squeeze the maximum out of life.

When they are not searching, many are fretting, fretting, fretting, especially over the environment. Save that tree, preserve that hill, don't you dare build that home or road. None of this is harmful but the wealth of the county makes some of it seem shallow.

Many of the residents are dedicated to living the good life. On any weekend night in Marin, the wine flows by the vat, the parties last into the wee hours, the feet dance, the voices sing. In many ways, it is a merry and ingratiating county, so much so that people mention it in their wills.

The Marin Community Foundation, $1.2 billion, funded by a widow for the benefit of Marin, every year dispenses millions to worthy causes — about $53 million in 2004. Ponce de Leon searched in vain for the Fountain of Youth. Marin may find it. The foundation has built in Novato a center to research aging.

The Real Marin

School rankings perhaps give a more accurate picture. They're quite high, which usually means someone at home is pushing the kids to study, that education is prized for itself. Almost every school district in recent years has won voter approval for more money for repairs, curriculum or new classrooms.

Crime, with the exception of a few neighborhoods, is very low. The entire county reported seven homicides in 1995, two in 1996, one in 1997, one in 1998, two in 1999, five in 2000, three in 2001, four in 2002, zero in 2003 and three in 2004. Nonetheless, Marin does have an excess of criminals: San Quentin, the famous prison, is located near the San Rafael-Richmond Bridge. It has about 6,000 inmates, including 560 on California's only death row. The state was thinking about closing San Quentin, which needs repairs, but changed its mind.

Towns like Tiburon, Belvedere, Mill Valley — well-to-do or rich — often seem to set the tone for the county. But the most populous towns, San Rafael and Novato, are generally middle-class with modest homes and many apartments.

Marin is one of the few counties that aptly can be described as cosmopolitan. Many residents are well-traveled and well-educated or bosses or managers. They stage plays, make movies and support the arts and progressive causes.

Rare for a small county, Marin fields a symphony orchestra.

Marin residents take stands, especially on environmental matters, and argue for their interests or hire a lawyer to do the same. By and large, they are not a bashful lot. If you enjoy stimulating conversation, Marin can oblige.

Not all are liberals. George Bush, the elder, got 32 percent of the county's ballots and Bush the younger, about 33,000 votes first, then 26,000. But most are the L people: Kerry 73 percent of the vote, Bush 25 percent.

Marin is a physically active county. People are hiking, biking, jogging, sailing in the Bay or Pacific, surfing, climbing Mount Tamalpais, dancing, skating, golfing, riding horses, playing tennis and softball, and more. According to one informal study done by the local newspaper, Marin spends more per capita on sporting goods and equipment than any other county in the state.

History

In the beginning, there were Indians, Miwoks, destined for tragedy. They fished, hunted, ground nuts for meal and lived in lodges made of willow.

Sir Francis Drake, of piratical and Armada fame, or a member of his crew may have been the first white to set foot in Marin. In June 1579, Drake's ship, the Golden Hinde, sailed into either San Francisco Bay or Drake's Bay, off Point Reyes, made contact with the Indians, and sailed off. Many dispute the landing of Sir Francis, but no matter. The buccaneer sailed into local lore.

The Spanish

Although Spanish captains sailed the coast of California in the 1500s, explorers did not arrive in the Bay Area until 1769. Distance and fierce Indians quickly choked the flow of settlers. Fifty years later Spanish-Hispanics in Northern California numbered below 2,000.

Church policy was to bring the Indians to the mission (in San Francisco) and instruct them in the habits of the field and the ways of God. Having no immunity to Western diseases, many contracted smallpox or measles and died. On the secular side, the rancheros, needing workers, indentured or enslaved Indians, further depleting their numbers.

Russians and Yankees

The Russians in 1812 built Fort Ross in Sonoma County, worrying the Californios. For this reason and others, the Spanish moved north from San

Francisco, opened a mission at San Rafael and divided the countryside into rancheros. Some Indians fought back. One band was led by a Chief Marin, defeated in the end but formidable enough for the tribute of having the county named in his honor.

Meanwhile, the United States ventured into the Midwest and trappers made their way over the mountains, followed a few years later by settlers. The Russians trapped the local otter out of existence, became discouraged, sold their cannons to John Sutter and left. Sutter took his arsenal, sailed up the Delta, founded Sacramento and went partners with John Marshall in a saw mill. Building the mill, Marshall looked in the stream and found gold. Whoopee!

The Yankee story: They came, they coveted, they conquered, more by numbers than anything else. Spain and Mexico (which took over from Spain in 1821) never put together a successful plan to colonize California — a great strategic failing. The Americans snared and shot the grizzly, cut the redwoods, farmed the land, fished the Bay and Pacific, ignored, swindled or bought the Californios into oblivion and apparently treated the remaining Indians with enough ill will to ensure the extinction of all but a few.

Railroads and Ferries

The arrival of the Yankees coincided with two great inventions of the 1800s: trains and steamships. Ferry slips were built at Sausalito and Tiburon. Rail lines, one even ascending Mount Tamalpais, snaked up the county. Train, ship and ferry allowed farmers to supply San Francisco with food and fish and opened Marin to excursions from the City.

About 1854, the state opened the prison at San Quentin, the first inmates coming from a ship that had been anchored off of Angel Island. In the beginning, the prison was far from secure. On one occasion about 400 inmates escaped and shot it out with local residents before surrendering.

When the businessman of old and his family wanted relief from the stink, noise and rush of San Francisco, they looked north to Marin. There they found shade of pine and redwood, burble of brook, diversions of hiking and fishing, and when they tired of all that, the pleasures of tippling, dining, carousing. About the turn of the century, Belvedere Cove was noted for its houseboats, called arks. Men rowed from ark to ark, sampling hospitality and parties. A launch deposited them in the morning at San Francisco and work.

The county's population at the turn of 1900 stood about 15,000.

Culture and Conservation

Marin in its formative years had the good fortune to attract the educated, the progressive, the wealthy and the cultivated. They bought land for parks, led the fight to conserve land, funded concerts and other musical events, patronized artists and instilled the idea that support for the arts and for conservation routinely should be enthusiastic, not occasional. Of special note, William Kent

Education Level of Population Age 25 & Older

City or Town	ND	HS	SC	AA	BA	Grad
Belvedere	1%	4%	16%	3%	41%	35%
Bolinas	3	11	20	8	30	24
Corte Madera	3	10	16	5	40	23
Fairfax	3	14	25	8	30	19
Inverness	0	7	23	4	36	30
Kentfield	1	9	16	5	34	34
Larkspur	2	10	19	6	36	26
Lucas Valley-Marinwood	3	10	23	5	35	23
Mill Valley	1	5	18	4	38	33
Pt. Reyes Station	2	15	22	11	29	16
Novato	6	18	28	8	25	12
Ross	5	5	7	5	38	37
San Anselmo	2	10	21	7	37	22
San Rafael	7	14	21	6	27	17
Santa Venetia	7	21	23	6	24	14
Sausalito	2	6	18	5	41	29
Stinson Beach	1	14	20	6	38	22
Strawberry	2	8	18	7	40	23
Tiburon	1	8	15	6	36	34
Tomales	6	24	17	6	22	21
Woodacre	2	16	25	5	32	19
Marin County	5	12	21	6	31	21

Source: 2000 Census. Figures are percent of population age 25 and older, rounded to the nearest whole number. Not shown are adults with less than a 9th grade education. **Key**: ND (high school, no diploma); HS (high school diploma or GED only, no college); SC (some college education); AA (associate degree); Bach. (bachelor's degree only); Grad (master's or higher degree).

purchased Muir Woods and donated it for a park and led the fight to preserve Mount Tamalpais. His mother, Adaline, donated the land for the College of Marin. The Marin Conservation League is a formidable organization.

Earthquake, Twenties and Thirties

The earthquake of 1906 leveled San Francisco and implanted in City dwellers an attitude of, "I'm getting outta here." Marin's population grew steadily and by 1930 stood at 41,648. Unfortunately, the logic behind the move was as faulty as the San Andreas. Marin, like the entire Bay Area, is very much earthquake country.

The San Andreas, the biggest fault, runs straight through Tomales Bay and, in fact, created the bay. **See map on page 141.** That long furrow running to Tomales Bay traces the San Andreas. Your phone book contains information about how to prepare for and what to do in a big quake — a prudent read.

The Golden Gate Bridge

The idea for spanning the Golden Gate dates back almost to the Forty Niners and retrospectively the bridge probably was inevitable. It opened on May 28, 1937, a feat of grace and engineering. "Paradise was lost," someone

Marin County Average Household Income

City or Area	1990	2000	*2005
Belvedere	$231,200	$303,400	$310,500
Corte Madera	84,900	105,900	109,100
Fairfax	76,500	93,800	97,100
Larkspur-Kentfield	117,600	144,600	147,800
Mill Valley	114,800	143,800	145,900
Novato	84,800	100,800	105,500
Ross	232,000	304,100	312,700
San Anselmo	90,600	114,100	116,000
San Rafael	85,600	105,500	107,700
Sausalito-Marin City	108,400	134,600	138,600
Tiburon	148,300	189,600	198,900
Remainder	80,500	95,900	100,600
Countywide	98,900	123,200	125,700

Source: Association of Bay Area Governments, "Projections 2002." Average income per household includes wages and salaries, dividends, interest, rent and transfer payments such as Social Security or public assistance. *Projections.

later wrote, a reference to the opening of Marin to great pressures to develop. But it might be argued that instead of lost, paradise was expanded. Tens of thousands now enjoy Marin. By 1940, the population had reached 52,907.

World War II

The World War boomed the West Coast, Marin no exception. Sausalito built ships, Novato flew planes (Hamilton Air Force Base). Men and women came from all over the country to work in the new industries. Marin got its first major infusion of African-Americans to work in local industries.

Highway 101

A logical addition to the Golden Gate Bridge, Highway 101, as a freeway, was started in the 1950s and in 1994 reached the northern end of Sonoma County. As revolutionary as the Golden Gate Bridge was, it could not realize its potential until feeder roads were improved. Highway 101 was one vast road improvement. From 1850 to 1950, Marin grew by 85,000 people. In the 20 years after 1950, it added 123,000 people.

The Great Slowdown

After the building boom of the 1960s and 1970s, Marin collectively said "Whoa." Of the county's 11 cities, five declined in population between the 1980 and 1990 census — Belvedere, Fairfax, Ross, San Anselmo and Sausalito. In 1998, in part because they feared more development, residents said no to funding road and freeway improvements through a half-cent sales tax.

Golden Gate National Recreational Area

In the early 1970s, Congressman Phil Burton pushed through one of the largest park purchases in the history of California. The result, called the Golden

Population by Age Groups in Marin County

City or Area	Under 5	5-19	20-34	35-54	55+
Belvedere	96	353	98	617	961
Bolinas	37	241	178	509	281
Corte MAdera	636	1,604	1,274	3,421	5,586
Fairfax	377	1,135	1,197	3,370	1,440
Inverness	46	176	131	522	576
Kentfield	387	1,282	600	2,771	1,911
Larkspur	560	1,509	1,597	4,406	3,942
Mill Valley	749	2,274	1,670	5,075	3,832
Novato	2,802	9,128	8,108	16,313	11,279
Ross	169	574	170	809	607
San Anselmo	725	2,130	1,734	5,132	2,657
San Rafael	3,271	8,903	12,587	18,005	13,297
Santa Venetia	191	661	561	1,554	1,331
Sausalito	222	354	1,465	3,203	2,086
Tiburon	520	1,456	819	3,157	2,714
Woodacre	64	277	147	602	303
County Total	13,396	40,771	41,648	90,178	61,296

Source: Census 2000

Gate National Recreational Area, includes the Marin headlands and Point Reyes, thousands of acres along the Pacific Coast, Muir Woods, Alcatraz and parts of the San Francisco coast.

The Marin County Open Space District has purchased almost 14,000 acres. Another group, the Marin Agricultural Land Trust, by payments to farmers and ranchers, has placed about 38,000 acres into preserve. West Marin, which was to have housed over 150,000 people, barely musters 10,000. The result: shortage of homes in the county, delightful vistas of sheep and lambs grazing in the hills and valleys.

Marin Today

More diverse and liberal. The census counted 194,254 Caucasians, 27,351 Hispanics, 11,203 Asians, 7,142 African-Americans and 1,061 American Indians. In the 1996 election, Marin voted to legalize marijuana for the terminally ill and to keep Affirmative Action.

Still attuned to the environment. Every December, members of the Audubon Society count the local birds, one the oldest studies in the U.S.

In 2004, to the shock of all, Marin voted to boost the sales tax a half cent to pay for transit improvements, something it had refused to do for decades. In 2005, those bad Republicans in Congress actually voted through a transit bill that includes money to widen Highway 101 north of Novato, the notorious Novato Narrows. If this keeps up, Marin may re-establish diplomatic relations with Washington.

Top 30 Baby Names

Marin County

Boys

Jack	23
John	23
William	23
Nicholas	21
Benjamin	19
James	19
Christopher	18
Daniel	17
Nathan	17
Ryan	17
Alexander	16
Andrew	15
Dylan	15
Jacob	15
Joshua	15
Lucas	14
Owen	14
Michael	13
Samuel	13
Luke	12
Joseph	11
Liam	11
Matthew	11
Zachary	11
Charles	10
Jackson	10
Aidan	9
Brian	9
Bryan	9
David	9

Girls

Isabella	21
Zoe	14
Ashley	13
Emma	13
Grace	13
Olivia	13
Alexandra	12
Emily	12
Elizabeth	11
Katherine	11
Sophia	11
Charlotte	10
Chloe	10
Lauren	10
Lily	10
Natalie	10
Sarah	10
Anna	9
Ava	9
Ella	9
Hannah	9
Julia	9
Avery	8
Kayla	8
Mia	8
Sofia	8
Stephanie	8
Abigail	7
Brooke	7
Nicole	7

California

Boys

Daniel	4157
Anthony	3797
Andrew	3464
Jose	3379
Jacob	3327
Joshua	3292
David	3246
Angel	3232
Matthew	2853
Michael	2844
Christopher	2754
Jonathan	2541
Ryan	2511
Alexander	2440
Joseph	2430
Ethan	2356
Nathan	2302
Brandon	2208
Kevin	2133
Juan	2106
Christian	2022
Jesus	2012
Nicholas	1999
Diego	1977
Luis	1957
Adrian	1824
Dylan	1757
Gabriel	1735
Isaac	1722
Carlos	1638

Girls

Emily	3388
Ashley	2922
Samantha	2474
Isabella	2435
Natalie	1942
Alyssa	1808
Emma	1740
Sophia	1715
Jessica	1700
Jasmine	1666
Elizabeth	1595
Madison	1572
Jennifer	1483
Kimberly	1460
Alexis	1434
Andrea	1374
Abigail	1314
Hannah	1310
Sarah	1304
Vanessa	1299
Mia	1270
Stephanie	1246
Brianna	1221
Michelle	1152
Olivia	1149
Kayla	1147
Leslie	1137
Grace	1127
Maria	1099
Victoria	1083

Source: California Department of Health Services, 2004 birth records. Number of children with the given name. Some names would move higher on the list if the state grouped essentially same names with slightly different spellings, for example, Sarah and Sara. But state computer goes by exact spellings.

MARIN COUNTY

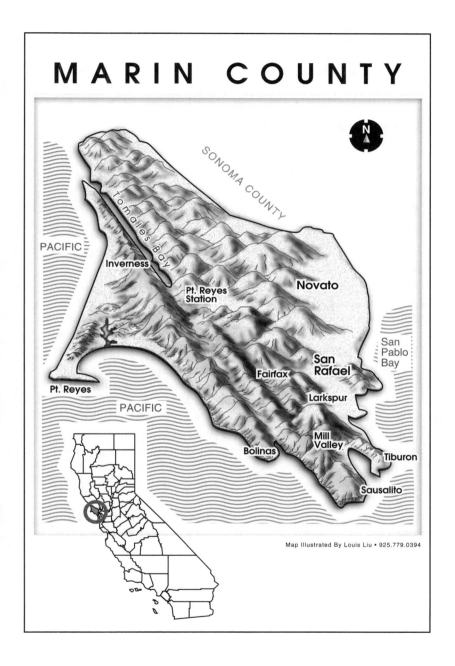

Map Illustrated By Louis Liu • 925.779.0394

Chapter 6

Marin City Profiles

Services

A WORD ABOUT what does what in Marin (and other counties). Two main agencies, the cities and the county, provide the bulk of government services. What they do not provide, small agencies or private parties do. For example, school boards, separately elected, set policy for local schools and school districts. Private firms collect garbage.

If you live in an incorporated city, city hall will fill the potholes, hire the cops, determine zoning, build and run the parks and other services. If you live in unincorporated areas, the board of supervisors and county government will hire sheriff's deputies to patrol the streets, public works people to fix roads, planners to work out zonings and land use.

Although both cities and county provide municipal services, they differ in important ways. Cities have been strong in parks and recreation, counties weak. County governments, in conjunction with the state, provide medical care for the poor and indigent. California cities rarely get involved in medical care.

Cities tend to be more hands-on, counties hands-off. Cities often employ code enforcers to prod property owners to clean up lots. Counties rarely do this. When new homes go in, cities require curbs and gutters. County governments do the same but if the home is out in the country, this condition is often waived.

To spruce up their downtowns, cities often create "redevelopment" agencies that fund infrastructure or cosmetic improvements and raise taxes to pay for these improvements. Counties rarely get into redevelopment.

City council members represent — and are elected by — only the people within the city's boundaries. County supervisors represent both city and county residents. Where services overlap or run close together, confusion sometimes follows. In some parts, city police will patrol one side of a street, sheriff's deputies the other. For more information, call your local supervisor or city hall.

BELVEDERE

Novato •

San Rafael •

Belvedere

SMALL CITY, AN APPENDAGE off the Tiburon peninsula. One of wealthiest cities in Bay Region. Although connected to the mainland since anyone can remember, Belvedere exudes appearance of an island. It rises abruptly from the water, climbs into a tall hill, then drops off on the other side.

Median age of residents is 53. Children and teens under 18 make up 20 percent of the town. Many adults and empty nesters. Many people work from home. Great views. Belvedere, which translates in Italian to "beautiful view," sticks out far enough to peek around Cavallo Point near Sausalito and glimpse the Golden Gate Bridge. Connected to Tiburon by two roads at either end of the "island." Between the roads shimmers a lagoon with housing. Expensive: prices for just about any home start at $2 million plus and in 2005 one home, 10,000 square feet, was going for $65 million.

The state in its 2005 tally counted 1,065 housing units: 874 single family, 54 single-family attached, 137 multiples, no mobile homes. Population 2,132. Between census 1990 and 2000, Belvedere dropped 22 residents. Built out. In the 1990s, Belvedere increased its housing stock by about 10 units.

Winding roads. No parking on some stretches. Land being scarce, cars are shoehorned into tight spaces. Hedges, walls and fences hide many homes from street. Very few lawns. Too steep, too short of land. Many shrubs, trees. Deer dance down hills. Nibble foliage. Design orients homes toward water, not street. Many homes small to middling, a few in mansion class, especially at the top. Probably the largest building in town is St. Stephen's Episcopal Church. Residents are burying utility lines. Leaf blowers banned.

Police station, a large Tudor building. California Crime Index shows zero homicides from 1994 through 2003 and one of lowest crime rates in U.S.

Academic rankings in elementary schools among highest in state. Voters have installed and renewed a parcel tax to pay for electives, teachers and a full curriculum. Bond passed in 2001 to renovate all schools in Reed Elementary District, which also serves Tiburon. Teens move up to Redwood High in Larkspur. High school district has passed several bonds, one recently to upgrade the campus with modern wiring, technology. Recreation department offers classes for kids and adults. Community center. Playground. Opera and summer concerts in park. Belvedere and Tiburon share stores and a library.

Chamber of Commerce: (415) 435-5633

BOLINAS

HERMIT HAMLET OF MARIN COUNTY. Hard to find because down through the years residents have torn down road signs and ripped out roadside phones with the intention of discouraging visitors. After a while, the road agency said, the hell with it, and stopped replacing the things.

The 2000 census tallied 1,246, an increase of 148 over the 1990 census. Bolinas is located on coast, off Highway 1, just above Stinson Beach, west of Bolinas Lagoon. On north side, Pt. Reyes national park. Median age of residents is 44. Children and teens under 18 make up 19 percent of town — a place for adults. Little parking. Small beach that locals use. Handful of stores, a saloon that doubles as town hall. Church, marine biology lab. Library. Post office. Wild berries brighten roadside. Homes along road are old and weather-beaten. Some homes near ocean stand on pilings. Away from the business strip, a few newer, larger, more expensive homes.

Other towns talk about protecting the environment, and some do a fair job. But it's a commitment with certain limits. It's all very nice to love the redwoods and deer but it's much more pleasant to love them if you have a glass of cabernet in hand and if, when inclined, you can stroll to the deli for a smoked turkey sandwich or whiz to San Francisco on Highway 101 to a play or movie. Marin owes much of its allure to the way it has mixed city and country.

Comes Bolinas. Its water system can't even support hot tubs. The town, through its control over water, has just about killed anything new. General plan opposes streets: "a waste of land and energy." In 2002, residents voted down the widening of the main street to add bicycle lanes (but in 2005, they said yes to resident-only parking spaces and to beach access.) More than any other town in the county, Bolinas has turned its back on the city and especially on the temptations of the tourist dollar. When Prince Charles, an environmentalist, and Camilla visited Marin in 2005, Bolinas was a ballyhooed stop. Locals pleased.

Kids attend Bolinas Elementary School. Many scores are landing in the 90th percentile, among tops in the state. School district passed parcel tax to keep classes small and programs intact. See Stinson Beach.

Bolinas has small-town, get-to-know-your-neighbors feeling. The 2000 census counted 629 residential units — 63 percent owner occupied, 37 percent rentals. Chamber of Commerce: (415) 663-9232.

CORTE MADERA

Novato ●

San Rafael

Corte Madera

BEDROOM TOWN of 9,378 residents that straddles Highway 101 just above Mill Valley and extends east to the Bay. Shopper's delight. Home to two malls. The stores pump tax revenue into the Corte Madera treasury and this helps fund many activities.

Used to be wooded. When Presidio in San Francisco was built, much of the timber came from Corte Madera, which translates to "cut wood."

Median age of residents is 41. Children and teens under 18 make up 23 percent of residents. In the 1990s, the town increased its population by 828.

Corte Madera snared the biggest shopping plaza in Marin County (The Village at Corte Madera: Nordstrom, Macys, about 90 other stores) and right across the freeway is another shopping plaza, Town Center, about 60 shops, restaurants.

The 2005 state count showed 3,977 housing units, of which 2,621 were single homes, 416 single attached, 930 multiples and 10 mobile homes. Corte Madera builds a few single homes every year, and that's about it. Proposals to build on the few remaining large lots often arouse strong opposition.

The 2000 census broke out Corte Madera housing as follows: 448 units built before World War II, 1,427 units built between 1940 and 1960, and 1,018 units between 1960 and 1970. The three decades after the war account for 64 percent of all housing in the town. In the following decades, 1970-2000, Corte Madera built, respectively, 389 units, 314 units and 245 units. What kind of housing will you find? Generally, tract models popular 1950-70, and this includes housing down on the Bay. All generally well-kept. Some lots command views; Corte Madera, for most part, is flat. City hall has spruced up the town's landscaping.

In 1970, a developer submitted a plan to build 528 homes on 81 acres just east of Highway 101. In 1995, a quarter century later, after many protests from residents, the project got under way — scaled down to 151 homes. Typical Marin approach to development.

Corte Madera shares police with Larkspur. Police department called "Twin Cities." Crime low. For both towns, zero homicides in 2004, 2003 and 2002, one in 2001, zero between 2000 and 1995. California Highway Patrol has station in town, near freeway. Gives Corte Madera more police presence.

Marin County Single-Family Home Prices

Place	Sales	Lowest	Median	Highest	Average
Belvedere Tiburon	55	$850,000	$2,005,000	$4,400,000	$2,245,540
Corte Madera	34	300,000	977,000	2,625,000	1,033,848
Dillon Beach	1	600,000	600,000	600,000	600,000
Fairfax	23	250,500	750,000	2,650,000	834,174
Forest Knolls	1	734,000	734,000	734,000	734,000
Greenbrae	37	191,400	1,285,000	6,050,000	1,671,365
Inverness	10	575,000	810,000	1,650,000	926,000
Lagunitas	1	678,000	678,000	678,000	678,000
Larkspur	12	400,000	1,310,000	2,200,000	1,406,550
Mill Valley	120	171,000	1,037,500	5,000,000	1,280,359
Novato	231	65,500	806,000	3,525,000	870,657
Ross	3	2,595,000	2,872,000	6,303,000	2,733,500
San Anselmo	69	640,000	863,000	2,600,000	1,032,485
San Rafael	169	38,500	870,000	3,503,000	1,044,583
Sausalito	30	643,000	1,420,000	3,295,000	1,404,241
Stinson Beach	3	225,000	1,600,000	3,750,000	1,858,333

Source: DataQuick Information Systems, Inc., La Jolla, Calif. **Key:** Resale single-family detached housing sales from May 1, 2005 to July 31, 2005.

Corte Madera shares schools with Larkspur. Most teens attend Redwood High, which, thanks to bonds, was renovated and equipped with modern technology. Academic rankings, with few exceptions, in the 90s, among tops in state. In recent years, voters also approved more money for elementary schools. Among recent additions, a computer lab, library and gym at Cummins school. Adults can use gym in evening. See Larkspur.

Eight parks, trails, ecological reserve on Bay, wildlife habitat. Excursions, tap, ballet, gymnastics, soccer, Little League baseball, aerobics, summer program for children, kids' basketball, adult softball leagues, town band. Bike path. On its south and east side, Corte Madera borders large park preserves with trails. Bike-foot bridge. Rail right of way turned into a trail. Flowers hanging from street lights.

In the evening, many residents stroll or jog on trails around Corte Madera Creek. Large old-fashioned movie house. Popular with locals.

Close to Marin General Hospital, Marin Catholic High School and College of Marin, which won a bond in 2004 and will overhaul its buildings. More classes.

By Marin standards, good commute. If freeway goes fast, you'll go fast. Short drive to Larkspur Terminal and commute ferries to San Francisco. Park and ride lot near dowtown.

Chamber of commerce: (415) 924-0441.

FAIRFAX

Novato ●
San Rafael ●
Fairfax ★
Mill Valley

LIVELY BEDROOM TOWN that frets occasionally about adding people and eroding its quality of life. So far little to worry about. In 1979 Fairfax had 7,391 residents. As of 2005, it had 7,309 residents. Median age of residents is 42. Children and teens under 18 make up 19 percent of town — low. Another town of empty nesters and adults.

Long-established restaurants. Pleasant place to sip and chat. All towns pride themselves on being friendly but Fairfax is small enough for residents to get to know one another. Fairfax pavilion offers activities from dance to basketball. Arts and Crafts Festival. Jazz festival. Live music at the clubs. Easter egg hunt. Many streets meander along canyon floors but Fairfax also rises into the hills. At top of Fairfax-Bolinas Road, a golf course. Three city parks. Old movie palace shows first-run films. Annual film festival. Town adjoins public watershed; miles of trails for bikes, horses, hiking.

Fairfax is anti-development, suffers from a weak tax base and is continually short of money. Residents voted in one tax to fix roads and drains. Nonetheless, in 2005, the town voted against more funding for municipal services. Needing 67 percent, the measure got only 57.

Housing units in 2005 totaled 3,421 — single homes 2,334, single attached 193, multiples 883, mobiles 11. Apartments near downtown. Many homes small and old and have one-car garages. About half predate 1950. Fairfax has its newer, more expensive homes but not many. In the 1980s, town added about 200 single homes, in the 1990s, about 110 single homes. Most of its "modern" construction took place in '50s and '60s — about 1,300 units.

Children attend schools in Ross Valley district. State academic rankings in the 90s, often the high 90s. You don't get rankings like this unless parents and the community value education and put a lot of energy into the schools. Teens move up to Drake High School in Tamalpais High School district, which also scores in the 90s. Voters have passed several improvement bonds for the elementary and the high schools, rebuilt their libraries and added high-tech where needed. They have also passed parcel taxes to maintain program quality at all the schools.

Zero homicides between 2003 and 1996, one in 1995, zero for 1994. Overall crime low. Fairfax is about six miles from freeway. Drake Boulevard, at times, can be congested. Chamber of Commerce: (415) 453-5928.

GREENBRAE

Novato ●

San Rafael ●

Greenbrae

A NEIGHBORHOOD that newspapers usually mention in a way that suggests it's a town. Close to freeway and Larkspur ferry wharf. Good commute. Upper middle-class. Well-kept. Very high academic rankings. Many homes have views of bay and Corte Madera Creek and lowlands. Views of Mt. Tamalpais.

Not tracked by FBI but demographics say low crime. Greenbrae, secluded and easily missed, enjoys the simple, effective defense of escaping attention.

Children attend Bacich Elementary and Kent Middle School, rankings in 98th and 99th percentiles, the highest scores possible.

The Greenbrae subdivision is located just west of Highway 101 and immediately north of Sir Francis Drake Boulevard. Its western border is approximately Wolf Grade Drive.

Most of the neighborhood has been annexed by the City of Larkspur, which adds to the confusion over Greenbrae's status and location, and some maps include the land immediately south of Sir Francis Drake in Greenbrae.

Entering Greenbrae at La Cuesta Drive, the homes start off modestly (one-story ranchers, two-car garages) then, in many instances, grow bigger as you ascend hills. Nothing showy. Large custom homes, tastefully landscaped (very few lawns), the decks and picture windows oriented to the prettiest views. Ravines divide the hills, allowing many homes to be positioned for views.

Where the streets narrow or prove difficult, the residents have worked out one-way or circle systems that keep the cars flowing. Plenty of shrubs, trees and foliage. Residents have imposed a neighborhood tax to maintain median strip and appearances. Down toward Sir Francis Drake, where the land flattens, mature trees line some of the streets. Utility lines run in back yards, hidden among trees. Some streets have street lights.

Shopping plaza directly across Sir Francis Drake Boulevard. Restaurants, shops in Larkspur.

About one minute to the freeway, two minutes to the ferry. For East Bay commuters, about five minutes to the San Rafael Bridge. Hiking trails, parks, recreation in Larkspur or just over the hill in San Rafael. In the evening, many people jog or stroll along Corte Madera creek. Greenbrae is the home of Barbara Boxer, U.S. senator.

INVERNESS,
OLEMA, PT. REYES STATION

Novato •

San Rafael

Mill Valley

INVERNESS, OLEMA AND PT. REYES STATION are three small towns at or near Tomales Bay.

Inverness, population 1,421, is a wooded hamlet sheltered on the west side of Tomales Bay. A few homes can be seen from the road but most are tucked among the trees. Many homes have been turned into weekend and vacation residences, retreats from the turmoil of the city. Town added about 130 homes in last decade. Median age of Inverness residents is 51. Children and teens under 18 make up 14 percent of village — about 200 kids.

In 1995, fire destroyed much of the woods and some of the homes. Periodic fires apparently are nature's way of clearing away the brush and undergrowth. If building or buying at Inverness, it might be prudent to make the house, as much as possible, fire resistant. Water supply from streams; sometimes a problem in summer.

Several restaurants have been built down by the water. Inverness, because of the pleasant way it mixes the hills and the water, is popular for weddings.

A long drive to San Francisco. Parcel tax to help school funding. Miles of open space around Inverness, which borders Point Reyes National Seashore Park. If you keep traveling west on Sir Francis Drake Boulevard, which serves Inverness, you hit the Pacific.

Pt. Reyes Station, 818 inhabitants in about 370 housing units, is a short hop away from Pt. Reyes Park and the Pacific. Small town at south end of Tomales Bay. Library. Shops, saloon. Just outside town limits, sheep graze. In spring and summer, many a traveler passes through Pt. Reyes Station.

Median age of residents is 45. Children and teens under 18 make up 19 percent of residents.

Olema, a cluster of homes and a few stores at Sir Francisco Drake Boulevard, is just to the south of Pt. Reyes Station.

Tule elk run wild in parts of Pt. Reyes National Park. In winter, elephant seals heave up on shore to breed and deliver pups. About half dozen oyster companies work Tomales Bay. Government is buying land or development rights. Marin Agricultural Land Trust, through purchase and other financial measures, has placed 38,000 acres in preserve. The goal is to put as much as possible of West Marin out of the reach of development. Chamber of Commerce: (415) 663-9232.

KENTFIELD

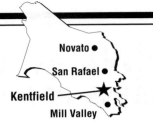

Novato ●

San Rafael ●

Kentfield

Mill Valley

UPPER MIDDLE CLASS-to-wealthy neighborhood, 6,351 residents, located in hills between Larkspur, San Rafael and Ross. Close to Mt. Tamalpais. Increased its population in the last decade by 321. Median age of residents is 45. Children and teens under 18 make up 25 percent of residents.

Homes set back from roads, among pine, redwood and manzanita. Low-profile roofs. Designed to blend in. No sidewalks. Meandering streets. Big lots. Many homes have views. Wooded. Country feeling. Because of its location, Kentfield gets more rain than most other Marin towns. Unincorporated, which means it's governed by the Marin County Board of Supervisors but, as typical in Marin, the supervisors pay close heed to the wishes of residents, especially on development.

Academic rankings in the 90s. Voters subscribe to parcel taxes to keep classes small, to avoid cuts in the curriculum, to retain drama and art programs and to fund Spanish instruction starting in kindergarten. Bonds have been passed to renovate and upgrade all the schools.

Kids move up to Redwood High School in the Tamalpais District. This district also taxes itself extra to maintain and improve programs. Redwood High in 1996 opened the unusual: outdoor roller rink for in-line skating and hockey. In 2000, voters approved a bond to renovate and "high tech" all the schools in the Tamalpais District. Marin Catholic, one of the most popular private high schools, is located in Kentfield.

Kentfield rarely makes the news. Being unincorporated, its crime is not tracked by the FBI but the demographics say very low. In 2001, residents renewed and increased tax to pay the sheriff for extra protection on their streets.

Commute not bad. Residents have to navigate Magnolia Avenue or Sir Francis Drake Boulevard to get to Highway 101 and at times those roads can tickle the nerve endings. But the ferry (at Larkspur) is close by and the freeway haul to the City is about a dozen miles. Restaurants, amenities in nearby towns.

College of Marin in Kentfield offers courses that appeal to many adults and opens its pool to the public. The college is being renovated and is adding classes.

LARKSPUR

MISNAMED BUT BELOVED, this city of 12,014 residents has one of the best commutes in Marin County, a charming downtown and a few streets that have all but surrendered to the forest primeval.

School rankings are high, crime low, activities many.

About ten years ago Larkspur made the New York Times with an article that purred over its restaurants and shops but rarely does it make headlines for anything else. It's a quiet burg.

Median age of residents is 46. Children and teens under 18 make up 16 percent of town. Translation: many mature adults and empty nesters, few kids.

Compared to other California schools, Larkspur elementary schools land in the 90th percentile, among the highest in the state.

The same for Redwood High School, which was once about to be closed until district residents voted to raise taxes to improve the place and the other schools in the Tamalpais Union High School District. Redwood High boasts five science-computer labs. In 1997 and 2004, the district won voter approval for more money to maintain and improve academic programs. In 2000, voters approved a $121 million bond to renovate and "high tech" all five high schools in the Tamalpais district.

Voters also approved more funds for the elementary district, which also serves Corte Madera, and in 2003 renewed a tax to avoid program cuts. In 2000, voters approved a $22 million bond to improve seismic safety at the elementary schools, to replace their roofs, wiring, and plumbing and heating and electrical systems, and to add classrooms, libraries and science labs.

In many ways, this attention to schools is routine Marin — strong support of education. One problem: homes are too expensive for some teachers.

Larkspur Landing, the neighborhood east of Highway 101, is served by the San Rafael Elementary School District. The older children attend San Rafael High.

Another choice, Marin Catholic, the largest private high school in the county, is located just over the Larkspur border. A drive of 5-10 minutes will bring you to the College of Marin.

In 2001, the city, the elementary district and the Marin Foundation chipped in to build a playing field and gym at Hall Middle School. Kids use gym days and afternoons, adults evenings and weekends.

Larkspur and Corte Madera are served by the same police department, called Twin Cities. Overall crime rate for both cities is low. Zero homicides in 2004, 2003 and 2002, one in 2001, zero between 2000 and 1995.

Larkspur is on Highway 101, about 10 miles from the Golden Gate Bridge. The city has buses and the largest ferry terminal in the county. The Golden Gate Transit District runs its commute ferries to downtown San Francisco out of Larkspur Landing, which has a large parking lot and is served by buses. The ferries and the buses ease the commute to the City.

Sheltered by Mt. Tamalpais and the hills, located on the Bay, Larkspur enjoys the typical Marin balm. On some streets the redwoods rule, to the point where they are allowed to grow right in the street. If you have ever wanted to live in a forest, drive west on Madrone or Baltimore avenues. Some streets are almost perpetually shaded by redwoods. Many people will love this, a few won't.

Clean, well-maintained, no graffiti. Housing, for the most part, is basic middle-class tract, but the lawns are mowed, the shrubs trimmed and so on, and many homes have been touched up with window boxes, solariums and ornaments.

Mt. Tamalpais, wooded and comforting, rises in the west, a few miles off.

Corte Madera Creek, fringed with trails, flows through the town, another pleaser.

City, adult school, College of Marin and private groups run a variety of sports and activities for adults and kids. Marin Cricket Club is out bowling almost every weekend. Among children, soccer is the most popular sport, among adults, softball. Redwood High School has an outdoor roller-skating rink for in-line skating and hockey. One of the few cities in the county with a dog park.

Restaurants, coffee shops, boutiques line Magnolia Street in the quaint downtown. Lark Theater converted to playhouse-cafe. More shopping choices, movies can be found at Larkspur Landing.

Larkspur got its start in the late 1880s when a developer bought a large ranch, subdivided it into lots, attracted a railroad station, and went along with his wife's idea to name the hamlet after a local flower that she thought was a larkspur. Turned out to be a lupine but the name stuck and ... what the hell ... Larkspur sounds better than Lupine.

The town incorporated as a city in 1908 and slowly began to grow. Many of the older homes can still be found in and around the downtown.

Following World War II, Larkspur shared in the great building boom that swept over Marin. In successive decades, the population went from 1,558 in 1940, to 2,905, to 5,710, to 10,487, to 11,065 residents in 1980. In the 1980s, the town increased its numbers by just six people and since 1990 has added about 1,000 residents.

Homes are still being built here and there but for all practical purposes this is another built-out Marin city. Typically even small projects arouse much opposition. In the 1990s, Larkspur built about 450 homes and apartments. The state in 2005 counted 6,427 residential units, of which 2,451 were single-family detached, 360 single attached, 3,377 apartments or condos, and 239 mobile homes (near the freeway).

Unusual for a small, upper-income city, Larkspur has more apartments than single homes.

Most of the apartments and condos, and a shopping-restaurant center, can be found in Larkspur Landing (east of Highway 101) and just west of Highway 101 in the hills overlooking Corte Madera Creek. The shopping center recently got a make-over. Marin General Hospital is at the base of the hills.

Behind Larkspur Landing is a quarry, famous for the finale of one of Clint Eastwood's "Dirty Harry" movies. A former brickyard in the area supplied many of the bricks used to rebuild San Francisco after the 1906 earthquake.

Years ago, Larkspur annexed much of Greenbrae and, accurately speaking, Greenbrae should be identified as a neighborhood of Larkspur. Many people, however, continue to speak of Greenbrae as if it were a separate town. Greenbrae is located just west of Highway 101 and north of Corte Madera Creek. It has a small mall with about 50 shops.

Chamber of commerce: (415) 663-9232

MARIN CITY

Novato ●

San Rafael

Marin City

DURING WORLD WAR II, poor people came to Marin County to work in shipyards at Sausalito. After the war, many stayed. Later eight five-story buildings, publicly funded, were erected to house them. Located just outside Sausalito, the community is called Marin City. About 2,000-2,700 residents.

Community Center. Baseball field. Boys and Girls Club. Seniors Center. Used to be well-known for its flea market but this event saw its last days in 1995.

Developers have built on the site 255 apartments and 85 townhouses, a shopping plaza (Ross store, PetsMart, food store), fast-food restaurants, a library and a fire station.

Good commute. Right off Highway 101, near Golden Gate Bridge. Bus station-transit center.

Patrolled by sheriff's deputies. Substation in neighborhood.

Marin City shares school district with Sausalito. Enrollment is low, about 265 students, grades kindergarten to eighth. One elementary and one charter elementary are located in Sausalito, middle school in Marin City. Voters in 2004 approved a bond to renovate the schools.

Some grades have only 30-40 students. In this situation, a few students scoring very high or very low can distort the overall scores.

Teenagers move up to Tamalpais High School in Mill Valley, very high scores. Residents tax themselves extra to maintain program quality at the high schools and to keep the buildings in good repair and equipped with the modern technology.

Marin City is unincorporated, which means governed by the county board of supervisors from San Rafael, but local groups wield a lot of influence. Apartment buildings designed by protege of Frank Lloyd Wright.

MARINWOOD, LUCAS VALLEY

LOCATED WEST OF Highway 101, between San Rafael and Novato, Marinwood is a subdivision that blends into the Lucas Valley subdivision. The 2000 census gave them both a combined population of 6,357.

Middle class. Mix of housing styles. Condos near freeway. Most just plain suburban tract, 3-4 bedroom, well-maintained. Plenty of empty and hilly land to west, north and south gives both a country feeling. A little more family oriented than most of Marin: the median age of residents is 43 and kids under 18 make up 23 percent of neighborhoods.

Children educated in Dixie school district, three elementary schools and a middle school. About $2 million was spent to upgrade the middle school and add a science building. Residents have voted to tax themselves extra for program quality. One private elementary.

Academic rankings compared to California schools land in the 80th and the 90th percentiles. Students move up to Terra Linda High in San Rafael, rankings also in the 80th and 90th percentiles. Some parents wanted to detach Terra Linda High from the San Rafael district and use it to convert Dixie into a unified district, kindergarten to 12th. But this idea flopped. The state approves very few reorganizations. The high school district has also passed tax measures to pay for small classes and enriched programs, and to renovate its buildings.

Both Marinwood and Lucas Valley are unincorporated, which means that they are under the jurisdiction of the county government. Marinwood has formed a tax district and raised money to provide parks, a swimming center, a community center, and recreational programs and classes. Also street lighting. The neighborhoods are within a few miles drive of downtown San Rafael, which has shops, restaurants, and of the Marin Civic Center, which books top-line performers.

Negotiations are under way to develop the 1,240 acres east of Highway 101. Not going to happen right away as several parties are involved and Marin does not rush into big projects. But something will be built, possibly before the next millennium. To reach these neighborhoods, take Miller Creek Road or Lucas Valley Road off of Highway 101.

MILL VALLEY

Novato ●

San Rafael

Mill Valley

PRETTY TOWN, SORT OF HOLLYWOOD HILLS NORTH, woodsy version. Attracts writers, artists. Sponsors annual film festival (but many of the movies are shown in San Rafael). Located in the shadow of Mt. Tamalpais. Crime low, school rankings high. Population 13,686.

Median age of residents is 44. Children and teens under 18 make up 21 percent of town. In the 1990s, increased its population by 562 people.

Quaint downtown, restaurants, delis, coffee shops, clothing stores, bookstores, a theater, art gallery, antique stores, small inn-lodge. Street layout gives a village square feeling, friendly, inviting. Mill Valley starts down on Richardson Bay, moves west into the valley floor and then rises into redwoods, a nice mix. On summer days, the fog will often break over the hills.

Town was named after lumber mill, which was later rebuilt to keep past alive. In the late 1800s, San Franciscans loved to camp in Mill Valley and take the train to the top of Mt. Tam. After the 1906 earthquake, Mill Valley redwoods helped rebuild San Francisco and some people fled San Francisco in the belief that Mill Valley was less prone to earthquakes.

The state in its 2005 count showed 6,341 housing units, of which 4,129 were single homes, 550 single attached, 1,662 multiples. Styles vary widely, a reflection of age of the town: cottages, condos, apartments, bungalows, Tudors, stately Victorians, small one-story homes in Tamalpais Valley (outside city limits), modern middle-class homes, large homes hidden behind long driveways in the wooded hills. Some homes just old and plain. But Mill Valley has knockout Victorian and custom homes. It also has fights over views and privacy. When property values soared, some people tore down small homes and replaced with giants. City council now limits size of new homes. Fewer than 100 buildable lots remain in the town.

The 2000 census showed this picture: about one-fourth of the housing units predated 1940, one fourth were built between 1940 and 1960 and 34 percent were evenly divided between the 1960s and 1970s. In the 1980s, Mill Valley built 560 homes and in the last decade, 255.

Many homes are surrounded by redwoods. Real feeling of the forests. Some roads narrow down to one lane as they move back into woods. Years ago Mill Valley gave parks and rec the highest priority. In recent years, however, it has spent more money on filling potholes and road improvements.

Except for 2002, when it had one, Mill Valley has not had a homicide since 1988 (and possibly earlier), FBI reports.

The elementary schools score generally in the middle to high 90s — the top 10 percent in California. Tamalpais High also scores in the 90s.

Local residents and businesses through a foundation raise thousands of dollars (some years over $600,000) for schools —strong support for education. Voters raised parcel tax to help elementary schools. Renovation bond, $18.6 million, approved in 1994. Much of the work was done on the schools in 1995. Tamalpais high school district approved another funding measure; more money for academics. Tax approved to repair and expand the town library, add more books. Job done in 1998. In 1998, more tax measures were approved to reopen and staff a school (opened in 2000 at Strawberry Point) to avoid crowding at the other schools, to improve the middle school and make general improvements. In 2000, Tamalpais district won voter approval to renovate and "high tech" all its schools. In 2003 , voters — surprise, surprise — turned down a school tax (needed two-thirds vote) to make up for money lost in the state budget crisis. But in 2004, they said yes. The same with more money for high school district.

Botanical gardens. Mt. Tam hiking. Nine-hole golf course. Dog park, trails at Bay Front Park. Bridge club. Seniors center. After-school child care, baby-care classes, aerobics, tennis, softball, soccer, usual kids' games. Little League season kicks off with a parade down Throckmorton Avenue. Supervised kiddie programs in summer. Skate park. City rec. department runs activities for kids, adults and seniors: line dancing, pre-ballet, gymnastics, fencing — to mention a few. Six parks with playgrounds. Muir Woods, Pacific close by. Restaurants, movies, bakeries, shops, cafes. Community center (pool, fitness rooms, fields). City is spending $1.5 million to improve bike trails and pedestrian walks. Film festival successful. Plays. Some TV-movie stars and writers settled in town. Arts festival. Festival of Wine and Gourmet Food every June. Big annual foot race: the Dipsea. Live music in some restaurants and bars. Annual Memorial Day parade.

Short hop to Golden Gate Bridge. Typical jams at bridge but a good commute. Mill Valley is one of the first cities over the Golden Gate. Money spent to synchronize traffic lights. Marin leads U.S. in home businesses and Mill Valley leads Marin. About 15 percent of Mill Valley workforce said they work at home (census).

Mill Valley worries about too many visitors. The stores like the dollars but visitors also bring traffic and parking problems. Chamber of commerce, phone (415) 388-9700.

NICASIO

HAMLET IN WEST MARIN. George Lucas, of "Star Wars" fame, lives at ranch near Nicasio. Action scenes from "Star Wars," "Indiana Jones" and "The Hunt for Red October" were put together at Lucas locations in Marin County.

Several years ago, Lucas won county approval to expand operations and build facilities for digital-film production and interactive media. The project covers 108 acres. In exchange, he placed 3,256 acres in open space.

In 2005, Lucas opened digital complex at the Presidio, the former military base in San Francisco that overlooks the Golden Gate. The facility employs about 1,500 and will probably absorb many of the Marin operations.

Town of Nicasio some distance removed. Historic Catholic Church. Post office. Fire station. Popular restaurant. Rolling countryside, gold in summer, green in winter and spring. Close to Samuel P. Taylor Park (many redwoods), Pt. Reyes Station and Tomales Bay. Golf course to the south at San Geronimo. Estate homes on ranches.

Children attend Nicasio Elementary, a K-8, enrollment about 70.

No crime stats but the entire county is low in crime.

NOVATO

Novato ★

San Rafael ●

Mill Valley

SECOND-MOST POPULOUS CITY in the county, and one of the few that is adding, by Marin standards, a great number of people, thanks to the development of a former military base.

In reality, Novato has swapped residents. The base provided housing for military personnel throughout the Bay Area. When it was turned over to the city, all but a few military personnel departed. This decreased the population of the town.

Over the past few years, new housing was built on the base, bringing in people. The result: over 15 years about 3,000 more residents. The 1990 census counted 47,585 residents in Novato. In 2005, the state estimated the population at 50,586.

Median age of residents is 40. Children and teens under 18 make up 23 percent of the town. Rounded demographics, even mix of groups.

In 1999, the Buck Institute for Age Research opened. This $100 million biomedical complex will probably make Marin noted for this kind of research and spur the construction of support facilities, such as medical offices and hotels. The institute sits atop a small mountain with sweeping views of San Pablo Bay and the Petaluma River. I.M Pei, an architect described accurately as world famous, designed the place.

Opened in 1932, Hamilton Air Field was deactivated in 1974. Novato was supposed to take over the base but arguments broke out and for about 20 years nothing happened. With the Cold War over, the military and Novato worked out their differences and the Coast Guard retained 282 homes for military personnel.

In 1997, ground was broken for the first phase of the Hamilton make-over: about 900 single and attached homes, 70 apartments for the elderly, and 535,000 square feet of commercial-industrial-office, almost all of the latter to be located in seven large hangars built by the military. Phase I also included a hotel, a supermarket, a drug store, a McDonald's and a rehab-training shelter housing up to 80 people down on their luck.

Developers call the neighborhood "Hamilton." Almost all of phase one has been completed. Construction has begun on more housing and, because it is so big, Hamilton will be a work in progress for several years. In 2004, the day care center was expanded. Over 2,500 acres adjoining the site are to be turned into wetlands and parks.

The Hamilton project generated considerable excitement because Marin has placed a great deal of its land in parks or open space and left very little for development. This is one of the largest projects to come on-line in decades. Novato hopes to attract more high-tech, bio-tech firms, and build a stronger financial foundation.

Hamilton is down near the water. Much of the infrastructure has been built and includes a school (opened in 2001), a community center and a community pool-fitness center. The city has converted the old administration building into art studios.

Without belaboring the obvious, the location is pretty and with the restoration and remodeling of many of the military buildings, no one will mistake Hamilton for just another housing tract. The place has charm.

East of Highway 101, on Ignacio Boulevard, more military housing was demolished and was replaced by 425 homes and 100 senior apartments.

The departure of almost all the military has changed the character of Novato. The military is one of the great social mixers of this country and it brought to Novato a diversity, ethnic and social, that may be lacking in the replacement housing.

School rankings generally high. Crime low. Novato, which was named after a Spanish land grant, Rancho de Novato, is built over small hills and valleys. Many homes have views of San Pablo Bay. A pretty town in a suburban way. The hills, ridges and freeways (seven exits) create distinct neighborhoods.

Of the 18,975 housing units counted in the 2000 census, about 550 were built before 1940 and 3,400 between 1940 and 1960. In the 1960s, Novato built 4,300 units, in the 1970s about 5,900 units and in the 1980s, about 3,100 units. In last decade, housing starts dropped to 1,800. To state this from another perspective: up to 2002, about two-thirds of all units were built in three decades, 1950 to 1980.

In 2005, the state tallied 20,317 units — single family detached 11,941 units, single attached 2,668, multiples 4,990, mobile homes 718.

Black Point, a Novato neighborhood, was famous for hosting the Renaissance Pleasure Faire, which drew thousands every summer. After years of arguing, the city gave the green light to build at Black Point 53 luxury homes, an 18-hole golf course (public), a clubhouse and restaurant.

Novato has a good deal of upscale housing: Bahia Park near Petaluma River, horse estates along Indian Valley Road, Partridge Knolls, new homes north of Fireman's Fund. Townhouses and custom homes are tucked away along Alameda Del Prado, woodsy. Deer nibble the lawns day and evening.

But much of the town was built for the middle-class. The most popular home is that workhorse of suburbia, the 3-bedroom tract model. If you take Marin Valley Drive, you'll find one of the prettiest mobile home parks in Bay Area.

Many people shop at a mall just off Highway 101: Macys, Target, Costco, Marshall's, Pier One. In 2003 and 2004, the city completed projects to make the downtown more inviting to shoppers. These included benches, ornamental street lights, bike racks, new sidewalks. On Saturday and Sunday mornings, people gather at Peet's to sip their coffee and read the papers. Noah's Bagels is located in the same complex. In 2000, voters approved a $15 million bond to repave streets. Much of the work was done in 2002. On the way in 2006, the dynamic duo of healthy and tasty, Whole Foods and Trader Joe's.

Novato is home to Marin's largest employer, Firemen's Fund. The city has been attracting — and losing to mergers — high-tech and software firms. Smith & Hawken, the firm that sells gardening tools, is headquartered in Novato, in one of the remodeled hangars on the air base.

One homicide in 2004, zero in 2003, one in 2002, zero in 2001, one in 2000, zero in 1999,1998, 1997 and 1996, three in 1995, zero in 1994 and 1993, three in 1992, two in 1991, zero in 1990, two in 1989. Curfew for kids after sundown.

About two dozen parks in the city. Bordering Novato are several large regional or state parks, a total 3,500 acres. Tennis courts, two golf courses, the traditional activities for the kids, two marinas, two museums, movie complex, seniors center. Summer academics for kids. Farmers' market. Local newspaper. Art, Wine, Music Festival. Fourth of July parade. Summer concerts in the park. Horse country. Gymnastics center. Teen center. Indian Valley Community College offers classes and activities and opens its pool for community use. Trails, wild flowers on Mt. Burdell, 1,565 feet, which overlooks Novato and the Bay. Skate park. Dog park.

School rankings generally in the top 20th percentile, many in the top 10th percentile. When program and curriculum cuts were threatened, voters in 1992 passed a $96 parcel tax that saved the day. In 1997, voters agreed to continue the tax. In 1999, voters trounced a $40 million bond to renovate the schools but in 2001 they came through with a $107 million renovation bond. In 2004, voters turned down another parcel tax but, revamped, it was passed in 2005. Every year, locals run a race called the "Stampede" to raise money for schools. Novato has several private schools.

Several schools run on year-round calendars. One regular school was turned into a charter school that emphasizes the Waldorf approach. Charter schools give teachers and parents more freedom than regular schools to decide instructional methods, extracurricular courses and how classes are staffed. Another charter school, called the Marin School of Art and Technology, is located at the community college campus.

Highest scoring school, Rancho Elementary, accepts students from around district but often gets an excess of applications. Lottery decides some admissions.

Indian Valley College has affiliated with San Francisco State University to offer several undergraduate and one graduate program at the college.

Commute so-so. Better than anything in neighboring Sonoma County but the 28 miles to San Francisco are often long miles. For commuters to the East Bay, there's the San Rafael Bridge and, out of Novato, Highway 37, another road from hell, but when it moves, you can make Concord in 45 minutes. Buses.

Highway 37, which has seen some horrible accidents, has been made safer with median dividers and lower speed limits. Plans are underway to improve Highway 37 and make it a 4-lane freeway.

Some improvements, with state money, are to be made to Highway 101. County airport north of Novato.

To control growth, Novato voters in 1997 established an urban limit line. The city can build within the line; anything outside must get voter approval.

Several neighborhoods on the Petaluma River or the bay have had silting problems. Solutions tough and expensive.

Bel Marin Keys is a large unincorporated neighborhood on the bay. In 2001, residents voted to pay for dredging.

For years, a developer tried to build housing near Bel Marin but residents fought all the way. With the help of state grants, the land in question was purchased and will be restored as wetlands. This land borders wetlands secured by Novato when the air base was closed. The result: miles of shore preserved and open for trails.

In 2002, voters approved a tax increase to staff a firehouse at Hamilton and to place paramedics at all stations.

• In 2004, the college district won a big bond, $250 million, to renovate its campuses, including Indian Valley.

• Among projects likely to be funded by the latest round of federal financing: the Novato Narrows, the two-lane stretch of Highway 101 to the north of town. One of these years, four lanes. Chamber of commerce: (415) 897-1164.

ROSS

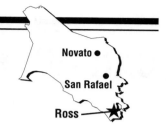

Novato •

San Rafael •

Ross ——

RICH, WOODED, SMALL, quiet, hilly, population 2,349. Tennis courts in back yards. Nannies and mothers stroll the streets with kiddies. Grocery, butcher, cafe. Town square. Golf course. In the 1980s, its population dropped from 2,801 to 2,123. In the 1990s, Ross added 206 residents. Median age of residents is 43. Children and teens under 18 make up 30 percent of town (census 2000). High percentage but it amounts to only 703 kids and teenagers.

Town took name from railroad station. Widow of land baron deeded station land to railroad on condition it would be named after departed hubby. Some homes fall into middle-class but Ross has a lot of big new and old stuff that without quibbling can be described as opulent. Art and Garden Center, two other parks. Lagunitas Country Club. About a mile to the College of Marin, which has many community activities. The state in 2005 tallied 814 units: 794 single homes, 0 single attached, 12 multiples, 8 mobile homes.

Zero homicides between 1994 and 2003. One of the lowest crime rates in county. Town contracts with sheriff for protection. Private security popular.

Kids attend Ross Elementary School, academic rankings high in the 90th percentile, among tops in the state. Child Magazine in 1991 named Ross Elementary one of top 10 schools in nation. Parents are asked to contribute voluntarily a "fair share" to fund that raises money for such programs as art, music and dancing. Parcel tax raises money for instructional program. Class sizes run about 17-to-1. In 2005, to the shock of many, the town turned down a construction-renovation bond for the single school, which enrolls 385. Needed 67 percent; got 59. Another try may made. Some opponents supposedly think that parents not the town should pay for the job. Graduates move up to Redwood High, scores in the high 90s. The high school is part of the Tamalpais District, which has won voter support to spend extra money on curriculum, programs and buildings. Voters have approved bonds to renovate and upgrade technology in all the schools in Tamalpais district. Branson, a private high school, is located in Ross.

Ross straddles Sir Francis Drake Boulevard, next to San Anselmo, Kentfield and San Rafael, and ascends into hills. Narrow streets, walls, gates protect privacy. No mail delivery; intrusive. Pickup at post office, which residents remodeled with own money. Some residents get irritated at outsiders who park on streets to get to park lands. Drake congests during peak hours but the distance to freeway and Larkspur Landing (ferries) is just a few miles.

SAN ANSELMO

SMALL, INTIMATE TOWN located between Ross and Fairfax, built for the blue- and white-collar middle class but, through remodelings and higher prices for homes, has moved up the scale. Many homes have been lovingly restored and improved. Median age of residents is 41. Children and teens under 18 make up 22 percent of town.

San Anselmo got its start about 1875 when the railroad arrived and built a junction at the location of the town. Residents incorporated the town as a legal city in 1907 and by 1940 San Anselmo had a population of 5,790 and a thriving business section along Anselmo Avenue.

Came the postwar boom, San Anselmo built tract single homes and apartment buildings and jumped to 13,031 residents by 1970. Then the baby boom collapsed and by 1990 the population had shrunk to 11,743. Since then, the number has eased up to 12,385. The state in 2005 counted 5,424 housing units, of which 3,995 were single homes, 186 single-family attached, 1,225 multiples, 18 mobile homes.

In this brief description lies the charm of San Anselmo. When the suburban splurge came, San Anselmo held on to its history and to its old town, which evolved into an antique center (over 100 stores) and a cozy mix of restaurants, art galleries, delis, bakeries, coffee shops, bookstores, banks, beauty parlors, etc., and government buildings, including city hall and the library. Also anchoring the downtown is a large Andronico's, an upscale supermarket. No giant box stores. Two schools and a religious seminary are located near the downtown. Also many single homes and some large apartment complexes.

Put the package together and you have a downtown that invites strolling and browsing and visitors and yet has enough variety to meet the daily needs of many residents. To recall the old days, the city has planted trees and installed decorative curbs, benches and old-fashioned street lights. San Anselmo also has a small shopping center with a supermarket on Drake Boulevard.

In its supermarket lots, San Anselmo is a town of Fords, Chevies, Civics and Accords — and BMWs and Mercedes. For a long while, the town was middle-class affordable and many of the buyers in the 1950s and 1960s probably used the G.I. Bill. Nowadays, even for a modest three-bedroom home, it's hard to find anything for less than $700,000. Inevitably, this is changing the town and attracting more double-income professionals with one or two kids. Many single homes are being remodeled, not into monster homes but into homes that have another bedroom and modern appliances and wiring. For the quaint and the restored, drive Ross Avenue and streets east of the downtown.

Much of San Anselmo was built in a bowl. The hills to the south generally have small homes tucked into oaks, the hills to the north have newer and larger homes, some custom designed, with views of the valley. If you take Butterfield Road north, you will find Sleepy Hollow, an unincorporated neighborhood of modern single homes, in size and appointments several notches above San Anselmo but not way off the scale. San Anselmo has about 240 grannie or second units tucked behind single homes. Rent controls have been placed on these units. Check with city hall for more info.

Half-dozen parks or preserves. Library. Community center. Tennis, baseball, softball, soccer (most popular sport), gymnastics, quilting, cooking, arts and crafts. Playing fields at the schools. Public swimming in summer at Drake High School. Summer camps for kids. Summer wine and food festival. Community parade. In 1999, residents, city hall and the Marin Land Trust chipped in to buy 22 acres, the largest remaining private parcel left in town. It was left in open space. Many parks close by; many trails.

Lacking big businesses and a strong tax base, San Anselmo runs a frugal operation at city hall. The city shares a fire department with Fairfax. In 2005, San Anselmo said no to higher municipal taxes.

Voters passed a bond for elementary school improvements in the early 1990s and in 1997 approved a renovation bond. San Anselmo also shares a school district with Fairfax (Ross Valley district). Another renovation bond was passed in 1999, indicating strong support for education. Kids move up to Drake High in the Tamalpais High School District. In 1997 and 2004, high school district increased parcel taxes to maintain and improve academic programs and in 2001 passed a bond to overhaul all high schools in the district. Academic rankings, state comparison, are landing generally in the 90th percentile in the elementary grades and the high school. San Anselmo has five private schools, one of them a high school (San Domenico).

Crime rate very low. Zero homicides between 1988 and 2003. "Kids leave their bikes out unlocked. People say hello to strangers," said one resident. San Anselmo has its own police department. City hall tries to handle city landscape without using herbicides or pesticides.

Peak hours, it's going to take 10-15 minutes to reach freeway, then it's up to Highway 101. Park-and-Ride lot. Transit center. Short drive to Larkspur and ferries. Buses to San Francisco and to Larkspur.

One striking site: The San Francisco Theological Seminary with Romanesque buildings that draw their inspiration from the Middle Ages. Chamber of commerce: (415) 454-2510.

SAN GERONIMO, WOODACRE

Novato ●

San Geronimo
Woodacre
Mill Valley

TWO HAMLETS in Western Marin, off Sir Francis Drake Boulevard. San Geronimo, 436 residents, Woodacre, 1,393.

Served by Lagunitas Elementary School District, enrollment 310. The district in 1995 passed a bond to build new classrooms and science and computer labs and bring facilities up to earthquake code. Also to build a new middle school, recently opened. In 2001, voters renewed a parcel tax to fund science, music and an environmental and technology programs.

Median age of San Geronimo and Woodacre residents is 44. Children under 18 make up 18 percent of San Geronimo and 23 percent of Woodacre.

Elementary rankings bounce around the upper percentiles, many of them landing in the 80th and 90th percentiles.

San Geronimo homes are single-family built in hills. Older ones small, newer big. After years of arguing, a developer won permission to build 32 homes on 550 acres, with much of the land put in open space. Golf course. School district runs Montessori classes. Cultural center.

Woodacre has many cottages and small homes that have been remodeled and expanded. Newer homes blended in.

Dogs and horses. Woodacre Improvement Club brings people together for swimming and fun. Little League field. Fourth of July parade. Redwood grove at the entrance to town. Small market. Trails meander through hills. In 1999, a fish ladder was built to help salmon move up stream to spawn. Seems to be working. Plenty of open space in West Marin. Country feeling. Thousands of acres have been placed in preserves. Shopping at Fairfax, which has movies and restaurants.

For decades, almost no crime. In 2000, however, a man and a woman were shot to death at night while they slept at the woman's Woodacre home. The woman's daughter was dating a Contra Costa man who was trying to extort money from an elderly Contra Costa couple. The couple were found in pieces in bags weighted and dropped into the Delta. Police say that the daughter, becoming suspicious, may have confided in her mother and the Contra Costa man found out. To cover his trail, he killed the daughter (and dropped her into the Delta) and shot the mother and her significant other. Three people were found guilty or confessed.

SAN RAFAEL

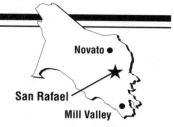

Novato ●

San Rafael

Mill Valley

THE COUNTY SEAT and most populous city in Marin County, San Rafael is a bedroom town of 57,224 people that provides housing for the rich and the middle class, and rare for Marin, the poor. Median age of residents is 39. Children and teens under 18 make up 19 percent of city. Translation: few kids, many singles and empty nesters.

In recent years San Rafael has put together one of the most entertaining and charming downtowns in the Bay Area. And it has attracted a few high-tech businesses that are making the commute shorter for some residents.

San Rafael has one low-income neighborhood, called the Canal, that over the past 30 years has attracted immigrants that work in service jobs throughout the county. San Rafael and its schools are working to integrate the new residents into town life and bring up their scores.

The town is served by two elementary school districts, San Rafael and Dixie. Compared against other schools in the state, Dixie schools land in the 80th and 90th percentiles, the top 20 percent.

In the San Rafael elementary district, state comparisons, two schools generally score in the 80th to 90th percentile, one in the 50th to 60th percentile, two in the 40th to 50th percentile, and two in the 10th to 30th percentile. The middle school, where all the children come together, lands in the 50th and 60th percentiles.

San Rafael High, state comparison, scores in the 50th to 70th percentile, Terra Linda High in the 90th percentile. In their SATs, both high schools score well above the state average.

In 1998, some parents petitioned to have their neighborhood transferred from the San Rafael district into the Dixie district. Request denied. In 1998, voters approved spending more money on both elementary districts, an indication that whatever the difficulties, residents continue to support their schools. In 2002, the San Rafael High School District and the San Rafael Elementary District approved more bonds for school improvements. Dixie district for years has carried an extra tax to maintain instructional quality. In 2005, voters in other two districts also raised their taxes to maintain program quality.

Private schools enroll about 1,700. In 2002, Marin Academy, a private school specializing in the arts, opened a performing arts center.

Dominican University and College of Marin (in bordering Kentfield) offer classes to general public. Kaiser Medical Center.

Pretty, well-kept town. San Rafael has been building for well over 100 years and some of the buildings, especially in the commercial section, show their age. But the residential sections come off well, in care and attention, painting, clipping, mowing, etc. San Rafael has its neighborhoods that bow-wow way up the scale (Peacock Gap) but most of the town was built for the middle class. Many tract homes, many Eichlers, a postwar design that used atriums and extra windows to bring in light. Hill homes look out on the Bay. Mount Tamalpais rises to the south and west and along with the coastal hills shelters San Rafael from the Pacific winds and, usually, fogs. On the ugly side, almost all of the town was built before it became fashionable to bury utility lines.

When Marin wanted a county government center built, it hired Frank Lloyd Wright to do the job. The result is many things to many people but no one can call it dull. In 2000, the county spent $1.3 million to restore the building and give the roof a new coat of blue. The civic center is the second-most popular tourist attraction in the county, after Muir Woods.

San Rafael has a convention center-auditorium that books touring shows and performers. It has marinas, trails, Falkirk Cultural Center (popular for parties and weddings), a renovated downtown library, and the usual roundup of sports, among which, says city hall, softball and basketball are the most popular. Also adult dance and music classes. Bingo for the elderly, soccer for the children, espresso and cafe au lait to prime the pump for the day's labors. Also, programs for the disabled. Farmers' market in spring. Dog park. Three community centers, public pool, day care centers. Just outside city limits at McInnis Park: a driving range, nine-hole golf course, miniature golf, batting cages, new skate park. Annual Youth and Arts Festival features street painting; it draws 400 artists and 20,000 spectators.

In 1817, seeking a healthy climate for the Indians, the Franciscans built a mission at San Rafael, the beginning of the town. San Rafael incorporated as a city in 1874 and by 1900 had 3,879 residents. By 1950, the population hit 13,848, by 1970 it had galloped to 38,977 and by 1990 it reached 48,404.

Imagine San Rafael in 1950, before the freeway was built. Movies, restaurants, shops, department stores, churches, bus station, train station, city hall, the library — all in the downtown, all patronized or visited by residents and workers. At that time, San Rafael was an intimate place where you knew your neighbors because you were always running into them in the downtown.

In the 1950s, housing jumped over the ridge into Lucas Valley. Stores and later a large mall followed. Two other large malls were erected at Corte

Home Price Sampler from Classified Ads

Belvedere
•4BR/2BA, $3 mil.
•8BR/8BA, $7 mil.

Corte Madera
•4BR/2BA, $919,000
•3BR/2BA, $849,000

Fairfax
•3BR/3BA, $949,000

Kentfield
•4BR/2BA, $2 mil.
•Condo, 2BR/1BA, $599,000

Larkspur
•4BR/3.5BA, $1.9 mil.

Mill Valley
•4BR/2.5BA, $3 mil.
•2BR/1BA, $745,000

Nicasio
•4BR/3BA, $2.2 mil.

Novato
•3BR/2BA, $639,000
•3BR/2BA, $779,000

Ross
•4BR/4BA, $4 mil.

San Anselmo
•3BR/2.5BA, $849,000
•2BR/2BA, $899,000

San Rafael
•3BR/1BA, $755,000
•3BR/3BA, $949,000
•4BR/2.5BA, $1.5 mil.

Sausalito
•2BR/2BA, $825,000
•4BR/3BA, $3.2 mil.

Stinson Beach
•3BR/2BA, $1.4 mil.
•Cottage, 1BR/1BA, $399,000

Tiburon
•3BR/1BA, $939,000
•3BR/2BA, $925,000

Madera, about five miles to the south. The freeway came and mercifully was run close to the downtown but it cut off the neighborhoods to the east. In the 1960s, the county center went up, over the ridges to the north and east of the freeway, removed from the downtown.

By 1980, the downtown was in decline — but it was far from dead. Many of the shops and restaurants drew enough customers to survive, the mission had gone to ruin but a replica was built and it attracted visitors as did the Victorians to the west. City hall and its functions supplied customers for the businesses. The downtown had a certain allure: old and historic in some ways was more inviting, more supportive of saloons, restaurants and nightclubs than malls, large, efficient and loaded with parking but curiously sterile.

Sentiment grew for a revival and when the effort came it tapped into new assets. Marin has a highly educated work force. San Rafael does not have much commercial land but it has more than almost all other Marin communities. Software and high-tech firms, liking the demographics, set up in San Rafael.

Retail shopping went through another mutation and began favoring large box stores that avoided the malls. Many Marin communities shut down or sharply curtailed residential construction and this created a demand for housing.

Marin's natural beauty and artistic inclinations began paying off in dollars. George Lucas opened a high-tech studio in Nicasio and rented supporting facilities in San Rafael. Mill Valley started a film festival that needed a movie house. Enter the Rafael, an art deco gem built in 1938 in the downtown and closed in 1989. Restored and fitted with modern sound, it was reopened in 1999 and serves as the main theater for the Film Festival and other events. There's another movie complex in downtown and two more nearby.

Finally, "redevelopment," a tax-capture, investment mechanism, allowed the city to secure the money necessary to overhaul the infrastructure.

To touch on the additions in and near the downtown: Borders bookstore, Staples, CompUSA, good sources of tax revenue. A private group opened "Art Works Downtown," a building with studio space for 30 artists, classrooms, a gallery, an art supply store and 17 studio apartments, many of them rented by artists. Old Macys store was demolished and was replaced by shops, offices and apartments. Streets were made one way to move traffic. More parking was provided. The restaurants are many and varied. Transit center near the freeway. The library is open Sunday afternoons. The result: a much livelier, attractive downtown that is winning many visitors and shoppers.

Fair, Isaac & Co., a firm specializing in credit checking technology, was to have built a large office complex south of the downtown but at the last minute backed out. Nonetheless, the site was later developed for offices.

Not all is rosy. Anti-development, Marin lacks workers and professionals to staff a great expansion in business. Many of the people who work in Marin live in west Contra Costa County. Lucas in 2005 opened a giant digital complex in San Francisco, at the Presidio. Some of the Lucas operations in San Rafael are moving to San Francisco. After the dotcom crash, the North Bay in general lost many high-tech jobs.

San Rafael is divided into distinct neighborhoods by hills, a peninsula, man-made obstacles, foremost Highway 101, political divisions and housing patterns. In 2005, the state counted 23,472 housing units: 10,624 single detached homes, 2,024 single attached, 10,335 apartments and condos, 489 mobile homes.

To the north, west of Highway 101, are the neighborhoods of Marin Wood and Terra Linda, mostly suburban tract, built in the 1950 and 1960s. Many of the homes are Eichlers.

Near the freeway, atop Quail Hill, sits a striking apartment complex that commands views of the Bay and countryside.

East of the freeway and Terra Linda are the county civic center, townhouses and some of the firms that are making Marin a high-tech address.

Immediately east of the downtown, on the other side of the freeway, Point San Pedro sticks its face and hooked nose into San Pablo Bay. Lovely neighborhoods are found here, the first including Dominican University, the last including Peacock Gap, custom and well-appointed tract homes surrounding an 18-hole golf course, the most upscale section of San Rafael.

Also east of the freeway is the Canal neighborhood. The city has opened a police substation in the neighborhood, built a community center and tightened code enforcement to prod landlords to make improvements. In 2001, two soccer fields and a baseball diamond were installed at a Canal park. To the south of the downtown is a neighborhood built in the 1920s and 1930s. Many of the homes here have been remodeled and enlarged.

One homicide in 2004, zero in 2003, two each in 2002 and 2001, zero in 2000, 1999, 1998 and 1997, one in 1996 and 1995, zero in 1994, two in 1993, zero in 1992, five in 1991, one each in 1990 and 1989, FBI reports.

Arguments occurring about developing two of the last big, available parcels in Marin, 1,240 acres on northeast side of San Rafael. One plan for part of the acreage calls for 766 housing units, 10 acres of commercial space, parks and a village center. The land was to have been annexed to San Rafael. In 2003, however, the city said no to annexation and in effect dumped the decision into the county's lap, a move interpreted as anti-development. This project promises to take forever.

Dominican University opened a recreational center and another dormitory and plans to build a science and technology center. The university enrolls 1,600 students, hopes to move up to 1,800 and has added international studies and business to its liberal arts curriculum.

The state was thinking about closing San Quentin prison, which is in need of expensive repairs. The possibility had locals salivating with plans: water-front village, transit terminal, hordes of tourists to see some of the salvaged buildings. The prison sits on 275 acres overlooking San Pablo Bay. It employs about 2,000, contains 6,000 prisoners, of whom about 560 have been condemned to death. Now the state people are saying, let's renovate and build a new compound. The locals are disappointed and are working on plan to transfer out some of the death penalty inmates. Chamber of commerce: (415) 454-4163.

• Best Buy may open a store in town.

SAUSALITO

Novato ●

San Rafael

Sausalito ➤

RESIDENTIAL-TOURIST TOWN, POPULATION 7,374, located just around the corner from the Golden Gate. Streets wind through hills, great views of Bay, Angel Island, and bridge to Oakland and, for some, downtown San Francisco. Discovered by explorer Juan de Ayala, first Spaniard to sail through Golden Gate. He dropped anchor near willows and named the spot, Sausalito, "place of little willows."

Median age of residents is 45. Few children, about 7 percent of the town. Lovely burg but there must be times when the residents wish tourists — about 1.5 million a year — would leave them in peace. Homes a mix: many well over 50 years old but here and there some spanking new ones. Large, small and tiny homes. Apartments near water. Townhouses near north entrance from freeway. Houseboats, about 350 of them, almost suburban in appearance.

On steeper hills, you park below and walk up, or you park above and walk down. Some streets in hills narrow to one lane. Street parking sparse. Few lawns, yards; can't spare the land. Many homes have balconies or decks; the views. State in 2005 counted 4,549 housing units: 1,725 of them single homes, 423 single attached, 2,177 multiples, 224 mobile homes.

Elementary district, which includes Marin City, enrolls only 265 students. Two schools in Sausalito, middle school in Marin City. Academic rankings bounce all over but many are below the 50th percentile. Bond passed in 2004 to renovate buildings. According to newspapers, many parents send their kids to private schools.

Commute excellent, a few minutes drive to Golden Gate. Ferries work the commute weekdays, serve tourists at other hours. On summer mornings, the fog often creeps over the hills but by midday it fades under the sunlight. Zero homicides from 1994 through 2003.

Few parks. Steep terrain makes them expensive. Lots of shops, movies, fishing, boating, arts, crafts. Nice town to stroll. Park for dogs. Great restaurants. Art galleries. Arts festival. Fort Baker, on north side, was given up by military and its 355 acres placed in parkland. After years of argument, an agreement was reached to build on the site a conference center with 225 rooms. For a small town, Sausalito has many businesses and fairly large commercial district. During World War II, the town built Liberty ships. This section stayed industrial-commercial. Chamber of commerce: (415) 331-7262.

STINSON BEACH

Novato •

San Rafael

Stinson Beach ★

SMALL BEACH TOWN on Highway 1, the yin to Bolinas' yang. Stinson, with one big exception, likes tourists. Couple dozen businesses cater to beach crowd. No sidewalks, little parking. Library. Post office. Away from the business section and the beach, older homes sit on unpaved streets.

Population 751. Median age of residents is 47. Children and teens under 18 make up 17 percent of residents. Not very many kids.

About 300 homes in the expensive and guarded Seadrift, which has sued to restrict access to its coast. So far, the rulings have gone in favor of Seadrift. For outsiders, no picnicking or sunbathing at Seadrift section.

Stinson exists solely for the lovely beach, which is well-kept, clean and accessible. No charge for admission, day use only, crowded on good weather days, somewhat crowded even in bad. Picnic tables, snack shop, lifeguards, signs warning you swim at own risk. Occasional shark warnings, often ignored. Every few years someone gets mauled and chewed by a shark. When a shark is sighted, the beach is occasionally closed for a few days. Further north, only when a shark bites someone are the beaches closed.

Incidentally, among the surfing cognoscenti, the great white is known as "the man in the gray suit," or "the landlord."

Every once in a while a dead whale washes ashore and is buried.

In El Niño storms, Stinson lost much of its beach and this hurt local businesses. The winter of 1998-99 was much milder; beach came back. Bolinas Lagoon has silting problems.

Kids attend Bolinas Elementary School. Scores are a little erratic but many are landing in the 90th percentile, among tops in the state. When enrollment is low, as it is in Bolinas district, a few kids scoring high or low can make a big difference.

School district passed parcel tax to maintain programs.

Borders Mt. Tamalpai State Park. Miles of woods. Many trails. Small basketball court.

Every year Marin runs the Dipsea, 7.1 miles of cross-country racing, hill and valley, finishing at Stinson Beach. Runners are handicapped according to age and sex. Chamber of Commerce: (415) 663-9232.

STRAWBERRY POINT

Novato ●

San Rafael

Strawberry Point

SMALL PENINSULA-NEIGHBORHOOD on Richardson Bay, near Tiburon. Site of Golden Gate Baptist Theological Seminary. The 2000 census counted 5,302 inhabitants. Median age of residents is 40. Children and teens under 18 make up 19 percent of the town.

Lovely views of Richardson Bay and the Bay panorama. Not every home has sweeping views but many are positioned to catch some vista. Bordered on three sides by water. Choice location.

Mix of apartments, modest homes, especially on the Tiburon border, and upper middle. A few executive homes. Also townhouses. The apartments are located right off Highway 101.

Strawberry is unincorporated, meaning it is governed by the Marin County Board of Supervisors and patrolled by sheriff's deputies. But the real governing is done by the locals through a taxing district with an elected board. The district raises about $600,000 annually to run a complex with a community center, two ball fields, lighted tennis courts, a pool and a gym. Monthly dances are held in the auditorium. Other amenities include four small parks, a playground and a boat dock. Lovely scenic walk along Seminary Drive.

Neither the state nor the FBI tracks Strawberry crime but it's probably very low. Some people contract for private security.

Some shops, stores and office buildings near Highway 101. After much hoo-hah, In 'N Out Burgers won permission to open a restaurant near freeway but no drive-through. Took the firm years to win approval. Typical Marin aversion to the exotic, in this case, a burger joint. Small shopping center with a large supermarket.

Other town problem: trees that get in way of Bay view. Residents are trying to forge some guidelines.

Served by Mill Valley Elementary School District, which has some of the highest scores in the state. The district in 2000 reopened Strawberry Elementary School. This shortened the drop-off for parents and relieved crowding at other schools. Teens move up to Tamalpais High. Both the school districts have passed funding measures to renovate schools and equip them for high tech. Also to keep class sizes low and retain electives and arts classes.

Short hop to Highway 101. Park-and-ride lot.

TIBURON

Novato ●

San Rafael

Tiburon ——

Mill Valley

ONE OF THE MOST PRESTIGIOUS addresses in the Bay Area, this city of 8,772 residents owes a great debt to Mother Nature.

She scooped out the terrain in such a manner as to create a hilly peninsula jutting into San Francisco Bay. Great views. She also erected coastal hills to buffer Tiburon from the fog and chilly winds of the Pacific.

Being omnipotent, Mother Nature threw in a reasonable commute, high-scoring schools and a small but pleasant downtown that is adding a statue in the town square.

Median age of residents is 45. Children and teens under 18 make up 22 percent of town. In the 1990s, Tiburon increased its population by 1,134 residents.

Low crime rate. Zero homicides between 1994 and 1998. One homicide in 1999. Man slain at home by his adult son, who was sentenced to 15 years to life. Zero homicides from 2000 to 2003.

Tiburon has its own police force. New police station opened in 1999.

Academic rankings among highest in state. Voters in 1990 agreed to raise taxes by $96 a parcel over five years to support school programs. In 2003, voters extended the tax. In 2001, residents approved a $38 million bond to renovate all the schools in the Reed district, which serves Tiburon and Belved-ere. In 2005, voters threw in another $13 million to upgrade science and technology facilities, build a gym at the middle school, renovate the playing fields and tidy up the landscaping.

Teens advance to Redwood High in Larkspur. High school district has passed bonds to rebuild schools and equip them for high tech. Scores in the high 90s, among tops in state.

Not too many controversies in Tiburon and when they come, they are often less than earth shattering — more classrooms and a gym for a private school, taxing residents in one neighborhood to underground utility lines, where to place a communications antennae and anything, however small, to do with development.

The town is served by Tiburon Boulevard, which runs along shore from Highway 101. Most homes are located on steep streets that ascend from the boulevard and look south toward Richardson Bay. At the tip of the peninsula, some homes line the shore.

The state in 2005 counted 3,950 residential units: single homes 2,412, single attached 237, multiples 1,301. About one-third of the housing stock is devoted to apartments or condos. Multiples include 102 apartments for low- and moderate-income residents and housing for elderly. No mobile homes. In single homes, Tiburon excels. Dotted over the hills, with their trees and shrubs and decorative touches, they please the eye. The more enchanting the view, the less enchanting the price (high). One Realtor said that anything going for less than $1 million would be a "fixer." In the 1990s, Tiburbon increased its housing stock by 470 units.

Many homes, apartments or condos offer inhabitants spectacular views of Richardson Bay, Raccoon Strait, Angel Island, San Rafael Bay and the towers of the Golden Gate Bridge. Some shore homes have own docks.

Streets clean, high level of general maintenance, a lot of pride (and work) in appearances. Much of the peninsula is wooded and the animals thrive — in part by eating flowers and gardens. Many people love the deer, a few find them less than endearing. Gas-powered leaf blowers have been banned — too noisy.

Commute fairly good. Highway 101 just down the road. Ferries to San Francisco from Tiburon.

Sister city to Belvedere, also rich. Both share a small downtown: super-market, beauty salons, clothing stores, banks, realty firms, antique shops, small movie house, restaurants and cafes. Small shopping plaza.

Tennis clubs, marina, yacht clubs, several parks, wildlife sanctuary. Fishing pier. Art and Garden Center. Local galleries host arts nights. Annual film festivals, low-keyed and fun. Angel Island across Raccoon Strait. Money enough for recreation at home. Wine festival in spring. Chili festival. Hallow-een pet parade. In the 1990s, residents voted to buy two large parcels and keep them in open space. County park on the north side of the Tiburon peninsula. Playing fields in short supply.

Soccer fields and park near Blackie's pasture. Blackie was a horse who whiled away his golden years munching hay in a field at the entrance to town. For many residents, he symbolized the unhurried, country ideal of what Tiburon should be and years after he died, the town commissioned a statue of Blackie and one of his beloved bales of hay. C. Gordon and Eleanore Knight loved to read. When they died, they left about $1 million for the Tiburon Peninsula Library Fund. The money was used to build a library at Tiburon Boulevard and Mar West Street, next to town hall.

Tiburon used to be railroad, working-class town. Ferries lugged trains down to San Francisco. Spanish called the peninsula "Punta de Tiburon (Shark Point)." Chamber of commerce: (415) 435-5633.

TOMALES

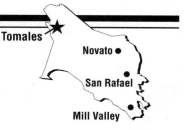

HISTORIC SMALL TOWN in northwest Marin, population about 210. Many homes restored. Farm country. Sheep graze in the fields.

Country town; a long commute. Residents have said good-bye to city and value rural obscurity. General store, Lady of Assumption Church built in 1860. Coffee house, deli. Nice town to visit.

Median age of residents is 46. Children and teens under 18 make up 22 percent of residents.

Children attend Tomales Elementary and Tomales High in the Shoreline Unified School District, which also takes in Pt. Reyes and crossed the county line to include Bodega and Bodega Bay. In 2000, district, which enrolls about 660 students, passed a tax to make improvements.

Tomales Elementary School enrolls about 215 pupils spread over grades kindergarten through eighth. The high school enrolls 220 students. Kids are not going to get lost in this setting but the low number of students makes it difficult to assess scores. A few children scoring high or low can made a big difference.

Scores in the elementary school range from the 30th to the 80th percentile. Scores at the high school land generally in the 70th to 80th percentile.

Bisected by Highway 1, the coastal road, favorite drive of tourists. Much of West Marin has been placed in open space or farm preserve. If you like the wide-open spaces, this is the place to look but not many homes come on the market. Chamber of Commerce: (415) 663-9232.

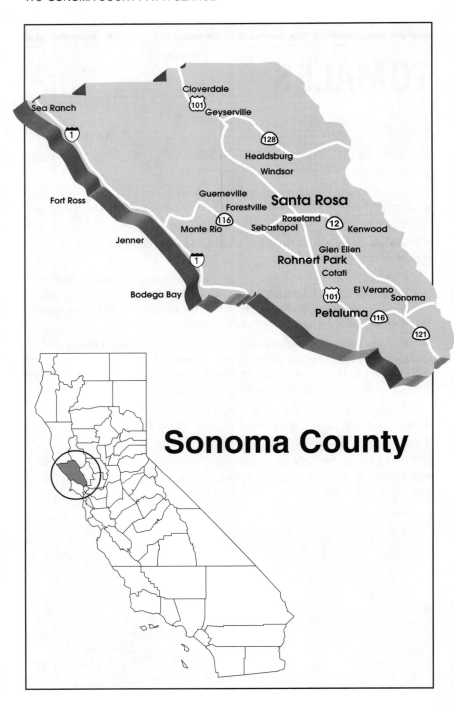

Sonoma County

Chapter **7**

Sonoma County at a Glance

LOCATED ON THE NORTH BORDER OF MARIN COUNTY, Sonoma mixes the ambiance of the wine country with the comforts of suburbia, an alluring concoction that is drawing residents by the tens of thousands. On the west border, the Pacific crashes against rocky cliffs and beaches. Through the middle of the county there meanders one of the prettiest and most accessible rivers in California — the Russian.

Zephyrs ease the summer heat. The Pacific warms the winters. Snow rarely falls. Rain confines itself to winter and spring. Flatlands give way gently to hills and valleys.

Between 1970 and 2000, Sonoma County's population has increased by about 124 percent, going from 204,885 residents to 458,614. Not surprisingly, a reaction has set in. Many cities are restricting new housing to infilling. More attention is being paid to preserving vineyards, farms and open space. Still the people come. The state in its annual estimates put the 2005 population of Sonoma at 478,440.

In land, lakes and rivers, Sonoma County covers 1,579 square miles, smaller than Delaware, larger than Rhode Island. Santa Rosa is its biggest city, Cloverdale its smallest.

For a long time, Mount Saint Helena was thought to be the highest peak. A recent survey gives the honor to Cobb Mountain, 4,480 feet, about 137 feet higher than Saint Helena, and highest mountain in nine-county Bay Area.

The 2000 census tallied 379,103 Caucasians, 63,879 people of Hispanic heritage, 14,098 Asians, 6,522 African-Americans, 5,389 American Indians and 934 Native Hawaiians or other Pacific Islanders.

The median age of residents is 38. Children and teens under age 18 make up 24 percent of the county, people over 55 account for 22 percent. Translation: rounded county, just about as many old as young.

The Coming of Highway 101

Following World War II, San Francisco, as a metropolis, spread to the East and South Bay and to Marin County, which gradually built Highway 101 to carry traffic to the City. The farther north 101 was extended, the more accessible Sonoma became and in the 1970s and 1980s the suburban swing became more pronounced.

Also pushing suburbia north was a sharp rise in the general population of California and housing costs that priced other sections, especially Marin, beyond the pocketbook of many home buyers.

Indeed, so favorable were home prices that many Marin residents and established residents from other counties sold their homes and with the equity bought bigger and better homes in Sonoma County. You will find in Sonoma many ideas and beliefs that Marin finds congenial.

Enticing for Home and Hearth

About 1990, the equity market began to dry up and with it went the roaring housing market of the 1980s. But about 1997, the market shifted into high gear again and for several years, prices increased sharply. Elevated by the low interest rates, home prices were still rising in 2004,

Beside the blessings of nature, the county offers many other enticements: classy restaurants, fresh farm produce, a state university, a community college, swimming, boating, fishing, golf, skating, softball — a wealth of activities.

School rankings are generally high, crime low. In 2003, the California Dept. of Justice recorded 12 homicides in Sonoma. The counts for the previous years are 16, 12, 11, 17 and 11. Services — hospitals, police and fire protection — in most cases, have kept pace with development.

But in one area, the whole North Bay has fallen down: traffic. Highway 101, which feeds to the Golden Gate, remains practically the only major road to San Francisco. Residents would love to widen it or duplicate it but cannot bring themselves to accept the population surge the improvements would bring.

In 1998, both Marin and Sonoma rejected a half-cent sales tax that would have brought sweeping relief to commuting problems. In 2004, another try was made. No one gave it much of a chance and lo and behold, it passed.

Meanwhile, dredging up of money wherever it can, the state has been gradually widening Highway 101. See commuting chapter.

History

Before the Europeans, there were the Indians: Pomos, Miwoks and others. They hunted, they fished, they ate acorns and berries and, fish from the Russian River, and foods derived from the wild fields. They were utterly unprepared for what was to befall them.

In 1492, Columbus, working for Spain, discovered America. The Spanish moved quickly into Mexico and other parts of Central and South America but they didn't get around to California, which they claimed, until the eve of the American Revolutionary War.

In 1769 Gaspar de Portola discovered the Bay. Once established in Northern California, the Spanish and their heirs (Mexico won independence in 1821 and took over the Spanish claim) moved energetically but the Southwest Indians again closed overland migration. On the eve of the Mexican-American War in 1846, fewer than 7,000 Spanish-Mexicans inhabited the entire state.

The Mission

Gradually, the first settlers moved north from the Presidio in San Francisco and in 1823 Father Jose Altimira opened the Mission of San Francisco de Solano at what is now the City of Sonoma.

From noble intentions — to care for and convert the Indians — came disastrous results. Having no immunity to European diseases, the Indians died in large numbers from measles and smallpox.

In 1834, Mariano Vallejo, commandant-general and a man of great energy, took over mission lands and built a small town and fort. The county, which is named after an Indian chief, was divided into great rancheros (Vallejo's covered 175,000 acres), soldiers were sent out to subdue the Indians and the great days of the Californios began.

Vast herds of cattle roamed the countryside. After vaqueros branded the cattle in the spring, fiestas were thrown that lasted for days. Music, dancing, barbecues, rodeos, unfettered hospitality — the Days of the Dons are still celebrated in California folklore.

But their time in the sun would quickly pass.

The Russians

As the Spanish were moving into Northern California, the Russians were crossing the Bering Strait and claiming Alaska. Not surprisingly, Russian explorers soon ventured down into California and in 1812, to the distress of the Spanish, built a settlement and fort on the Sonoma coast.

The Spanish hinted it would be nice if the Russians returned from whence they came. But, behind their cannons, the Russians chose not to hear. They muddled along, trading with Indians and Californios, exploring the countryside and taking care not to rile authorities. Spanish-Mexican distrust of the Russians soon receded before fears of the Yankees.

The Yankee Invasion

Although nominally Spanish or Mexican, California in the early 1800s was claimed by several nations. A sparsity of settlers created a situation where the country that could field the largest numbers would probably carry the day.

In 1803, Thomas Jefferson purchased the Midwest and as it was settled, mountain men and pioneers began pushing west toward California. The Monroe Doctrine — no more European colonies in the Americas — apparently impressed the czar and nothing was done to expand the settlement at Fort Ross.

SONOMA COUNTY

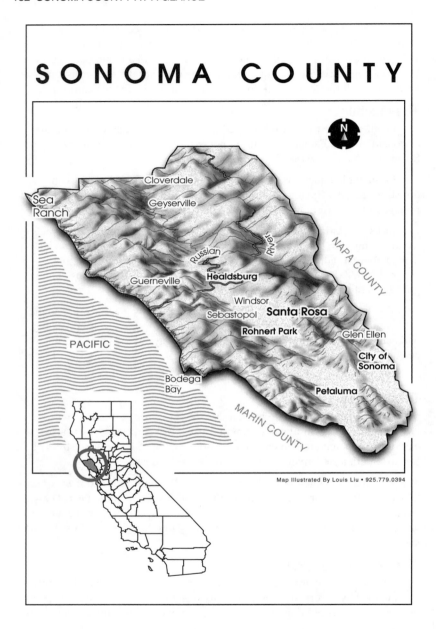

Cloverdale

Geyserville

Sea Ranch

Russian River

NAPA COUNTY

Guerneville

Healdsburg

Windsor

Sebastopol Santa Rosa

Rohnert Park

Glen Ellen

City of Sonoma

PACIFIC

Bodega Bay

Petaluma

MARIN COUNTY

Map Illustrated By Louis Liu • 925.779.0394

Sonoma County Population

City or Area	1990	2000	2005*
Bodega Bay	1,127	1,423	NA
Boyes Hot Springs	5,973	6,665	NA
Cloverdale	4,924	6,831	8,241
Cotati	5,714	6,471	7,337
El Verano	3,498	3,954	NA
Fetters Hot Springs/Agua Caliente	2,024	2,505	NA
Forestville	2,443	2,370	NA
Glen Ellen	1,191	992	NA
Guerneville	1,966	2,441	NA
Healdsburg	9,469	10,722	11,711
Monte Rio	1,058	1,104	NA
Occidental	1,300	1,272	NA
Petaluma	43,184	54,548	56,632
Rohnert Park	36,326	42,236	42,445
Roseland	8,779	6,369	NA
Santa Rosa	113,313	147,595	156,268
Sebastopol	7,004	7,774	7,794
Sonoma	8,121	9,128	9,834
Windsor	13,371	22,744	25,475
Countywide	388,222	458,614	478,440

Source: 1990 Census, 2000 Census. *California Dept. of Finance annually updates the populations of legal cities. These figures are from Jan. 2005.

The Russians hunted the local otter to extinction and in 1841, after selling the fort and its cannon to John Sutter, of golden fame, sailed off. As more Americans arrived, disputes arose. The Californios claimed all; the Yankees saw land poorly defended, sparsely inhabited, ideal for trade and farming. They began plotting.

On June 11, 1846, buckskinned Americans, many shoeless, seized Vallejo at Sonoma and took him to Sutter's Fort in Sacramento — the Bear Flag Revolt, which preceded but soon became part of the war between Mexico and the United States.

Skirmishes were fought up and down the state, but almost all the blood was shed in the invasion of Mexico. Two years after the shooting stopped, California, in 1850, was admitted into the Union.

Squatters and settlers moved onto the great rancheros. Vallejo, who died poor, is remembered in local histories as a great man and a tragic figure.

Taking the long view, the true victims of the era were the Indians. They preceded the Californios (and the Americans, who also were cruel) by a thousand years. Few escaped with their lives. The Californio interlude in Northern California lasted less than 80 years, in Sonoma County less than 25 years.

Average Household Income in Sonoma County

City or Area	1990	2000	*2005
Cloverdale	$76,500	$92,500	$96,400
Coastal-Gualala	80,900	91,500	91,500
Cotati	63,900	73,500	78,100
Healdsburg	61,800	70,200	75,800
Healdsburg, Rural	81,500	85,000	86,500
Petaluma	68,600	81,000	82,600
Petaluma, Rural	69,900	82,600	84,300
Rohnert Park	60,700	69,200	73,300
Rohnert Park, Rural	56,100	59,000	60,100
Rural Northeast	80,700	92,600	99,900
Russian River	52,500	56, 900	59,600
Santa Rosa	64,100	72,400	74,600
Santa Rosa, Rural	71,000	90,900	92,100
Sebastopol	62,000	72,500	75,200
Sebastopol, Rural	72,900	84,900	87,500
Sonoma	62,000	71,100	77,500
Sonoma Valley, Rural	65,900	77,000	81,000
Windsor	69,100	73,800	74,900
Countywide	65,600	75,900	77,400

Source: Association of Bay Area Governments, "Projections 2002." Average income per household includes wages and salaries, dividends, interest, rent and transfer payments such as Social Security or public assistance.

The New Californians

First almost all headed for the gold fields after the strike of 1848, then, having struck out, they came to Sonoma in the Fifties and took up farming.

Hay and wheat, beef and potatoes, cheese, eggs and milk — from the fields and farms of Sonoma to the bellies and ships of San Francisco. Redwoods grew in great abundance in west Sonoma. With the exceptions of a few groves, all were felled to help build the West. Second-growth redwoods, however, have restored much of the forested look.

The Railroad

In 1870, the San Francisco and Northern Pacific Railroad laid a line between Petaluma (accessible to ship) and Santa Rosa, and within a few years the line was extended to Cloverdale.

What the freeway is to Sonoma now, the railroad was to Sonoma in the late 19th century. Within five years, Santa Rosa shot from 1,000 to 6,000 residents. Perhaps more important, rails gave Sonoma County much better access to the commerce of the world.

Wine

The mission padres dabbled in grapes and produced simple, sweet wines, better than nothing but incapable of exciting the palate.

Education Level of Population Age 25 & Older

City or Town	ND	HS	SC	AA	BA	Grad
Bodega Bay	7%	14%	20%	4%	23%	25%
Boyes Hot Spring	11	26	23	8	15	8
Cloverdale	16	22	27	9	11	4
Cotati	9	21	31	11	16	7
Eldridge	9	15	21	6	15	7
El Verano	8	18	34	9	16	8
Fetters Hot Springs/Agua Caliente	15	19	29	7	15	7
Forestville	4	18	25	9	25	16
Glen Ellen	6	16	16	7	39	6
Graton	12	20	18	5	26	10
Guerneville	9	23	28	8	20	10
Healdsburg	8	19	24	9	20	9
Larkfield-Wikiup	4	18	29	13	21	12
Monte Rio	7	17	32	14	22	7
Occidental	7	10	21	14	31	17
Petaluma	9	19	27	9	21	9
Rohnert Park	8	24	30	10	18	7
Roseland	15	27	21	6	6	3
Santa Rosa	9	21	27	9	19	9
Sebastopol	6	17	29	8	23	13
Sonoma City	6	19	27	7	26	13
Temelec	8	19	31	4	17	18
Windsor	9	21	28	10	17	7
Sonoma County	8	20	27	9	19	10

Source: 2000 Census. Figures are percent of population age 25 and older, rounded to the nearest whole number. **Key**: ND (high school, no diploma); HS (adults with high school diploma or GED only, no college); SC (adults with some college education); AA (adults with an associate degree); BA (adults with a bachelor's degree only); Grad (adults with a master's or higher degree).

In the early 1800s in Hungary, a showdown pitted Liberals against Conservatives. Agoston Haraszthy, a nobleman, threw in with the Libs, and when they lost, packed his bags and headed for the New World.

After an adventuresome and prosperous sojourn in Wisconsin, he made for California, was elected sheriff of San Diego County and in 1856 wound up in Sonoma County. The colonel, the title which he claimed, knew his wines and what he didn't know about grape growing he remedied during an 1861 tour of European wine countries. Returning with 300 varieties of vines, Haraszthy planted, literally, the foundation of the California wine industry.

Chickens and Eggs

Thousands of chicken farms flourished in and about Petaluma, which even had a pharmacy for chickens. Some years, the town shipped out over 600 million eggs, all over the world. It was touted as "The Egg Basket of the World."

Rising labor and feed costs in the 1930s started the industry on a slow decline. Many farms were consolidated into few. Cattle, sheep and homes replaced hens and roosters but it's still possible to get fresh eggs and every May the town celebrates with the Butter and Eggs Parade. Kids one to eight, if costumed, get a chance to win the title of "Cutest Little Chick in Town."

Golden Gate Bridge, World War II

Completed in 1937, the Golden Gate Bridge began what Highway 101 finished, the development of Sonoma County as a suburb. World War II, following four years later, brought millions to the West Coast — soldiers, sailors and marines in transit to the Pacific, workers for the war industries.

Many of former came back, many of the latter stayed. The population boomed but not until the '50s was the key built to open the door: Highway 101.

Present Sonoma

Uneasy over growth but still growing. Many of the cities have established urban growth lines to protect the vineyards.

Sonoma is growing more cosmopolitan, more interested in the arts. The state university at Rohnert Park has nudged the county in this direction. But much of this interest is coming naturally. Sonoma is being discovered by the educated and the affluent. The university is building a concert hall that will be used by both student and county groups. Marin is building very little new housing and has priced many young professionals out of the housing market. Sonoma increasingly is filling the market that Marin used to control.

Sonoma is capturing high-tech firms from Marin. Or getting firms that might have favored Marin but were put off by insufficient land or high rents or land prices. But in the nasty economy of recent years, many firms bit the dust or cut back. One estimate put the number of high-tech manufacturing jobs lost between 2001 and 2004 at 6,000.

Most of the firms are located in what's called "Telecom Valley," the stretch along Highway 101, from Petaluma to Santa Rosa. North Santa Rosa, off of Fountaingrove Parkway, has a cluster of high-tech firms. The largest private employer in the county is Agilent Technologies (Santa Rosa).

Tourism is bringing about 6 million visitors a year and encouraging the construction of hotels, spas and resorts.

Santa Rosa Junior College has added classes and programs in high tech. Sonoma State University has created a master's degree in computers and engineering science and has opened a program to train high school students.

Sonoma taxes itself to buy development rights of ranchers and keep land in farming or open space. So far the trust has locked up over 36,000 acres.

Presidential Voting in Sonoma County

Year	Democrat	Votes	Republican	Votes
1948	Truman*	16,026	Dewey	22,077
1952	Stevenson	17,046	Eisenhower*	34,088
1956	Stevenson	20,616	Eisenhower*	33,659
1960	Kennedy*	29,147	Nixon	34,641
1964	Johnson*	44,354	Goldwater	27,677
1968	Humphrey	33,587	Nixon*	38,088
1972	McGovern	43,746	Nixon*	57,697
1976	Carter*	50,353	Ford	50,555
1980	Carter	45,596	Reagan*	60,722
1984	Mondale	71,295	Reagan*	76,447
1988	Dukakis	91,262	Bush*	67,625
1992	Clinton*	97,207	Bush	43,381
1996	Clinton*	100,738	Dole	53,555
2000	Gore	106,490	Bush*	57,834
2004	Kerry	119,821	Bush*	55,541

Source: California Secretary of State. *Election winner.

Sonoma County Voter Registration

City	Demo.	Repub.	NP
Cloverdale	1,812	191	617
Cotati	1,931	740	665
Healdsburg	2,927	1,623	919
Petaluma	14,220	7,397	4,668
Rohnert Park	8,784	4,939	3,385
Santa Rosa	37,662	21,175	12,296
Sebastopol	2,635	780	703
Sonoma	3,151	1,688	937
Windsor	5,575	3,986	1,810
Unincorporated	40,738	21,397	12,724
Countywide	119,435	64,916	38,724

Source: California Secretary of State, October 2004. Key: Demo. (Democrat), Repub. (Republican), NP (Declined to state).

Wine (about 210 wineries and 960 grape growers cultivating 57,570 acres), high tech, wi-fi at the libraries, culture, lovely country, close to ocean — delightful enticements. More people and firms are welcome in some ways but they bring worries about too much development.

Among the latest arrivals: Indian casinos, which will bring in thousands of job and, people fear, social problems and more traffic.

Top 30 Baby Names

Sonoma County

Boys

Anthony	37
Daniel	37
Jose	36
Diego	34
David	33
Ryan	33
Alexander	32
Jonathan	32
Jacob	31
Jesus	30
Alexis	29
Angel	28
Joseph	28
Joshua	28
Nicholas	28
Aidan	27
Christian	27
Christopher	27
Tyler	27
Andrew	26
Juan	26
Ethan	25
Alejandro	23
Dominic	23
Dylan	23
Jack	23
Samuel	23
Benjamin	21
Gabriel	21
Michael	20

Girls

Isabella	42
Emily	37
Sophia	37
Ashley	35
Emma	33
Madison	28
Olivia	25
Samantha	24
Jessica	22
Vanessa	22
Jasmine	21
Elizabeth	20
Jennifer	19
Alyssa	18
Grace	17
Jocelyn	17
Leslie	17
Alexis	16
Ava	16
Evelyn	16
Ella	15
Maria	15
Andrea	14
Hannah	14
Sofia	14
Gabriela	13
Kayla	13
Stephanie	13
Diana	12
Jacqueline	12

California

Boys

Daniel	4157
Anthony	3797
Andrew	3464
Jose	3379
Jacob	3327
Joshua	3292
David	3246
Angel	3232
Matthew	2853
Michael	2844
Christopher	2754
Jonathan	2541
Ryan	2511
Alexander	2440
Joseph	2430
Ethan	2356
Nathan	2302
Brandon	2208
Kevin	2133
Juan	2106
Christian	2022
Jesus	2012
Nicholas	1999
Diego	1977
Luis	1957
Adrian	1824
Dylan	1757
Gabriel	1735
Isaac	1722
Carlos	1638

Girls

Emily	3388
Ashley	2922
Samantha	2474
Isabella	2435
Natalie	1942
Alyssa	1808
Emma	1740
Sophia	1715
Jessica	1700
Jasmine	1666
Elizabeth	1595
Madison	1572
Jennifer	1483
Kimberly	1460
Alexis	1434
Andrea	1374
Abigail	1314
Hannah	1310
Sarah	1304
Vanessa	1299
Mia	1270
Stephanie	1246
Brianna	1221
Michelle	1152
Olivia	1149
Kayla	1147
Leslie	1137
Grace	1127
Maria	1099
Victoria	1083

Source: California Department of Health Services, 2004 birth records. Number of children with the given name. Some names would move higher on the list if the state grouped essentially same names with slightly different spellings, for example, Sarah and Sara. But state computer goes by exact spellings.

Chapter **8**

Sonoma City Profiles

FOR A BRIEF DISCUSSION of the roles of local governments, see the beginning of Marin City Profiles.

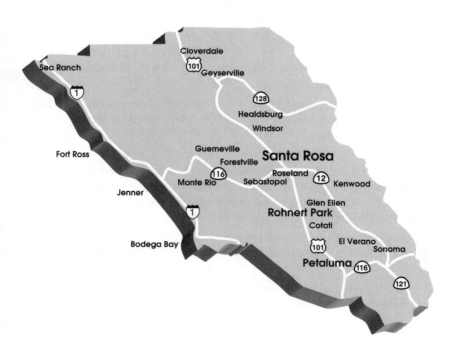

AGUA CALIENTE, BOYES HOT SPRINGS, EL VERANO, FETTERS HOT SPRINGS

Santa Rosa

Petaluma

HAMLETS TO NORTH of City of Sonoma. Quiet, generally well-kept in most parts, rundown in a few (but improvements are being made), noted for their spas, restaurants and resorts. Golf course. Several parks.

Although they claim separate identities and are unincorporated and therefore governed from Santa Rosa by the board of supervisors, these neighborhoods should be considered part of greater (city of) Sonoma. Contiguous to the city, they follow the same pursuits (tourism, government work, commuting, retirement) and shop in Sonoma. Just north of these towns, the wine country picks up in earnest. Lovely drive.

Census 2000 populations: Boyes Hot Springs, 6,665, El Verano, 3,954, Fetters Hot Springs-Agua Caliente, 2,505.

Median age of Boyes residents is 32. Children and teens under 18 make up 28 percent of village. Agua Caliente and Fetters Hot Springs median age is 34. Children and teens under 18 make up 27 percent of neighborhood. El Verano, median 36, kids 27 percent.

Over the last 10 years, people have been adding townhouses and single homes and moving the area upscale, and this in turn has encouraged more building. The Sonoma Mission Inn in Boyes Hot Springs does the spa thing in grand style and has made itself famous as a luxury resort.

About $9 million was spent to improve the looks of Highway 12 from Boyes Hot Springs to Kenwood. In the towns, sidewalks, trees and bikeways were added. Among recent additions: coffee houses and movies.

All the towns, including Sonoma, are part of the Sonoma Valley Unified School District. Academic rankings range from 30th to 90th percentile.

In 1995, in Agua Caliente, the school district opened the county's first charter school, called Sonoma Charter School. These schools require students to master a basic curriculum but give teachers a great deal of flexibility to structure teaching to the individual needs of students. The schools go out of their way to encourage parents to get active in their children's education.

School district passed a bond, which was used to renovate Sonoma Charter. In 2004, a parcel tax was passed to retain programs and teachers.

BODEGA BAY, JENNER

Jenner ★
Bodega Bay ★
Rohnert Park ➤
Petaluma

COASTAL TOWNS. Bodega Bay, a fishing-tourist-second-home town on the south Sonoma coast. Tiny sister village of Bodega located a few miles inland. Jenner, farther north, a small town built on the side of a wind-protected hill overlooking the mouth of Russian River.

Bodega Bay, named after a Spanish captain who sailed into the bay in 1775, is a good place for a salmon or crab dinner. One of the largest "small" harbors on the West Coast. Many fishing boats. Also, boats for whale watching and . Fresh crab for three-four months every year.

Population 1,423 (census 2000). Few kids, many mature adults and retirees. A place for weekend retreats, close enough to San Francisco for a Friday afternoon cutout, but too distant for a commute, although no doubt some manage it. Many people rent their homes by the weekend or month. Bodega Harbor, a 750-home tract, provides most of housing. Few homes for sale and those that are often run from $700,000 to over $1 million. Town, which has almost no sidewalks, is working on plan for pedestrian and bike trails.

Windy and mostly clear in summer, often foggy in winter. Mix of homes, many on bluff overlooking Bay. Coast Guard station. Marine lab. North of town, in the 1998 storms, some homes built on bluffs over the Pacific had to be shored up to keep from falling into the ocean. Sand dune park, salt marshes, tidal flats, sea birds, abalone for divers, a lot of outdoorsy stuff, beaches. In 2003, shark tasted and rejected surfer; 80 stitches. Public golf course, 18 holes. Spring Fishermen's Festival. Kite Festival. Sheep graze in hills. Hitchcock shot scenes for "The Birds" in Bodega Bay and Bodega. During their annual migration, Monarch butterflies set down on state land to take a breather.

Children attend Bodega Bay Elementary, enrollment 42, and move up to Tomales High, enrollment 220. Both schools are in the Shoreline Unified School District, which passed parcel tax and bond in 2000 to help the schools.

Jenner, chilly in summer, mild in winter, is picturesque. Couple of restaurants, shops. About 60 homes. Goat Rock, south of the river mouth, dominates the landscape. Seals loll on a sandbar where the river meets the ocean. No dogs allowed. Watch the waves, often powerful. To north, scenic road with ocean views occasionally washes out. In 2004, young man and woman murdered on beach. Shot in their sleeping bags. No arrests.

CLOVERDALE

COUNTRY TOWN GOING SUBURBAN. Last town in Sonoma County traveling north on Highway 101, about 27 north of Santa Rosa. Surrounded by vineyards or redwoods. Borders the Russian River. Just about doubled its population over the past 25 years. Now has 8,241 residents.

Median age of residents is 36. Children and teens under 18 make up 27 percent of town. Among recent additions, Clover Springs, a retirement community, 362 single homes. More homes under consideration.

Pomo Indians have built the River Rock Casino in Alexander Valley, a few miles outside of town.

They also want to build a casino in Cloverdale, on the south side. But some locals have a different idea — no casino.

In 1991, the last lumber mill was closed and about six years later Highway 101 was extended and routed around the downtown. This hurt some businesses and forced the town into adjustments. In 1997, Cloverdale opened a large supermarket, a drug store and miscellaneous stores. Downtown was spruced up, though it retains its history with diners and older shops. Movie complex, fitness club added, new hotel. Seniors center.

At Cloverdale, you pick up Highway 128 to Boonville and Albion, redwood country and coastal Mendocino. Lake Sonoma is close by. Hills to east and west. The metropolis is growing out. Cloverdale probably will continue to go suburban while retaining its wine country, small-town flavor.

Cloverdale hopes to get itself deeper in the wine country tourist loop that runs through Healdsburg and Alexander Valley. Shady streets, city pool, farmers' market. Downtown park with ball field. Planted median strip. Ornamental lights. Small movie house called, "The Clover." New sidewalks and street lights.

Park along the river. Youth Center. Annual citrus fair. Annual fiddle contest. End-of-Harvest Fiesta. Library. Post office. Transit center for bus riders and car poolers. Public art; 19 sculptures scattered around town.

Mix of housing, '50s tract types, bungalows, Victorians, trailers, some new one- and two-story stuccos north of town, and Clover Springs to the south. In

2005, housing units totaled 3,192, of which 2,416 were single family, 155 single attached, 413 apartments, 208 mobiles.

School district enrolls 1,600. School rankings from 40th to 80th percentile, California comparisons. In 1999, voters raised taxes to renovate the schools, replace portables and add or improve libraries and science labs.

Zero homicides in 2003 and 2002, one each in 2001 and 2000, and zero in the eight preceding years. Cloverdale has own police and fire departments. Chamber of commerce: (707) 894-4470.

• Work began in 2005 on development consisting of hotel, spa, golf course, bungalows, single homes, mansions (about 175 units), restaurants, stores. Located north of airport.

• Town is revising its general plan to control growth, which is making some residents uneasy. City leaders say that over next 20 years population could rise to 12,000 and another 1,500 homes could be added.

• Cloverdale has rail station but no trains. For years, North Bay has been trying to come up with, and fund, rail service that would please a variety of interest groups. Another funding vote may be held in 2006.

COTATI

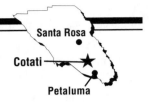

Santa Rosa

Cotati

Petaluma

SMALL BEDROOM TOWN with unusual design. Named after Indian chief. Population 7,337. Added 757 residents in the 1990s. Straddles Highway 101 just south of Rohnert Park.

Cotati has been growing rapidly — doubled its population over last 20 years — but is overshadowed by Rohnert Park and you might say they are joined at the hip.

The two towns share the same school district and in many ways blend in with one another.

When a region grows, it's important for cities to secure businesses to raise tax revenues to pay for roads and services. Rohnert Park has played this game well, attracting Wal-mart, Target, Costco, etc., and Cotati, poorly. Cotati's turn, has arrived. After years of arguing and lawsuits, Lowe's got the green light to build a giant home improvement store near Highway 101. Opening in 2006.

The state in 2005 tallied 2,956 housing units: 1,623 single homes, 506 single attached, 706 apartments, 121 mobile homes. Urban line limits growth. Median age of residents is 34. Children and teens under 18 make up 26 percent of town; over age 55, about 14 percent. Rounded burg.

Sonoma state university at city limits. Cotati has its recreational offerings, including a jazz festival, an accordion festival (waltzes and polkas), an Indian Summer festival. Bookstore, restaurants, cafes. Some bars book bands and singers that attract the college students. For many college students, Cotati serves as the night life (modest) that can't be found in Rohnert Park.

Zero homicides in 2003, 2002 and 2001, one in 2000, zero in 1999, 1998, 1997 and 1996, one in 1995, zero in 1994. New police station opened in 2003.

Bond passed in 1990 to build schools, improve high school. Rancho-Cotati High opened math and science building, cost $2.4 million. School district has spent $5 million to open classrooms at Sonoma State University so students can use facilities to study science, computers and technology. In 2005, parcel tax for programs lost by about 60 votes; another try probable.

The Cotati downtown is designed around a hexagon and efforts have been made to build on the town's history. Statute of Chief Cotati in La Plaza Park. Sidewalks built, traffic signals installed, streets repaved, roses and flowers planted. Chamber of commerce: (707) 795-5508.

FORESTVILLE, GEYSERVILLE

Rohnert Park
Petaluma

RURAL HAMLETS. Forestville along Highway 116, Geyserville, just off Highway 101, north of Healdsburg.

Trees and brush on outskirts of Forestville, some fields in farming. Coastal redwoods thicken as one heads west on Highway 116. Claims to be named after a guy named Forest, never mind the trees. Population 2,370. Median age of residents is 43. Children and teens under 18 make up 25 percent of town.

Downtown covers a few blocks: dentists, lawyers, restaurants, hardware, real estate, bank, post office, general store-market, shops. Bus service to other towns. Churches, baseball diamond, volunteer fire dept. Wineries. Canoeing. Ordinary town with sense of community. Many visitors.

One school, Forestville Elementary, about 620 students. Academic rankings from the 60th to 90th percentile, California comparisons. Parcel tax passed to maintain and improve programs and to retain music and art. In 2001, another tax was passed to renovate school buildings and add classrooms. But in 2005, by a few percent, residents turned down a tax to maintain programs. Teens move up to El Molino High in Forestville; scores in 80th percentile.

About 1.5 to 2 hours from San Francisco. Residents a mix of homeowners, renters, retirees, vacationers. Modest homes, mobile homes downtown, further out, larger, newer homes.

In the northeast portion of Sonoma County, Geyserville has — geysers. Wine country village. Russian River ambles by just east of town. Restaurants. Quality wineries.

Geyserville runs its own kindergarten-through-grade-12 school district, a rarity for a village. Total enrollment is 275 including 93 kids at Geyserville High. The senior class can fit into one classroom. Academic rankings bounce all over; with small schools a few kids scoring high or low can skew percentiles. Residents passed bond to improve schools.

East of Geyserville in the Alexander Valley, the Pomo Indians have erected a casino on their 75-acre reservation. The casino has come with arguments, some over traffic and infrastructure.

As much as these places are criticized, they often prove to be quite popular. If successful, the casino will bring in more visitors to north Sonoma. Cloverdale, just up the road, may add a casino.

GLEN ELLEN, KENWOOD

Santa Rosa

WINERY HAMLETS in the Sonoma Valley, about 7-12 miles north of City of Sonoma, off of Highway 12. Historical and gastronomic draw for visitors.

Glen Ellen homes tucked out of sight in the middle of miles of orchards and vineyards. Population was 1,191 in 1990 and 992 in 2000. A few shops.

Median age of residents is 41. Children and teens under 18 make up 29 percent of area.

In recent years, popular with the custom-home crowd. They like the country. One family built a striking country estate with blue slate, 12,000 square feet, then decided to use it for events, not for a home. Visible from Highway 12. Locals are getting prickly about development — the inescapable in Sonoma County.

Jack London Park. Museum. London, entranced with the nearby Valley of the Moon, built Wolf House here, 26 rooms, nine fireplaces, volcanic rock and redwood. Shortly before he was to move in, the place burned down. Its ruins still stand. An exciting writer ("The Call of the Wild") and a native son, London is remembered with great fondness in California and indeed many parts of the world. For London fans, Wolf House has become a sort of pilgrimage.

Still a lot of country here. In 1999, a bear ventured down from the mountains and climbed a tree in back of a restaurant. Wildlife people tranquillized it and turned it loose in the back country.

Glen Ellen kids attend Dunbar Elementary in the Sonoma Valley district. Scores in 30th to 70th percentile.

Kenwood, along with wineries, has plaza, small park. Shops, stores, restaurants. Noted for wine and restaurants. About a dozen luxury hotels have opened between Kenwood and the City of Sonoma. Volunteer firefighters sponsor Fourth of July Pillow Fight. Contestants sit astride a horizontal pole placed over a large pool of mud. Whack, whack, whack and splash to the loser.

Kenwood has own school district, one elementary school, kindergarten through sixth, enrollment 150. Academic rankings in 80s and 90s, California comparisons. In 2001 residents renewed a parcel tax to maintain programs and lower class sizes. Teens advance to Carrillo High in Santa Rosa.

GUERNEVILLE

RUSSIAN RIVER VILLAGE. Population About 2,500. Pronounced Gurn-ville. After a founding father who cut down many of the giant redwoods in the vicinity. A resort town, fetching in a quiet way. In the summer a dam usually is thrown across the river, backing it up so swimmers and canoeists won't scrape bottom. Lovely town in summer, spring and fall but soggy in winter.

Median age of residents is 42. Children and teens under 18 make up 20 percent of town, those over age 55 about 21 percent.

Vacation homes line the river. Some condos, some hotels, cabins for rent. Housing mixed. Many older homes. Restaurants, saloons, shops, a bakery, video rentals, a Safeway with a deli, small amusements scattered around town. Summer jazz festival. Seniors center.

A popular town with gays. Generally low key, don't-flaunt-it style but no apologies. Annual Women's Weekend, lesbian event. Also many straights.

Rarely makes the headlines for crime. The California Dept. of Justice reported zero homicides for the Russian River area from 1998 to 2001. One homicide in 2004; suspect convicted..

The Russian is one of five California rivers designated "wild," meaning no dams to prevent floods. Thus ... floods. In wet winters, the river rises into the streets and homes. About 250 homes along the river are built with floods in mind; the first story is a kiss-off, the second holds the valuables. Despite the known regularity of the floods, a few people always suffer serious losses. If you want to move to area, do your research on flooding.

Guerneville school district, enrollment 336, also serves nearby Rio Nido, another victim of floods and slides. Academic rankings in the last round of tests landed in the 40th to 70th percentile. Teens attend El Molino High in Forestville, scores in the 80th and 90th percentiles.

Armstrong Redwoods State Preserve, a short hike up, is a pleasing remnant of the ancient giants, some over 1,000 years old. Many second-growth redwoods. Another ancient grove a little to north was saved in 1998.

New bridge over river. Old bridge saved for pedestrians and cyclists. A little plaza — trees, fountain, benches, chess table — at the foot of the old bridge. Town is working on a plan to define and implement beauty in future buildings. Chamber of commerce: (707) 869-9000.

HEALDSBURG

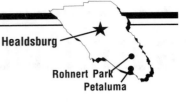

Healdsburg

Rohnert Park
Petaluma

RIVER TOWN noted for charm, 11,711 residents. Increased its population in the 1990s by 1,250. Many people would like to move to Healdsburg but the city, to protect the environment and way of life, has restricted the construction of homes.

Located north of Santa Rosa, just east of Highway 101, part of the wine-tourist circuit. Westside Road, dotted with wineries, leads right into Healdsburg. Many visitors stop in the downtown for meals and shopping between tastings. Fitch Mountain rises 991 feet to the east. The Russian River takes a pleasantly wide loop around the east side of town.

Healdsburg, which has preserved its history, was designed along lines that 30 or 40 years ago would have brought snorts of derision from any city planner but now strike us moderns as quaint and reassuring. The downtown has a square and, in the middle, a gazebo. Antique shops, art galleries, book stores, boutiques, a hotel, restaurants travel around the square and into adjoining streets. Wineries have opened tasting rooms and wine shops around town-square.

City spent about $2 million on downtown landscaping, parking and antique street lights, and on burying power lines. Old neighborhoods and downtown have been discovered by Hollywood for movies and commercials.

The streets are laid out on a grid pattern — logical, few suburban curli-cues. Around the old town are scattered homes from around the turn of the century and the early 1900s: Queen Annes, bungalows, cottages, homes built in the styles of Italianate, Greek, Mediterranean. Lived in, well-cared-for, cherished, a few catering to the bed-and-breakfast trade. Most of the apartments are clustered near center of town.

As you travel east on Fitch Mountain Road, the homes get newer and near the river custom homes and middle-class tracts can be found, the latter well-kept. Further out, vacation cottages line the river. State in 2005 counted 4,538 housing units: 3,255 single homes, 254 single attached, 930 apartments, 99 mobile homes.

Median age of residents is 37. Children and teens under 18 make up 26 percent of town. Rounded, the age groups about evenly divided.

In the 1980s, Healdsburg added about 2,200 people. Residents argued that the city was growing too fast and in danger of losing its charm. Developers have won permission to build at least 300 homes on the north. City officials say that within 10-15 years the town may have 13,000 residents. In 2000, residents voted to slow the pace of new homes: only 30 building permits to be issued each year. Hardly a year goes by when Healdsburg doesn't get into some argument over development.

School rankings range generally from the 30th to the 80th percentile. Town is moving toward upper middle class, which usually means high rankings.

Not too long ago, Healdsburg ran two separate elementary districts and a junior high-high school district, which also served Windsor. Now Healdburg's schools have been combined into a unified district. In 1999, Windsor opened its own high school, severing the last academic connection between the towns. In 1994, voters approved a $19.5 million bond to improve and expand Healdsburg Junior High and the high school.

In 2002, yet another bond was passed: $4 million to renovate more school facilities, replace the high-school track, fix up a kindergarten complex and install high-tech wiring.

Baseball, soccer, swimming (river and city pool), fishing, canoeing, nine-hole golf course, the wineries. Six parks, a museum. Farmers' market. Boys and Girls Club. Seniors' center. Annual guitar festival. Skate park. The latest park, 17 acres along the river, includes sports fields. Dog run at Badger Park.

Development rights to top of Fitch Mountain were purchased in 1994 by county government. An effort is being made to buy the mountain to keep it in open space. River is dammed in the spring to raise the water level for swimming and boating. Over a dozen bed-and-breakfast places. In 2005, downtown opened another upscale restaurant and more wine-food shops.

Library. Summer concerts in the gazebo park. Raven theater for community events, live comedy and music. Lots of cultural stuff: chamber music group, town band, town chorus, ballet, galleries, art shows. Small airport on the other side of the freeway. River Rock casino, Las Vegas gambling, has opened in Alexander Valley, a 15 minute drive from town.

New city hall, located about four blocks from plaza. Old city hall at the plaza was turned into a food store and cafe. Freeway bridge over river was replaced in 1999. Another bridge, a favorite of the town, was to have been replaced but residents rallied for an overhaul (seismic safety) and the state agreed.

Zero homicides between 1995 and 2004, one in 1994, zero for at least preceding three years, state Dept. of Justice and local newspaper reports. Chamber of commerce: (707) 433-6935.

MONTE RIO, OCCIDENTAL

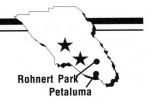

Rohnert Park
Petaluma

SMALL TOWNS that draw visitors and vacationers — Monte Rio, a resort that straddles the Russian River west of Guerneville, and Occidental, a tourist village on Route 116 between Sebastopol and Russian River. Monte Rio, population 1,104 (census 2000), is one of the few towns where men outnumber women, 579 to 525. Median age is 44. Kids make up 18 percent of town.

Every summer for about two weeks the world's movers and shakers gather at the nearby Bohemian Grove to play and to plot God knows what. Men only. Mucho secret. Among the participants in recent years, according to the locals, were the Bushes: George, ex pres, George W, pres, and Jeb, gov of Florida.

When the rains fall heavily, parts of Monte Rio flood, one of the drawbacks to living so close to the river. A nice place to drive to: vineyards, lots of pine, redwood, poppies, wild fern and laurel. In 2003, residents voted to build a sewage collection-treatment system.

Crime generally very low.

Occidental, population 1,272 (census 2000), is surrounded by redwood forest and ridges that, locals say, hold back fog and define neighborhoods: upper ridge, lower ridge. In 2000, the county government and a private group purchased 28 acres of old-growth redwoods near Occidental.

Median age of residents is 41. Children and teens under 18 make up 23 percent of hamlet.

Shops, restaurants along three blocks. Tiny library. Victorians peek out of hillsides, horses and sheep graze the upper ridges. Picturesque town, a favorite of people who want to drive the redwoods and take in a family-style Italian dinner. In 2003, the town, which occasionally runs out of water in the summer, secured a more reliable source.

One-school, Harmony-Salmon Creek, about 290 students. When enrollment declined, the second school was sold and is to be turned to live-work homes and offices and Victorian style homes. Money from sale went to improve the remaining school.

Rankings generally high, 50th to 80th percentile, California comparisons. Parcel tax to support curriculum, programs. Older children attend either El Molino High (Forestville) or Analy High (Sebastopol).

PETALUMA

Santa Rosa

Rohnert Park
Petaluma

RIVER TOWN, SECOND-LARGEST CITY in Sonoma County. Located near the southern border, straddling Highway 101. Best commute in the county to San Francisco but still a long 35 miles. Population 56,632. In the 1990s, Petaluma added 9,400 residents. Median age of residents is 37. Children and teens under 18 make up 26 percent of town. Rounded demographics.

Picturesque town, popular with the winers and diners and culturati. And becoming more so. Recently overhauled its downtown (again), cleaning up the riverfront and building a river promenade. More apartments, restaurants, amusements and a movie complex. Theater district.

Many arguments over growth, how to handle it and how to develop the downtown and preserve its history.

Petaluma also has some high tech and business parks on south and north.

New Petaluma to the east of the freeway, old Petaluma to the west. New suburban, old quaint, and the "location" for several movies, including "American Graffiti," "Peggy Sue Got Married," and many commercials. Liberal town, interested in the arts. City council has extended benefits to partners of unwed employees and registers the union of same-sex or unmarried couples.

Several years ago, one of our researchers visited Petaluma when a fire broke out in the downtown. Big fire. Loads of water pumped on it. One resident stationed himself by a storm drain and picked out the plastic and garbage before it could wash below (and ultimately out to sea). That kind of town; people care about the little things that add up to big things.

Mariano Vallejo, commandante of the Mexican excursion, built a hacienda-fort at Petaluma. It has been restored and is now a park. In the latter half of the 19th century, Petaluma was a farming center. Mansions, many still standing, were built in the old town. The 20th century saw Petaluma become probably the egg capital of the world. Eventually feed and labor costs drastically reduced the trade. Every May, Petaluma residents dress up in costumes of eggs, cows and chickens and celebrate the past with a Butter and Eggs Parade.

The town and its environs are served by seven elementary school districts, several consisting of just one school. Two largest are Old Adobe and Petaluma. After elementary, kids attend either Kenilworth or Petaluma junior highs, then either Casa Grande or Petaluma Union high schools. Academic rankings land

Sonoma County Single Family Home Prices

Place	Sales	Lowest	Median	Highest	Average
Bodega Bay	20	$525,000	$1,056,250	$1,650,000	$1,040,200
Camp Meeker	2	$380,000	$415,000	$450,000	$415,000
Cazadero	8	$330,000	$407,000	$599,000	$442,875
Cloverdale	50	$103,000	$474,000	$880,000	$480,006
Cotati	27	$160,000	$587,500	$900,000	$619,846
Forestville	31	$150,000	$450,000	$1,499,000	$508,940
Geyserville	6	$275,000	$875,000	$1,108,000	$783,250
Glen Ellen	15	$53,000	$622,000	$1,505,000	$705,000
Graton	6	$310,000	$545,000	$670,000	$508,600
Guerneville	55	$67,536	$430,000	$1,850,000	$448,331
Healdsburg	68	$87,000	$599,000	$1,895,000	$684,177
Kenwood	7	$132,818	$579,000	$2,870,000	$931,617
Monte Rio	12	$160,000	$450,000	$732,000	$451,818
Occidental	4	$569,000	$815,000	$900,000	$774,750
Penngrove	13	$307,500	$967,500	$2,025,000	$1,045,958
Petaluma	226	$85,000	$630,000	$1,700,000	$660,164
Rio Nido	6	$275,000	$354,000	$420,000	$349,600
Rohnert Park	125	$43,245	$555,000	$799,000	$568,948
Santa Rosa	814	$30,000	$562,500	$3,113,000	$626,720
Sebastopol	88	$237,500	$750,000	$2,000,000	$777,607
Sonoma	141	$45,000	$665,000	$3,650,000	$874,389
Windsor	153	$125,000	$627,477	$1,295,000	$641,158

Source: DataQuick Information Systems, Inc., La Jolla, Calif. **Key:** Resale single-family detached housing sales from May 1, 2005 to July 31, 2005.

generally well above the 50th percentile, California comparisons. The school district closed Kenilworth, sold the land for stores and mall and built a new junior high on the east side. Opened in 2005. Down through years, voters have approved renovation-construction bonds for almost every school in the region. Now the schools are trying for parcel taxes to retain programs. Some have failed, some passed. Parents are expected to chip in for programs.

Santa Rosa Junior College has opened in Petaluma two campuses: one with classrooms, computer and science labs and a library; the second, a tech academy in the Redwood Business Park. The college also rents classrooms at Casa Grande High School for night and weekend classes and for dance and exercise classes. More facilities, classes to be added.

Petaluma is part of what is called Telecom Valley, the Highway 101 corridor that extends to Santa Rosa. Rough economic times have shaken the valley but the region has retained its high-tech core and is still attracting firms. Municipal airport on the city's eastern border. Hangars. Tie-downs.

In 1993, Petaluma was made famous, sadly, by the kidnapping-killing of Polly Klaas, a local girl. Suspect, an ex-con, was arrested, tried and condemned to death. Despite this, Petaluma is not a high-crime town. Zero homicides in

2004, one in 2003, two in 2002, one each in 2001 and 2000, zero in 1999, two in 1998, one in 1997. The counts for previous years are two, one, two, two, zero, one, zero, zero, one.

For recreation: 22 tennis courts, two baseball fields, two softball, plus fields for kids (soccer, baseball, etc.), about 20 parks (one with lake), dog park, swim center, three gyms, bowling alley, three golf courses, driving range, hockey rink. Boys and Girls clubs. Community pool and skate park. City recreation programs. Teen center. BMX park (private). Fishing, boating, marina. Rowing, sculling. Christmas parade. County fair, summer music festival, farmers' market, library, museum, two playhouses (opera, drama, ballet), car races at the fairgrounds, river festival, ugly dog contest, quilt show, Heritage tours, poetry walk, arm wrestling championship, delis, good mix of (120) restaurants, art galleries, antique stores. Genuine night life: dining, dancing, drinking, chatting, plays, meeting people. Meryvns, Penneys near freeway. Auto mall pumps sales tax dollars into city amenities. Hotel and conference center at the marina. Trader Joe's. Whole Foods. Bookstore. Outlet mall that wants to expand. Recently added, Kohl's department store.

Housing units in 2005 totaled 21,265, of which 15,334 were single homes, 1,652 single-family attached, 3,348 apartments, 931 mobiles. If shopping for a home and wanting to avoid tract look, drive the downtown neighborhoods. You'll find the old, the ornate and the quaint, but mostly an assortment of ordinary homes, many built before World War II, that have been remodeled. Petaluma, east of the freeway, has been building tracts for decades. The farther east (and north) you travel, the newer the homes, but almost all fall within the description of middle class (with upper middle to rich prices).

Just west of Petaluma, at Two Rock, the Coast Guard runs an 800-acre training facility with a clinic that helps veterans. About 700 employees and families live on base, which trains about 4,000 personnel in a year and pumps about $30 million a year into the local economy. Children attend Two Rock elementary, scores in 70s and 80s, state comparison, then Petaluma schools.

After blowup over potholes, city council voted spent millions to fill and repave the streets. Chamber of commerce: (707) 762-2785. Visitor info: (707) 769-0429.

• One park is almost entirely planted in majestic walnut trees. After a branch fell and hit a woman (no injury), it was discovered that many trees were diseased. Most to be removed; replaced by yet-to-be majestic walnuts.

• Petaluma school district is debating when to start school year, mid or late August.

• New movie complex devotes some of its 12 screens to art and independent films.

• City hall trying to find ways to expedite downtown traffic.

ROHNERT PARK

Santa Rosa

Rohnert Park
Petaluma

MODERN SUBURB WITH A STATE UNIVERSITY. Started from scratch in the 1950s. Cleverly designed for kids and family life. Many retired. Many students. Low crime. May get an Indian casino. Population 42,445.

Like many towns in the county, Rohnert Park professes itself anti-growth but still manages to keep the hammers nailing. In the 1990s, Rohnert Park built about 1,500 housing units and increased its population by 6,000. Their median age is 32. Children and teens under 18 make up 25 percent of town. Rounded demographics.

Almost 100 percent suburb, which invites slurs of being dull and bland. No history or traditions worthy of note. No downtown or heart of town, although city is working to create one. Built on flat land, purchased from a farmer named Rohnert. Tract after tract of middle-class housing, located between Petaluma and Santa Rosa. Surrounded by open fields. Oriented to the car and the freeway. Not San Francisco, Toto, but not Kansas either. In a subdued and complicated way, sophisticated. Sonoma state students roll their eyes over Rohnert Park — definitely not cool. On weekends, many head for Santa Rosa or Petaluma or San Francisco.

But if you're older and can survive without a rollicking night life, Rohnert Park offers a lot. The shopping is convenient. The amusements are many. And the university, with its many activities, makes a big difference. Some of the city's characteristics:

• Sonoma State University, which plans to open a music center in 2008. Sonoma is attracting more professionals, more college educated and its interest in the arts has been increasing steadily.

Music and theater lovers, many in number, and university want to make the center a facility that will not only showcase the musical arts but encourage them. All this will benefit Rohnert Park and its smaller sibling, Cotati. The university through its lectures, its extension classes open to public, and its library and facilities also enriches local life. In 2000, thanks in large measure to the generosity of the late Charles Schulz ("Peanuts" and Charlie Brown) and his wife, Jean, the university opened a library tech center. It holds 450,000 books plus tapes, CDs, videos, etc.

About 8,000 students attend the university. More coming. University is moving from a traditional to an all-year program.

• Academic rankings middling to fairly high, mostly 50th to 80th percentile, California comparisons. Rohnert Park and Cotati share the school district and have demographics that mix kids from diverse backgrounds. This in part explains the rankings that jump all round. The towns in 1990 passed an $85 million bond to buy land, build schools and renovate existing ones. High school added a math and science building. Elementary schools offer before and after child care. In 2005, district lost a tax election by about 60 votes. Another try will probably be made.

School district spent $5 million to open high-school classrooms at Sonoma State University. This way, students can take advantage of university's science and computer labs and technology. Schools are pushing high-tech instruction. High school joined International Baccalaureate Program. Allows school to offer tough math, science and liberal arts classes.

• Commute awful, if employed in San Francisco, about 40 miles to the south. But Rohnert Park has a giant local employer in the university.

• Zero homicides in 2004, two in 2003, one each in 2002 and 2001, two in 2000, one in 1999, zero in 1998. The counts for previous years are zero, one, zero, zero, one. In the eight preceding years, zero.

• Parks, recreational activities many, another strong point of the city. Twelve parks, community center, seniors center, two 18-hole golf courses (city owned, just rebuilt), tennis, racquetball, and basketball courts, five public pools, roller skating rink, miniature golf, soccer and softball fields (popular sports), bowling alley, ballet, gymnastic and acting classes. Movie plex, 16 screens. Pools in the apartment complexes. Skate park. Teen center. Plus all the university offers: libraries, plays, college sports, summer sports clinics for kids. Unusually plentiful and, in fact, city hall says the town has more parks and recreational facilities than many cities twice its size. New library. Rohnert Park also has its own performing arts center, which stages plays and musicals and presents recitals and other artistic events.

• Shopping. Wal-Mart, Target, Home Depot, Costco, a giant supermarket and more, all located west of the freeway. Sales taxes help pay for city programs. Lowe's is building giant home improvement store in Cotati; to open in 2006.

• Good housing mix. The state in 2005 counted 16,020 housing units, 7,660 single-family detached, 1,699 single attached, 5,248 apartments or condos, 1,413 mobiles.

Some homes in the southern section, the oldest neighborhoods, are showing their age — paint peeling, weeds thriving — but these are the exceptions. For the most part, the city appears well-kept: median strips planted and litter free, lawns mowed, parks maintained, utility lines, on most streets, buried. Many of the apartments have been built along Snyder Way, which runs near the university. In 1999, the university added more apartment dorms. One or two of the tracts have gone upscale: brick and slate and three-car garages. But if ever a city deserved the title "middle America," Rohnert Park is it.

To understand the novelty of Rohnert Park it's necessary to emphasize what it isn't: old and established.

Many of the older suburban towns in the Bay Region started off as farming centers and railroad depots. So vital was the train that wherever the depot was built, the downtown — shops, restaurants, businesses, city hall, government buildings — followed. When the freeways came, they pulled so many shoppers to the malls and stores at their access ramps that the downtowns went into decline. There followed countless "redevelopment" or salvage efforts as the cities, loath to abandon their centers, tried to revamp them back to vitality. A few efforts succeeded, some failed, many are muddling through.

Rohnert Park, starting with 2,600 acres of grazing land, missed all this. It lacks the charm and pleasant (and not-so-pleasant) disarray of the old and the decayed. The university, in off-campus facilities, suffers from a dearth of boola-boola: very little or nothing in the way of cafes, beer and pizza joints, book and music stores.

In compensation, Rohnert Park boasts a clever, enlightened and comprehensive design that draws on the power of the freeway, slows the car and builds neighborhood intimacy. Following a master plan, the developer divided the city into neighborhood units, 200-250 homes per unit, each with a park and rec center and in combinations of several units, a school. The kids play, walk to school, and grow up with each other and, in the natural course of this arrangement, the parents come to know each other. Scattered through the neighborhoods are churches, a few stores and a medical complex — social glue of another sort.

Just about everything else that makes money — offices, businesses, hotels, stores — was zoned into the land near Highway 101. The Rohnert Park expressway moves arterial traffic from east to west, Snyder Lane and the freeway move it from north to south. Off the main roads, in the residential sections, curving streets, cul-de-sacs and the golf courses force drivers to slow their speeds. The library, post office and chamber of commerce were built near the expressway, close to the freeway. Also on the expressway but away from the freeway are the civic center and the performing arts center. No section calls attention to itself as a "downtown" but all are easily accessible. Cops and firefighters, called public safety officers, are one and the same and serve in a public safety department. The city created 12 full-time firefighting positions to improve protection at night. Two stations are staffed 24 hours a day.

The complaints and drawbacks: Some people don't like the universal suburban look. For those who do, for families, a town with a lot to offer.

Chamber of commerce: (707) 584-1415.

• In 2003, Kaiser opened medical offices in Rohnert Park. Kaiser is the largest medical-care provide in Sonoma County.

• City limits home construction to about 250 units a year. Frustrated developers would like to build thousands.

• In 2005 Agilent, which used to employ 2,000 in Rohnert Park, closed its plant and moved the remaining 400 jobs to Santa Rosa. Local developer, Coddington, and other firms purchased the 200 acres and plan to turn place into a high-tech business park mixed with housing. Plan to get people to walk to work and shop locally.

• Big fight over casino that has a good chance of going in west of town. Las Vegas slots, hotel, auditorium with 2,000 seats. Many details to be worked out. Casino would pump a lot of money into Rohnert Park but many residents oppose the place. Arguments continued through 2005.

Population by Age Groups in Sonoma County

City or Area	Under 5	5-19	20-34	35-54	55+
Agua Caliente-Fetters Hot Springs	181	589	527	840	368
Bodega Bay	51	151	215	401	605
Boyes Hot Springs	516	1,582	1,578	2,029	960
Cloverdale	478	1,583	1,279	1,942	1,549
Cotati	416	1,400	1,540	2,243	872
El Verano	258	902	743	1,334	717
Forestville	99	540	284	945	502
Guerneville	103	439	385	1,009	505
Healdsburg	632	2,492	1,908	3,315	2,375
Monte Rio	51	163	161	472	257
Occidental	53	267	204	514	234
Petaluma	3,612	11,967	9,653	18,720	10,596
Rohnert Park	2,656	10,006	10,643	12,824	6,107
Santa Rosa	9,606	30,180	31,142	44,502	32,165
Sebastopol	340	1,704	1,090	2,720	1,920
Sonoma	450	1,393	1,152	2,821	3,312
Windsor	1,818	5,744	3,716	7,445	4,021
County Total	27,597	97,238	86,212	149,452	98,115

Source: 2000 Census.

SANTA ROSA

Santa Rosa

Rohnert Park
Petaluma

LARGEST CITY, COUNTY SEAT of Sonoma County. Flat lands, hills and valleys. Split by Highway 101. Named by a padre who had a narrow escape from Indians on feast day of St. Rose of Lima. Population 156,268.

Median age of residents is 36. Children and teens under 18 make up 24 percent of town. Middle aged, the age groups about evingly divided.

A changing city that added about 30,000 people in the 1980s and 34,000 in the 1990s, became more sophisticated but still retains much of its small-town flavor. Used by Alfred Hitchcock in "Shadow of a Doubt" to symbolize the virtues of small-town America (Evil uncle flees big city, comes to Santa Rosa where he is undone by niece and cops.)

Charles Schulz, creator of the Peanuts comic strip (Lucy and Charlie Brown), lived in town and was generous in his support of community endeavors. Schulz died in 2000. In his memory, the town erected a statue near the old train depot. Before he died, Schulz funded a museum to display his collection of art and memorabilia and offer cartoon lessons to kids and adults.

Civic leaders and business people are doing a nice job of making the downtown pleasant and inviting. Movies, restaurants, shops, delis, etc. Opened in 2002: hotel with 155 rooms, restaurant and conference center for the downtown neighborhood west of Highway 101 and near railroad depot (Railroad Square).

In the population numbers, you can see the arguments that irritate the city and the region. Over the last 20 years, Santa Rosa, by itself, has added three times as many residents as all of neighboring Marin County.

The reason: pretty town with homes priced lower and apartments rented cheaper than just about any place in Marin County.

When you say Santa Rosa and Sonoma County, you're saying, choice, selection, variety. And middle- to upper middle-class "affordable" — by California's standard. Iowans and Texans would cringe at these prices.

The trade-off: If you work in San Fran (46 miles thither), you'll spend a good hour or more mornings and evenings on the freeway. Many people, however, have local jobs. And a different, though hard to pin down, style of life. Take a look at the Marin school rankings. A lot of 90s. In Santa Rosa, a lot of 90s, but also scores that bounce across the spectrum, especially in the elementary grades. More variety, more middle America, more ethnic diversity, yet still much support for education.

Santa Rosa is served by one high school-middle school district that is coupled to an elementary district, and by several elementary districts. All or almost all the elementary districts and the high school district in the 1990s have passed bonds to renovate or construct facilities. Several have passed parcel taxes to maintain programs.

Elsie Allen High School (after a Pomo Indian basket weaver) was opened in 1994. Maria Carrillo High School was opened in 1996. Santa Rosa High, with its classic front, was renovated at a cost of $8 million. Montgomery High School added a performing arts center. More improvements and additions are being made.

In 1993, after much debate, the high school district decided to leave students in their neighborhoods but with rapid growth school officials may have to change attendance boundaries. Check with school districts. In 1999, the high-school trustees voted to add more advanced placement courses.

In 1992, a school (kindergarten to third grade) opened in Agilent complex. Instead of neighborhood oriented, workplace oriented. The better for working parents to visit and pick up kids. University of San Francisco opened a satellite campus in downtown.

Close to wine country. Two centers for the arts. Two libraries, about 40 parks, two public lakes, ice arena, teen center, seniors center, aquatic center, summer camps for kids, roller-skating arena, movie theaters, bowling, softball, basketball, tennis, volleyball. Miles and miles of trails. Rose Festival Parade in May. Symphony orchestra. Sailing on Lake Ralphine. Fair grounds hosts the annual county fair, which draws 400,000, and other events. State university in nearby Rohnert Park. In 2003, San Jose Junior College opened a culinary center in the downtown; trains chefs and waiters.

Santa Rosa Junior College, enrollment about 40,000 per semester, offers classes at its downtown campus and at locations around the county. In summer, it offers classes for kids.

Neighborhood shopping plazas and two regional plazas: the downtown (Macy's, Sears, Mervyn's) and Coddingtown Center (Macy's, Penneys), located west of 101 and about a mile north of the downtown. A Costco and two Trader Joe's. Whole Foods market.

Santa Rosa has done a good job of reviving its downtown: stores, mall, restaurants, sidewalk cafes, Barnes and Noble bookstore, gym-health spa, billiard parlor, movie complexes and more. Ornamental brickwork, fountains, trees, artwork, flowers. On a Sunday morning, many head to Railroad Square, centered on the train depot, now a historical museum. Between antique shops and vintage stores, Omelette Express is popular for breakfast and A'roma

Home Price Sampler from Classified Ads

Forestville
- 3BR/2BA, $529,000
- 2BR/2BA, $475,000

Guerneville
- 2BR/2BA, $699,000
- 3BR/2BA, $615,000

Healdsburg
- 4BR/2.5BA, $655,000
- 4BR/3BA, $1.6 mil.

Occidental
- 2BR/2BA, $358,000

Petaluma
- 3BR/2BA, $579,000
- 4BR/3BA, $750,000

Rohnert Park
- 3BR/2.5BA, $585,000
- 3BR/2BA, $595,000

Santa Rosa
- 3BR/2BA, $519,000
- 3BR/2.5BA, $500,000
- 3BR/2.5BA, $889,000

Sebastopol
- 3BR/2BA, $699,000
- 4BR/3BA, $810,000

Sonoma
- 3BR/2BA, $600,000
- 3BR/2.5BA, $629,000
- 3BR/1BA $460,000

Windsor
- 3BR/2BA, $545,000
- 2BR/1BA, $440,000

Roasters draws a young crowd that chats over lattes and cappuccinos. Museum for kids. Downtown trolley for shoppers. In summer, on a weekday evening, thousands jam the downtown for festivities and the farmers' market. City is building a linear park along Santa Rosa Creek in the downtown.

For years, city has been tinkering with the downtown and fretting that it could not do more. With Petaluma and Windsor making drastic and generally well-received changes to their downtowns, Santa Rosa is thinking about moving faster.

Best choice of housing in the county: 61,586 housing units: 37,030 single homes, 5,760 single attached, 16,102 apartments, 2,694 mobile homes (2005 state count). In many towns, the higher the elevation, the better the view, the higher the price. To some extent, Santa Rosa follows this rule. Fountaingrove, probably the ultimate in Santa Rosa housing, looks down from the north hills. But a fair amount of first-class stuff was plopped on the valley floor west of Highway 101. And on some eastern hills, the housing runs suburban tract. Market forces greatly influenced Santa Rosa housing. When plain sold, it built plain. When fancy sold, it built fancy. If your budget says 1950 flattop, two bedrooms, drive some of the downtown neighborhoods. East of Highway 101, the town sends fingers down into valleys. Drive Bennett Valley Road, Yulupa Avenue, Summerfield Road. Lot of fairly new stuff. Some lovely old mansions and bungalows on and near McDonald Avenue (downtown).

Oakmont, a retirement community, jumped down Highway 12 into the Sonoma Valley, wine country. City is pushing development east of Highway 101 in the southern section. In 1996, Santa Rosa voted for tighter controls on growth.

Five homicides in 2004, two in 2003. Counts for previous years, 6, 3, 2, 5, 4, 10, 2, 4, 5, 7, 2, 6. Police substation in downtown mall. Trouble with teens. In 2004, the city voted in a quarter-cent sales tax to improve public safety and suppress gangs. In 2005, after a graduation party, four graduates and a mom were shot. None died but the town was shocked.

Two big unincorporated neighborhoods to south of city. Roseland, west of Highway 101, and South Santa Rosa. Older homes, many 1950s. Many kids. Good place to look if you lack bucks and want to break into housing market. Sheriff's substation in Roseland. County is spending $30 million to improve Roseland housing, get rid of toxic soil and upgrade the roads. Chamber of commerce: (707) 545-1414

• Believe it. One of the more famous local sons: Robert Ripley of Ripley's Believe It or Not.

• Work completed in 2003 on widening of Highway 101 to Rohnert Park. The job laid in car-pool lanes in each direction, new ramps, metering lights and sound walls. Money permitting, Highway 101 to the north will be widened. Federal dollars are now finding their way to Highway 101, which over the next few years should be widened in several spots along the journey to the Golden Gate Bridge. Highway 12 splits the town west to east and ends abruptly a few miles east of Highway 101, then picks up three or four miles to east.

• Sutter Health in 2004 won county permission to build medical center a few miles north of town, near Burbank Cultural Center. Construction to start in 2007; open 2009. Sutter also runs med center in downtown Santa Rosa; it will remain open but give up some beds.

• Opened in 2004, Santa Rosa Breast Care Center — screening, diagnosis, treatment, surgery, followup.

• High school district , concerned about losing enrollment to charter schools, is beefing up advanced academics at several schools to appeal to college-prep crowd.

• Not too long ago Santa Rosa allowed July Fourth fireworks. In 2003, a smoke bomb ignited a fire that destroyed a home. Bye-bye fireworks.

• Worries about high-tech quitting the county and sending jobs overseas. In recent years, Agilent has lost over 1,100 jobs in the county. The company has consolidated its operations into Santa Rosa, where it employs about 2,600.

• In 2005, city council passed an ordinance to classify graffiti as a misdemeanor, part of an effort to discourage taggers. The city also has imposed restrictions on the sale of aerosol paints and other graffiti tools.

Sea Ranch

Santa Rosa

Rohnert Park

Petaluma

SEA RANCH

SECOND-HOME COMMUNITY on the north coast. About 2,400 lots on 1,200 acres with another 4,000 acres or so set aside for buffer. Sea Ranch runs about 11 miles along the coast. Active resale-rental market. Many homes rented out weekends and holidays.

Diverse group of residents, many educators, doctors, professionals, some artists. One fellow described them as a "community of overachievers."

Some of the homes were designed by famous architects in the stovepipe style. Sea Ranch shows up in coffee table books: the homes, the Pacific, the bluffs, a pretty package.

Many of the homes are by the beach, many in the hills. The hill homes command great views of the Pacific. The shore homes also have their views, a different kind of spectacular. A small bluff rises from the Pacific and flattens out. Many of the homes are built back from the bluff; you can see the Pacific but not the crashing surf. But the shore homes are more intimate with the Pacific. Morning and evening you will see dozens of people hiking or jogging the shore trail or just watching the surf spray against the rocks.

About 600 people, half of them retired, live year-round. The two dozen or so kids attend Horicon Elementary in Annapolis; high school in Pt. Arena. Horicon passed a $4.2 million bond to make improvements.

Small landing strip but most come by car, up Route 1. When the roads are clear, 2 hours and 10 minutes from Golden Gate, about 90 miles to the south.

Community is run by homeowners group, which employs about two dozen and assesses fee on property owners for common maintenance. Design committee reviews plans for new homes; picky lot. You can't just throw up any old home in Sea Ranch.

Summer fog but real estate agents say that winds allow more sunshine than other locations on coast. Trails. Stables. Golf course. Recreation centers, restaurant. Tennis. Fishing. Two swimming pools. Gualala, a small trendy town, located to immediate north. Motels, stores, some restaurants. Watch the waves and surf.

SEBASTOPOL

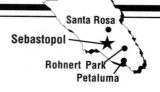

Santa Rosa
Sebastopol
Rohnert Park
Petaluma

COUNTRY CITY, ENTICING. Quietly upscale and artsy-progressive. Used to be famous for Gravenstein apples but these days seemingly everyone is growing grapes. Added about 1,400 residents in the 1980s and 774 in the 1990s. Population 7,794. Favors slow growth, small toilets and "green" construction.

Median age of residents is 42. Children and teens under 18 make up 24 percent of residents. Rounded demographics.

In and about the downtown, a good many ordinary homes, nice but not distinctive. Away from Main Street, custom homes pop up here and there, and the town has many well-kept older homes. Clean. Built over gentle hills. Open fields and orchards on edge of town but you can find horses grazing a few blocks from Main Street. Little nippy when fog creeps in from the ocean. Safe prediction: many will find Sebastopol charming.

The 2005 state count showed 3,358 housing units, of which 2,013 were single homes, 254 single attached, 1,032 apartments, 59 mobile homes. In the last decade, Sebastopol increased its housing stock by about 350 units and is working to bring in what is considered affordable homes. Also energy-efficient housing built with non-toxic materials. The city passed an ordinance requiring new homes to install dual-flush toilets. These toilets allow for one flush, if that's all required, or more if necessary.

In 1854, during the Crimean War, the British and French laid siege to the Russian fort at Sebastopol but were repulsed. About a year, later two men got into a fight near a general store in Sonoma County. One man took refuge in the store while the other man, forbidden to enter, stalked back and forth outside. Finally, he got tired and left. Just like the siege of Sebastopol, said a local wit. The remark amused residents and they decided to call their hamlet Sebastopol.

Served by Sebastopol Elementary District and West Sonoma High District, which runs Analy High in Sebastopol. Just about all the school rankings, compared to other California schools, are landing in the top 20th percentile.

In 1998, voters approved a parcel tax for Sebastopol Elementary District. Money was used for music, fine arts and instruction. The elementary district in 2001 followed up with a renovation-construction bond. Brook Haven Middle School was demolished and a new school built. Twin Hills school district, located to west, in 1999 won approval of a $4 million bond to renovate its two schools. In 2001, Gravenstein Elementary District approved a tax that will raise $60,000 a year for computers, library services and music. The high school district has also passed taxes to retain programs and renovate buildings.

In 2005, the Sebastopol elementary district and the high-school district again passed program-quality bonds, which require two-thirds approval. Other districts in the county attempted these bonds and failed and in many parts of California two-thirds bonds rarely pass.

This speaks well for the academic ambitions and values of Sebastopol and it reflects the changing demographics of Sebastopol. When they pass, these taxes usually find favor in high-income, high-education towns.

Sebastopol has its own police department. Overall crime rate is low. Zero homicides between 1994 and 2003, except for 1998, one homicide.

Six parks, including a preserve, five playgrounds, public swimming pool, public tennis courts. Bike-hiking path around town that may one day connect to Forestville. Bookstore, movies, at least two saloons, restaurants from fast food to haute cuisine. Antique stores. Deli. Farmers market. Some hot spots: Food for Thought, organic vegetables, Whole Foods, Screaming Mimi's ice cream shop. Lucy's Cafe for breakfast. Live music at Coffee Catz.

Swimming, soccer, Little League baseball. Teen center: games, pool table, large-screen TV, computers, dance and concert hall. Plaza with fountain, gazebo, benches, small pavilion. Holiday Inn with 82 rooms. Close to Russian River and Pacific and wineries. Santa Rosa offers mall shopping and more movies and restaurants. Celtic festival, Apple Blossom Festival. Repertory theater. Old rail line converted into bike trail. County animal shelter.

An intimate town. If your house catches fire in Sebastopol, your neighbors put out the blaze. Volunteer fire department (headed by a professional, full-time chief).

Town also has a small hospital, which ran into financial problems but seems to have weathered them. Residents in 2000 and 2004 approved taxes to give the town a say over the hospital's future and to expand the emergency room and improve its facilities and earthquake durability.

Highways 12 and 116 shoot over to Highway 101, a distance of about seven miles along Highway 12. One-way streets in the downtown to move traffic. Highway 12 sometimes gets overloaded with traffic.

Sebastopol, which has acre-plus zoning for some parcels, has been holding the line on big-time development and trying to fine tune the smaller commerce to give the town's economy a stronger footing. Artists have set up shop in some buildings. The apple businesses are closing, bringing to market parcels that might be turned to a mix of residential, retail and light industry. On wish list: a small department store. Chamber of commerce: (707) 823-3032.

SONOMA

Santa Rosa

Sonoma

Petaluma

WHEN IT COMES TO HISTORY, California cities rarely cough up anything worth a second look but this small city, population 9,834, is an exception.

At Sonoma, Spain's (and later Mexico's) reach into California ended with the construction of a mission, barracks and the home of Mariano Vallejo, one of the great figures of the Hispanic era.

Here the Bear Flag was raised for the first time and the first blow struck for the U.S. conquest of California. Some historians take a dim view of the insurrection, arguing it was unnecessary, clumsy and fueled by liquor. Others see the Bear Flaggers as heroes.

Decades later the mission and barracks and other buildings were restored with the happy result that Sonoma has one of most pleasing town squares in California. Throw in the fields, vineyards, wineries and horse ranches of the Sonoma Valley and the green hills that almost ring the town and you come up with oodles of charm.

Academic scores range from the 50th to 80th percentile. Residents in 1994 came through with a $27 million bond that was used to renovate all the schools in the district, rewire them for high-tech equipment and purchase land to expand the high school. In 2004 , they came through again with a parcel tax for libraries and teacher retention. For parents dissatisfied with the customary ways of public education, the school district runs a charter school that gives teachers and parents more freedom to decide how the students will be taught.

Median age of residents is 47. Children and teens under 18 make up 19 percent of town. Many empty nesters, retirees and adults, few children.

Zero homicides 1996 through 2004. In 2004, city disbanded its police department and contracted with sheriff for protection. Station remains in town.

The Golden Gate is 45 tedious miles to the southwest but, according to local Realtors, some buyers are softening the commute by "telecommuting" at home a few days a week. For East Bay cities, the miles are slightly fewer (about 35 to Walnut Creek) but often the freeways are congested.

Typical sports and activities for kids, adults and seniors: soccer and football, social and service clubs. Boys and Girls Club. Community center. Good mix of first-class restaurants, sustained by tourists. Wine tastings. Spas. Festivals and events that spin off the history and wine-country ambiance.

Californians are notoriously indifferent to history. Temperamentally we feel more comfortable with the modern and the novel and what history we have lacks blood and glory — no Valley Forge, no Gettysburg, no Wild Bill or Geronimo or cattle drives to Abilene or Wyatt Earp blazing away at the OK Corral. About the best we can muster is Zorro. Nonetheless, the history is there, in its own way fascinating: the race for empire, the hubris of the Californios, the tragedy of the Indians, the misguided courage of the padres, the dash and the deviousness of the Yankees. Sonoma, with its restorations, calls up this past and invites us to find out more about ourselves and how we got where we are.

The town, however, is not a postcard re-creation of Old California. Sonoma incorporated as a city in 1900 but almost all its residential development came after World War II. In appearance and design, most of the streets and homes can be described as suburban presentable: clean, lawns mowed, flowers planted, etc. And in its habits, the town is moving toward a suburban pattern: more residents are commuting. But Sonoma is not a typical bedroom community. For one thing, the mission and historical buildings give it a sense of continuity that's lacking in many suburban towns. For another, its parts hang together differently. Only in the late 20th century has Sonoma become commute reachable and this means that it developed as a small country town.

Sebastiani runs its winery almost within a block of the mission and the town square. Other wineries are located nearby. Within a mile or two of the downtown and close to housing tracts, cattle moo, sheep baaa, horses whinny. Restaurants, shops, bookstores and a movie theater ring the town square. Besides city hall, the square itself contains duck ponds and several playgrounds with swings and slides and a small museum.

Other towns stick work in one corner and play in another and the homes somewhere else. Sonoma jumbles them together, in an old-fashioned way — to a more noticeable extent. The suburban feel is there but so is the country. The state in 2005 counted 5,071 residential units: 2,876 single homes, 698 single attached, 1,060 apartments or condos, 437 mobile homes.

For years, Sonoma attracted retirees. The 1990 census placed 40 percent of residents over age 55, but by 2000 this number had slipped to 36 percent. Several family tracts were erected in the 1990s. The town added about 550 housing units in the 1990s. Although much of the new housing is aimed at the upper middle class, Sonoma is getting its upscale and $1 million plus homes..

In summer and on many weekends, the town is loaded with tourists. Chamber of commerce: (707) 996-1033.

• Sonoma County taxes itself to raise money for parks and open space. A private group, called the Coastal Conservancy, also buys land or development rights. The two and the City of Sonoma got together in 2005 to buy 157 acres overlooking the historic district. The purchase will spare the parcel from development and, it is hoped, keep the city and the region pretty and scenic. Hikers welcome.

WINDSOR

NEWEST CITY IN SONOMA COUNTY, formed 13 years ago. Spent the 1990s catching up on schools and roads and stores, the latter for ease of shopping and for a stronger tax base. Many new or fairly new homes. Population 25,475.

Charming and interesting downtown, modern shops, restaurants and townhomes in "vintage" buildings, circa 1900, around a town square. One of the most innovative downtowns in Northern California. Even if you are not buying in Windsor, the downtown is worth a visit.

Median age of residents is 35. Children and teens under 18 make up 31 percent of Windsor. This is a lot of kids and marks Windsor as a family town.

Served by Windsor district, which has built several schools and in 1999 opened its own high school. In statewide comparisons, scores are landing generally in the 60th and 70th percentiles but some scores are erratic. Windsor educates many limited-English kids from the wine country. This affects the scores but for the most part the district posts what's expected from a middle-class community.

Kindergartners and first-graders attend one school, second- and third-graders another, fourth- and fifth-graders, yet another. Then there's the middle school and the high school. Windsor district also runs a charter school, Cali Calmecac, grades kindergarten to eighth, that offers Spanish-English immersion. School wants all kids speaking both languages by sixth grade.

Two homicides in 2004, one each in 2003, 2002 and 2001, zero in 2000, 1999, 1998 and 1997, two in 1996, zero in 1995 and 1994. Windsor contracts with the sheriff's office to run and staff its police department. New police station. New fire station.

If you have a job in Sonoma County, the commute is congested but short. If you work in Marin and can get on the freeway just a little before peak hours, the commute is endurable, 30-40 minutes each way. If you work in downtown San Francisco, 60 miles off, we're talking stomach acid by the bucket.

Nice-looking town that is receiving a lot of the old tender loving from residents: lawns mowed, streets clean, homes and businesses well kept, graffiti absent. Some homes are built around small lakes. Gated community in the center of town. Hills on east border, hills to distant west. Small vineyards. Open country at the borders.

Many recreational choices. About 10 parks, mix of neighborhood, community and regional. Russian River to the west and the Pacific is within a half-hour drive. Public golf course, 18 holes. Seniors' center with pool and spa. Community gym. Boys and Girls Club, next to middle school. Water slides, Library. Usual sports: soccer, baseball, football. City hall runs programs and activities for all ages: aerobics, computer classes, dancing, karate, kinder club, gymnastics, dancing, guitar, etc. Starbucks, restaurants, shops, several supermarkets, Home Depot, Wal-Mart. Santa Rosa and all its offerings are about seven miles to the south. About 100 wineries in the region. Cinco De Mayo Celebration.

Nourished by the railroad, Windsor came to life in the last century as a farming hamlet. Supposedly the fields and hills reminded an early resident of the lands around Windsor Castle — hence the name. In the 1950s and 1960s the town, which was unincorporated and under the jurisdiction of the county government, added a few two- and three-bedroom tracts and by 1980 the population had risen to 6,100.

In the 1980s, Sonoma County residents began to protect vineyards and farms and limit growth. At the same time, the forces for development were strong and the demand for housing was hot.

Caught in the middle, county supervisors backed away from the vineyards and shunted a lot of growth into Windsor, which is split by Highway 101 and probably would have been developed in any event. There was a good market for modestly upscale single homes and that's pretty much what Windsor got, laid out in tracts that used modern planning techniques.

Homes were buffered from arterial traffic, land was set aside for schools and parks, the shops and stores were placed near the freeway. The new residents, many of them middle-class professionals, soon became disenchanted with how things were run. Homes went up quickly, roads and freeway ramps were improved not so quickly, causing traffic jams.

In 1992, voters said "enough of this" and incorporated Windsor into a legal city, taking control of planning, zoning, building permits, parks and recreation, police protection and more. Residents passed a $28.5 million bond to build schools. After incorporation, a lot of energy went into building the city's infrastructure. The state in 2005 counted 8,731 housing units, of which 6,803 were single homes, 460 single attached, 646 apartments, and 822 mobiles.

Voters approved a measure establishing an urban limit and the city council slowed the pace of construction. Civic leaders favor home designs that blend past and present. Some newer homes recall porches of yesterday and are built among older farm houses. In 2002, a measure to slow construction even more was rejected by voters.

In the old Windsor downtown, west of the freeway, the city has been working to create a true heart. To this end, it has built a civic center, a library and installed a village green with a fountain and bandstand. It has also welcomed homes and apartments and businesses that complement the desired style, approximately Old West with a modern twist — live-work units, a condo building with a clock tower, a bookstore, a gym, a wine boutique and more.

The description might come across as presenting the downtown as something different but not that different. Actually, it is quite different, and illustrates the new thinking of smart growth and designs that encourage walking (as opposed to hopping in the car) and community friendliness.

Another section to the south may get similar treatment, and about 1,800 housing units. In 2005, plans were being discussed.

Chamber of commerce: (707) 838-7285.

• In 2003, the Sonoma Open Space District, supported by local taxes, purchased a gravel mine located on the Russian River, two miles west of Windsor. Open to the public, the 305 acres take in three man-made lakes and hundreds of tall redwoods. Trails, picnic grounds, boat launch.

• Wish list: town pool, better fire protection. Money short; arguments and agonizing over what should be funded first.

• Old railroad right-of-way winds through countryside. Windsor and other communities are talking about using the rail path as a hiking path.

Chapter **9a**

State School Rankings

HERE ARE COMPARISON RANKINGS from the 2005 STAR tests taken by almost every public-school student in California. This test is administered annually by the California Department of Education.

We have broken out the results in a way that makes comparisons between schools easy.

The rankings, based on the scores, range from 1 (the lowest) to 99 (the highest). A school that scores in the 20th percentile is landing in the bottom 20 percent of the state. A school that scores in the 95th percentile is placing among the top 5 percent of schools in the state.

These rankings should be considered rough measures of how the schools and their students are performing.

Many low- and middle-scoring schools have students who score high. Many high-scoring schools have students who land below the 25th percentile.

A few schools post average scores but turn out many high-scoring students. These schools often will have many students at the bottom and many at the top and few in the middle.

For more information, visit the school or go on the web and check out reports about individual schools. For more test results, go to www.star.cde.ca.gov. See also the school accountability reports.

To flesh out these scores, we are including in Chapter 9B a ranking system issued by the California Department of Education and in Chapter 10 the SAT scores, math and verbal, for the regular high schools. These scores and a chart that presents SAT scores by state will give you some idea of how local schools compare to schools nationwide.

Scores range from 1-99. A school scoring 75 has done better than 75 percent of other public schools in California.
Key: Eng (English), Ma (Math), Sci (Science).

San Francisco County

San Francisco Unified School Dist.

A. P. Giannini Middle

Grade	Eng	Ma	Sci
6	79	85	
7	85	93	
8	86		

Abraham Lincoln High

Grade	Eng	Ma	Sci
9	68		
10	79		
11	87		

Aim High Academy

Grade	Eng	Ma	Sci
6	28	21	
7	36	22	

Alamo Elem.

Grade	Eng	Ma	Sci
2	86	82	
3	83	90	
4	86	88	
5	89	87	74

Alvarado Elem.

Grade	Eng	Ma	Sci
2	73	76	
3	80	77	
4	66	52	
5	69	69	61

Aptos Middle

Grade	Eng	Ma	Sci
6	72	64	
7	82	84	
8	79		

Argonne Elem.

Grade	Eng	Ma	Sci
2	79	86	
3	81	86	
4	87	85	
5	89	85	80

Balboa High

Grade	Eng	Ma	Sci
9	49		
10	41		
11	35		

Benjamin Franklin Middle

Grade	Eng	Ma	Sci
6	2	12	
7	6	19	
8	9		

Bryant Elem.

Grade	Eng	Ma	Sci
2	27	11	
3	15	38	
4	28	24	
5	10	15	14

Buena Vista Annex

Grade	Eng	Ma	Sci
2	10	11	
3	52	33	
4	43	46	
5	39	36	67

Burton Acad.

Grade	Eng	Ma	Sci
9	39		
10	58		
11	54		

Cabrillo Elem.

Grade	Eng	Ma	Sci
2	51	77	
3	72	92	
4	56	53	
5	45	43	33

Carmichael Elem.

Grade	Eng	Ma	Sci
2	57	46	
3	34	39	
4	20	8	
5	34	26	16

Carver Elem.

Grade	Eng	Ma	Sci
2	85	88	
3	21	17	
4	34	36	
5	17	4	15

Chavez Elem.

Grade	Eng	Ma	Sci
2	28	44	
3	51	57	
4	20	25	
5	23	25	27

Chin Elem.

Grade	Eng	Ma	Sci
2	75	94	
3	56	85	
4	86	97	
5	82	99	72

Chinese Education Center

Grade	Eng	Ma	Sci
2	1	3	
3	1	13	
4	1	71	
5	2	67	1

City Arts and Tech High

Grade	Eng	Ma	Sci
9	60		

Clarendon Elem.

Grade	Eng	Ma	Sci
2	89	88	
3	92	83	
4	95	88	
5	89	75	83

Cleveland Elem.

Grade	Eng	Ma	Sci
2	30	46	
3	26	7	
4	28	36	
5	45	47	74

Cobb Elem.

Grade	Eng	Ma	Sci
2	78	82	
3	49	13	
4	21	4	
5	32	18	36

Commodore Sloat Elem.

Grade	Eng	Ma	Sci
2	91	85	
3	69	83	
4	83	81	
5	76	78	77

Scores range from 1-99. A school scoring 75 has done better than 75 percent of other public schools in California.

Key: Eng (English), Ma (Math), Sci (Science).

Grade	Eng	Ma	Sci
Creative Arts Char.			
2	2	44	
3	73	48	
4	53	16	
5	78	35	75
6	85	63	
7	69	72	
8	68		
Cross Cultural Academy			
9	56		
10	48		
Davis Middle			
7	7	8	
8	12		
Downtown High (Cont.)			
9	2		
10	7		
11	8		
Drew Elem.			
2	10	9	
3	29	29	
El Dorado Elem.			
2	21	22	
3	39	41	
4	27	27	
5	39	37	27
Everett Middle			
6	4	5	
7	15	9	
8	15		
Fairmount Elem.			
2	12	19	
3	14	10	
4	18	6	
5	20	6	27
Flynn Elem.			
2	6	13	
3	20	25	
4	21	12	
5	12	16	14
Francis Scott Key Elem.			
2	73	63	
3	79	94	
4	80	88	
5	82	90	84
Francisco Middle			
6	27	30	
7	44	59	
8	34		
Galileo High			
9	74		
10	73		
11	63		
Garfield Elem.			
2	81	88	
3	75	98	
4	87	97	
5	82	96	80

Grade	Eng	Ma	Sci
Gateway High			
9	87		
10	78		
11	84		
George Washington High			
9	78		
10	80		
11	89		
Glen Park Elem.			
2	35	19	
3	79	42	
4	55	52	
5	57	43	51
Golden Gate Elem.			
2	86	90	
4	74	90	
5	49	63	38
Grattan Elem.			
2	65	40	
3	81	70	
4	41	28	
5	62	43	66
Guadalupe Elem.			
2	56	71	
3	62	70	
4	60	58	
5	57	58	63
Harte Elem.			
2	17	7	
3	33	24	
4	8	13	
5	36	11	5
Herbert Hoover Middle			
6	86	85	
7	87	88	
8	92		
Hillcrest Elem.			
2	20	22	
3	12	12	
4	14	6	
5	19	21	32
Horace Mann Middle			
6	11	8	
7	20	17	
8	35		
Independence High (Alt.)			
10	47		
11	38		
Intl Studies Academy			
9	43		
10	35		
11	44		
James Denman Middle			
6	41	22	
7	44	33	
8	55		

Scores range from 1-99. A school scoring 75 has done better than 75 percent of other public schools in California.

Key: Eng (English), Ma (Math), Sci (Science).

Grade	Eng	Ma	Sci
James Lick Middle			
6	26	47	
7	15	22	
8	17		
Jefferson Elem.			
2	85	90	
3	80	82	
4	91	85	
5	92	94	89
King Middle			
6	30	30	
7	41	54	
8	55		
KIPP Bayview Academy			
5	22	28	23
6	57	71	
KIPP S.F. Bay Academy			
5	40	54	23
6	43	29	
Lafayette Elem.			
2	61	72	
3	66	73	
4	77	66	
5	78	61	75
Lakeshore Elem.			
2	54	61	
3	61	57	
4	83	80	
5	73	86	76
Lau Elem.			
2	69	85	
3	63	86	
4	55	82	
5	55	62	38
Lawton Elem.			
2	83	90	
3	82	79	
4	86	87	
5	84	80	80
6	97	98	
7	90	96	
8	94		
Leadership High (Char.)			
9	67		
10	65		
11	80		
Life Learning Acad. Char.			
9	26		
10	28		
11	39		
Lilienthal Elem.			
2	83	91	
3	97	98	
4	91	88	
5	92	73	84
6	86	86	
7	96	97	
8	82		

Grade	Eng	Ma	Sci
Longfellow Elem.			
2	56	72	
3	81	89	
4	83	94	
5	71	77	50
Lowell High			
9	99		
10	99		
11	99		
Luther Burbank Middle			
6	13	9	
7	23	18	
8	19		
Malcolm X Academy (Elem.)			
2	21	44	
3	15	32	
4	2	3	
5	8	14	26
Marina Middle			
6	48	68	
7	65	78	
8	65		
Marshall Elem.			
2	23	33	
3	4	16	
4	5	11	
5	21	8	21
Marshall High			
9	37		
10	42		
11	44		
Maxwell Middle			
6	4	4	
7	10	8	
8	25		
McCoppin Elem.			
2	53	68	
3	51	73	
4	52	62	
5	78	38	49
McKinley Elem.			
2	61	62	
3	47	35	
4	78	78	
5	22	12	25
Milk Civil Rights Elem.			
2	53	24	
3	72	68	
4	72	81	
5	33	38	42
Miraloma Elem.			
2	58	42	
3	60	39	
4	26	7	
5	62	57	81
Mission Education Center			
2	1	1	
3	1	1	
4	1	2	
5	1	2	1

Scores range from 1-99. A school scoring 75 has done better than 75 percent of other public schools in California.
Key: Eng (English), Ma (Math), Sci (Science).

Grade	Eng	Ma	Sci
Mission High			
9	33		
10	30		
11	41		
Monroe Elem.			
2	27	24	
3	39	47	
4	46	63	
5	39	61	55
Moscone Elem.			
2	72	78	
3	78	94	
4	67	74	
5	76	83	60
Muir Elem.			
2	5	3	
3	18	10	
4	13	6	
5	34	55	35
New Traditions Elem.			
2	82	53	
3	51	60	
4	85	76	
5	52	28	15
Newcomer High			
9	1		
10	2		
11	1		
O'ConnellHigh			
9	25		
10	43		
11	64		
Ortega Elem.			
2	62	75	
3	70	81	
4	31	51	
5	52	51	44
Parker Elem.			
2	73	87	
3	72	93	
4	36	71	
5	25	39	31
Parks Elem.			
2	4	2	
3	33	33	
4	12	4	
5	74	83	83
Peabody Elem.			
2	59	43	
3	58	65	
4	81	92	
5	76	74	71
Presidio Middle			
6	81	90	
7	90	96	
8	88		
Raoul Wallenberg Traditional High			
9	56		
10	57		
11	83		

Grade	Eng	Ma	Sci
Redding Elem.			
2	49	55	
3	29	55	
4	50	78	
5	62	55	53
Revere Elem.			
2	5	6	
3	17	13	
4	12	16	
5	15	46	17
Rooftop Elem.			
2	79	84	
3	81	47	
4	85	82	
5	82	83	74
6	83	87	
7	98	97	
8	98		
Roosevelt Middle			
6	72	82	
7	67	88	
8	65		
San Francisco Comm. Alt.			
2	86	92	
3	82	71	
4	55	70	
5	37	55	54
6	54	50	
7	65	58	
8	64		
Sanchez Elem.			
2	22	10	
3	37	60	
4	54	37	
5	34	40	21
School of the Arts (High)			
9	98		
10	93		
11	92		
Serra Elem.			
2	49	64	
3	32	25	
4	36	22	
5	26	25	28
Sheridan Elem.			
2	97	83	
3	91	72	
4	63	75	
5	27	38	63
Sherman Elem.			
2	89	94	
3	80	91	
4	66	59	
5	61	69	77
Small School for Equity High			
9	35		
10	50		

Scores range from 1-99. A school scoring 75 has done better than 75 percent of other public schools in California.

Key: Eng (English), Ma (Math), Sci (Science).

Grade	Eng	Ma	Sci
Spring Valley Elem.			
2	73	77	
3	55	75	
4	87	95	
5	68	77	62
Starr King Elem.			
2	7	7	
3	47	25	
4	23	22	
5	14	21	15
Stevenson Elem.			
2	95	96	
3	82	92	
4	82	89	
5	91	88	95
Sunnyside Elem.			
2	54	57	
3	66	69	
4	41	49	
5	53	45	42
Sunset Elem.			
2	74	80	
3	58	76	
4	67	66	
5	73	91	75
Sutro Elem.			
2	56	51	
3	64	69	
4	73	76	
5	82	89	65
Swett Elem.			
2	19	21	
3	4	5	
4	14	3	
5	22	13	14
Taylor Elem.			
2	63	79	
3	64	84	
4	77	84	
5	57	76	47
Tenderloin Comm.			
2	11	21	
3	36	48	
4	17	7	
5	37	79	51
Treasure Island Elem.			
2	23	17	
3	3	3	
4	4	3	
5	13	6	8
6	16	24	
7	55	71	
8	53		
Twenty-First Century Elem.			
4	4	3	
5	6	8	2
6	4	4	

Grade	Eng	Ma	Sci
Ulloa Elem.			
2	89	89	
3	82	91	
4	84	86	
5	88	91	85
Visitacion Valley Elem.			
2	58	78	
3	50	70	
4	45	63	
5	54	70	56
Visitacion Valley Middle			
6	24	21	
7	49	48	
8	29		
Webster Elem.			
2	24	43	
3	44	70	
4	9	39	
5	21	50	29
Wells Alt. High			
9	25		
10	23		
11	16		
West Portal Elem.			
2	95	97	
3	96	97	
4	85	88	
5	93	93	91
William de Avila Elem.			
2	37	21	
3	30	13	
4	32	28	
5	21	22	20
Yick Wo Elem.			
2	64	87	
3	72	96	
4	76	95	
5	76	95	88
Yu Elem.			
2	93	93	
3	85	91	
4	86	96	
5	98	98	89
6	96	98	
7	99	99	
8	97		

SBE-Edison Char. Academy Sch. Dist.

SBE-Edison Char. Academy

Grade	Eng	Ma	Sci
2	34	41	
3	61	52	
4	31	43	
5	37	22	28
6	29	22	

Scores range from 1-99. A school scoring 75 has done better than 75 percent of other public schools in California.
Key: Eng (English), Ma (Math), Sci (Science).

Grade	Eng	Ma	Sci	Grade	Eng	Ma	Sci

San Mateo County

Bayshore Elem. School Dist.
Bayshore Elem. (Daly City)

Grade	Eng	Ma	Sci
2	27	12	
3	45	50	
4	11	18	

Robertson Int. (Daly City)

Grade	Eng	Ma	Sci
4	65	64	
5	35	34	37
6	32	38	
7	64	86	
8	50		

Belmont-Redwood Shores Elem. Dist.
Central Elem. (Belmont)

Grade	Eng	Ma	Sci
2	92	94	
3	94	95	
4	87	75	
5	94	91	92

Cipriani Elem. (Belmont)

Grade	Eng	Ma	Sci
2	85	70	
3	91	84	
4	72	78	
5	57	62	72

Fox Elem. (Belmont)

Grade	Eng	Ma	Sci
2	87	86	
3	96	97	
4	90	91	
5	88	84	87

Nesbit Elem. (Belmont)

Grade	Eng	Ma	Sci
2	78	82	
3	52	63	
4	65	56	
5	19	26	29

Ralston Int. (Belmont)

Grade	Eng	Ma	Sci
6	89	93	
7	91	89	
8	93		

Sandpiper Elem. (Redwood City)

Grade	Eng	Ma	Sci
2	91	91	
3	89	86	
4	92	80	
5	87	85	86

Brisbane Elem. School Dist.
Brisbane Elem. (Brisbane)

Grade	Eng	Ma	Sci
2	71	65	
3	44	22	
4	67	50	
5	79	36	73

Lipman Middle (Brisbane)

Grade	Eng	Ma	Sci
6	60	65	
7	75	72	
8	78		

Panorama Elem. (Daly City)

Grade	Eng	Ma	Sci
2	54	42	
3	62	41	
4	60	44	
5	49	49	48

Burlingame Elem. School Dist.
Burlingame Int.

Grade	Eng	Ma	Sci
6	93	81	
7	93	82	
8	89		

California Virtual Academy

Grade	Eng	Ma	Sci
2	66	27	
3	81	21	
4	89	22	
5	67	12	69
6	87	59	
7	77	32	
8	78		

Franklin Elem.

Grade	Eng	Ma	Sci
2	93	90	
3	89	93	
4	98	98	
5	95	96	90

Lincoln Elem.

Grade	Eng	Ma	Sci
2	91	89	
3	93	82	
4	93	87	
5	91	84	86

McKinley Elem.

Grade	Eng	Ma	Sci
2	84	80	
3	73	66	
4	71	50	
5	86	71	86

Roosevelt Elem.

Grade	Eng	Ma	Sci
2	90	97	
3	92	87	
4	75	76	
5	83	76	79

Washington Elem.

Grade	Eng	Ma	Sci
2	65	69	
3	66	35	
4	75	34	
5	81	85	67

Cabrillo Unified School Dist.
Cunha Int. (Half Moon Bay)

Grade	Eng	Ma	Sci
6	64	63	
7	73	66	
8	85		

El Granada Elem. (El Granada)

Grade	Eng	Ma	Sci
2	31	40	
3	56	63	
4	69	68	
5	68	74	67

Scores range from 1-99. A school scoring 75 has done better than 75 percent of other public schools in California.
Key: Eng (English), Ma (Math), Sci (Science).

Grade	Eng	Ma	Sci
Farallone View Elem. (Montara)			
2	52	52	
3	66	50	
4	68	68	
5	61	52	62
Half Moon Bay High (Half Moon Bay)			
9	72		
10	83		
11	80		
Hatch Elem. (Half Moon Bay)			
2	20	46	
3	59	64	
4	59	58	
5	53	52	34
Kings Mountain Primary			
2	90	98	
4	97	99	
Pilarcitos High (Cont.) (Half Moon Bay)			
11	17		

Hillsborough City Elem. Sch. Dist.

Grade	Eng	Ma	Sci
Crocker Middle			
6	99	98	
7	99	99	
8	99		
North Hillsborough Elem.			
2	99	99	
3	99	98	
4	99	85	
5	99	97	97
South Hillsborough Elem.			
2	99	99	
3	99	99	
4	99	98	
5	97	97	92
West Hillsborough Elem.			
2	96	99	
3	99	99	
4	98	99	
5	99	98	96

Jefferson Elem. School Dist.

Grade	Eng	Ma	Sci
Anthony Elem. (Daly City)			
2	36	29	
3	46	42	
4	49	45	
5	53	45	55
Brown Elem. (Daly City)			
2	48	56	
3	73	63	
4	52	31	
5	68	64	58
6	53	56	
Edison Elem. (Daly City)			
2	54	41	
3	61	66	
4	49	46	
5	68	73	76
6	71	71	

Grade	Eng	Ma	Sci
Franklin Int. (Colma)			
7	54	50	
8	59		
Garden Village Elem. (Colma)			
2	54	61	
3	52	51	
4	66	64	
5	46	64	41
6	72	82	
John F. Kennedy Elem. (Daly City)			
2	36	35	
3	51	51	
4	50	55	
5	42	14	39
Pollicita Middle (Daly City)			
6	33	23	
7	43	33	
8	52		
Rivera Int. (Daly City)			
7	73	70	
8	55		
Roosevelt Elem. (Daly City)			
2	67	56	
3	57	22	
4	69	37	
5	49	22	68
6	41	23	
Tobias Elem. (Daly City)			
2	41	29	
3	71	70	
4	76	70	
5	63	33	67
6	73	79	
Washington Elem. (Daly City)			
2	80	79	
3	67	82	
4	66	61	
5	83	67	77
Webster Elem. (Daly City)			
2	54	46	
3	71	52	
4	48	52	
5	67	67	59
6	66	75	
Westlake Elem. (Daly City)			
2	48	31	
3	57	66	
4	48	70	
5	51	49	47
6	51	54	
Woodrow Wilson Elem. (Daly City)			
2	22	35	
3	61	61	
4	32	36	
5	38	39	28
6	36	40	

Scores range from 1-99. A school scoring 75 has done better than 75 percent of other public schools in California.

Key: Eng (English), Ma (Math), Sci (Science).

Grade	Eng	Ma	Sci

Jefferson Union High
Jefferson High (Daly City)

Grade	Eng	Ma	Sci
9	50		
10	43		
11	51		

Oceana High (Pacifica)

Grade	Eng	Ma	Sci
9	78		
10	80		
11	76		

Terra Nova High (Pacifica)

Grade	Eng	Ma	Sci
9	88		
10	81		
11	80		

Thornton High (Cont.) (Daly City)

Grade	Eng	Ma	Sci
10	12		
11	5		

Westmoor High (Daly City)

Grade	Eng	Ma	Sci
9	74		
10	78		
11	74		

La Honda-Pescadero Unified Sch. Dist.
La Honda Elem. (La Honda)

Grade	Eng	Ma	Sci
2	94	98	
3	95	93	
4	97	88	

Pescadero Elem. (Pescadero)

Grade	Eng	Ma	Sci
2	4	38	
3	17	9	
4	13	10	
5	11	2	30
6	75	60	
7	58	63	
8	72		

Pescadero High (Pescadero)

Grade	Eng	Ma	Sci
9	73		
10	83		
11	58		

Las Lomitas Elem. School Dist.
La Entrada Middle (Menlo Park)

Grade	Eng	Ma	Sci
4	98	98	
5	97	97	97
6	98	98	
7	99	99	
8	99		

Las Lomitas Elem. (Atherton)

Grade	Eng	Ma	Sci
2	98	99	
3	97	98	

Menlo Park City Elem. School Dist.
Encinal Elem. (Atherton)

Grade	Eng	Ma	Sci
3	97	94	
4	96	91	
5	98	88	99

Hillview Middle

Grade	Eng	Ma	Sci
6	97	97	
7	97	97	
8	98		89

Laurel Elem. (Atherton)

Grade	Eng	Ma	Sci
2	94	89	

Oak Knoll Elem.

Grade	Eng	Ma	Sci
2	95	91	
3	94	90	
4	97	96	
5	96	93	94

Millbrae Elem. School Dist.
Green Hills Elem.

Grade	Eng	Ma	Sci
2	74	31	
3	77	90	
4	78	66	
5	72	71	71

Lomita Park Elem. (San Bruno)

Grade	Eng	Ma	Sci
2	40	32	
3	65	79	
4	77	75	
5	76	51	69

Meadows Elem.

Grade	Eng	Ma	Sci
2	85	85	
3	86	89	
4	79	63	
5	76	44	67

Spring Valley Elem.

Grade	Eng	Ma	Sci
2	84	91	
3	72	86	
4	88	87	
5	89	97	84

Taylor Middle

Grade	Eng	Ma	Sci
6	80	89	
7	91	94	
8	89		

Pacifica School Dist.
Cabrillo Elem.

Grade	Eng	Ma	Sci
2	81	84	
3	85	87	
4	86	81	
5	91	93	91
6	91	92	
7	86	79	
8	93		

Ingrid B. Lacy Middle

Grade	Eng	Ma	Sci
6	74	62	
7	78	47	
8	78		

Ocean Shore Elem.

Grade	Eng	Ma	Sci
2	95	92	
3	84	62	
4	91	83	
5	96	78	88
6	80	85	
7	90	84	
8	96		

Ortega Elem. School

Grade	Eng	Ma	Sci
2	73	82	
3	81	68	
4	64	38	
5	66	19	44

Scores range from 1-99. A school scoring 75 has done better than 75 percent of other public schools in California.
Key: Eng (English), Ma (Math), Sci (Science).

Grade	Eng	Ma	Sci
Sunset Ridge Elem.			
2	57	40	
3	54	37	
4	51	36	
5	56	63	46
Vallemar Elem.			
2	89	79	
3	85	86	
4	82	68	
5	88	95	94
6	87	77	
7	86	93	
8	94		

Portola Valley Elem. School Dist.
Corte Madera Elem.

Grade	Eng	Ma	Sci
4	97	87	
5	99	98	99
6	99	96	
7	99	98	
8	99		
Ormondale Elem.			
2	98	96	
3	99	97	

Ravenswood City Elem. School Dist.
Belle Haven Elem. (Menlo Park)

Grade	Eng	Ma	Sci
2	11	13	
3	8	11	
4	5	3	
5	8	6	17
6	3	5	
7	40	35	
8	15		
Chavez Academy (Elem.) (East Palo Alto)			
4	7	29	
5	5	18	9
6	7	17	
7	15	22	
8	13		
Costano Elem. (East Palo Alto)			
2	91	96	
3	27	8	
4	10	6	
5	21	7	15
6	14	4	
7	25	9	
8	13		
East Palo Alto Char. (East Palo Alto)			
2	74	94	
3	61	78	
4	57	89	
5	52	88	65
6	46	68	
7	21	97	
8	39		
East Palo Alto High (East Palo Alto)			
9	28		
10	27		
11	9		

Grade	Eng	Ma	Sci
Edison-Brentwood Academy			
2	40	53	
3	12	26	
Edison-McNair Academy (East Palo Alto)			
4	11	13	
5	9	11	11
6	14	22	
7	17	31	
8	13		
Flood Elem. (Menlo Park)			
2	55	74	
3	60	57	
4	39	29	
5	59	35	36
6	35	49	
7	54	52	
8	41		
Forty-Niner Academy (East Palo Alto)			
6	2	4	
7	12	13	
8	21		
Green Oaks (East Palo Alto)			
2	2	4	
3	2	2	
Willow Oaks Elem. (Menlo Park)			
2	9	4	
3	9	4	
4	2	3	
5	4	4	7
6	6	7	
7	28	58	
8	28		

Redwood City Elem. School Dist.
Adelante Span. Imm. Elem.

Grade	Eng	Ma	Sci
2	24	45	
3	38	49	
4	38	61	
5	67	85	77
6	54	43	
7	67	57	
8	56		
Clifford Elem.			
2	77	79	
3	72	84	
4	65	70	
5	80	77	73
6	76	82	
7	89	83	
8	75		
Cloud Elem.			
2	85	80	
3	86	88	
4	77	79	
5	76	81	67
6	89	86	
7	98	97	
8	91		

Scores range from 1-99. A school scoring 75 has done better than 75 percent of other public schools in California.

Key: Eng (English), Ma (Math), Sci (Science).

Grade	Eng	Ma	Sci
Fair Oaks Elem.			
2	5	6	
3	15	10	
4	6	11	
5	15	11	8
Ford Elem.			
2	40	46	
3	40	31	
4	49	65	
5	47	55	59
Garfield Char. (Elem.)			
2	8	26	
3	5	17	
4	18	23	
5	11	44	9
6	11	16	
7	16	54	
8	51		
Gill Elem.			
2	63	61	
3	51	47	
4	62	63	
5	53	52	25
Hawes Elem.			
2	32	18	
3	20	30	
4	21	31	
5	22	34	17
Hoover Elem.			
2	15	53	
3	15	45	
4	15	42	
5	18	39	25
6	11	11	
7	30	50	
8	33		
Kennedy Middle			
6	39	52	
7	55	64	
8	50		
McKinley Institute of Tech.			
6	15	12	
7	24	25	
8	15		
North Star Academy (Elem.)			
3	99	99	
4	99	97	
5	99	99	98
6	99	98	
7	99	99	
8	99		
Orion Alt.			
2	46	46	
3	79	71	
4	86	69	
5	87	80	73

Grade	Eng	Ma	Sci
Roosevelt Elem.			
2	17	15	
3	7	6	
4	51	72	
5	44	26	29
Selby Lane Elem. (Atherton)			
2	55	72	
3	30	46	
4	45	78	
5	19	35	14
6	32	27	
7	33	29	
8	55		
Taft Elem.			
2	9	21	
3	4	11	
4	12	22	
5	3	12	4
San Bruno Park Elem. School Dist.			
Allen Elem.			
2	71	47	
3	63	57	
4	52	40	
5	39	30	33
6	48	59	
Belle Air Elem.			
2	33	33	
3	52	55	
4	58	69	
5	49	70	30
6	66	65	
Crestmoor Elem.			
2	93	85	
3	90	83	
4	88	88	
5	83	78	79
6	88	94	
El Crystal Elem.			
2	73	33	
3	76	85	
4	66	66	
5	61	62	50
6	64	78	
John Muir Elem.			
2	76	65	
3	77	78	
4	80	83	
5	86	72	70
6	87	88	
Parkside Int.			
7	59	59	
8	56		
Portola Elem.			
2	89	95	
3	75	70	
4	77	89	
5	55	58	45
6	74	77	

Scores range from 1-99. A school scoring 75 has done better than 75 percent of other public schools in California.

Key: Eng (English), Ma (Math), Sci (Science).

Rollingwood Elem.

Grade	Eng	Ma	Sci
2	54	32	
3	59	56	
4	75	76	
5	70	60	51
6	80	81	

San Carlos Elem. School Dist.

Arundel Elem.

Grade	Eng	Ma	Sci
2	85	94	
3	75	72	
4	86	83	

Brittan Acres Elem.

Grade	Eng	Ma	Sci
2	91	90	
3	93	86	
4	83	69	

Central Middle

Grade	Eng	Ma	Sci
5	86	69	83
6	86	80	
7	92	91	
8	89		

Char. Learning Center

Grade	Eng	Ma	Sci
2	84	85	
3	92	62	
4	90	65	
5	97	77	93
6	97	90	
7	95	87	
8	99		

Heather Elem.

Grade	Eng	Ma	Sci
2	80	90	
3	81	68	
4	89	71	

San Carlos High

Grade	Eng	Ma	Sci
9	64		
10	52		

Tierra Linda Middle

Grade	Eng	Ma	Sci
5	94	92	89
6	86	87	
7	95	96	
8	96		

White Oaks Elem.

Grade	Eng	Ma	Sci
2	83	80	
3	90	81	
4	97	94	

San Mateo Union High School Dist.

Aragon High

Grade	Eng	Ma	Sci
9	92		
10	94		
11	95		

Burlingame High (Burlingame)

Grade	Eng	Ma	Sci
9	92		
10	91		
11	89		

Capuchino High

Grade	Eng	Ma	Sci
9	69		
10	72		
11	74		

Hillsdale High

Grade	Eng	Ma	Sci
9	81		
10	80		
11	67		

Mills High (Millbrae)

Grade	Eng	Ma	Sci
9	92		
10	96		
11	94		

Peninsula High Cont.

Grade	Eng	Ma	Sci
10	31		
11	47		

San Mateo High

Grade	Eng	Ma	Sci
9	87		
10	87		
11	80		

San Mateo-Foster City Elem. Sch. Dist.

Abbott Middle (San Mateo)

Grade	Eng	Ma	Sci
6	67	47	
7	60	49	
8	67		

Audubon Elem. (Foster City)

Grade	Eng	Ma	Sci
2	83	82	
3	88	83	
4	85	73	
5	80	68	66

Bayside Middle (San Mateo)

Grade	Eng	Ma	Sci
6	45	24	
7	36	39	
8	36		

Baywood Elem. (San Mateo)

Grade	Eng	Ma	Sci
2	90	91	
3	96	96	
4	96	94	
5	91	90	92

Beresford Elem. (San Mateo)

Grade	Eng	Ma	Sci
2	26	34	
3	34	54	
4	22	38	
5	42	58	45

Borel Middle (San Mateo)

Grade	Eng	Ma	Sci
6	75	72	
7	72	60	
8	74		

Bowditch Middle (Foster City)

Grade	Eng	Ma	Sci
6	92	91	
7	92	89	
8	94		

Brewer Island Elem. (Foster City)

Grade	Eng	Ma	Sci
2	95	91	
3	97	92	
4	97	96	
5	97	95	97

Fiesta Gardens Int. Elem. (San Mateo)

Grade	Eng	Ma	Sci
2	7	44	
3	55	62	
4	64	59	
5	77	40	61

Scores range from 1-99. A school scoring 75 has done better than 75 percent of other public schools in California.

Key: Eng (English), Ma (Math), Sci (Science).

Grade	Eng	Ma	Sci
Foster City Elem. (Foster City)			
2	79	80	
3	85	90	
4	92	87	
5	92	92	89
George Hall Elem. (San Mateo)			
2	31	57	
3	43	55	
4	46	36	
5	62	86	53
Highlands Elem. (San Mateo)			
2	78	72	
3	91	92	
4	91	85	
5	91	97	96
Horrall Elem. (San Mateo)			
2	26	8	
3	32	27	
4	40	61	
5	28	22	28
Laurel Elem. (San Mateo)			
2	63	60	
3	74	83	
4	89	87	
5	92	88	85
Meadow Heights Elem. (San Mateo)			
2	66	72	
3	76	94	
4	93	97	
5	96	98	94
North Shoreview Elem. (San Mateo)			
2	49	50	
3	34	64	
4	45	26	
5	42	14	34
Park Elem. (San Mateo)			
2	32	31	
3	64	39	
4	47	45	
5	53	52	37
Parkside Elem. (San Mateo)			
2	58	44	
3	65	69	
4	57	45	
5	60	49	68
Sunnybrae Elem. (San Mateo)			
2	49	59	
3	64	59	
4	43	39	
5	29	24	43
Turnbull Learning Academy (San Mateo)			
2	4	7	
3	7	7	
4	14	13	
5	10	10	10

Grade	Eng	Ma	Sci
Sequoia Union High			
Carlmont High (Belmont)			
9	90		
10	90		
11	84		
Menlo-Atherton High (Atherton)			
9	86		
10	87		
11	83		
Redwood High (Cont.) (Redwood City)			
10	1		
11	14		
Sequoia District Comm. (Redwood City)			
9	8		
Sequoia High (Redwood City)			
9	63		
10	59		
11	62		
Woodside High (Woodside)			
9	77		
10	83		
11	75		

South San Francisco Unified Sch. Dist.

Grade	Eng	Ma	Sci
Alta Loma Middle			
6	48	42	
7	58	53	
8	57		
Baden High (Cont.)			
8	15		
10	26		
11	32		
Buri Buri Elem.			
2	66	54	
3	72	71	
4	73	69	
5	73	85	78
El Camino High			
9	78		
10	82		
11	68		
Hillside Elem.			
2	46	49	
3	26	12	
4	26	7	
5	45	29	40
Junipero Serra Elem. (Daly City)			
2	65	59	
3	60	67	
4	68	46	
5	70	77	69
Los Cerritos Elem.			
2	35	18	
3	41	42	
4	56	52	
5	38	56	58

Scores range from 1-99. A school scoring 75 has done better than 75 percent of other public schools in California.
Key: Eng (English), Ma (Math), Sci (Science).

Grade	Eng	Ma	Sci
Martin Elem.			
2	39	42	
3	33	50	
4	23	49	
5	62	81	76
Monte Verde Elem. (Daly City)			
2	72	70	
3	73	74	
4	68	60	
5	75	67	78
Parkway Heights Middle			
6	34	26	
7	46	34	
8	33		
Ponderosa Elem.			
2	84	87	
3	77	78	
4	60	49	
5	79	78	86
Skyline Elem. (Daly City)			
2	70	66	
3	56	79	
4	60	44	
5	51	46	48
South San Francisco High			
9	74		
10	68		
11	74		

Grade	Eng	Ma	Sci
Spruce Elem.			
2	41	59	
3	38	50	
4	36	52	
5	43	81	54
Sunshine Gardens Elem.			
2	35	23	
3	46	48	
4	50	26	
5	52	59	69
Westborough Middle			
6	61	65	
7	63	78	
8	66		
Woodside Elem. School Dist.			
Woodside Elem. (Woodside)			
2	87	86	
3	99	90	
4	99	99	
5	98	97	96
6	98	96	
7	99	98	
8	99		

Scores range from 1-99. A school scoring 75 has done better than 75 percent of other public schools in California.
Key: Eng (English), Ma (Math), Sci (Science).

Grade	Eng	Ma	Sci

Marin County

Bolinas-Stinson Union Elem. Sch. Dist.
Bolinas Elem.

Grade	Eng	Ma	Sci
3	84	51	
4	87	64	
5	83	57	77
6	77	44	
7	73	80	
8	88		

Dixie Elem. School Dist. (San Rafael)
Dixie Elem.

Grade	Eng	Ma	Sci
2	98	98	
3	97	96	
4	83	84	
5	96	91	93

Miller Creek Middle

Grade	Eng	Ma	Sci
6	91	95	
7	95	93	
8	92		

Silveira Elem.

Grade	Eng	Ma	Sci
2	73	74	
3	85	79	
4	82	90	
5	81	75	78

Vallecito Elem.

Grade	Eng	Ma	Sci
2	90	85	
3	91	90	
4	93	85	
5	98	95	92

Kentfield Elem. School Dist.
Bacich Elem.

Grade	Eng	Ma	Sci
2	94	94	
3	99	97	
4	98	89	

Kent Middle

Grade	Eng	Ma	Sci
5	98	96	94
6	98	93	
7	99	98	
8	98		

Lagunitas Elem. School Dist.
Lagunitas Elem. (San Geronimo)

Grade	Eng	Ma	Sci
3	44	20	
4	80	41	
5	73	11	89
6	82	48	
7	85	67	
8	61		

Larkspur Elem. School Dist.
Hall Middle (Larkspur)

Grade	Eng	Ma	Sci
6	98	94	
7	95	96	
8	98		

Neil Cummins Elem. (Corte Madera)

Grade	Eng	Ma	Sci
2	91	90	
3	89	84	
4	97	97	
5	93	91	88

Mill Valley Elem. School Dist.
Maguire Elem.

Grade	Eng	Ma	Sci
2	96	96	
3	96	95	
4	98	92	
5	97	97	99

Mill Valley Middle

Grade	Eng	Ma	Sci
6	97	94	
7	97	95	
8	97		

Old Mill Elem.

Grade	Eng	Ma	Sci
2	94	96	
3	95	92	
4	98	85	
5	95	86	96

Park Elem.

Grade	Eng	Ma	Sci
2	84	92	
3	96	96	
4	92	81	
5	92	86	93

Strawberry Point

Grade	Eng	Ma	Sci
2	91	98	
3	98	96	
4	88	90	
5	94	92	97

Tamalpais Valley Elem.

Grade	Eng	Ma	Sci
2	97	96	
3	99	99	
4	99	88	
5	98	96	97

Nicasio Elem. School Dist.
Nicasio Elem.

Grade	Eng	Ma	Sci
4	94	93	

Novato Unified School Dist.
Hamilton Meadow Park Elem.

Grade	Eng	Ma	Sci
2	69	39	
3	60	55	
4	78	82	
5	34	37	37

Hill Middle

Grade	Eng	Ma	Sci
6	70	69	
7	82	83	
8	89		

Loma Verde Elem.

Grade	Eng	Ma	Sci
2	72	71	
3	55	72	
4	64	69	
5	75	71	68

Scores range from 1-99. A school scoring 75 has done better than 75 percent of other public schools in California.
Key: Eng (English), Ma (Math), Sci (Science).

Grade	Eng	Ma	Sci
Lu Sutton Elem.			
2	74	83	
3	72	68	
4	63	58	
5	71	51	59
Lynwood Elem.			
2	50	44	
3	41	20	
4	83	84	
5	93	90	89
Marin Oaks High			
11	36		
Marin School of Arts & Tech.			
9	87		
10	94		
Nova Ed. Ctr. (Ind. Study)			
10	86		
11	59		
Novato Char. (Elem.)			
2	80	73	
3	95	73	
4	83	92	
5	89	57	79
6	93	85	
7	84	71	
8	98		
Novato High			
9	80		
10	83		
11	86		
Olive Elem.			
2	73	61	
3	65	67	
4	63	82	
5	73	61	66
Pleasant Valley Elem.			
2	97	97	
3	93	86	
4	93	98	
5	88	86	96
Rancho Elem.			
2	98	93	
3	99	98	
4	96	97	
5	91	95	93
San Jose Middle			
6	83	84	
7	65	82	
8	84		
San Marin High			
9	89		
10	91		
11	91		
San Ramon Elem.			
2	64	51	
3	88	88	
4	82	85	
5	85	88	84

Grade	Eng	Ma	Sci
Sinaloa Middle			
6	91	92	
7	92	97	
8	90		

Reed Union Elem. School Dist. (Tiburon)

Grade	Eng	Ma	Sci
Bel Aire Elem.			
3	97	94	
4	99	93	
5	96	87	95
Del Mar Int.			
6	98	92	
7	99	97	
8	98		
Reed Elem.			
2	96	96	

Ross Elem. School Dist.

Grade	Eng	Ma	Sci
Ross Elem.			
2	88	86	
3	99	98	
4	99	96	
5	99	91	98
6	99	99	
7	98	96	
8	99		

Ross Valley Elem. School Dist.

Grade	Eng	Ma	Sci
Brookside Elem. (San Anselmo)			
2	89	82	
3	98	98	
4	98	98	
5	95	92	97
Manor Elem. (Fairfax)			
2	81	92	
3	90	75	
4	91	79	
5	80	69	91
Wade Thomas Elem. (San Anselmo)			
2	97	98	
3	99	95	
4	98	94	
5	90	86	91
White Hill Middle (Fairfax)			
6	96	81	
7	98	93	
8	95		

San Rafael City Elem. School Dist.

Grade	Eng	Ma	Sci
Bahia Vista Elem.			
2	6	33	
3	23	39	
4	46	55	
5	23	53	18
Coleman Elem.			
2	64	95	
3	48	27	
4	55	68	
5	61	86	84

Scores range from 1-99. A school scoring 75 has done better than 75 percent of other public schools in California.

Key: Eng (English), Ma (Math), Sci (Science).

Grade	Eng	Ma	Sci
Gallinas Elem.			
2	37	54	
3	40	26	
4	65	82	
5	72	80	40
6	56	69	
7	46	72	
8	54		
Glenwood Elem.			
2	99	99	
3	99	99	
4	94	94	
5	93	89	81
James B. Davidson Middle			
6	49	56	
7	67	71	
8	66		
Laurel Dell Elem.			
2	19	55	
3	51	64	
4	53	39	
5	23	48	31
San Pedro Elem.			
2	47	49	
3	9	27	
4	3	4	
5	13	27	6
Sun Valley Elem.			
2	85	87	
3	91	82	
4	98	98	
5	93	78	94

San Rafael City High School Dist.

Grade	Eng	Ma	Sci
Madrone High (Cont.)			
11	20		
San Rafael High			
9	69		
10	74		
11	80		
Terra Linda High			
9	89		
10	94		
11	81		

Sausalito Marin City School Dist.

Grade	Eng	Ma	Sci
Bayside Elem.			
2	58	64	
3	67	94	
4	32	32	
5	49	15	53
6	36	11	
King Academy			
7	19	12	
8	59		
Willow Creek Academy			
2	24	34	
4	45	8	

Shoreline Unified School Dist.

Grade	Eng	Ma	Sci
Tomales Elem. (Tomales)			
2	56	59	
3	64	84	
4	48	43	
5	80	91	82
6	63	62	
7	71	70	
8	76		
Tomales High (Tomales)			
9	75		
10	82		
11	64		
West Marin Elem. (Pt. Reyes)			
2	94	97	
3	61	54	
4	70	13	
5	62	26	66
6	69	53	
7	75	67	
8	55		

Tamalpais Union High School Dist.

Grade	Eng	Ma	Sci
Redwood High (Larkspur)			
9	97		
10	98		
11	97		
San Andreas High (Cont.) (Larkspur)			
10	51		
11	42		
Sir Francis Drake High (San Anselmo)			
9	95		
10	95		
11	96		
Tamalpais High (Mill Valley)			
9	94		
10	95		
11	93		
Tamiscal High (Alt.) (Larkspur)			
10	99		
11	99		

Scores range from 1-99. A school scoring 75 has done better than 75 percent of other public schools in California.

Key: Eng (English), Ma (Math), Sci (Science).

Sonoma County

Alexander Valley Union Elem. Sch. Dist.
Alexander Valley Elem.

Grade	Eng	Ma	Sci
2	57	63	
3	84	45	
4	80	60	
5	65	14	69
6	43	42	

Bellevue Union Elem. School Dist.
Bellevue Elem. (Santa Rosa)

Grade	Eng	Ma	Sci
2	30	38	
3	12	13	
4	36	32	
5	40	47	38
6	29	33	

Kawana Elem. (Santa Rosa)

Grade	Eng	Ma	Sci
2	6	12	
3	10	12	
4	37	26	
5	11	21	4
6	31	38	

Meadow View Elem. (Santa Rosa)

Grade	Eng	Ma	Sci
2	27	39	
3	20	27	
4	34	21	
5	21	39	18
6	31	41	

Bennett Valley Union Elem. School Dist.
Strawberry Elem. (Santa Rosa)

Grade	Eng	Ma	Sci
4	86	72	
5	84	83	88
6	86	93	

Yulupa Elem. (Santa Rosa)

Grade	Eng	Ma	Sci
2	87	72	
3	87	71	

Cinnabar Elem. School Dist.
Cinnabar Elem.

Grade	Eng	Ma	Sci
2	65	60	
3	49	25	
4	75	70	
5	69	78	75
6	77	79	

Cloverdale Unified School Dist.
Cloverdale High

Grade	Eng	Ma	Sci
9	77		72
10	78		75
11	71		

Jefferson Elem.

Grade	Eng	Ma	Sci
2	38	60	
3	38	36	

Washington

Grade	Eng	Ma	Sci
4	49	58	
5	51	40	57
6	45	46	
7	69	61	
8	46		

Cotati-Rohnert Park Unified School Dist.
Comm. Day

Grade	Eng	Ma	Sci
8	5		
9	10		

Creekside Middle (Rohnert Park)

Grade	Eng	Ma	Sci
6	68	43	
7	68	72	
8	75		

El Camino High

Grade	Eng	Ma	Sci
10	42		
11	4		

Evergreen Elem. (Rohnert Park)

Grade	Eng	Ma	Sci
2	72	70	
3	81	89	
4	63	59	
5	66	33	54

Gold Ridge Elem. (Rohnert Park)

Grade	Eng	Ma	Sci
2	63	76	
3	69	65	
4	47	61	
5	67	61	70

Hahn Elem. (Rohnert Park)

Grade	Eng	Ma	Sci
2	73	70	
3	92	90	
4	79	69	
5	91	81	80

La Fiesta Elem. (Rohnert Park)

Grade	Eng	Ma	Sci
2	45	65	
3	50	50	
4	51	37	
5	52	16	50

Monte Vista Elem. (Rohnert Park)

Grade	Eng	Ma	Sci
2	77	67	
3	74	84	
4	70	66	
5	71	68	78

Mountain Shadows Middle (Rohnert Park)

Grade	Eng	Ma	Sci
6	40	30	
7	55	54	
8	43		

Page Elem. (Cotati)

Grade	Eng	Ma	Sci
2	53	49	
3	76	65	
4	44	48	
5	60	26	51

Phoenix High (Cont.)

Grade	Eng	Ma	Sci
10	11		

Scores range from 1-99. A school scoring 75 has done better than 75 percent of other public schools in California.
Key: Eng (English), Ma (Math), Sci (Science).

Grade	Eng	Ma	Sci
Rancho Cotate High (Rohnert Park)			
9	73		
10	59		
11	63		
Reed Elem. (Rohnert Park)			
2	18	19	
3	37	29	
4	31	27	
5	48	37	64
Rohnert Elem. (Rohnert Park)			
2	52	53	
3	38	21	
4	51	34	
5	56	52	57
Technology High (Rohnert Park)			
9	95		
10	96		
11	96		

Dunham Elem. School Dist.
Dunham Elem. (Petaluma)

Grade	Eng	Ma	Sci
2	69	52	
3	86	76	
4	95	96	
5	76	59	79
6	87	81	

Forestville Union Elem. School Dist.
Forestville Elem.

Grade	Eng	Ma	Sci
2	71	69	
3	74	74	
4	84	74	
5	75	66	77
6	80	86	
7	84	57	
8	78		

Fort Ross Elem. School Dist.
Fort Ross Elem.

Grade	Eng	Ma	Sci
6	68	70	

Geyserville Unified School Dist.
Geyserville Educational Park High

Grade	Eng	Ma	Sci
9	42		
10	77		
11	76		
Geyserville Elem.			
2	28	7	
3	23	3	
4	30	8	
5	37	29	37
Geyserville Middle			
6	65	72	
7	32	41	
8	52		

Gravenstein Union Elem.
Gravenstein Elem. (Sebastopol)

Grade	Eng	Ma	Sci
2	75	84	
3	82	73	
4	83	89	
5	68	64	62
Hillcrest Middle			
4	97	93	
5	96	94	95
6	97	87	
7	81	65	
8	80		

Guerneville Elem. School Dist.
Guerneville Elem.

Grade	Eng	Ma	Sci
2	65	88	
3	43	57	
4	53	48	
5	59	70	77
6	63	56	
7	89	91	
8	79		

Harmony Union Elem. School Dist.
Harmony Elem. (Occidental)

Grade	Eng	Ma	Sci
2	57	59	
3	77	45	
4	66	37	
Pathways Char. (Occidental)			
2	31	43	
3	59	12	
4	63	10	
5	73	15	76
6	73	39	
7	87	43	
8	74		
9	73		
10	75		
11	59		
Salmon Creek Middle (Occidental)			
5	89	80	90
6	86	86	
7	87	86	
8	87		

Healdsburg Unified School Dist.
Foss Creek Elem.

Grade	Eng	Ma	Sci
2	7	20	
3	10	20	
4	11	13	
5	18	22	18
6	49	36	
Healdsburg Elem.			
2	51	47	
3	45	21	
4	47	13	
5	67	31	66
6	72	45	

Scores range from 1-99. A school scoring 75 has done better than 75 percent of other public schools in California.
Key: Eng (English), Ma (Math), Sci (Science).

Grade	Eng	Ma	Sci
Healdsburg High			
9	72		
10	86		
11	92		
Healdsburg Jr. High			
7	65	52	
8	72		
Marce Becerra Academy (Cont.)			
9	11		
10	10		

Horicon Elem. School Dist.
Horicon Elem.

Grade	Eng	Ma	Sci
2	32	38	
3	29	9	

Kenwood Elem. School Dist.
Kenwood Elem.

Grade	Eng	Ma	Sci
2	78	97	
3	92	84	
4	96	80	
5	80	74	84
6	88	94	

Liberty Elem. School Dist.
Calif. Virtual Academy@Sonoma

Grade	Eng	Ma	Sci
2	57	36	
3	66	14	
4	73	26	
5	75	8	69
6	78	46	
7	91	66	
8	81		
Liberty Elem. (Petaluma)			
2	90	88	
3	99	99	
4	92	91	
5	95	98	96
6	91	95	

Mark West Union Elem. School Dist.
Mark West Char. (Santa Rosa)

Grade	Eng	Ma	Sci
7	74	65	
Mark West Elem. (Santa Rosa)			
2	63	61	
3	73	49	
4	83	86	
5	76	62	79
6	76	68	
Riebli Elem. (Santa Rosa)			
2	87	85	
3	70	35	
4	81	80	
5	76	52	59
6	88	82	

Grade	Eng	Ma	Sci
San Miguel Elem. (Santa Rosa)			
2	81	66	
3	88	76	
4	84	64	
5	69	38	73
6	87	81	

Monte Rio Union Elem. School Dist.
Monte Rio Elem.

Grade	Eng	Ma	Sci
3	62	45	
4	56	22	
7	77	81	

Oak Grove Union Elem. School Dist.
Oak Grove Elem. (Sebastopol)

Grade	Eng	Ma	Sci
2	45	33	
3	74	71	
4	90	93	
5	78	74	72
Willowside Middle (Santa Rosa)			
6	79	77	
7	82	83	
8	86		

Old Adobe Union Elem. School Dist.
Eldredge Elem. (Petaluma)

Grade	Eng	Ma	Sci
2	39	37	
3	31	13	
4	33	27	
5	36	17	57
6	53	47	
La Tercera Elem. (Petaluma)			
2	57	46	
3	69	33	
4	82	72	
5	65	30	77
6	80	63	
Miwok Valley Elem. (Petaluma)			
2	58	68	
3	58	49	
4	49	31	
5	61	17	48
6	87	80	
Old Adobe Elem. (Petaluma)			
2	62	55	
3	73	71	
4	88	72	
5	78	61	89
6	75	61	
Sonoma Mountain Elem. (Petaluma)			
2	83	80	
3	77	67	
4	79	37	
5	78	50	79
6	90	87	

Scores range from 1-99. A school scoring 75 has done better than 75 percent of other public schools in California.

Key: Eng (English), Ma (Math), Sci (Science).

Grade	Eng	Ma	Sci
Petaluma City Elem. School Dist.			
Grant Elem.			
2	76	89	
3	93	95	
4	85	72	
5	93	74	91
6	84	73	
Live Oak Elem.			
2	34	32	
3	41	21	
4	56	16	
6	90	77	
McDowell Elem.			
2	10	9	
3	15	6	
4	11	61	
5	19	8	17
6	14	10	
McKinley Elem.			
2	12	14	
3	14	16	
4	2	3	
5	41	25	17
6	34	51	
McNear Elem.			
2	78	82	
3	70	52	
4	91	86	
5	89	70	91
6	95	93	
Penngrove Elem.			
2	84	91	
3	70	43	
4	51	45	
5	77	36	67
6	77	28	
Valley Vista Elem.			
2	76	74	
3	60	38	
4	83	84	
5	71	52	61
6	76	75	
Petaluma Joint Union High School Dist.			
Casa Grande High			
9	68		
10	79		
11	76		
Crossroads			
8	7		
Kenilworth Jr. High			
7	72	71	
8	74		

Grade	Eng	Ma	Sci
Mary Collins/Cherry Valley			
2	53	79	
3	66	24	
4	78	45	
5	80	27	71
6	86	58	
7	95	72	
8	84		
Petaluma High			
9	79		55
10	88		42
11	88		16
Petaluma Jr. High			
7	74	68	
8	71		68
San Antonio High (Cont.)			
9	28		
10	37		
11	22		
Sonoma Mountain High			
11	26		
Valley Oaks High (Alt.)			
8	60		
10	34		
Piner-Olivet Union Elem. School Dist. (Santa Rosa)			
Career Academy at Piner-Olivet			
7	55	30	
8	60		
Jack London Elem.			
2	82	81	
3	63	61	
4	60	34	
5	84	54	69
6	67	67	
Olivet Elem.			
2	53	41	
3	76	66	
4	56	57	
5	67	68	57
6	73	83	
Piner Elem.			
2	71	66	
3	73	79	
4	66	71	
5	70	42	64
6	60	62	
Piner-Olivet Char.			
7	78	87	
8	87		
Schaefer Elem.			
2	64	57	
3	45	18	
4	74	80	
5	77	83	63
6	65	84	

Scores range from 1-99. A school scoring 75 has done better than 75 percent of other public schools in California.
Key: Eng (English), Ma (Math), Sci (Science).

Grade	Eng	Ma	Sci
Rincon Valley Union Elem. (Santa Rosa)			
Austin Creek Elem.			
2	95	93	
3	98	98	
4	99	99	
5	98	98	97
6	98	99	
Binkley Elem.			
2	91	82	
3	70	72	
4	90	77	
5	74	59	81
6	92	84	
Madrone Elem.			
2	73	76	
3	91	84	
4	82	65	
5	89	97	93
6	84	98	
Matanzas Elem.			
2	93	82	
3	95	84	
4	79	68	
5	85	94	74
6	92	88	
Rincon Valley Char.			
7	91	87	
Sequoia Elem.			
2	85	90	
3	94	91	
4	84	70	
5	92	92	88
6	91	96	
Spring Creek Elem.			
2	49	55	
3	73	75	
4	76	50	
5	75	87	74
6	84	83	
Village Elem.			
2	86	80	
3	91	83	
4	57	64	
5	86	86	80
6	78	75	
White Elem.			
2	81	61	
3	88	94	
4	76	44	
5	72	64	72
6	69	65	
Roseland Elem. School Dist.			
Roseland Char.			
7	26	67	
8	28		
9	51		

Grade	Eng	Ma	Sci
Roseland Elem. (Santa Rosa)			
2	7	10	
3	13	16	
4	8	9	
5	12	8	5
6	20	17	
Sheppard Elem. (Santa Rosa)			
2	34	77	
3	51	63	
4	15	37	
5	12	56	33
6	10	18	
Santa Rosa Elem. School Dist.			
Biella Elem.			
2	28	11	
3	43	37	
4	44	27	
5	80	80	69
6	64	66	
Brook Hill Elem.			
2	16	9	
3	35	51	
4	30	40	
5	39	36	39
6	47	37	
Burbank Elem.			
2	38	54	
3	20	18	
4	9	6	
5	13	31	20
6	28	51	
Doyle Park Elem.			
2	27	33	
3	56	47	
4	48	64	
5	28	22	12
6	31	26	
Fremont Elem.			
2	31	29	
3	45	51	
4	20	12	
5	33	26	29
6	29	35	
Hidden Valley Elem.			
2	85	77	
3	91	86	
4	93	86	
5	93	91	91
6	92	92	
Lehman Elem.			
2	40	24	
3	43	53	
4	42	32	
5	10	4	5
6	20	21	

Scores range from 1-99. A school scoring 75 has done better than 75 percent of other public schools in California.
Key: Eng (English), Ma (Math), Sci (Science).

Grade	Eng	Ma	Sci

Lincoln Elem.

Grade	Eng	Ma	Sci
2	10	44	
3	17	46	
4	11	47	
5	14	24	9
6	10	31	

Monroe Elem.

Grade	Eng	Ma	Sci
2	12	12	
3	14	9	
4	13	13	
5	10	12	11
6	15	26	

Proctor Terrace Elem.

Grade	Eng	Ma	Sci
2	72	59	
3	82	67	
4	81	75	
5	88	68	74
6	91	90	

Santa Rosa Char.

Grade	Eng	Ma	Sci
2	41	43	
3	70	35	
4	80	65	
5	93	68	77
6	92	77	
7	77	85	
8	88		

Steele Lane Elem.

Grade	Eng	Ma	Sci
2	22	12	
3	17	14	
4	36	42	
5	24	27	12
6	21	14	

Santa Rosa High School Dist.

Allen High

Grade	Eng	Ma	Sci
9	43		
10	45		
11	44		

Carrillo High

Grade	Eng	Ma	Sci
9	91		
10	90		
11	94		

Cook Middle

Grade	Eng	Ma	Sci
7	23	24	
8	35		

Grace High (Cont.)

Grade	Eng	Ma	Sci
11	40		

Hilliard Comstock Middle

Grade	Eng	Ma	Sci
7	25	35	
8	49		

Mesa High (Cont.)

Grade	Eng	Ma	Sci
11	82		

Midrose High (Cont.)

Grade	Eng	Ma	Sci
11	26		

Montgomery High

Grade	Eng	Ma	Sci
9	78		
10	77		
11	87		

Nueva Vista High

Grade	Eng	Ma	Sci
11	11		

Piner High

Grade	Eng	Ma	Sci
9	60		
10	70		
11	62		

Ridgway High (Cont.)

Grade	Eng	Ma	Sci
7	4	3	
8	11		
9	22		
10	25		
11	30		

Rincon Valley Middle

Grade	Eng	Ma	Sci
7	90	84	
8	89		

Santa Rosa Accelerated Char.

Grade	Eng	Ma	Sci
5	97	85	91
6	98	91	

Santa Rosa High

Grade	Eng	Ma	Sci
9	86		
10	89		
11	85		

Santa Rosa Middle

Grade	Eng	Ma	Sci
7	61	73	
8	66		

Slater Middle

Grade	Eng	Ma	Sci
7	72	82	
8	67		

Sebastopol Union Elem. Sch. Dist.

Brook Haven Elem.

Grade	Eng	Ma	Sci
6	68	50	
7	71	79	
8	73		

Park Side Elem.

Grade	Eng	Ma	Sci
2	76	87	
3	56	22	

Pine Crest Elem.

Grade	Eng	Ma	Sci
3	73	51	
4	71	52	
5	84	70	75

Sebastopol Ind. Char.

Grade	Eng	Ma	Sci
2	5	58	
3	71	31	
4	62	35	
5	85	19	61
6	92	45	
7	98	85	
8	99		

Sonoma Valley Unified School Dist.

Altimira Middle (Sonoma)

Grade	Eng	Ma	Sci
6	53	52	
7	66	66	
8	55		

Creekside High (Cont.)

Grade	Eng	Ma	Sci
10	4		

Scores range from 1-99. A school scoring 75 has done better than 75 percent of other public schools in California.

Key: Eng (English), Ma (Math), Sci (Science).

Dunbar Elem. (Glen Ellen)

Grade	Eng	Ma	Sci
2	60	50	
3	79	70	
4	53	39	
5	64	30	53

El Verano Elem. (El Verano)

Grade	Eng	Ma	Sci
2	31	36	
3	7	21	
4	23	30	
5	43	49	45

Flowery Elem. (Boyes Hot Springs)

Grade	Eng	Ma	Sci
2	2	8	
3	7	6	
4	20	6	
5	32	37	24

Harrison Adele (Sonoma)

Grade	Eng	Ma	Sci
6	57	51	
7	60	60	
8	74		

Prestwood Elem. (Sonoma)

Grade	Eng	Ma	Sci
2	62	58	
3	79	68	
4	70	42	
5	81	80	86

Sassarini Elem. (Sonoma)

Grade	Eng	Ma	Sci
2	40	27	
3	33	28	
4	55	59	
5	59	53	50

Sonoma Char. (Elem.) (Sonoma)

Grade	Eng	Ma	Sci
2	56	68	
3	92	81	
4	70	20	
5	63	26	69
6	88	74	
7	85	68	
8	86		

Sonoma Valley High (Sonoma)

Grade	Eng	Ma	Sci
9	71		
10	72		
11	86		

Woodland Star Char.

Grade	Eng	Ma	Sci
2	2	2	
3	18	2	
4	52	6	
7	97	81	

Twin Hills Union Elem. School Dist.

Apple Blossom Elem. (Sebastopol)

Grade	Eng	Ma	Sci
2	71	56	
3	62	15	
4	86	71	
5	69	43	76

Orchard View (Sebastopol)

Grade	Eng	Ma	Sci
5	86	21	92
6	97	55	
7	94	74	
8	88		
9	83		
10	74		
11	78		

Sunridge Char. (Sebastopol)

Grade	Eng	Ma	Sci
2	1	28	
3	31	10	
4	40	25	
5	78	21	48
8	98		

Twin Hills Middle (Sebastopol)

Grade	Eng	Ma	Sci
6	76	51	
7	95	83	
8	90		

Two Rock Union Elem. School Dist.

Two Rock Elem. (near Petaluma)

Grade	Eng	Ma	Sci
2	52	66	
3	61	70	
4	69	82	
5	75	88	91
6	73	70	

Waugh Elem. School Dist. (Petaluma)

Corona Creek Elem.

Grade	Eng	Ma	Sci
2	89	75	
3	93	96	
4	95	95	
5	81	71	70
6	89	78	

Meadow Elem.

Grade	Eng	Ma	Sci
2	95	89	
3	87	87	
4	97	97	
5	93	91	95
6	74	65	

West Side Union Elem. School Dist.

West Side Elem. (Healdsburg)

Grade	Eng	Ma	Sci
2	33	69	
3	81	61	
4	82	51	
5	44	20	49
6	74	66	

West Sonoma County High Sch. Dist.

Analy High (Sebastopol)

Grade	Eng	Ma	Sci
9	93		
10	92		
11	92		

El Molino High (Forestville)

Grade	Eng	Ma	Sci
9	82		
10	84		
11	87		

Scores range from 1-99. A school scoring 75 has done better than 75 percent of other public schools in California.

Key: Eng (English), Ma (Math), Sci (Science).

Grade	Eng	Ma	Sci
Laguna High (Cont.)			
10	40		52
11	27		36
Russian River Char.			
9	18		
10	47		
11	49		

Wilmar Union Elem. School Dist.
Wilson Elem. (Petaluma)

Grade	Eng	Ma	Sci
2	36	43	
3	56	49	
4	61	55	
5	63	88	78
6	91	91	

Windsor Unified School Dist.
Brooks Elem.

Grade	Eng	Ma	Sci
4	72	48	
5	56	26	57
Cali Calmecac Char.			
2	6	31	
3	24	31	
4	47	67	
5	57	39	42
6	39	31	
7	74	89	
8	64		
Windsor Creek Elem.			
2	58	54	
3	63	52	
Windsor High			
9	74		48
10	83		66
11	71		48
Windsor Middle			
6	65	55	
7	66	53	
8	77		
Windsor Oaks Academy			
10	22		

Wright Elem. School Dist. (Santa Rosa)
Stevens Elem.

Grade	Eng	Ma	Sci
2	51	33	
3	63	66	
4	46	75	
5	41	32	34
6	73	85	
Wilson Elem.			
2	64	81	
3	65	68	
4	80	95	
5	70	73	57
6	53	61	
Wright Elem.			
2	40	43	
3	55	47	
4	53	72	
5	59	80	81
6	22	19	

Chapter **9b**

State 1 to 10 Rankings

FOR EASE OF COMPREHENSION, the California Department of Education has worked out a system to rank schools by their test scores.

This system takes several forms, the simplest of which is a ranking of 1 to 10.

One is the lowest score, ten is the highest.

This chapter lists the rankings for just about every school in the county.

Keep in mind that this is a crude representation of how the schools are scoring. If you combine this data with the rankings in Chapter 9b and the SAT scores and other data in Chapter 10, you will have a more rounded picture of the scores at each school.

Nonetheless, the scores can still mislead. Almost every school, even those at the bottom, will graduate students who score at the top.

Almost every school with scores at the top will graduate kids who score at the bottom and the middle.

For a general discussion of scores and what they mean, read the chapter on How Public Schools Work.

San Francisco County

School	District	City/Town	Rank
Alamo Elem.	San Francisco Unif.	San Francisco	10
Alvarado Elem.	San Francisco Unif.	San Francisco	7
Argonne Elem.	San Francisco Unif.	San Francisco	9
Bryant Elem.	San Francisco Unif.	San Francisco	2
Buena Vista Annex	San Francisco Unif.	San Francisco	4
Cabrillo Elem.	San Francisco Unif.	San Francisco	7
Carmichael Elem.	San Francisco Unif.	San Francisco	5
Carver Elem.	San Francisco Unif.	San Francisco	3
Chavez Elem.	San Francisco Unif.	San Francisco	3
Chin Elem.	San Francisco Unif.	San Francisco	9
Clarendon Elem.	San Francisco Unif.	San Francisco	10
Cleveland Elem.	San Francisco Unif.	San Francisco	1
Cobb Elem.	San Francisco Unif.	San Francisco	3
Commodore Sloat Elem.	San Francisco Unif.	San Francisco	9
Creative Arts Char.	San Francisco Unif.	San Francisco	5
Drew Elem.	San Francisco Unif.	San Francisco	1
El Dorado Elem.	San Francisco Unif.	San Francisco	4
Fairmount Elem.	San Francisco Unif.	San Francisco	1
Flynn Elem.	San Francisco Unif.	San Francisco	2
Francis Scott Key Elem.	San Francisco Unif.	San Francisco	8
Garfield Elem.	San Francisco Unif.	San Francisco	9
Glen Park Elem.	San Francisco Unif.	San Francisco	5
Grattan Elem.	San Francisco Unif.	San Francisco	6
Guadalupe Elem.	San Francisco Unif.	San Francisco	6
Harte Elem.	San Francisco Unif.	San Francisco	1
Hillcrest Elem.	San Francisco Unif.	San Francisco	2
Jefferson Elem.	San Francisco Unif.	San Francisco	9
Lafayette Elem.	San Francisco Unif.	San Francisco	8
Lakeshore Elem.	San Francisco Unif.	San Francisco	8
Lau Elem.	San Francisco Unif.	San Francisco	7
Lawton Elem.	San Francisco Unif.	San Francisco	9
Lilienthal Elem.	San Francisco Unif.	San Francisco	9
Longfellow Elem.	San Francisco Unif.	San Francisco	8
Malcolm X Acad.	San Francisco Unif.	San Francisco	1
Marshall Elem.	San Francisco Unif.	San Francisco	3
McCoppin Elem.	San Francisco Unif.	San Francisco	7
McKinley Elem.	San Francisco Unif.	San Francisco	5
Milk Civil Rights Elem.	San Francisco Unif.	San Francisco	3
Miraloma Elem.	San Francisco Unif.	San Francisco	3
Monroe Elem.	San Francisco Unif.	San Francisco	4
Moscone Elem.	San Francisco Unif.	San Francisco	8
Muir Elem.	San Francisco Unif.	San Francisco	2
New Traditions Elem.	San Francisco Unif.	San Francisco	3
Ortega Elem.	San Francisco Unif.	San Francisco	5
Parker Elem.	San Francisco Unif.	San Francisco	7
Parks Elem.	San Francisco Unif.	San Francisco	4
Peabody Elem.	San Francisco Unif.	San Francisco	6
Redding Elem.	San Francisco Unif.	San Francisco	6

School	District	City/Town	Rank
Revere Elem.	San Francisco Unif.	San Francisco	1
Rooftop Elem.	San Francisco Unif.	San Francisco	9
San Fran. Comm. Alt.	San Francisco Unif.	San Francisco	6
Sanchez Elem.	San Francisco Unif.	San Francisco	2
Serra Elem.	San Francisco Unif.	San Francisco	3
Sheridan Elem.	San Francisco Unif.	San Francisco	5
Sherman Elem.	San Francisco Unif.	San Francisco	8
Spring Valley Elem.	San Francisco Unif.	San Francisco	7
Starr King Elem.	San Francisco Unif.	San Francisco	3
Stevenson Elem.	San Francisco Unif.	San Francisco	9
Sunnyside Elem.	San Francisco Unif.	San Francisco	5
Sunset Elem.	San Francisco Unif.	San Francisco	6
Sutro Elem.	San Francisco Unif.	San Francisco	8
Swett Elem.	San Francisco Unif.	San Francisco	2
Taylor Elem.	San Francisco Unif.	San Francisco	7
Tenderloin Comm.	San Francisco Unif.	San Francisco	4
Treasure Island Elem.	San Francisco Unif.	San Francisco	2
21st Century Acad.	San Francisco Unif.	San Francisco	1
Ulloa Elem.	San Francisco Unif.	San Francisco	9
Visitacion Valley Elem.	San Francisco Unif.	San Francisco	5
Webster Elem.	San Francisco Unif.	San Francisco	2
West Portal Elem.	San Francisco Unif.	San Francisco	9
William de Avila Elem.	San Francisco Unif.	San Francisco	2
Yick Wo Elem.	San Francisco Unif.	San Francisco	9
Yu Elem.	San Francisco Unif.	San Francisco	10
A.P. Giannini Middle	San Francisco Unif.	San Francisco	9
Aptos Middle	San Francisco Unif.	San Francisco	7
Burbank Middle	San Francisco Unif.	San Francisco	2
Davis Middle	San Francisco Unif.	San Francisco	1
Denman Middle	San Francisco Unif.	San Francisco	5
Everett Middle	San Francisco Unif.	San Francisco	2
Francisco Middle	San Francisco Unif.	San Francisco	4
Franklin Middle	San Francisco Unif.	San Francisco	1
Hoover Middle	San Francisco Unif.	San Francisco	9
King Acad. Middle	San Francisco Unif.	San Francisco	5
Lick Middle	San Francisco Unif.	San Francisco	1
Mann Middle	San Francisco Unif.	San Francisco	2
Marina Middle	San Francisco Unif.	San Francisco	7
Maxwell Middle	San Francisco Unif.	San Francisco	1
Presidio Middle	San Francisco Unif.	San Francisco	10
Roosevelt Middle	San Francisco Unif.	San Francisco	8
Visitacion Valley Middle	San Francisco Unif.	San Francisco	3
Abraham Lincoln High	San Francisco Unif.	San Francisco	9
Balboa High	San Francisco Unif.	San Francisco	2
Burton Acad. High	San Francisco Unif.	San Francisco	5
Galileo High	San Francisco Unif.	San Francisco	6
Gateway High	San Francisco Unif.	San Francisco	8
George Washington High	San Francisco Unif.	San Francisco	9
Int'l Studies Acad.	San Francisco Unif.	San Francisco	1
Leadership High	San Francisco Unif.	San Francisco	6

School	District	City/Town	Rank
Lowell High	San Francisco Unif.	San Francisco	10
Marshall Acad. High	San Francisco Unif.	San Francisco	3
Mission High	San Francisco Unif.	San Francisco	1
Newcomer High	San Francisco Unif.	San Francisco	1
O'Connell High	San Francisco Unif.	San Francisco	2
School of the Arts	San Francisco Unif.	San Francisco	9
Wallenberg Trad. High	San Francisco Unif.	San Francisco	7

San Mateo County

School	District	City/Town	Rank
Robertson Int.	Bayshore Elem.	Daly City	7
Central Elem.	Belmont-Redwood Shores	Belmont	10
Cipriani Elem.	Belmont-Redwood Shores	Belmont	8
Fox Elem.	Belmont-Redwood Shores	Belmont	9
Nesbit Elem.	Belmont-Redwood Shores	Belmont	4
Sandpiper Elem.	Belmont-Redwood Shores	Redwood City	10
Ralston Int.	Belmont-Redwood Shores	Belmont	9
Brisbane Elem.	Brisbane Elem.	Brisbane	7
Panorama Elem.	Brisbane Elem.	Daly City	5
Lipman Middle	Brisbane Elem.	Brisbane	8
Franklin Elem.	Burlingame Elem.	Burlingame	10
Lincoln Elem.	Burlingame Elem.	Burlingame	10
McKinley Elem.	Burlingame Elem.	Burlingame	8
Roosevelt Elem.	Burlingame Elem.	Burlingame	9
Washington Elem.	Burlingame Elem.	Burlingame	8
Burlingame Int.	Burlingame Elem.	Burlingame	9
El Granada Elem.	Cabrillo Unified	El Granada	6
Farallone View Elem.	Cabrillo Unified	Montara	6
Hatch Elem.	Cabrillo Unified	Half Moon Bay	4
Cunha Int.	Cabrillo Unified	Half Moon Bay	7
Half Moon Bay High	Cabrillo Unified	Half Moon Bay	7
N. Hillsborough Elem.	Hillsborough City Elem.	Hillsborough	10
S. Hillsborough Elem.	Hillsborough City Elem.	Hillsborough	10
W. Hillsborough Elem.	Hillsborough City Elem.	Hillsborough	10
Crocker Middle	Hillsborough City Elem.	Hillsborough	10
Anthony Elem.	Jefferson Elem.	Daly City	4
Brown Elem.	Jefferson Elem.	Daly City	6
Colma Elem.	Jefferson Elem.	Daly City	6
Columbus Elem.	Jefferson Elem.	Daly City	4
Edison Elem.	Jefferson Elem.	Daly City	8
Garden Village Elem.	Jefferson Elem.	Colma	6
Kennedy Elem.	Jefferson Elem.	Daly City	5
Roosevelt Elem.	Jefferson Elem.	Daly City	6
Tobias Elem.	Jefferson Elem.	Daly City	8
Washington Elem.	Jefferson Elem.	Daly City	8
Webster Elem.	Jefferson Elem.	Daly City	7
Westlake Elem.	Jefferson Elem.	Daly City	5
Wilson Elem.	Jefferson Elem.	Daly City	5
Franklin Int.	Jefferson Elem.	Colma	6
Pollicita Middle	Jefferson Elem.	Daly City	4
Rivera Int.	Jefferson Elem.	Daly City	7
Jefferson High	Jefferson Union High	Daly City	3
Oceana High	Jefferson Union High	Pacifica	8
Terra Nova High	Jefferson Union High	Pacifica	8
Westmoor High	Jefferson Union High	Daly City	8
Pescadero Elem.	La Honda-Pescadero Unified	Pescadero	4
Las Lomitas Elem.	Las Lomitas Elem.	Atherton	10
La Entrada Middle	Las Lomitas Elem.	Menlo Park	10
Encinal Elem.	Menlo Park City Elem.	Atherton	10

School	District	City/Town	Rank
Laurel Elem.	Menlo Park City Elem.	Atherton	10
Oak Knoll Elem.	Menlo Park City Elem.	Menlo Park	10
Hillview Middle	Menlo Park City Elem.	Menlo Park	10
Green Hills Elem.	Millbrae Elem.	Millbrae	8
Lomita Park Elem.	Millbrae Elem.	Millbrae	8
Meadows Elem.	Millbrae Elem.	Millbrae	8
Spring Valley Elem.	Millbrae Elem.	Millbrae	9
Taylor Middle	Millbrae Elem.	Millbrae	9
Cabrillo Elem.	Pacifica School	Pacifica	9
Linda Mar Elem.	Pacifica School	Pacifica	6
Ocean Shore Elem.	Pacifica School	Pacifica	9
Oddstad Elem.	Pacifica School	Pacifica	8
Sunset Ridge Elem.	Pacifica School	Pacifica	6
Vallemar Elem.	Pacifica School	Pacifica	9
Lacy Middle	Pacifica School	Pacifica	7
Ormondale Elem.	Portola Valley Elem.	Portola Valley	10
Corte Madera Elem.	Portola Valley Elem.	Portola Valley	10
Belle Haven Elem.	Ravenswood City Elem.	Menlo Park	1
Costano Elem.	Ravenswood City Elem.	East Palo Alto	2
East Palo Alto Char.	Ravenswood City Elem.	East Palo Alto	5
Edison-Brentwood Acad.	Ravenswood City Elem.	East Palo Alto	1
Flood Elem.	Ravenswood City Elem.	Menlo Park	6
Green Oaks Elem.	Ravenswood City Elem.	East Palo Alto	1
Willow Oaks Elem.	Ravenswood City Elem.	Menlo Park	1
Chavez Acad.	Ravenswood City Elem.	East Palo Alto	1
Edison-McNair Acad.	Ravenswood City Elem.	East Palo Alto	3
East Palo Alto High	Ravenswood City Elem.	East Palo Alto	1
Adelante Span. Immersion	Redwood City Elem.	Redwood City	4
Clifford Elem.	Redwood City Elem.	Redwood City	7
Cloud Elem.	Redwood City Elem.	Redwood City	9
Fair Oaks Elem.	Redwood City Elem.	Redwood City	1
Ford Elem.	Redwood City Elem.	Redwood City	5
Garfield Char.	Redwood City Elem.	Redwood City	1
Gill Elem.	Redwood City Elem.	Redwood City	7
Hawes Elem.	Redwood City Elem.	Redwood City	4
Hoover Elem.	Redwood City Elem.	Redwood City	3
North Star Acad.	Redwood City Elem.	Redwood City	10
Roosevelt Elem.	Redwood City Elem.	Redwood City	4
Selby Ln. Elem.	Redwood City Elem.	Atherton	3
Taft Elem.	Redwood City Elem.	Redwood City	1
Kennedy Middle	Redwood City Elem.	Redwood City	4
McKinley Inst. Of Tech.	Redwood City Elem.	Redwood City	3
Allen Elem.	San Bruno Park Elem.	San Bruno	6
Belle Air Elem.	San Bruno Park Elem.	San Bruno	5
Crestmoor Elem.	San Bruno Park Elem.	San Bruno	9
El Crystal Elem.	San Bruno Park Elem.	San Bruno	7
John Muir Elem.	San Bruno Park Elem.	San Bruno	8
Portola Elem.	San Bruno Park Elem.	San Bruno	6
Rollingwood Elem.	San Bruno Park Elem.	San Bruno	8
Parkside Int.	San Bruno Park Elem.	San Bruno	6
Arundel Elem.	San Carlos Elem.	San Carlos	9

School	District	City/Town	Rank
Brittan Acres Elem.	San Carlos Elem.	San Carlos	8
Charter Lrng. Ctr.	San Carlos Elem.	San Carlos	9
Heather Elem.	San Carlos Elem.	San Carlos	9
White Oaks Elem.	San Carlos Elem.	San Carlos	10
Central Middle	San Carlos Elem.	San Carlos	9
Tierra Linda Middle	San Carlos Elem.	San Carlos	10
Aragon High	San Mateo Union High	San Mateo	9
Burlingame High	San Mateo Union High	Burlingame	9
Capuchino High	San Mateo Union High	San Bruno	6
Hillsdale High	San Mateo Union High	San Mateo	6
Mills High	San Mateo Union High	Millbrae	10
San Mateo High	San Mateo Union High	San Mateo	8
Audubon Elem.	San Mateo-Foster City	Foster City	9
Baywood Elem.	San Mateo-Foster City	San Mateo	10
Beresford Elem.	San Mateo-Foster City	San Mateo	5
Brewer Island Elem.	San Mateo-Foster City	Foster City	10
Fiesta Gardens Int'l Elem.	San Mateo-Foster City	San Mateo	5
Foster City Elem.	San Mateo-Foster City	Foster City	10
Hall Elem.	San Mateo-Foster City	San Mateo	6
Highlands Elem.	San Mateo-Foster City	San Mateo	10
Horrall Elem.	San Mateo-Foster City	San Mateo	4
Laurel Elem.	San Mateo-Foster City	San Mateo	9
Meadow Heights Elem.	San Mateo-Foster City	San Mateo	9
N. Shoreview Elem.	San Mateo-Foster City	San Mateo	5
Park Elem.	San Mateo-Foster City	San Mateo	5
Parkside Elem.	San Mateo-Foster City	San Mateo	6
Sunnybrae Elem.	San Mateo-Foster City	San Mateo	5
Turnbull Lrng. Acad.	San Mateo-Foster City	San Mateo	1
Abbott Middle	San Mateo-Foster City	San Mateo	8
Bayside Middle	San Mateo-Foster City	San Mateo	5
Borel Middle	San Mateo-Foster City	San Mateo	8
Bowditch Middle	San Mateo-Foster City	Foster City	10
Carlmont High	Sequoia Union High	Belmont	8
Menlo-Atherton High	Sequoia Union High	Atherton	6
Sequoia High	Sequoia Union High	Redwood City	3
Woodside High	Sequoia Union High	Woodside	5
Hillside Elem.	South San Francisco Unif.	S. San Francisco	3
Junipero Serra Elem.	South San Francisco Unif.	Daly City	7
Los Cerritos Elem.	South San Francisco Unif.	S. San Francisco	6
Martin Elem.	South San Francisco Unif.	S. San Francisco	4
Monte Verde Elem.	South San Francisco Unif.	San Bruno	9
Ponderosa Elem.	South San Francisco Unif.	S. San Francisco	8
Skyline Elem.	South San Francisco Unif.	Daly City	7
Spruce Elem.	South San Francisco Unif.	S. San Francisco	6
Sunshine Gardens Elem.	South San Francisco Unif.	S. San Francisco	5
Alta Loma Middle	South San Francisco Unif.	S. San Francisco	6
Parkway Heights Middle	South San Francisco Unif.	S. San Francisco	3
Westborough Middle	South San Francisco Unif.	S. San Francisco	8
El Camino High	South San Francisco Unif.	S. San Francisco	8
S. San Francisco High	South San Francisco Unif.	S. San Francisco	6
Woodside Elem.	Woodside Elem.	Woodside	10

Marin County

School	District	City/Town	Rank
Bolinas Elem.	Bolinas-Stinson Union Elem.	Bolinas	7
Dixie Elem.	Dixie Elem.	San Rafael	10
Silveira Elem.	Dixie Elem.	San Rafael	9
Vallecito Elem.	Dixie Elem.	San Rafael	10
Miller Creek Middle	Dixie Elem.	San Rafael	10
Bacich Elem.	Kentfield Elem.	Kentfield	10
Kent Middle	Kentfield Elem.	Kentfield	10
Lagunitas Elem.	Lagunitas Elem.	San Geronimo	8
Cummins Elem.	Larkspur Elem.	Corte Madera	10
Hall Middle	Larkspur Elem.	Larkspur	10
Maguire Elem.	Mill Valley Elem.	Mill Valley	10
Old Mill Elem.	Mill Valley Elem.	Mill Valley	10
Park Elem.	Mill Valley Elem.	Mill Valley	9
Strawberry Point Elem.	Mill Valley Elem.	Strawberry	10
Tamalpais Valley Elem.	Mill Valley Elem.	Mill Valley	10
Mill Valley Middle	Mill Valley Elem.	Mill Valley	10
Hamilton Meadow Park Elem.	Novato Unified	Novato	7
Loma Verde Elem.	Novato Unified	Novato	7
Lu Sutton Elem.	Novato Unified	Novato	8
Lynwood Elem.	Novato Unified	Novato	8
Novato Char.	Novato Unified	Novato	9
Olive Elem.	Novato Unified	Novato	7
Pleasant Valley Elem.	Novato Unified	Novato	10
Rancho Elem.	Novato Unified	Novato	10
San Ramon Elem.	Novato Unified	Novato	9
Hill Middle	Novato Unified	Novato	9
San Jose Middle	Novato Unified	Novato	9
Sinaloa Middle	Novato Unified	Novato	10
Marin Sch. Of Arts & Tech.	Novato Unified	Novato	6
Novato High	Novato Unified	Novato	9
Bel Aire Elem.	Reed Union Elem.	Tiburon	10
Reed Elem.	Reed Union Elem.	Tiburon	10
Del Mar Int.	Reed Union Elem.	Tiburon	10
Ross Elem.	Ross Elem.	Ross	10
Brookside Elem.	Ross Valley Elem.	San Anselmo	10
Manor Elem.	Ross Valley Elem.	Fairfax	8
Thomas Elem.	Ross Valley Elem.	San Anselmo	10
White Hill Middle	Ross Valley Elem.	Fairfax	10
Bahia Vista Elem.	San Rafael City Elem.	San Rafael	4
Coleman Elem.	San Rafael City Elem.	San Rafael	5
Gallinas Elem.	San Rafael City Elem.	San Rafael	4
Glenwood Elem.	San Rafael City Elem.	San Rafael	10
San Pedro Elem.	San Rafael City Elem.	San Rafael	1
Sun Valley Elem.	San Rafael City Elem.	San Rafael	9
Davidson Middle	San Rafael City Elem.	San Rafael	6
San Rafael High	San Rafael City High	San Rafael	6
Terra Linda High	San Rafael City High	San Rafael	9
Bayside Elem.	Sausalito Marin City	Sausalito	2
Tomales Elem.	Shoreline Unified	Tomales	6

School	District	City/Town	Rank
West Marin Elem.	Shoreline Unified	Pt. Reyes	5
Tomales High	Shoreline Unified	Tomales	6
Redwood High	Tamalpais Union High	Larkspur	10
Sir Francis Drake High	Tamalpais Union High	San Anselmo	10
Tamalpais High	Tamalpais Union High	Mill Valley	10

Sonoma County

School	District	City/Town	Rank
Bellevue Elem.	Bellevue Union Elem.	Santa Rosa	2
Kawana Elem.	Bellevue Union Elem.	Santa Rosa	2
Meadow View Elem.	Bellevue Union Elem.	Santa Rosa	3
Strawberry Elem.	Bennett Valley Union Elem.	Santa Rosa	9
Yulupa Elem.	Bennett Valley Union Elem.	Santa Rosa	9
Cinnabar Elem.	Cinnabar Elem.	Petaluma	6
Jefferson Elem.	Cloverdale Unified	Cloverdale	3
Washington Middle	Cloverdale Unified	Cloverdale	6
Cloverdale High	Cloverdale Unified	Cloverdale	5
Evergreen Elem.	Cotati-Rohnert Park Unified	Rohnert Park	8
Gold Ridge Elem.	Cotati-Rohnert Park Unified	Rohnert Park	8
Hahn Elem.	Cotati-Rohnert Park Unified	Rohnert Park	9
La Fiesta Elem.	Cotati-Rohnert Park Unified	Rohnert Park	4
Monte Vista Elem.	Cotati-Rohnert Park Unified	Rohnert Park	7
Page Elem.	Cotati-Rohnert Park Unified	Cotati	5
Reed Elem.	Cotati-Rohnert Park Unified	Rohnert Park	4
Rohnert Elem.	Cotati-Rohnert Park Unified	Rohnert Park	5
Creekside Middle	Cotati-Rohnert Park Unified	Rohnert Park	8
Mountain Shadows Middle	Cotati-Rohnert Park Unified	Rohnert Park	6
Rancho Cotate High	Cotati-Rohnert Park Unified	Rohnert Park	6
Technology High	Cotati-Rohnert Park Unified	Rohnert Park	10
Dunham Elem.	Dunham Elem.	Petaluma	9
Forestville Elem.	Forestville Union Elem.	Forestville	8
Gravenstein Elem.	Gravenstein Union Elem.	Sebastopol	9
Hillcrest Middle	Gravenstein Union Elem.	Sebastopol	9
Guerneville Elem.	Guerneville Elem.	Guerneville	6
Pathways Char.	Harmony Union Elem.	Occidental	5
Salmon Creek Middle	Harmony Union Elem.	Occidental	9
Fitch Mountain Elem.	Healdsburg Unified	Healdsburg	1
Foss Creek Elem.	Healdsburg Unified	Healdsburg	3
Healdsburg Elem.	Healdsburg Unified	Healdsburg	5
Healdsburg Jr. High	Healdsburg Unified	Healdsburg	6
Healdsburg High	Healdsburg Unified	Healdsburg	5
Kenwood Elem.	Kenwood Elem.	Kenwood	9
Liberty Elem.	Liberty Elem.	Petaluma	10
Mark West Elem.	Mark West Union Elem.	Santa Rosa	8
Riebli Elem.	Mark West Union Elem.	Santa Rosa	8
San Miguel Elem.	Mark West Union Elem.	Santa Rosa	9
Oak Grove Elem.	Oak Grove Union Elem.	Sebastopol	9
Willowside Middle	Oak Grove Union Elem.	Santa Rosa	8
Eldredge Elem.	Old Adobe Union Elem.	Petaluma	4
La Tercera Elem.	Old Adobe Union Elem.	Petaluma	7
Miwok Valley Elem.	Old Adobe Union Elem.	Petaluma	7
Old Adobe Elem.	Old Adobe Union Elem.	Petaluma	7
Sonoma Mountain Elem.	Old Adobe Union Elem.	Petaluma	8
Grant Elem.	Petaluma City	Petaluma	9
Mary Collins School	Petaluma City	Petaluma	6
McDowell Elem.	Petaluma City	Petaluma	3
McKinley Elem.	Petaluma City	Petaluma	3

School	District	City/Town	Rank
McNear Elem.	Petaluma City	Petaluma	8
Penngrove Elem.	Petaluma City	Petaluma	7
Valley Vista Elem.	Petaluma City	Petaluma	7
Kenilworth Jr. High	Petaluma City	Petaluma	7
Petaluma Jr. High	Petaluma City	Petaluma	7
Casa Grande High	Petaluma City	Petaluma	8
Petaluma High	Petaluma City	Petaluma	8
Jack London Elem.	Piner-Olivet Union Elem.	Santa Rosa	7
Olivet Elem.	Piner-Olivet Union Elem.	Santa Rosa	8
Piner Elem.	Piner-Olivet Union Elem.	Santa Rosa	7
Schaefer Elem.	Piner-Olivet Union Elem.	Santa Rosa	8
Piner-Olivet Char.	Piner-Olivet Union Elem.	Santa Rosa	10
Austin Creek Elem.	Rincon Valley Union Elem.	Santa Rosa	10
Binkley Elem.	Rincon Valley Union Elem.	Santa Rosa	8
Madrone Elem.	Rincon Valley Union Elem.	Santa Rosa	9
Matanzas Elem.	Rincon Valley Union Elem.	Santa Rosa	10
Sequoia Elem.	Rincon Valley Union Elem.	Santa Rosa	10
Spring Creek Elem.	Rincon Valley Union Elem.	Santa Rosa	9
Village Elem.	Rincon Valley Union Elem.	Santa Rosa	9
Whited Elem.	Rincon Valley Union Elem.	Santa Rosa	9
Roseland Elem.	Roseland Elem.	Santa Rosa	2
Sheppard Elem.	Roseland Elem.	Santa Rosa	4
Roseland Char.	Roseland Elem.	Santa Rosa	4
Biella Elem.	Santa Rosa City	Santa Rosa	6
Brook Hill Elem.	Santa Rosa City	Santa Rosa	3
Burbank Elem.	Santa Rosa City	Santa Rosa	2
Doyle Park Elem.	Santa Rosa City	Santa Rosa	5
Fremont Elem.	Santa Rosa City	Santa Rosa	4
Hidden Valley Elem.	Santa Rosa City	Santa Rosa	10
Lehman Elem.	Santa Rosa City	Santa Rosa	2
Lincoln Elem.	Santa Rosa City	Santa Rosa	1
Monroe Elem.	Santa Rosa City	Santa Rosa	2
Proctor Terrace Elem.	Santa Rosa City	Santa Rosa	9
Santa Rosa Ed. Co-op	Santa Rosa City	Santa Rosa	9
Steele Ln. Elem.	Santa Rosa City	Santa Rosa	2
Cook Middle	Santa Rosa City	Santa Rosa	3
Hilliard Comstock Middle	Santa Rosa City	Santa Rosa	4
Rincon Valley Middle	Santa Rosa City	Santa Rosa	9
Santa Rosa Middle	Santa Rosa City	Santa Rosa	7
Slater Middle	Santa Rosa City	Santa Rosa	6
Carrillo High	Santa Rosa City	Santa Rosa	10
Montgomery High	Santa Rosa City	Santa Rosa	9
Piner High	Santa Rosa City	Santa Rosa	4
Santa Rosa High	Santa Rosa City	Santa Rosa	8
Pine Crest Elem.	Sebastopol Union Elem.	Sebastopol	6
Sebastopol Ind. Char.	Sebastopol Union Elem.	Sebastopol	7
Brook Haven Elem.	Sebastopol Union Elem.	Sebastopol	8
Altimira Middle	Sebastopol Union Elem.	Sebastopol	5
Dunbar Elem.	Sebastopol Union Elem.	Sebastopol	6
El Verano Elem.	Sebastopol Union Elem.	Sebastopol	3
Flowery Elem.	Sebastopol Union Elem.	Sebastopol	3

School	District	City/Town	Rank
Prestwood Elem.	Sebastopol Union Elem.	Sebastopol	8
Sassarini Elem.	Sebastopol Union Elem.	Sebastopol	6
Sonoma Char.	Sebastopol Union Elem.	Sebastopol	7
Harrison Middle	Sebastopol Union Elem.	Sebastopol	6
Sonoma Valley High	Sebastopol Union Elem.	Sebastopol	5
Apple Blossom Elem.	Twin Hills Union Elem.	Sebastopol	7
Sunridge Char.	Twin Hills Union Elem.	Sebastopol	6
Twin Hills Middle	Twin Hills Union Elem.	Sebastopol	9
Two Rock Elem.	Two Rock Elem.	Petaluma	8
Corona Creek Elem.	Waugh Elem.	Petaluma	9
Meadow Elem.	Waugh Elem.	Petaluma	9
West Side Elem.	West Side Union Elem.	Healdsburg	7
Analy High	W. Sonoma Co. Union High	Sebastopol	7
El Molino High	W. Sonoma Co. Union High	Forestville	8
Wilson Elem.	Wilmar Union Elem.	Petaluma	8
Brooks Elem.	Windsor Unified	Windsor	6
Cali Calmecac Char.	Windsor Unified	Windsor	3
Windsor Creek Elem.	Windsor Unified	Windsor	7
Windsor Middle	Windsor Unified	Windsor	8
Windsor High	Windsor Unified	Windsor	7
Stevens Elem.	Wright Elem.	Santa Rosa	6
Wilson Elem.	Wright Elem.	Santa Rosa	7
Wright Elem.	Wright Elem.	Santa Rosa	6

Chapter 10

How Public Schools Work

SCORES MEASURE ACADEMIC success but they have their shortcomings. Some students know the material but are not adept at taking tests and some tests are so poorly designed that they fail to assess what has been taught. The rankings in the previous chapter do not break out students as individuals. A basic exam tests the least the children should know, not the most. Scores cannot assess goodness, kindness or wisdom or predict how helpful students will be to society.

There are other legitimate criticisms of probably every test given to California school children. Nonetheless, the tests have their value and except for a few cases probably give an accurate picture of how the schools are doing academically. Students who do well in elementary school generally do well in high school and score high on the SAT and go on to succeed in college. With rare exceptions, the scores correlate with teacher assessments, and so on. The exceptions cannot be ignored. A student who does poorly in one educational arrangement may thrive in another.

When your children attend a school with high test scores, they are not assured of success. These schools have their failures. Neither can you be certain that your children will get the best teachers or the right programs. Other schools with lower scores might do better on these points. What you can be certain of is that your children are entering a setting that has proven successful for many students.

The main problem with making sense out of scores concerns what is called socioeconomics, a theory educators love, hate and widely believe.

Socioeconomics — The Bottom Line

In its crudest form, socioeconomics means rich kids score high, middle-class kids score about the middle and poor kids score low. Not all the time, not predictably by individual. Many children from poor and middle-class homes succeed in school and attend the best colleges. But as a general rule socioeconomics enjoys much statistical support.

Compare San Mateo school rankings with income by cities. Hillsborough, Atherton, Woodside, rich or well-to-do, high scores; East Palo Alto, low

Scholastic Aptitude Test (SAT) Scores

San Francisco

High School	Enrollment*	% Tested	Verbal	Math
Abraham Lincoln	516	64	452	545
Balboa	175	58	362	433
Burton	352	52	411	485
Galileo	344	63	386	478
Geo. Washington	513	65	462	548
International	121	46	386	442
Lowell	652	97	590	643
Marshall	261	74	382	455
Mission	207	29	386	479
O'Connell	173	23	438	477
Raoul Wallenberg	176	66	437	515
School Of The Arts	127	70	559	539

San Mateo County

High School	Enrollment*	% Tested	Verbal	Math
Aragon High	359	62	543	577
Burlingame High	321	67	521	557
Capuchino High	256	32	483	512
Carlmont High	444	53	533	560
El Camino High	317	36	466	503
Half Moon Bay High	270	43	536	535
Hillsdale High	269	52	510	544
Jefferson High	276	26	431	451
Menlo-Atherton High	495	55	550	558
Mills High	342	70	540	589
Oceana High	112	44	477	499
San Mateo High	307	53	546	578
Sequoia High	295	34	489	511
So. San Francisco High	325	40	480	515
Terra Nova High	363	46	507	522
Westmoor High	408	38	462	511
Woodside High	404	49	489	491

Source: California Department of Education, 2004 tests. SAT scores are greatly influenced by who and how many take the test. The state education department has been pushing schools to have more students take the SAT. A school that has more marginal students taking the test will, by one line of reasoning, be doing a good job but the scores are likely to be lower. *Senior class enrollment.

income or poor, low scores; Half Moon Bay and Daly City, middle-class towns, middling to upper middle s scores. Marin, in median income the highest among the state's 58 counties, has many high-scoring schools. The exceptions show up in the few low-income neighborhoods. The same for Sonoma County.

Scholastic Aptitude Test (SAT) Scores

Marin County

High School Sr.	Senior Class	% Tested	Verbal	Math
Novato	232	56	539	545
Redwood	299	82	567	578
San Marin	258	62	545	568
San Rafael	208	50	544	525
Sir Francis Drake	236	70	556	556
Tamalpais	237	68	578	573
Terra Linda	236	72	566	576
Tomales	61	56	514	499

Sonoma County

High School	Senior Class	% Tested	Verbal	Math
Allen	362	18	477	493
Analy	364	53	556	563
Carrillo	342	52	563	579
Casa Grande	327	48	500	521
Cloverdale	96	25	490	510
El Molino	248	36	573	578
Healdsburg	200	41	548	556
Montgomery	417	47	549	555
Petaluma	321	49	543	533
Piner	290	27	492	506
Rancho Cotate	387	35	511	529
Santa Rosa	458	42	571	570
Sonoma Valley	357	35	545	543
Windsor	302	34	507	427

Source: California Department of Education, 2004 tests. **Note**: SAT scores are greatly influenced by who and how many take the test. The California Department of Education has been pushing schools to have more students take the SAT. A school that has more marginal students taking the test will, by one line of reasoning, be doing a good job but the scores are likely to be lower.

Where there are differences in schools in the same district, often the higher-scoring students will be from higher-income neighborhoods. The SAT scores reflect the basic test scores.

San Francisco correlations are masked somewhat by the school district's attendance policy: many kids attend schools outside their neighborhoods. But the overall correlation holds: Children from Twin Peaks and Pacific Heights score higher than children from the Mission and Bayview.

The same pattern shows up in the nation and in other countries. The federal study, "Japanese Education Today," notes a "solid correlation between poverty and poor school performance ...."

National Scholastic Aptitude Test (SAT) Scores

State	*Tested (%)	Verbal	Math
Alabama	10	560	553
Alaska	53	518	514
Arizona	32	523	524
Arkansas	6	569	555
California	**49**	**501**	**519**
Colorado	27	554	553
Connecticut	85	515	515
Delaware	73	500	499
Dist. of Columbia	77	489	476
Florida	67	499	499
Georgia	73	494	493
Hawaii	60	487	514
Idaho	20	540	539
Illinois	10	585	597
Indiana	64	501	506
Iowa	5	593	602
Kansas	9	584	585
Kentucky	12	559	557
Louisiana	8	564	561
Maine	76	505	501
Maryland	68	511	515
Massachusetts	85	518	523
Michigan	11	563	573
Minnesota	10	587	593
Mississippi	5	562	547
Missouri	8	587	585
Montana	29	537	539
Nebraska	8	569	576
Nevada	40	507	514
New Hampshire	80	522	521
New Jersey	83	501	514
New Mexico	14	554	543
New York	87	497	510
North Carolina	70	499	507
North Dakota	5	582	601
Ohio	28	538	542
Oklahoma	7	569	566
Oregon	56	527	528
Pennsylvania	74	501	502
Rhode Island	72	503	502
South Carolina	62	491	495
South Dakota	5	594	597
Tennessee	16	567	557
Texas	52	493	499
Utah	7	565	556
Vermont	66	516	512
Virginia	71	515	509
Washington	52	528	531
West Virginia	19	524	514
Wisconsin	7	587	596
Wyoming	12	551	546
Nationwide	**48**	**508**	**518**

Source: California Dept. of Education, 2004 tests. *Percentage of class taking the test.

Family and Culture

In its refined form, socioeconomics moves away from the buck and toward culture and family influence.

Note the chart on page 71. The towns with the highest number of college educated are generally also the towns with the highest scores. If your mom or dad attended college, chances are you will attend college or do well at school because in a thousand ways while you were growing up they and their milieu pushed you in this direction. Emphasis on "chances are." Nothing is certain when dealing with human beings.

What if mom and dad never got beyond the third grade? Or can't even speak English?

In many statistical studies, scores correlate closely with family income and education. So thoroughly does the California Department of Education believe in these correlations that it has worked socioeconomics into a mathematical model. Teachers collect data on almost all students: Are they on welfare, do they have language problems (immigrants), how educated are their parents? The information is fed to computers and used to predict how students will score on tests.

These correlations cannot be ignored — often they predict scores accurately — but they have contradictions. Historically, many poor and immigrant children have succeeded at school. Asian kids are the latest example of poor kids succeeding but we can also point to the children of peasant Europeans and of Africans brought to this country as slaves. This suggests that the money correlation — rich kids score high, middle at the middle, poor at the low end — is more complicated than first appears. Money is certainly a factor, but so is tradition and culture, family and neighborhood history and stability, the influence of peers, the values of the times, and technology. Before television and radio, people got much of their news and sports information from newspapers. Like it or not, you had to read just about every day. In modern times, you don't have to read to get the news or scores, and this has weakened perhaps the most important fundamental of school success, ability to read.

One of the biggest problems California schools have is children who enter school unprepared to do the rudimentary academics required in kindergarten or the first grade. The children start behind and often stay behind.

Does it make a difference if the child is English proficient? Immigrant children unfamiliar with English will have more difficulties with literature and language-proficient courses than native-born children. They will need extra or special help in schools.

Another Socioeconomic Flaw

If you carry the logic of socioeconomics too far, you may conclude that schools and teachers and teaching methods don't matter: Students succeed or fail according to their family or societal backgrounds.

California College Admissions of Public School Graduates

San Francisco Schools

High School	UC	CSU	CC
Balboa	20	14	71
Burton	47	69	110
Gateway	15	16	1
Galileo	58	66	123
Int'l Studies Academy	13	14	18
Leadership	11	13	NA
Lincoln	87	95	208
Lowell	326	82	125
Marshall	51	57	47
Mission	15	8	46
O'Connell	8	18	26
School of the Arts	17	4	28
Wallenberg	39	20	57
Washington	91	105	175

San Mateo County Schools

High School	UC	CSU	CC
Aragon (San Mateo)	72	34	87
Burlingame	42	59	62
Capuchino (San Bruno)	11	25	79
Carlmont (Belmont)	56	69	123
El Camino (So. San Francisco)	19	38	103
Half Moon Bay	17	27	98
Hillsdale (San Mateo)	25	36	66
Jefferson (Daly City)	8	29	56
Menlo-Atherton (Atherton)	20	43	103
Mills (Millbrae)	83	59	75
Oceana (Pacifica)	9	12	33
San Mateo	45	28	79
Sequoia (Redwood City)	13	25	119
South San Francisco	21	51	115
Terra Nova (Pacifica)	24	61	90
Westmoor (Daly City)	27	48	124
Woodside (Woodside)	23	61	128

Source: California Dept. of Education. The chart lists local public high schools and shows how many students they advanced in 2004 into California public colleges and universities. The state does not track graduates enrolling in private or out-of-state colleges. Continuation schools not included. **Key:** UC (University of California); CSU (Cal States) CC (Community Colleges).

California College Admissions of Public School Graduates

Marin County

High School	UC	CSU	CC
Novato	24	32	77
Redwood (Larkspur)	51	31	21
San Marin (Novato)	30	45	78
San Rafael	27	23	21
Sir Francis Drake (San Anselmo)	28	43	22
Tamalpais (Mill Valley)	43	21	23
Terra Linda (San Rafael)	46	52	33
Tomales	5	13	20

Sonoma County

High School	UC	CSU	CC
Allen (Santa Rosa)	7	13	154
Analy (Sebastopol)	34	55	153
Carrillo (Santa Rosa)	35	32	157
Casa Grande (Petaluma)	27	42	171
Cloverdale	5	8	30
El Molino (Forestville)	20	22	101
Geyserville Ed. Pk.	0	1	2
Healdsburg	13	14	95
Montgomery (Santa Rosa)	40	32	178
Petaluma	27	44	150
Piner (Santa Rosa)	7	18	157
Rancho Cotate (Rohnert Park)	20	49	211
Santa Rosa	28	24	210
Sonoma Valley (Sonoma)	22	33	164
Windsor	0	21	2

Source: California Department of Education. The chart lists the local public high schools and shows how many students they advanced in the year 2004 into California public colleges and universities. The state does not track graduates enrolling in private or out-of-state colleges. Continuation schools not included. **Key**: UC (University of California); CSU (Cal State system); CC (Community Colleges). *NA Not Available. In 2002, New Technology in Napa sent 7 students to a UC, 17 to CSU and 3 to community colleges.

Just not the case! No matter how dedicated or well-intentioned the parent, if the teacher is grossly inept the child probably will learn little. If material or textbooks are out-of-date or inaccurate, what the student learns may be useless or even damaging.

Conversely, if the teacher is dedicated and knowledgeable, if the material is well-presented and appropriate, what the child comes away with will be helpful and, to society, more likely to be beneficial.

Where the Confusion Enters

It's difficult, if not impossible, to separate the influence of home-society and schools. Many parents try hard with disappointing results. Some experts argue that friends and peer groups exercise greater influence than the home.

UCs Chosen by Public School Graduates

San Francisco

School	Berk	Davis	Irv	UCLA	Riv	SD	SB	SC	Total
Balboa	7	5	0	0	0	1	1	6	20
Burton	9	20	0	1	0	4	1	12	47
Galileo	12	27	0	5	4	1	0	9	58
Int'l Acad	3	8	0	0	0	0	1	1	13
Lincoln	8	32	4	4	8	4	5	22	87
Lowell	51	110	17	24	27	26	10	61	326
Marshall	14	17	0	0	1	0	2	17	51
Mission	3	9	0	2	0	0	1	0	15
O'Connell	5	0	0	2	0	0	1	0	8
School of the Arts	2	2	1	2	0	0	2	8	17
Wallenberg	2	20	3	2	2	0	0	10	39
Washington	13	40	2	6	0	7	4	16	91

San Mateo County

School	Berk	Davis	Irv	UCLA	Riv	SD	SB	SC	Total
Aragon	11	23	4	5	6	8	5	10	72
Burlingame	6	10	2	2	3	5	3	11	42
Capuchino	4	2	0	0	1	0	1	3	11
Carlmont	16	12	1	8	3	4	7	5	56
El Camino	5	6	3	1	0	1	2	1	19
Half Moon Bay	2	1	2	2	0	2	5	3	17
Hillsdale	2	9	1	0	0	1	6	6	25
Jefferson	4	2	0	2	0	0	0	0	8
Menlo-Atherton	2	1	3	4	0	4	3	3	20
Mills	11	22	7	9	9	9	3	13	83
Oceana	0	4	0	0	0	0	0	5	9
Pescadero	NA	NA	NA	NA	NA	NA	NA	NA	NA
San Mateo	10	10	8	5	1	4	3	4	45
Sequoia	5	2	0	0	2	0	1	3	13
So. San Fran.	2	4	8	1	0	3	1	2	21
Terra Nova	2	8	1	0	3	4	1	5	24
Westmoor	3	5	4	6	2	1	2	4	27
Woodside	10	6	0	0	0	0	3	4	23

Source: California Dept. of Education. The chart shows the University of California choices by local public high school graduates of 2004. The state does not track graduates enrolling in private or out-of-state colleges. Continuation schools not included in list. **Key**: Berk (Berkeley), Irv (Irvine), Riv (Riverside), SD (San Diego), SB (Santa Barbara), SC (Santa Cruz).

UCs Chosen by Public School Graduates

Marin County

School	Berk	Davis	Irv	LA	Riv	SD	SB	SC	Total
Novato	5	10	1	0	0	2	3	3	24
Redwood	9	19	1	3	2	1	8	8	51
San Marin	4	12	1	0	6	0	2	5	30
San Rafael	3	2	0	0	3	6	3	10	27
Sir Fr. Drake	4	5	1	3	0	3	3	9	28
Tamalpais	5	5	0	13	0	3	7	10	43
Terra Linda	6	7	2	2	2	6	6	15	46
Tomales	1	1	0	0	0	0	1	2	5

Sonoma County

School	Berk	Davis	Irv	LA	Riv	SD	SB	SC	Total
Allen (Elsie)	1	2	0	1	1	0	2	0	7
Analy	4	10	1	1	0	1	3	14	34
Carrillo	4	6	3	4	0	2	6	10	35
Casa Grande	6	8	1	1	0	1	1	9	27
Cloverdale	0	2	0	0	0	0	3	0	5
El Molino	4	7	0	0	0	0	1	8	20
Geyserville	NA	NA	NA	NA	NA	NA	NA	NA	NA
Healdsburg	1	2	1	3	1	0	0	5	13
Montgomery	4	13	1	1	0	3	8	10	40
Petaluma	1	3	0	4	0	5	2	12	27
Piner	2	3	0	0	1	0	1	0	7
Rancho Cotate	4	4	0	1	1	2	4	4	20
Santa Rosa	4	2	1	2	0	4	3	12	28
Sonoma Valley	1	6	1	0	0	2	4	8	22
Windsor High	1	4	3	0	0	2	4	0	14

Source: California Dept. of Education. The chart shows the University of California choices by local public high school graduates of 2004. The state does not track graduates enrolling in private or out-of-state colleges. Continuation schools not included in list. **Key**: Berk (Berkeley), Irv (Irvine), LA (UCLA), Riv (Riverside), SD (San Diego), SB (Santa Barbara), SC (Santa Cruz).

When scores go up, often principals or superintendents credit this or that instructional program, or extra efforts by teachers. But the scores may have risen because mom and dad cracked down on excessive TV. Or a city with old and faded low-income housing (low scores) approves a high-end development. The new residents are more middle class, more demographically inclined to push their kids academically.

One last joker-in-the-deck, mobility. Johnny is doing great at his school, which has low to middling scores, but programs that seem to be working. And his family is doing better. Mom has a job, Dad a promotion. What does the family do? It moves. Happens all the time in the U.S.A. and this also makes precise interpretation of scores difficult.

Back to Scores

If a school's scores are middling, it may still be capable of doing an excellent job, if it has dedicated teachers and sound programs. The middling scores may reflect socioeconomics, not instructional quality.

Don't judge us by our overall scores, many schools say. Judge us by our ability to deliver for your son or daughter.

This gets tricky because the children do influence one another and high-income parents often interact differently with schools than low-income parents. To some extent, the school must structure its programs to the ability of the students. But schools with middling and middling-plus grades can point to many successes.

Basic Instruction-Ability Grouping

California and American schools attempt to meet the needs of students by providing a good basic education and by addressing individual and subgroup needs by special classes and ability grouping.

In the first six years in an average school, children receive some special help according to ability but for the most part they share the same class experiences and get the same instruction.

About the seventh grade, until recently, students were divided into classes for low achievers, middling students and high achievers, or low-middle and advanced — tracking. Texts, homework and expectations were different for each group. High achievers were on the college track, the low, the vocational.

Pressured by the state, schools are curtailing this practice, but many schools retain accelerated English and math classes for advanced seventh and eighth graders. Parents can always request a transfer from one group to another (whether they can get it is another matter). The reality often is, however, that remedial and middle children can't keep pace with the high achievers.

In the last 40 years or so schools introduced into the early grades special programs aimed at low achievers or children with learning difficulties. Although they vary greatly, these programs typically pull the children out of class for instruction in small groups then return them to the regular class.

Many schools also pull out gifted (high I.Q.) students and a few cluster them in their own classes.

College Influence

The junior high divisions sharpen at high school. Colleges exercise great influence over what students are taught in high school. So many local students attend the University of California and California State University schools that public and private high schools must of necessity teach the classes demanded by these institutions.

So the typical high school will have a prep program that meets University of California requirements. The school also will offer general education classes in math and English but these will not be as tough as the prep courses and will not be recognized by the state universities. And usually the school will teach some trades and technical skills so those inclined can secure jobs upon graduation.

Can a school with mediocre or even low basic scores field a successful college prep program? With comprehensive programs, the answer is yes.

How Middling Schools Succeed — College Admissions

Freshmen attending a California State University, a public community college or a University of California (Berkeley, Los Angeles, San Diego, Davis, Santa Cruz, etc.) are asked to identify their high schools. In this way and others, the state finds out how many students the individual high schools are advancing to college.

The charts on pages 262, 263, 264 and 265 break out the high schools and community colleges in the four counties (data collected fall 2004) and shows how many students from each school went on to the public colleges.

The UCs generally restrict themselves to the top 13 percent in the state. The Cal States take the top third.

Every school on the chart is graduating kids into college but obviously some are more successful at it than others. Does this mean that the "lesser" schools have awful teachers or misguided programs? We have no idea. It simply may be socioeconomics at work.

Parents with college ambitions for their children should find out as much as possible about prospective schools and their programs and make sure that their kids get into the college-track classes.

Where does the chart mislead? Students who qualify for a Cal State or even a UC often take their freshman and sophomore years at a community college. It's cheaper and closer to home.

To secure a more diverse student mix, the UCs have selectively lowered their admission scores, a practice that has critics and supporters. The numbers mentioned above and listed in the accompanying chart do not consist of the top students as defined by tests and grade point. In 2004, the UCs raised their admission scores but the last word has not been said on this matter.

The chart does not track private colleges. It doesn't tell us how many local students went to Mills College or the University of San Francisco or Stanford or Harvard. Or public colleges out of the state.

Many college students drop out. These numbers are not included.

The chart does confirm the influence of socioeconomics: the rich towns, the educated towns or neighborhoods, send more kids to the UCs than the poorer ones.

But socioeconomics does not sweep the field. Not every student from a high-scoring school goes on to college. Many students from low- and middle-income towns come through.

Dissatisfaction

If high schools can deliver on college education and train students for vocations, why are so many people dissatisfied with public schools? These schools can cite other accomplishments: Textbooks and curriculums have been improved, the dropout rate has been decreased and proficiency tests have been adopted to force high school students to meet minimum academic standards.

Yet almost every year of so, some group releases a study showing many California children are scoring below expectations or doing poorly as compared to Japanese or European children.

The California system is expensive, over $55 billion annually just for the K-12 system, three fourths from the state, one fourth from the feds.

Comparisons between countries are tricky. If Japanese or European high school students fail or do poorly on their tests, they are often denied admission to college. Those who do well, however, are marked not only for college but the higher-paying jobs. Our system gives second and third chances and allows easy admission to colleges, but bears down on students during college and after they graduate. Then they have to prove themselves at work to get ahead, and this forces many to return to college or get training. Their system pressures teenagers; ours pressures young adults. Some studies suggest that by age 30 the differences even out.

As intriguing as this theory is, many parents and teachers would feel much better if the learning curve showed a sharper rise for the high-school scholars and, of course, our top universities — Cal, Stanford, Harvard — demand high scores for admission.

Registering For School

To get into kindergarten, your child must turn five before Dec. 3 of the year he or she enters the grade. For first grade, your child must be six before Dec. 3. If he is six on Dec. 4, if she is a mature Jan. 6 birthday girl, speak to the school. There may be some wiggle room. The law gives schools some say over whether the child is mature enough for school.

For registration, you are required to show proof of immunization for polio, diphtheria, hepatitis B, tetanus, pertussis (whooping cough), measles, rubella and mumps. If the kid is seven or older, you can skip mumps and whooping cough. Students entering the seventh grade must show proof of being immunized against hepatitis B.

San Francisco School Choices

San Francisco educates its children in unusual and changing ways. For parents new to the City, it is important to register your children with the schools right away. This may decide what school they are assigned to.

Although liberal in politics, San Francisco leads all other counties in the state in educating students at private schools — about 30 percent of the enrollments. In the 19th and early 20th centuries, the Catholic community built schools all around town. These schools, which now enroll many non-Catholics, make up the majority of private schools. As for the others, a wide choice. See directory of private schools in this guide.

About three decades ago, the federal court, to remedy segregation, imposed upon the public school system an integration plan that was amended several times in major ways but was never fully accepted by key groups. The plan and its revisions bused many kids out of their neighborhood schools and introduced uncertainty into the usually simple business of registering for school. Many parents were never sure where their children would be assigned. Some assignments were made by lottery.

In 2005, the court ended its supervision over the schools and told the district draw up its own plan.

At the same time, Arlene Ackerman, the superintendent, in an unrelated action, quit the district. Chances are the revised enrollment procedures will not be worked out until a new superintendent is hired and gets acquainted with the district.

One practice is firmly and traditionally grounded and unlikely to be changed — Lowell High admits by competitive exam and takes only the top students. For this reason, Lowell, which has the highest enrollment of any school in the district, for as long as anyone can remember has been one of the highest-scoring schools in the state. It graduates many of its students into the top universities and in 2002 won a national Blue Ribbon for academic excellence.

This is all well and good but it complicates enrollments for the other public high schools (and illustrates the contrary nature of San Francisco. Ultra liberal city subscribes to elite school education.) In recent years, to help its struggling students, the district has created learning academies with uniforms and more instructional time.

San Francisco has the lowest percentage of school-age children of any county in the state, and this is showing itself by declining enrollments. Several schools have been closed; more closings are expected. The private sector is also closing schools.

(San Francisco Continued) Despite all this, the schools systems, public and private, may be doing a good job. Yes, San Francisco has its failing students (who should not be ignored.) Every major city in the U.S. has many failing students. But San Francisco has many students who score well above the 50th percentile and 75th percentile. Several years ago, our editors informally crunched a few numbers to determine which Bay Area counties and cities, per capita, were sending the most students to the UCs (top 13 percent). San Francisco numbers were close to Marin's and about equal to upper-middle towns of the East Bay.

Most adults in San Francisco don't have children and many never will. Nonetheless, San Francisco over the last 17 years has never turned down a bond or money request for the schools. The district in that period made six requests. For school funding in California, San Francisco leads the pack — by miles.

All schools will be able to give you enrollment information and application papers. Parents should call the enrollment office at (415) 241-6085 for information. Or visit the office at 555 Franklin St., near city hall. The office is staffed with counselors who can give you advice. For web advice, search under San Francisco Unified School District.

Register Early

Just because you enroll your child first does not necessarily mean that you will get your first choice of schools or teachers. But in some school districts first-come does mean first-served. Enrollment and transfer policies change from year to year in some districts, depending on the number of children enrolled and the space available. When new schools are opened, attendance boundaries are often changed.

Even if the school district says, "There's plenty of time to register," do it as soon as possible. If a dispute arises over attendance — the school might get an unexpected influx of students — early registration might give you a leg up in any negotiations. Persistence sometimes helps in trying for transfers.

Choosing the "Right" School

Almost all public schools have attendance zones, usually the immediate neighborhood. The school comes with the neighborhood; often you have no choice. Your address determines your school.In San Francisco, there are many exceptions to this approach. See San Francisco School Choices in this chapter.

Always call the school district to find out what school your children will be attending. Sometimes school districts change attendance boundaries and do not inform local Realtors. Sometimes crowding forces kids out of their neighborhood schools. It's always good to go to the first source.

Just say something like, "I'm Mrs. Jones and we're thinking about moving into 1234 Main Street. What school will my six-year-old attend?"

Ask what elementary school your child will attend and what middle school and high school. Keep in mind that although a district scores high, not all the schools in the district may score high. In some districts, scores vary widely.

Several districts may serve one town, another reason to nail down your school of attendance.

Transfers

If you don't like your neighborhood school, you can request a transfer to another school in the district or to a school outside the district. But the school won't provide transportation.

Transfers to schools inside the district are easier to get than transfers outside the district. New laws supposedly make it easier to transfer children to other districts. In reality, the more popular (high scoring) districts and schools, lacking space, rarely accept "outside" students. New federal laws supposedly make it easier to transfer out of schools that do not meet academic standards.

A few parents use the address of a friend or relative to smuggle their child into a high-scoring school or district. Some districts make an effort to ferret out these students and give them the boot.

If your child has a special problem that may demand your attention, speak to the school administrators about a transfer to a school close to your job.

Does a Different School Make a Difference?

This may sound like a dumb question but it pays to understand some of the thinking behind choosing one school or school district over another. Two stories:

Researching our guides, we contacted a school district that refused to give us test results. This stuff is public information.

In so many words, the school administrator said, look, our scores are lousy because our demographics are awful: low income, parents poorly educated, etc. But our programs and staff are great. I'm not giving out the scores because parents will get the wrong idea about our district and keep their kids out of our schools. (He later changed his mind and gave us the scores.)

Second story, while working as a reporter, one of our editors covered a large urban school district and heard about a principal who was considered top notch. An interview was set up and the fellow seemed as good as his reputation: friendly, hard-working, supportive of his staff, a great role model for his students, many of whom he knew by their first names. But scores at the school were running in the 10th to 20th percentile, very low.

Although neither person said this, the clear implication was that if the demographics were different, scores would be much higher. And they're probably right. If these schools got an influx of middle- and upper middle-class children, their scores would dramatically increase.

Why don't schools tell this to the public, to parents? Probably because socioeconomics is difficult to explain. Teachers want to work with parents, not alienate them with accusations of neglect. Some educators argue that even with poor socioeconomics, teachers should be able to do an effective job — controversy. Socioeconomics focuses attention on the problems of home and society to the possible detriment of schools (which also need help and funds). School, after all, is a limited activity: about six hours a day, about 180 teaching days a year.

When you strip away the fluff, schools seem to be saying that they are in the business of schools, not in reforming the larger society, and that they should be held accountable only for what they can influence: the children during the school day, on school grounds.

For these reasons — this is our opinion — many teachers and school administrators think that scores mislead and that parents often pay too much attention to scores and not enough to programs and the background and training of personnel. This is not to say that teachers ignore scores and measurements of accomplishment. They would love to see their students succeed. And schools find tests useful to determine whether their programs need changes.

No matter how low the scores, if you, as a parent, go into any school and ask — can my child get a good education here — you will be told, probably invariably, often enthusiastically, yes. First, there's the obvious reason: if the principal said no, his or her staff and bosses would be upset and angry. Second, by the reasoning common to public schools, "yes" means that the principal believes that the school and its teachers have the knowledge, training and dedication to turn out accomplished students. And the programs. Schools stress programs.

Is all this valid? Yes. Programs and training are important. Many schools with middling scores do turn out students that attend the best universities.

But this approach has its skeptics. Many parents and educators believe that schools must be judged by their scores, that scores are the true test of quality.

Some parents fear that if their child or children are placed in classes with low-achieving or even middle-achieving children they will not try as hard as they would if their friends or classmates were more academic, or that in some situations their children will be enticed into mischief. In some inner-city districts, the children, for misguided reasons, pressure each other not to do well in school.

Some parents do not believe that a school with many low-scoring students can do justice to its few middle- and high-scoring students. To meet the needs of the majority, instruction might have to be slowed for everyone.

Discipline is another problem. Teachers in low-scoring schools might have to spend more time on problem kids than teachers in high-scoring schools.

There's much more but basically it comes down to the belief that schools do not stand alone, that they and their students are influenced by the values of parents, of classmates and of the immediate neighborhood.

To continue this logic, schools and school districts are different from one another and for this reason it pays to move into a neighborhood with high-scoring schools or one with at least middling-plus scores. Or to somehow secure a transfer to one of the schools in these neighborhoods.

To an unknown extent, the marketplace has reinforced this belief. It rewards neighborhoods and towns with high-scoring schools by increasing the value (the price) of their homes. Woven into all this is the suspicion, held by many in California, that public schools have failed to dismiss incompetent teachers and have become inflexible and unable to address problems. California for decades has been wracked by arguments over the power of the teachers' union, and over testing and teaching methods, and curriculum.

The parents who seem to do best at this business find out as much as possible about the schools, make decisions or compromises based on good information and work with the schools and teachers to advance their children's interests. Each school should be publishing an "accountability report." Ask for it.

Year-Round Schools

Year-round schools are becoming increasingly popular as a way to handle rapidly increasing enrollments. Schedules, called "tracks," vary from district to district but all students attend a full academic year (about 180 teaching days).

Traditional holidays are observed. One group may start in summer, one in late summer and so on. A typical pattern is 12 weeks on, four weeks off. One track is always off, allowing another track to use its class space. For more information, call the school districts.

Ability Grouping

Ask about the school's advancement or grouping policy or gifted classes. Some California schools, responding to parents' wishes, group them for part of the day in gifted classes (the college track). At the middle schools, advanced students might be tracked into algebra, other students into everyday math. At high school, this type of dividing becomes more prevalent.

Without getting into the pros and cons of these practices, schools often tiptoe around them because they upset some parents and frankly because some children have to be slighted. Say the ideal situation in a middle school is three levels of math: low, middle and high. But funds will allow only two levels. So low is combined with middle or middle with high. If you know the school is being forced into compromises, you might choose to pay for tutoring.

Miscellaneous

- For much of the 1990s, California, in a tough economy, pulled the purse strings tight against school spending. Teacher salaries fell behind what was paid in other states. Programs were cut. Quality, many believe, suffered. In the late 1990s, the economy came roaring back and pushed billions of extra dollars into the state treasury.

- Teacher salaries were raised (tops in U.S.), class sizes in the first three grades were lowered (to 20-1), programs were restored.

- In 2001 and 2002, the dot coms crashed and tax revenues plummeted. California has burned through its budget surplus and is saddled with a large deficit. We have entered another era of stingy state spending that is spilling into cuts for education.

- On the positive side, several years ago voters dropped the approval vote for local bonds for school construction from two-thirds of ballots cast to 55 percent. School districts that had lost several bond elections went back to the voters and won approval. On the state level, voters in 2002 and 2004 approved construction bonds worth $24 billion. Many school districts have become skilled at squeezing developers for building costs.

- The contradiction: after decades of neglect, California is renovating thousands of its schools and building more. The state in 2004 settled a law suit that will inject more fixing-up money into the poorest and most run-down schools. At the same time, school districts are finding it harder to come up with operational funds — salaries, programs, books, etc. Extra operational money generally requires a two-thirds vote; hard to win. Many school districts have turned to parental and community fund raising to come up with operational money. This often amounts to a parental tax, usually collected by a "foundation" run by the parents.

- What if you or your neighborhood can't afford voluntary fees? Shop for bargains. Community colleges, in the summer, often run academic programs for children. Local tutors might work with small groups. Specific tutoring, say just in math, might be used to get the student over the rough spots. For information on tutors, look in the Yellow Pages under "Tutoring."

- Private vs. public. A complex battle, it boils down to one side saying public schools are the best and fairest way to educate all children versus the other side saying public education is inefficient and will never reform until it has meaningful competition. The state has allowed over 560 schools to restructure their programs according to local needs — an effort at eliminating unnecessary rules. These institutions are called charter schools.

- Once tenured, teachers are almost impossible to fire, which opens schools to accusations of coddling incompetents. If your child gets a sour teacher, request a transfer. Better still, become active in the PTA or talk to other parents and try to identify the best teachers. Then ask for them.

- Over the past several years, the state Dept. of Education has adopted standards for science, history, math and reading. These standards define what the students are supposed to master at every grade level. Now the state has introduced texts and tests based on the standards. If students don't pass the tests, they may not be promoted. How much of this will be implemented remains to be seen. The feds, through No Child Left Behind, are demanding tougher penalties on low-scoring schools and programs that do not improve. Testing is touchy in California.

- Courts and school districts have sorted out Proposition 227, which curtailed non-English instruction in public schools. Parents can request a waiver, which under certain conditions allows instruction in the native language. Some schools are embracing dual immersion as a way to teach Spanish and English. The kids start with almost all Spanish and gradually introduce English until the ratio is 50-50.

- Busing. School districts can charge and several do. Some low-income and special education kids ride free.

- Uniforms. Schools have the discretion to require uniforms, an effort to discourage gang colors and get the kids to pay more attention to school than to how they look. "Uniforms" are generally interpreted to mean modest dress; for example, dark pants and shirts for boys, plaid skirts and light blouse for girls.

- Closed campus vs. open campus. The former stops the students from leaving at lunch or at any time during the school day. The latter allows the kids to leave. Kids love open, parents love closed.

- Grad night. Not too many years ago, graduating seniors would whoop it up on grad night and some would drink and then drive and get injured or killed. At many high schools now, parents stage a grad night party at the school, load it with games, raffles and prizes, and lock the kids in until dawn. A lot of work but it keeps the darlings healthy.

- T-P. California tradition. Your son or daughter joins a school team and it wins a few games or the cheerleaders win some prize — any excuse will do — and some parent will drive the kids around and they will fling toilet paper over your house, car, trees and shrubs. Damn nuisance but the kids love it.

- The number of teaching days has been increased, from about 172 to 180.

- Open Houses, Parents Nights. One study, done at Stanford, concluded that if parents will attend these events, the students, or at least some of them, will be impressed enough to pay more attention to school.

- Rather than lug around books, lunches, gym gear, etc., students these days are using rolling suitcases similar to carry-on luggage. "They help your back," said one student. The outfits seem to be particularly popular in schools that have done away with lockers.

- More kids are being pushed into algebra, not only in high school but in the seventh and eighth grades. New law requires all students to take algebra before graduating from high school.

- Exit exam. Starting in 2006, students must pass an exit exam to receive a high school diploma. To get the kids prepared, all of them must take the exam by their sophomore year. If they fail, the high school will offer extra help.

- Every year the California Dept. of Education honors certain schools as "Distinguished." This means that the department thinks they are well run. In one year, middle and high schools are singled out, the following year, elementary schools.

In San Mateo County, Hillview Middle – Menlo Park, Central Middle – San Carlos, Bowditch Middle – Foster City.

In Sonoma County, Technology High – Rohnert Park, Hillcrest Middle – Sebastopol, Windsor High – Windsor.

In Marin County, Miller Creek Middle, Terra Linda High – San Rafael, Sir Francis Drake High – San Anselmo, Tamalpais High – Mill Valley.

In San Francisco, Galileo Acad., Lowell High and Presidio Middle.

In 2005, the national Blue Ribbon for academic excellence, a rare award, went to Chin Elementary and Yick Wo Elementary in San Francisco and Meadow Elementary in Petaluma.

Community College Transfers

ALTHOUGH PRIMARILY trade schools, community colleges are a major source of students for the University of California and for the California State universities. The students usually take freshman and sophomore classes at a community college, then transfer to a university.

Community colleges are cheap a nd often conveniently located. Many community colleges have worked out transfer agreements with local state universities and with the UCs. The data below shows how many students each sector advances.

Tracking San Francisco County Students to UCs & CSUs

By High Schools and Community Colleges

Student Sector	Graduates	To UC	To CSU
Public High Schools	3,812	804	595
Community Colleges	-----	289	614

By Community College Campus

Community College	To UC	To CSU
City College of San Francisco	289	614

Tracking all San Mateo County Students to UCs & CSUs

By High Schools and Community Colleges

Student Sector	Graduates	To UC	To CSU
Public High Schools	5,289	515	706
Community Colleges	-----	236	473

Tracking all Marin & Sonoma Students to UCs & CSUs

By Community College Campuses

Community College	To UC	To CSU
Canãda College	14	64
College of San Mateo	144	192
Skyline College	78	217

Source: California Postsecondary Education Commission, Student Profile 2004. **Note**: Enrolling students counted in 2003-2004 by UCs and Cal States.

School Accountability Report Card

Want more information about a particular school or school district?

Every public school and district in the state is required by law to issue an annual School Accountability Report Card. The everyday name is the SARC report or the SARC card (pronounced SARK). SARCs include:

- The ethnic makeup of the school and school district.

- Test results. The results may be presented in several ways but almost without exception the formats follow the presentation methods of the California Dept. of Education.

- A description of the curriculum and the programs.

- Class sizes, teacher-pupil ratios.

- Description of the teaching staff. How many have teaching credentials.

- Description of facilities.

To obtain a SARC, call the school and if the person answering the phone can't help you, ask for the superintendent's secretary or the curriculum department. Many schools post their SARCS on the web. If you don't know the name of the neighborhood school, start with the school district. See following.

Local School Districts

San Francisco is served by one school district. For enrollment information, call (415) 241-6085

San Mateo County (see chart on page 279) is divided into elementary districts, high school districts and unified districts. Unified districts cover grades K-12; they have their own elementary, middle (or junior high) and high schools. San Mateo County has three unified districts: Cabrillo, La Honda-Pescadero, South San Francisco. In the other arrangements, the elementary districts advance their children into the high school districts. For example, students attending schools in the Bayshore, Brisbane, Jefferson and Pacifica Elementary districts move up to schools in the Jefferson Union High School District. Each district sets its own attendance policies. Call the districts for more information.

San Mateo County

ELEMENTARY, HIGH SCHOOL & UNIFIED SCHOOL DISTRICTS

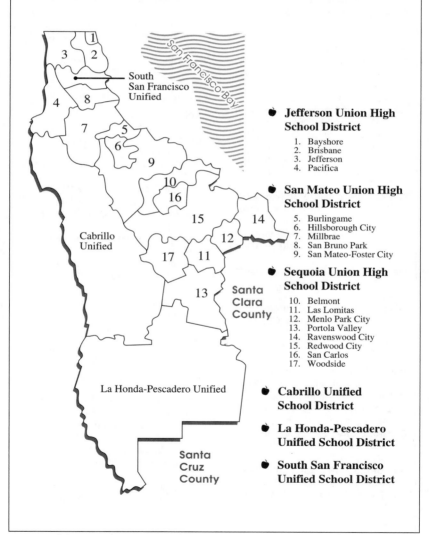

Jefferson Union High School District

1. Bayshore
2. Brisbane
3. Jefferson
4. Pacifica

San Mateo Union High School District

5. Burlingame
6. Hillsborough City
7. Millbrae
8. San Bruno Park
9. San Mateo-Foster City

Sequoia Union High School District

10. Belmont
11. Las Lomitas
12. Menlo Park City
13. Portola Valley
14. Ravenswood City
15. Redwood City
16. San Carlos
17. Woodside

Cabrillo Unified School District

La Honda-Pescadero Unified School District

South San Francisco Unified School District

San Francisco and San Mateo School Districts

San Francisco Unified School District (all of San Francisco) (415) 241-6000.

Bayshore Elementary District (Daly City) (415) 467-5443

Belmont-Redwood Shores Elementary District (Belmont, Redwood City) (650) 637-4800

Brisbane Elementary District (Brisbane, Daly City) (415) 467-0550

Burlingame Elementary District (Burlingame) (650) 259-3800

Cabrillo Unified School District (Half Moon Bay, El Granada, Montera, Woodside) (650) 712-7100

Hillsborough City School District (Hillsborough) (650) 342-5193

Jefferson Elementary District (Daly City, Colma) (650) 991-1200

Jefferson Union High School District (Daly City, Pacifica) (650) 550-7900

La Honda-Pescadero Unified School District (La Honda, Pescadero) (650) 879-0286

Las Lomitas Elementary District (Atherton, Menlo Park) (650) 854-2880

Menlo Park City Elementary District (Atherton, Menlo Park) (650) 321-7140

Millbrae Elementary District (Millbrae, San Bruno) (650) 697-5693

Pacifica School District (Pacifica) (650) 738-6600

Portola Valley Elementary District (Portola Valley) (650) 851-1777

Ravenswood City Elementary District (East Palo Alto, Menlo Park) (650) 329-2800

Redwood City Elementary District (Atherton, Menlo Park, Redwood City) (650) 423-2200

San Bruno Park Elementary District (San Bruno) (650) 624-3100

San Carlos Elementary District (San Carlos) (650) 508-7333

San Mateo-Foster City (Foster City, San Mateo) (650) 312-7700

San Mateo Union High School District (Burlingame, Millbrae, San Bruno, San Mateo) (650) 762-0200

Sequoia Union High School District (Atherton, Belmont, Redwood City, Woodside) (650) 369-1411

South San Francisco Unified School District (Daly City, San Bruno, South San Francisco) (650) 877-8700

Woodside Elementary District (Woodside) (650) 851-1571

Marin School Districts

- Bolinas-Stinson School Elementary (415) 868-1603
- Dixie Elementary District (San Rafael) (415) 492-3700
- Kentfield School District (415) 925-2230
- Laguna School Elementary (rural, north county) (707) 762-6051
- Lagunitas District (San Geronimo) (415) 488-4118
- Larkspur District Office (415) 927-6960
- Lincoln School Elementary District (rural, north county) (707) 763-0045
- Mill Valley School District (415) 389-7700
- Nicasio Elementary (415) 662-2184
- Novato Unified (415) 897-4201
- Reed Union Elementary (Tiburon-Belvedere) (415) 435-7840
- Ross Elementary District (415) 457-2705
- Ross Valley District (San Anselmo and Fairfax) (415) 454-2162
- San Rafael Elementary and High School District (415) 492-3233
- Sausalito Elementary District (includes Marin City) (415) 332-3190
- Shoreline Unified (Tomales, Bodega Bay, Pt. Reyes Station) (707) 878-2266

- **Tamalpais Union High (Larkspur, San Anselmo, Corte Madera, Mill Valley)** (415) 945-3737
- **Union Joint Elementary (rural, north county)** (707) 762-2047

Sonoma School Districts

- **Alexander Union Elementary** (707) 433-1375
- **Bellevue Union Elementary (Santa Rosa)** (707) 542-5197
- **Bennett Valley Union Elem. (Santa Rosa)** (707) 542-2201
- **Cinnabar Elementary (Petaluma)** (707) 765-4345
- **Cloverdale Unified** (707) 894-1920
- **Cotati-Rohnert Park Unified** (707) 792-4722
- **Dunham Elementary (Petaluma)** (707) 795-5050
- **Forestville Union Elem.** (707) 887-9767
- **Fort Ross Elem.** (707) 847-3390
- **Geyserville Unified** (707) 857-3592
- **Gravenstein Union Elem.** (Sebastopol), (707) 823-5361
- **Guerneville Elem.** (707) 887-7762
- **Harmony School District (Occidental)** (707) 874-3280
- **Healdsburg Unified** (707) 431-3117
- **Horicon Elementary (Sea Ranch)** (707) 886-5322
- **Kashia Elementary (rural)** (707) 785-9682
- **Kenwood Elem.** (707) 833-2500
- **Liberty Elem. (Petaluma)** (707) 795-4380
- **Mark West Union (Santa Rosa)** (707) 524-2970
- **Monte Rio Union Elem.** (707) 865-2266
- **Montgomery Elem. (Cazadero)** (707) 632-5221
- **Oak Grove Union Elem. (Santa Rosa)** (707) 545-0171
- **Old Adobe Union Elem. (Petaluma)** (707) 765-4321
- **Petaluma Elem. and High** (707) 778-4604.
- **Piner-Olivet School District (Santa Rosa)** (707) 522-3000
- **Rincon Valley Union Elem. (Santa Rosa)** (707) 542-7375
- **Roseland Elem. (Santa Rosa area)** (707) 545-0102
- **Santa Rosa Elem and High Dist.** (707) 528-5181
- **Sebastopol Elem.** (707) 829-4570
- **Sonoma Valley (Sonoma, El Verano, Boyes Hot Springs)** (707) 935-6000
- **Twin Hills Elem. (near Sebastopol)** (707) 823-0871
- **Two Rock Elem. (near Petaluma)** (707) 762-6617
- **Waugh (near Petaluma)** (707) 765-3331
- **West Side Union Elem. (near Healdsburg)** (707) 433-3923
- **West Sonoma Union High (Sebastopol, Forestville)** (707) 824-6403
- **Wilmar Elem. (near Petaluma)** (707) 765-4340
- **Windsor** (707) 837-7700
- **Wright District (Santa Rosa)** (707) 542-0550

SAT Test Scores By County 2004

County	Enroll.	% Tested	Verbal	Math
Alameda	13,522	48	504	537
Alpine	3	33	NA	NA
Amador	476	31	520	506
Butte	2,688	26	503	517
Calaveras	556	30	526	531
Colusa	337	26	449	454
Contra Costa	11,834	41	530	548
Del Norte	589	14	511	517
El Dorado	2,348	33	538	556
Fresno	11,569	29	468	487
Glenn	463	25	465	478
Humboldt	1,651	30	537	543
Imperial	2,257	27	449	459
Inyo	257	37	500	500
Kern	11,057	22	481	494
Kings	1,746	18	474	476
Lake	740	22	512	509
Lassen	579	18	477	486
Los Angeles	94,377	40	473	499
Madera	1,683	18	477	497
Marin	2,031	59	557	561
Mariposa	200	23	531	544
Mendocino	1,194	32	508	523
Merced	3,700	23	453	464
Modoc	190	29	466	466
Mono	170	44	522	500
Monterey	4,487	32	463	473
Napa	1,463	32	515	527
Nevada	2,275	18	551	548
Orange	32,337	40	523	557
Placer	4,657	33	522	539
Plumas	245	33	505	491
Riverside	21,643	31	474	489
Sacramento	15,080	30	495	512
San Benito	646	32	495	504
San Bernardino	24,828	27	475	489
San Diego	31,968	40	508	524
San Francisco	4,376	58	471	536
San Joaquin	8,645	24	472	491
San Luis Obispo	3,100	32	537	539
San Mateo	6,023	45	513	541
Santa Barbara	4,505	32	529	543
Santa Clara	17,231	47	528	565
Santa Cruz	2,891	36	519	531
Shasta	2,470	21	517	526
Sierra	70	40	514	501
Siskiyou	517	24	508	524
Solano	5,109	32	489	510
Sonoma	5,249	34	538	546

(Continued on next page)

(Continued from previous page)

SAT Test Scores By County 2004

County	Enroll.	% Tested	Verbal	Math
Stanislaus	7,210	21	499	507
Sutter	1,203	23	496	530
Tehama	806	18	512	512
Trinity	199	23	567	571
Tulare	5,772	23	462	478
Tuolumne	608	26	533	526
Ventura	10,317	31	528	543
Yolo	2,064	39	536	561
Yuba	983	18	461	486
Statewide:	395,194	35	496	519

Source: California Dept. of Education, 2004 School year.

High School Graduates College Choice By County

County	UC	CSU	CC
Alameda	1,679	1,898	5,203
Alpine	0	0	0
Amador	13	40	91
Butte	75	246	730
Calaveras	19	54	68
Colusa	7	36	73
Contra Costa	1,078	1,222	2,217
Del Norte	9	18	60
El Dorado	131	190	615
Fresno	320	1,247	1,175
Glenn	4	60	126
Humboldt	62	161	437
Imperial	82	133	1,595
Inyo	13	15	60
Kern	263	906	2,461
Kings	36	88	241
Lake	12	52	184
Lassen	6	13	103
Los Angeles	7,113	9,713	28,916
Madera	25	131	55
Marin	345	299	323
Mariposa	5	6	20
Mendocino	32	102	372
Merced	90	286	151
Modoc	5	6	30
Mono	4	17	36
Monterey	254	421	1,355
Napa	90	137	202
Nevada	49	100	338
Orange	2,937	3,060	15,172
Placer	223	434	1,365
Plumas	6	10	64
Riverside	1,056	1,402	4,661
Sacramento	882	1,398	5,178
San Benito	24	61	229
San Bernardino	959	1,821	5,805
San Diego	2,020	3,061	9,197
San Francisco	1,093	813	1,353
San Joaquin	217	524	2,008
San Luis Obispo	148	295	1,120
San Mateo	707	638	1,733
Santa Barbara	306	256	1,680
Santa Clara	2,226	2,182	4,185
Santa Cruz	234	298	969
Shasta	42	146	98
Sierra	2	7	10
Siskiyou	12	28	163
Solano	242	423	1,395
Sonoma	332	469	2,058
Stanislaus	187	553	1,642

High School Graduates Choice of School By County

County	UC	CSU	CC
Sutter	42	99	496
Tehama	14	61	83
Trinity	6	7	23
Tulare	134	395	1,537
Tuolumne	12	34	145
Ventura	541	656	4,193
Yolo	204	192	578
Yuba	9	47	278

Source: California Postsecondary Education Commission, 2004. Number of public and private high-school students moving up as freshmen to a UC or a California State University.

Chapter **11**

Private Schools

ALTHOUGH PRIVATE SCHOOLS often enjoy a better reputation than public, they are not without problems. The typical private or parochial school is funded way below its public school counterpart.

In size, facilities and playing fields, and in programs, public schools usually far outstrip private schools. Private school teachers earn less than public school teachers.

"Typical" has to be emphasized. Some private schools are well-equipped, offer exceptional programs, pay their teachers competitively and limit class sizes to fewer than 15 students.

Private schools vary widely in funding. But even when "typical," private schools enjoy certain advantages over public schools.

The Advantages

Public schools must accept all students, have almost no power to dismiss incompetent teachers and are at the mercy of their neighborhoods for the quality of students — the socioeconomic correlation. The unruly often cannot be expelled or effectively disciplined.

Much has been said about the ability of private schools to rid themselves of problem children and screen them out in the first place. But tuition, even when modest, probably does more than anything else to assure private schools quality students.

Parents who pay extra for their child's education and often agree to work closely with the school are, usually, demanding parents. The result: fewer discipline problems, fewer distractions in the class, more of a willingness to learn.

When you place your child in a good private school, you are, to a large extent, buying him or her scholastic classmates. They may not be the smartest children — many private schools accept children of varying ability — but generally they will have someone at home breathing down their necks to succeed in academics.

College Admissions of Private School Graduates

San Francisco Schools

High School	UC	CSU	CC
Arch. Riordan	20	45	44
Bridgemont	1	0	1
Conv. of Sacred Heart	8	3	1
Cornerstone Academy	4	0	NA
Drew College Prep	11	4	2
Hebrew Academy	5	0	4
Immaculate Conception	6	16	13
Lick-Wilmerding	12	3	2
Lycee-Francais	5	0	3
Mercy	18	23	45
Sacred Heart	64	26	39
St. Ignatius	107	31	20
San Francisco University	15	0	2
Urban	10	3	4
Wildshaw	3	0	5

San Mateo County Schools

High School	UC	CSU	CC
Alma Heights	1	0	3
Alpha Beacon Christian	1	0	1
Crystal Springs	15	0	NA
Junipero Serra	39	40	33
Menlo School	76	2	6
Mercy	19	22	14
Notre Dame	18	28	15
Sacred Heart	19	4	4
Woodside Priory	4	1	NA

The same attitude, a reflection of family values, is found in the high-achieving public schools.

When a child in one of these schools or a private school turns to his left and right, he will see and later talk to children who read books and newspapers. A child in a low-achieving school, public or private, will talk to classmates who watch a lot of television and rarely read.

(These are, necessarily, broad generalizations. Much depends on whom the children pick for friends. High-achieving students certainly watch television but, studies show, much less than low-achieving students. Many critics contend that even high-scoring schools are graduating students poorly prepared for college.)

The Quality of Teaching

Do private schools have better teachers than public schools? Impossible to tell. Both sectors sing the praises of their teachers. (Cont. on P. 290)

A Profile of Catholic Schools

THE LARGEST PRIVATE system, Catholic schools enroll about 15,000 students in San Francisco and 10,000 in San Mateo County. About 25 percent of the students are non Catholic. Data from 2000-2001 school year. Sorry no data on Marin and Sonoma schools but the policies described below will give you some idea of how Catholic schools are run.

- **All races, creeds welcome.** Where schools are full, preference is given first to Catholic children from families active in parish. After that, to active Catholics unable to get into own parish schools.

- **High schools recruit regionally for students.** Admissions and placement tests but all accept average students. Standards vary by school. Recommendations by parish pastors, principals, eighth-grade teachers carry clout.

- **Why parents send kids to Catholic schools.** A survey: 1. Religious tradition, moral and spiritual values. 2. Academics. 3. Discipline.

- **Curriculum.** Elementary schools cover same basic subjects as public schools but weave in religious-moral viewpoint. "Philosophy based in Jesus Christ. Religious values are integral to learning experience." State textbooks often used. Each school picks texts from list approved by diocese. High school instruction, although varied, is greatly influenced by requirements of University of California. Strong emphasis on technology in elementary and secondary schools.

Educators advise parents to approach high schools as they would any educational institution: ask about grades, what percentage of students go on to college.

- **Non-Catholics.** Get same instruction as Catholics, including history of Church and scripture. Attend Mass but not required to take sacraments. "We don't try to convert them," said one nun.

- **Corporal punishment.** Thing of past. More aware now of child abuse. Stress positive discipline, name on board, detention, probation. Try to work problems through, few expulsions.

- **Class sizes.** Before 40, now 30 to 32. Somewhat smaller for high schools because of special classes, e.g. French.

Would like smaller but point out that with well-behaved students, teachers can accomplish a lot. Matter of economics. If parents wanted smaller classes, they would have to pay more. "We want to keep affordable prices so all people can choose us, not just rich."

Catholic Schools

- **Tuition.** See directory of private schools at the end of this chapter.

- **Schedule.** Similar to public schools. 180 teaching days, minimum of five hours, 10 minutes a day. Many go longer.

- **Ability grouping.** In elementary grades (K-8) not done by class. Grouping within classes, advanced children working at one level, slow children at another. Tutoring after class. "You're not going to walk in and find 35 children on the same page."

  All high schools run prep programs, tend to attract prep students, but will accept remedial students, if they have remedial instruction. Admission standards vary by high school.

- **Homework.** Each school sets policy but diocese suggests guidelines: Grades one and two, 20 minutes; three and four, 30-45 minutes; five and six, 45 to 60 minutes; seven and eight, 60-90 minutes. None on weekends and vacations. High schools require more homework, may assign on weekends and holidays. Teacher's choice.

- **Report cards.** Four a year plus results of diocesan tests. Parents are expected to attend conferences, back-to-school nights.

- **Teacher quality.** Bachelor's degree required. Most credentialed. Hired for competence, commitment to Catholic educational philosophy. A few non-Catholic teachers but system tends to attract Catholic educators.

- **Uniforms.** Yes. Generally plaid skirts, blouses and sweaters for girls, collared shirts, sweaters and cords for boys.

- **Extended care.** All schools offer before- and after-school care, 7 a.m. to 6 p.m. Ask.

- **Drugs.** "Not major problem but when it happens we do everything to work with student."

- **Extracurricular activities.** Although campuses small, schools try to offer variety of activities, sports, arts, music. At elementary school, much depends on work of parents. "Parents are expected to do a lot." High schools offer good variety: music, band, arts, intramural sports, many club activities, computers, science. Catholic high schools usually field very competitive football and basketball teams.

- **For more information,** admissions, call school directly. Most registrations in spring but earlier for high schools. Education office at diocese, (415) 614-5660.

College Admissions of Private School Graduates

Marin County

High School	UC	CSU	CC
Branson	15	0	NA
Marin Academy	16	3	4
Marin Catholic	41	25	12
North Bay Marin	3	8	NA
San Domenico	11	1	3

Sonoma County

High School	UC	CSU	CC
Cardinal Newman	9	14	22
Nonesuch	0	2	NA
Rincon Valley	4	3	2
Rio Lindo Adventist	0	1	11
St.Vincent	0	23	12
Summerfield	1	0	NA
Ursuline	10	16	13

Source: California Dept. of Education. The chart tracks California public colleges or universities, and high school graduates from private schools. It shows how many students from these high schools enrolled as college freshmen in the year 2004. The state does not track graduates enrolling in private colleges or out-of-state colleges.
Key: UC (University of California system); CSU (Cal State system); CC (Community Colleges).

(Cont. from P. 287)

Private schools, compared to public, have much more freedom to dismiss teachers but this can be abused. The private schools themselves advise parents to avoid schools with excessive teacher turnover.

Although most can't pay as much as public schools, private institutions claim to attract people fed up with the limitations of public schools, particularly the restrictions on disciplining and ejecting unruly children. Some proponents argue that private schools attract teachers "who really want to teach."

Religion and Private Schools

Some private schools are as secular as any public institution. But many are religious-oriented and talk in depth about religion or ethics, or teach a specific creed. Or possibly they teach values within a framework of western civilization or some other philosophy.

Until recently, public schools almost never talked about religion or religious figures. They now teach the history of major religions and the basic tenets of each, and they try to inculcate in the children a respect for all religions.

It's hard, if not impossible, however, for public schools to talk about values outside of a framework of religion or a system of ethics. Often, it's difficult for them to talk about values. Some people argue that this is major failing.

UCs Chosen by Private School Graduates

Marin County

High Sch.	Berk	Davis	Irv	LA	Riv	SD	SB	SC	Total
Branson	4	1	0	3	0	2	3	2	15
Marin Academy	2	5	0	3	1	2	0	3	16
Marin Catholic	3	14	4	5	1	3	3	8	41
North Bay Marin	0	0	0	0	0	0	2	1	3
San Domenico	3	2	0	4	0	0	1	1	11

Sonoma County

High Sch.	Berk	Davis	Irv	LA	Riv	SD	SB	SC	Total
Cardi. Newman	0	4	1	0	0	0	3	1	9
Rincon	0	4	0	0	0	0	0	0	4
Summerfield	1	0	0	0	0	0	0	0	1
Ursuline	0	6	0	1	0	0	2	1	10

Many religious schools accept students of different religions or no religion. Some schools offer these students broad courses in religion — less dogma. Ask about the program.

Money

Private-school parents pay taxes for public schools and they pay tuition. Public-school parents pay taxes but not tuition. Big difference.

Ethnic Diversity

Many private schools are integrated and the great majority of private-school principals — the editor knows no exceptions — welcome minorities. Some principals fret over tuition, believing that it keeps many poor students out of private schools.

Money, or lack of it, weighs heavily on private schools. Scholarships, however, are awarded, adjustments made, family rates offered. Never hurts to ask.

What's in San Francisco, San Mateo, Marin and Sonoma

San Francisco has about 90 private schools, San Mateo about 65, Marin 35, Sonoma 43. These are regular schools, enrolling at least 25 students.

They do not include the one-family "schools" (that are recognized by the state as schools) of mother or father or both teaching their own children at home. These family schools, incidentally, have a support network and are able in many instances to get some help (books, advice) from local public schools.

Some private schools have low teacher-pupil ratios, fewer than 15 students per teacher, occasionally around 10 to 1. Public school classes usually go 25 to

UCs Chosen by Private School Graduates

San Francisco Schools

High Sch.	Berk	Davis	Irv	UCLA	Riv	SD	SB	SC	Total
Archbishop Riordan	3	5	1	0	6	1	0	5	26
Bridgemont	1	0	0	0	0	0	0	0	1
Conv. of Sac. Ht.	0	2	0	3	0	1	1	1	8
Cornerstone Acad.	1	2	0	0	0	0	0	1	4
Drew College	2	3	1	0	0	0	1	4	11
Hebrew Acad.	0	4	0	0	0	0	0	1	5
Immaculate Con.	1	1	1	0	0	2	1	0	6
Lick-Wilmerding	0	4	1	1	1	0	3	2	12
Lycee-Francais	1	2	0	0	0	1	0	1	5
Mercy	3	2	1	0	2	1	0	9	18
Sacred Heart	7	27	5	0	6	6	2	11	64
St. Ignatius	19	28	6	16	4	11	6	17	107
SF Univ.	1	3	0	5	2	2	2	0	15
Urban	3	3	0	0	1	0	1	2	10
Wildshaw	1	0	0	1	0	0	1	0	3

San Mateo County Schools

High Sch.	Berk	Davis	Irv	UCLA	Riv	SD	SB	SC	Total
Alma Heights	0	0	0	0	0	0	0	1	1
Alpha Beacon	0	0	0	0	0	0	1	0	1
Crystal Springs	5	2	0	3	0	1	2	2	15
Junipero Serra	5	9	1	4	2	3	9	6	39
Menlo	17	11	4	8	2	8	12	14	76
Mercy	1	4	4	1	1	4	2	2	19
Notre Dame	1	4	2	1	0	2	4	4	18
Sacred Heart	0	4	1	6	0	1	7	0	19
Woodside Priory	0	0	0	0	1	1	0	2	4

Source: California Dept. of Education. The chart tracks the Universities of California and high school graduates from private schools. It shows how many students from these schools enrolled as UC freshmen in fall 2004. The state does not track graduates enrolling in private colleges or out-of-state colleges. **Key**: Berk (Berkeley), Irv (Irvine), Riv (Riverside), SD (San Diego), SB (Santa Barbara), SC (Santa Cruz).

30 per teacher, sometimes higher (new funding has reduced sizes in grades 1-3). Class sizes in Catholic schools generally run higher than what's found in public schools. Catholic schools, nonetheless, are the most popular, a reflection in part of the high number of Catholics in the Bay Area and the high number of Catholic schools.

Private schools in both counties come in great variety, Christian, Jewish, Montessori, Carden (schools with different teaching approaches), prep schools, schools that emphasize language or music, boarding and day schools, schools that allow informal dress, schools that require uniforms.

Choosing a Private School

1. Inspect the grounds, the school's buildings, ask plenty of questions. "I would make myself a real pest," advised one private school official. The good schools welcome this kind of attention.

2. Choose a school with a philosophy congenial to your own, and your child's. Carden schools emphasize structure. Montessori schools, while somewhat structured, encourage individual initiative and independence.

   Ask whether the school is accredited. Private schools are free to run almost any program they like, to set any standards they like, which may sound enticing but in some aspects might hurt the schools. A few bad ones spoil the reputation of the good.

   To remedy this, many private schools sign up for inspections by independent agencies, such as the Western Association of Schools and Colleges and the California Association of Independent Schools. These agencies try to make sure that schools meet their own goals. Some good schools do not seek accreditation.

3. Get all details about tuition carefully explained. How is it to be paid? Are there extra fees? Book costs? Is there a refund if the student is withdrawn or dropped from the school?

4. Progress reports. Parent conferences. How often are they scheduled?

5. What are the entrance requirements? When must they be met? Although many schools use entrance tests, often they are employed to place the child in an academic program, not exclude him from the school.

6. For prep schools, what percentage of the students go on to college and to what colleges?

7. How are discipline problems handled?

8. What are the teacher qualifications? What is the teacher turnover rate?

9. How sound financially is the school? How long has it been in existence? There is nothing wrong per se with new schools. But you want a school that has the wherewithal to do the job.

10. Do parents have to work at functions? Do they have to "volunteer"?

11. Don't choose in haste but don't wait until the last minute. Some schools fill quickly, some fill certain classes quickly. If you can, call the school the year before your child is to enter, early in the year.

12. Don't assume that because your child attends a private school you can expect everything will go all right, that neither the school nor the student needs your attention. The quality of private schools in California varies widely.

Susan Vogel has written "Private High Schools of the San Francisco Bay Area," "Private Schools of the San Francisco Peninsula and Silicon Valley" (Kinder-8th) and "Private Schools of San Francisco and Marin Counties Kindergarten-8th." All are well researched, comprehensive. Check with bookstores or call (415) 267-5978.

Directory of Private Schools

The directory contains the most current information available at press time.

In California, tuition ranges widely in private schools. Many Catholic elementaries charge from about $2,400 to $3,400. Some non-denominational schools go as high as $12,000, and a few higher.

High schools range generally from $7,500 to $13,000 but a few in the peninsula-Silicon Valley are hitting $18,000. Discounts are often given for siblings.

Don't let these numbers discourage you. Call the schools. If strapped, ask about financial help.

San Francisco County

San Francisco

Adda Clevenger Jr .Prep. and Theater Sch., 180 Fair Oaks, (415) 824-2240, Enroll: 125, K-8th.

Archbishop Riordan High, 175 Phelan Ave., (415) 586-8200, Enroll: 788, 9th-12th .

Brandeis Hillel Day, 655 Brotherhood Way, (415) 406-1035, Enroll: 344, K-8th.

Bridgemont Sr. & Jr. High, 777 Brotherhood Way, (415) 333-7600, Enroll: 87, 6th-12th.

Cathedral Sch. for Boys, 1275 Sacramento St., (415) 771-6600, Enroll: 245, K-8th.

Challenge to Lrng., 924 Balboa St., (415) 221-9200, Enroll: 27, 5th-12th.

Children's Day Sch., 333 Dolores St., (415) 861-5432, Enroll: 107, K-8th.

Chinese American Int'l, 150 Oak St., (415) 865-6000, Enroll: 310, K-8th.

Convent of the Sacred Heart Elem., 2200 Broadway, (415) 563-2900, Enroll: 335, K-8th.

Convent of the Sacred Heart High, 2222 Broadway, (415) 563-2900, Enroll: 204, 9th-12th.

Cornerstone Acad., 801 Silver Ave., (415) 587-7256, Enroll: 1,138, K-12th.

Corpus Christi Elem., 75 Francis St., (415) 587-7014, Enroll: 295, K-8th.

De Marillac Middle Sch., 175 Golden Gate Ave., (415) 552-5220, Enroll: 60, 6th-8th.

Discovery Ctr., 65 Ocean Ave., (415) 333-6609, Enroll: 178, K-8th.

Drew Sch., 2901 California St., (415) 409-3739, Enroll: 238, 9th-12th.

Ecole Notre Dame Des Victoires, 659 Pine St., (415) 421-0069, Enroll: 251, K-8th.

Edgewood Ctr. for Children & Families, 1801 Vicente St., (415) 681-3211, Enroll: 49, 1st-9th.

Epiphany Elem., 600 Italy Ave., (415) 337-4030, Enroll: 601, K-8th.

Fellowship Acad., 495 Cambridge St., (415) 239-0511, Enroll: 75, PreK-8th.

French-American Int'l., 150 Oak St., (415) 558-2000, Enroll: 832, K-12th.

Hamlin Sch., 2120 Broadway, (415) 922-0300, Enroll: 402, K-8th .

Hebrew Acad., 645 14th Ave., (415) 752-7333, Enroll: 174, K-12th.

Hillwood Academic Day, 2521 Scott St., (415) 931-0400, Enroll: 36, 1st-8th.

Holy Name Elem., 1560 40th Ave., (415) 731-4077, Enroll: 461, K-8th.

Holy Trinity Orthodox Elem., 999 Brotherhood Way, (415) 584-8451, Enroll: 36, K-8th.

Immaculate Conception Acad., 3625 24th St., (415) 824-2052, Enroll: 257, 9th-12th.

Int'l Christian, 42 Waller St., (415) 863-1691, Enroll: 60, K-5th.

Jewish Comm. High Sch., 1835 Ellis St., (415) 345-9777, Enroll: 110, 9th-11th.

Katherine Delmar Burke, 7070 California St., (415) 751-0177, Enroll: 400, K-8th.

Kittredge Sch. Inc., 2355 Lake St., (415) 750-8390, Enroll: 73, K-8th.

Krouzian-Zekarian of St. Gregory Armenian Ch., 825 Brotherhood Way, (415) 586-8686, Enroll: 121, K-8th.

Lakeside Pres. Ctr. for Children, 201 Eucalyptus Dr., (415) 564-5044, Enroll: 25, K.

Laurel, 350 Ninth Ave., (415) 752-3567, Enroll: 63, K-8th.

Lick-Wilmerding High, 755 Ocean Ave., (415) 333-4021, Enroll: 397, 9th-12th.

Live Oak Sch., 1555 Mariposa St., (415) 861-8840, Enroll: 216, K-8th.

Living Hope Christian, 1209 Geneva Ave., (415) 586-4320, Enroll: 29, K-12th.

Lycee Francais la Perouse, 755 Ashbury St., (415) 661-5232, Enroll: 334, K-12th.

Mercy High, 3250 19th Ave., (415) 334-0525, Enroll: 576, 9th-12th.

Mission Dolores Elem., 3371 16th St., (415) 861-7673, Enroll: 214, K-8th.

Muhammad Univ., 5048 3rd St., (415) 822-0828, Enroll: 95, K-12th.

Our Lady of the Visitation Elem., 785 Sunnydale Ave., (415) 239-7840, Enroll: 259, K-8th.

Presidio Hill, 3839 Washington St., (415) 751-9318, Enroll: 180, K-8th.

Rise Inst., 1760 Cesar Chavez, (415) 641-1878, Enroll: 35, K-12th.

S.R. Martin College Prep., 2660 San Bruno Ave., (415) 715-0102, Enroll: 42, 5th-12th.

Sacred Heart Cathedral Prep., 1055 Ellis St., (415) 775-6626, Enroll: 1,218, 9th-12th.

Sacred Heart/St. Dominic's Elem., 735 Fell St., (415) 621-8035, Enroll: 200, K-8th.

San Francisco Adventist Sch., 66 Geneva Ave., (415) 585-5550, Enroll: 61, K-10th.

San Francisco Christian Acad., 230 Jones St., (415) 345-0924, Enroll: 32, K-12th.

San Francisco Christian Elem., 25 Whittier St., (415) 586-1117, Enroll: 260, K-12th.

San Francisco Day, 350 Masonic Ave., (415) 931-2422, Enroll: 395, K-8th.

San Francisco Friends Sch., 117 Diamond St., (415) 552-8500, Enroll: 73, K-1st.

San Francisco University High, 3065 Jackson St., (415) 447-3100, Enroll: 404, 9th-12th.

San Francisco Sch., 300 Gaven St., (415) 239-5065, Enroll: 217, K-8th.

San Francisco Waldorf, 2938 Washington St., (415) 931-2750, Enroll: 363, K-12th.

Sand Paths Acad., 1218 S. Van Ness Ave., (415) 826-2662, Enroll: 30, 3rd-12th.

St. Anne Elem., 1320 14th Ave., (415) 664-7977, Enroll: 502, K-8th.

St. Anthony's/Immaculate Conception Elem., 299 Precita Ave., (415) 648-2008, Enroll: 321, K-8th.

St. Brendan Elem., 940 Laguna Honda Blvd., (415) 731-2665, Enroll: 346, K-8th.

St. Brigid Sch., 2250 Franklin St., (415) 673-4523, Enroll: 291, K-8th.

St. Cecilia Elem., 660 Vicente St., (415) 731-8400, Enroll: 575, K-8th.

St. Charles Elem., 3250-18th St., (415) 861-7652, Enroll: 309, K-8th.

St. Elizabeth's Elem., 450 Somerset St., (415) 468-3247, Enroll: 238, K-8th.

St. Emydius Elem., 301 De Montfort Ave., (415) 333-4877, Enroll: 151, K-8th.

St. Finn Bar, 419 Hearst Ave., (415) 333-1800, Enroll: 179, K-8th.

St. Gabriel Elem., 2550 41st Ave., (415) 566-0314, Enroll: 473, K-8th.

St. Ignatius College Prep., 2001-37th Ave., (415) 731-7500, Enroll: 1,415, 9th-12th.

St. James Elem., 321 Fair Oaks St., (415) 647-8972, Enroll: 202, K-8th.

St. John of S.F. Orthodox Acad., 6210 Geary Blvd., (415) 221-3484, Enroll: 47, K-12th.

St. John's Elem., 925 Chenery St., (415) 584-8383, Enroll: 243, K-8th.

St. Mary's Chinese Day, 910 Broadway , (415) 929-4690, Enroll: 233, K-8th.

St. Monica Elem., 5450 Geary Blvd., (415) 751-9564, Enroll: 213, K-8th.

St. Paul Elem., 1690 Church St., (415) 648-2055, Enroll: 268, K-8th.

St. Peter's Parish Sch., 1266 Florida St., (415) 647-8662, Enroll: 497, K-8th.

St. Philip Elem., 665 Elizabeth St., (415) 824-8467, Enroll: 213, K-8th.

St. Stephen's Elem., 401 Eucalyptus Dr., (415) 664-8331, Enroll: 300, K-8th.

St. Thomas More, 50 Thomas More Way, (415) 337-0100, Enroll: 312, K-8th.

St. Thomas The Apostle Elem., 3801 Balboa St., (415) 221-2711, Enroll: 292, K-8th.

St. Vincent de Paul Elem., 2350 Green St., (415) 346-5505, Enroll: 257, K-8th.

Star of the Sea Elem., 360-9th Ave., (415) 221-8558, Enroll: 250, K-8th.

Sterne Sch., 2690 Jackson St., (415) 922-6081, Enroll: 54, 5th-12th.

Sts. Peter & Paul Elem., 660 Filbert St., (415) 421-5219, Enroll: 280, K-8th.

Stuart Hall for Boys, 2252 Broadway St., (415) 563-2900, Enroll: 317, K-8th.

Stuart Hall High Sch., 1715 Octavia St., (415) 345-5811, Enroll: 161, 9th-11th.

Sunset Bible Sch., 1690 21st Ave., (415) 682-9572, Enroll: 29, K-12th.

Synergy Sch., 1387 Valencia St., (415) 567-6177, Enroll: 183, K-8th.

Town Sch. for Boys, 2750 Jackson St., (415) 921-3747, Enroll: 400, K-8th.

Urban Sch. of San Francisco, 1563 Page St., (415) 626-2919, Enroll: 257, 9th-12th.

Voice of Pentecost Acad., 1970 Ocean Ave., (415) 334-0105, Enroll: 140, K-12th.

West Portal Luth. Elem., 200 Sloat Blvd., (415) 665-6330, Enroll: 513, K-8th.

Woodside Int'l Sch., 1555 Irving St., (415) 564-1063, Enroll: 74, 6-12th.

Zion Lutheran, 495 9th Ave., (415) 221-7500, Enroll: 186, K-8th.

San Mateo County
Atherton

Menlo Sch., 50 Valparaiso Ave., (650) 330-2000, Enroll: 755, 6th-12th.

Sacred Heart Schs., 150 Valparaiso Ave., (650) 322-1928, Enroll: 918, K-12th.

St. Joseph's Elem., 50 Emilie Ave., (650) 322-9931, Enroll: 520, PreK-8th.

Belmont

Belmont Oaks Acad., 2200 Carlmont Dr., (650) 593-6175, Enroll: 198, K-6th.

Charles Armstrong, 1405 Solana Dr., (650) 592-7570, Enroll: 238, 1st-8th.

Immaculate Heart of Mary, 1000 Alameda de las Pulgas, (650) 593-4265, Enroll: 307, K-8th.

Notre Dame Elem., 1200 Notre Dame Ave., (650) 591-2209, Enroll: 255, 1st-8th.

Notre Dame High, 1540 Ralston Ave., (650) 595-1913, Enroll: 735, 9th-12th.

Serendipity Sch., 2820 Ponce Ave., (650) 596-9100, Enroll: 53, K-5th.

Burlingame

Hope Tech. Sch., 2303 Trousdale Dr., (650) 259-0566, Enroll: 39, K-4th.

Mercy High, 2750 Adeline Dr., (650) 343-3631, Enroll: 461, 9th-12th.

Our Lady of Angels Elem., 1328 Cabrillo Ave., (650) 343-9200, Enroll: 311, K-8th.

St. Catherine of Siena Elem., 1300 Bayswater Ave., (650) 344-7176, Enroll: 302, K-8th.

Colma

Holy Angels Elem., 20 Reiner St., (650) 755-0220, Enroll: 273, K-8th.

Daly City

Christian Life Acad., 310 Ottilia, (415) 468-1732, Enroll: 33, K-12th.

Hilldale, 79 Florence St., (650) 756-4737, Enroll: 104, K-7th.

Hope Lutheran Elem., 55 San Fernando Way., (650) 991-4673 Enroll: 73, K-4th.

Our Lady of Mercy Elem., 7 Elmwood Dr., (650) 756-5872, Enroll: 563, K-8th.

Our Lady of Perpetual Help Elem., 80 Wellington Ave., (650) 755-4438, Enroll: 281, K-8th.

East Palo Alto

Eastside College Prep., 2101 Pulgas Ave., (650) 688-0850, Enroll: 171, 6th-12th.

Foster City

Ronald C. Wernick Jewish Day Sch., 800 Foster City, (650) 345-8900, Enroll: 173, K-6th.

Kid's Connection, 1998 Beach Park Blvd., (650) 578-9696, Enroll: 228, K-5th.

Newton, 1157 Chess Dr. #100, (650) 345-4043, Enroll: 315, K-9th.

Half Moon Bay

Sea Crest Sch., 901 Arnold Way, (650) 712-9892, Enroll: 246, K-8th.

Hillsborough

Crystal Springs Uplands, 400 Uplands Dr., (650) 342-4175, Enroll: 357, 6th-12th.

Nueva Sch., 6565 Skyline Blvd., (650) 348-2272, Enroll: 327, K-8th.

Menlo Park

Beechwood, 50 Terminal Ave., (650) 327-5052, Enroll: 150, K-8th.

German-American Int'l Sch., 275 Elliott Dr., (650) 324-8617, Enroll: 82, K-8th.

Mid-Peninsula Ed. Ctr., 1340 Willow Rd., (650) 321-1991, Enroll: 134, 9th-12th.

Nativity Elem., 1250 Laurel St., (650) 325-7304, Enroll: 300, K-8th.

Peninsula Sch., 920 Peninsula Way, (650) 325-1584, Enroll: 183, K-8th.

Phillips Brooks, 2245 Avy Ave., (650) 854-4545, Enroll: 196, K-5th.

St. Raymond's, 1211 Arbor Rd., (650) 322-2312, Enroll: 259, K-8th.

Trinity, 2650 Sand Hill Rd., (650) 854-0288, Enroll: 123, K-5th.

Millbrae

Mills Montessori, 1 Alp Way, (650) 697-5561, Enroll: 53, K-5th.

St. Dunstan's Elem., 1150 Magnolia Ave., (650) 697-8119, Enroll: 293, K-8th.

Pacifica

Alma Heights Christian Acad., 1030 Linda Mar Blvd., (650) 355-1935, Enroll: 315, K-12th.

Good Shepherd Elem., 909 Oceana Blvd., (650) 359-4544, Enroll: 309, K-8th.

Portola Valley

Woodland, 360 La Cuesta Dr., (650) 854-9065, Enroll: 228, K-8th.

Woodside Priory, 302 Portola Rd., (650) 851-8221, Enroll: 338, 6th-12th.

Redwood City

Our Lady of Mt. Carmel, 301 Grand St., (650) 366-6127, Enroll: 290, K-8th.

Peninsula Christian Sch., 1305 Middlefield Rd., (650) 366-3842, Enroll: 101, K-8th.

Redeemer Lutheran Elem., 468 Grand St., (650) 366-3466, Enroll: 125, K-8th.

St. Pius Elem., 1100 Woodside Rd., (650) 368-8327, Enroll: 304, K-8th.

West Bay Christian Acad., 233 Topaz St., (650) 568-9222, Enroll: 81, K-12th.

San Bruno

Highlands Christian Schs., 1900 Monterey Dr., (650) 873-4090, Enroll: 571, K-8th.

St. Robert's Elem., 345 Oak Ave., (650) 583-5065, Enroll: 306, K-8th.

San Carlos

Kindercourt Acad., 1225 Greenwood, (650) 591-4882, Enroll: 45, K.

St. Charles Elem., 850 Tamarack Ave., (650) 593-1629, Enroll: 305, K-8th.

West Bay High, 1482 Laurel St., (650) 595-5022, Enroll: 43, 9th-12th.

San Mateo

Alpha Beacon Christian, 1950 Elkhorn Ct., (650) 212-4222, Enroll: 182, K-12th.

Carey School, 1 Carey Sch. Ln., (650) 345-8205, Enroll: 160, K-5th.

Grace Lutheran Sch., 2825 Alameda de las Pulgas, (650) 345-9082, Enroll: 83, K-8th.

Junipero Serra High, 451 W. 20th Ave., (650) 345-8207, Enroll: 987, 9th-12th.

Odyssey Sch., 201 Polhemus Rd., (650) 212-6868, Enroll: 37, 6th-8th.

St. Gregory Elem., 2701 Hacienda St., (650) 573-0111, Enroll: 318, K-8th.

St. Matthew's Catholic, 910 S. El Camino Real, (650) 343-1373, Enroll: 594, K-8th.

St. Matthew's Episcopal Day Sch., 16 Baldwin Ave., (650) 342-5436, Enroll: 215, K-9th.

St. Timothy, 1515 Dolan Ave., (650) 342-6567, Enroll: 280, K-8th.

Stanbridge Acad., 515 E. Poplar Ave., (650) 375-5860, Enroll: 75, K-12th.

So. San Francisco

All Souls Catholic Elem., 479 Miller Ave., (650) 583-3562, Enroll: 299, K-8th.

Mater Dolorosa Sch., 1040 Miller Ave., (650) 588-8175, Enroll: 216, K-8th.

Roger Williams Acad., 600 Grand Ave., (650) 589-1081, Enroll: 46, K-12th.

St. Veronica's Elem., 434 Alida Way, (650) 589-3909, Enroll: 324, K-8th.

Marin County

Corte Madera

Lycee Francais LaPerouse, 330 Golden Hind Passage, (415) 924-1737, Enroll: 152, K-5th.

Marin Country Day Elem., 5221 Paradise Dr., (415) 927-5900, Enroll: 540, K-8th.

Marin Montessori, 5200 Paradise Dr., (415) 924-5388, Enroll: 105, K-6th.

Fairfax

Cascade Canyon, 2626 Sir Francis Drake Blvd., (415) 459-3464, Enroll: 60, K-8.

St. Rita Elem., 102 Marinda Dr., (415) 456-1003, Enroll: 207, K-8th.

Kentfield

Marin Catholic High, 675 Sir Francis Drake Blvd., (415) 461-8844, Enroll: 724, 9th-12th.

Larkspur

Marin Primary & Middle Sch., 20 Magnolia Ave., (415) 924-2608, Enroll: 350, K-8th .

St. Patrick, 120 King St., (415) 924-0501, Enroll: 262, K-8th.

Mill Valley

Greenwood Sch., 17 Buena Vista Ave., (415) 388-0495, Enroll: 76, K-8th.

Marin Horizon, 305 Montford Ave., (415) 388-8408, Enroll: 180, K-8th.

Marin Sch., 70 Lomita Dr., (415) 381-3003, Enroll: 89, 9th-12th.

Mount Tamalpais, 100 Harvard Ave., (415) 383-9434, Enroll: 240, K-8th.

Ring Mountain Day, 104 Tiburon Blvd., (415) 381-8183, Enroll: 54, K-9th.

Novato

Good Shepherd Lutheran, 1180 Lynwood Dr., (415) 897-2510, Enroll: 110, K-5th.

Marin Christian Acad., 1370 S. Novato Blvd., (415) 892-5713, Enroll: 140, K-8th.

North Bay Christian Acad., 6965 Redwood Blvd., (415) 892-8921, Enroll: 90, K-12th.

Our Lady of Loretto, 1811 Virginia Ave., (415) 892-8621, Enroll: 248, K-8th.

Ross

Branson Sch., 39 Fernhill, (415) 454-3612, Enroll: 320, 9th-12th.

San Anselmo

San Domenico Upper Sch., 1500 Butterfield Rd., (415) 258-1939, Enroll: 142, 9th-12th.

San Domenico Lower-Middle, 1500 Butterfield Rd., (415) 454-1900, Enroll: 380, K-8th.

St. Anselm Elem., 40 Belle Ave., (415) 454-8667, Enroll: 264, K-8th.

Star Acad., 921 Sir Francis Drake Blvd., (415) 456-8727, Enroll: 35, 1st-12th.

Sunny Hills Children's Garden, 300 Sunny Hills Dr., (415) 457-3200, Enroll: 60, 6th-12th.

San Rafael

Brandeis Hillel Day, 180 N. San Pedro Rd., (415) 472-1833, Enroll: 210, K-8th.

Marin Acad., 1600 Mission Ave., (415) 453-4550, Enroll: 402, 9th-12th.

Marin Acad. Ctr., 755 Idylberry Rd., (415) 457-3200, Enroll: 43, K-7th.

Marin Waldorf, 755 Idylberry Rd., (415) 479-8190, Enroll: 1950, K-8th.

Montessori De Terra Linda, 620 Del Ganado, (415) 479-7373, Enroll: 56, K-6th.

St. Isabella's Parochial Elem., 1 Trinity Way, (415) 479-3727, Enroll: 256, K-8th.

St. Mark's Sch., 39 Trellis Dr., (415) 472-8000, Enroll: 379, K-8th.

St. Raphael's Elem., 1100 Fifth Ave., (415) 454-4455, Enroll: 182, K-8th.

Timothy Murphy, 1 St. Vincent Dr., (415) 499-7616, Enroll: 75, 1st-12th.

Tiburon

St. Hilary's Elem., 765 Hilary Dr., (415) 435-2224, Enroll: 240, K-8th.

Sonoma County

Cotati

Rancho Bodega Sch., 8297 Old Redwood Hwy., (707) 795-7166, Enroll: 28, 1st-12th.

Forestville

American Christian Acad., 6782 1st St., (707) 887-8328, Enroll: 35, 1st-12th.

Healdsburg

Rio Lindo Adventist. Acad., 3200 Rio Lindo Ave., (707) 431-5100, Enroll: 165, 9th-12th.

St. John's the Baptist Cath Sch., 217 Fitch St., (707) 433-2758, Enroll: 260, K-8th.

Petaluma

Family Life Ctr., 365 Kuck Ln., (707) 795-6954, Enroll: 47, 7th-12th.

Montessori Schools of Petaluma, 211 Springhill Rd., (707) 763-9222, Enroll: 32, 1st-6th.

Oaks Preparatory, 100 Gnoss Concourse, (707) 778-0400, Enroll: 43, 6th-9th.

Petaluma Christian Acad., 175 Fairgrounds Dr. Pk. Lot B, (707) 763-7908, Enroll: 93, K-8th.

St. Vincent Elem., Union & Howard Sts., (707) 762-6426, Enroll: 307, 1st.-8th.

St. Vincent High, 849 Keokuk St., (707) 763-1032, Enroll: 379, 9th-12th.

Rohnert Park

Berean Baptist Christian Acad., 6298 Country Club Dr., (707) 584-1376, Enroll: 98, K-12th.

Cross and Crown Lutheran, 5475 Snyder Ln., (707) 795-7863, Enroll: 186, K-8th.

Santa Rosa

Cardinal Newman High, 50 Ursuline Rd., (707) 546-6470, Enroll: 419, 9th-12th.

Covenant Christian Acad., 1315 Pacific Ave., (707) 579-0661, Enroll: 67, 1st-12th .

Guadalupe Pvt., 4614 Old Redwood Hwy, (707) 546-5399, Enroll: 52, K-8th.

Lattice Ed. Srvcs., 3273 Airway Dr. #A, (707) 571-1234, Enroll: 31, 1st-12th.

Merryhill Sch., 4580 Bennett View Dr., (707) 575-0910, Enroll: 160, K-8th.

North Valley, 3164 Condo Ct., (707) 523-2334, Enroll: 77, K-12th.

Redwood Adventist Acad., 385 Mark West Springs Rd., (707) 545-1697, Enroll: 173, K-12th.

Rincon Valley Christian, 4585 Badger Rd., (707) 539-1486, Enroll: 493, K-12th.

Santa Rosa Christian Sch., 350 S. Wright Rd., (707) 542-6414, Enroll: 416, K-12th.

Shady Oaks Elem., 1281 Edwards Ave., (707) 579-1883, Enroll: 54, K-6th

Sonoma Academy, 50 Mark West Springs Road, (707) 545-1770, Enroll: 130, 9th-11th.

Sonoma Country Day, 4400 Day Sch. Place, (707) 284-3200, Enroll: 286, K-8th.

St. Eugene's Elem., 300 Farmers Ln., (707) 545-7252, Enroll: 350, K-8th.

St. Luke Lutheran Elem., 905 Mendocino Ave., (707) 545-0526, Enroll: 137, K-8.

St. Rose Elem., 4300 Old Redwood Hwy, (707) 545-0379, Enroll: 341, K-8th.

Stuart Prep. Sch., 431 Humboldt St., (707) 528-0721, Enroll: 40, K-8th.

Summerfield Waldorf, 655 Willowside Rd., (707) 575-7194, Enroll: 353, K-12.

Ursuline High, 90 Ursuline Rd., (707) 524-1130, Enroll: 368, 9th-12th.

Sebastopol

Greenacre Homes, Inc., 7590 Atkinson Rd., (707) 823-8722, Enroll: 28, 5th-12th.

Journey High, 1800 N. Gravenstein, (707) 824-5418, Enroll: 35, 7th-12th.

Nonesuch, 4004 Bones Rd., (707) 823-6603, Enroll: 40, 7th-12th.

Pleasant Hill Christian, 1782 Pleasant Hill Rd., (707) 823-5868, Enroll: 74, K-6th.

Plumfield Acad., 9360 Occidental Rd., (707) 824-1414, Enroll: 29, K-12th.

Sebastopol Christian , 7789 Healdsburg Ave., (707) 823-2754, Enroll: 78, K-8th.

Sonoma

Hanna Boys Ctr., 17000 Arnold Dr., (707) 996-6767, Enroll: 86, 6th-12th.

New Song I.S.P., 18925 Lomita Ave., (707) 935-3359, Enroll: 146, K-12th.

Presentation, 276 E. Napa St., (707) 996-2496, Enroll: 145, K-8th.

Sonoma Valley Acad., 276 E. Napa St., (707) 996-2881, Enroll: 27, K-12th.

Sonoma Valley Christian, 542 1st St. East, (707) 996-1853, Enroll: 35, K-9th.

St. Francis Solano Sch., 342 W. Napa St., (707) 996-4994, Enroll: 327, K-8th.

Windsor

Windsor Christian Schs., 10285 Starr Rd., (707) 838-3757, Enroll: 262, K-12th.

Chapter 12

Infant-Baby Care

FOR LICENSING, CALIFORNIA divides child-care facilities into several categories:

- Small family: up to 6 children in the providers's home.
- Large family: 7-12 children in the provider's home.
- Nursery Schools or Child-Care centers.

A child is considered an infant from birth to age 2. No category has yet been established for toddler.

Individual sitters are not licensed and neither are people whom parents arrange for informally to take care of their children. But if a person is clearly in the business of child care from more than one family, he or she should be licensed. Each of the three categories has restrictions. For example, the small-family provider with six children cannot have more than three under age 2.

In everyday reality, many of the larger facilities tend to limit enrollments to children over age 2, and some have even higher age limits. The state and its local umbrella agencies maintain referral lists of local infant and day-care providers. All you have to do is call and they will send a list of the licensed providers and suggestions on how to make a wise choice. The names of the agencies and their numbers are:

• Children's Council of San Francisco, 575 Sutter St., 2nd Floor, San Francisco. (415) 276-2900.

• Wu Yee Resource and Referral, 777 Stockton St., Room 202, San Francisco. (415) 391-8993.

• Child Care Coordinating Council of San Mateo County, Inc., 2121 South El Camino Real, Suite A-100, San Mateo, 94403. (650) 655-6770.

• 4C's of Sonoma County, 396 Tesconi Ct., Santa Rosa, (707) 544-3084.

• Marin Child Care Council, 555 Northgate Dr., San Rafael, (415) 472-1092.

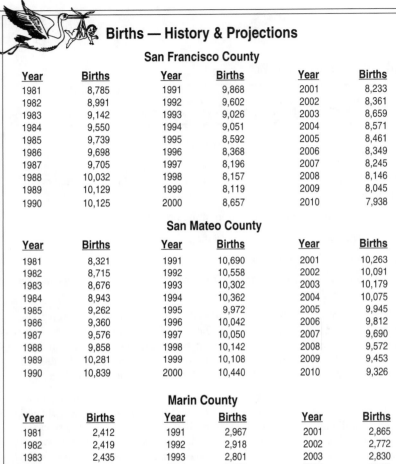

Births — History & Projections

San Francisco County

Year	Births	Year	Births	Year	Births
1981	8,785	1991	9,868	2001	8,233
1982	8,991	1992	9,602	2002	8,361
1983	9,142	1993	9,026	2003	8,659
1984	9,550	1994	9,051	2004	8,571
1985	9,739	1995	8,592	2005	8,461
1986	9,698	1996	8,368	2006	8,349
1987	9,705	1997	8,196	2007	8,245
1988	10,032	1998	8,157	2008	8,146
1989	10,129	1999	8,119	2009	8,045
1990	10,125	2000	8,657	2010	7,938

San Mateo County

Year	Births	Year	Births	Year	Births
1981	8,321	1991	10,690	2001	10,263
1982	8,715	1992	10,558	2002	10,091
1983	8,676	1993	10,302	2003	10,179
1984	8,943	1994	10,362	2004	10,075
1985	9,262	1995	9,972	2005	9,945
1986	9,360	1996	10,042	2006	9,812
1987	9,576	1997	10,050	2007	9,690
1988	9,858	1998	10,142	2008	9,572
1989	10,281	1999	10,108	2009	9,453
1990	10,839	2000	10,440	2010	9,326

Marin County

Year	Births	Year	Births	Year	Births
1981	2,412	1991	2,967	2001	2,865
1982	2,419	1992	2,918	2002	2,772
1983	2,435	1993	2,801	2003	2,830
1984	2,502	1994	2,750	2004	2,760
1985	2,560	1995	2,614	2005	2,681
1986	2,637	1996	2,642	2006	2,601
1987	2,786	1997	2,651	2007	2,523
1988	2,796	1998	2,569	2008	2,445
1989	2,938	1999	2,650	2009	2,366
1990	3,042	2000	2,824	2010	2,283

(Continued)

Sonoma County

Year	Births	Year	Births	Year	Births
1981	4,713	1991	6,096	2001	5,706
1982	4,818	1992	5,804	2002	5,679
1983	4,803	1993	5,614	2003	5,843
1984	4,872	1994	5,507	2004	5,915
1985	5,266	1995	5,442	2005	5,975
1986	5,228	1996	5,503	2006	6,036
1987	5,329	1997	5,409	2007	6,106
1988	5,474	1998	5,472	2008	6,183
1989	6,056	1999	5,420	2009	6,262
1990	6,113	2000	5,651	2010	6,341

Source: California Dept. of Finance, Demographic Research Unit.

• River Child Care, P.O. Box 1060, Guerneville, (707) 887-1809.

Some Advice

This advice comes from a licensing agency:

- Plan ahead. Give yourself one month for searching and screening.

- Contact the appropriate agencies for referrals.

- Once you have identified potential caregivers, phone them to find out about their services and policies. For those that meet your needs, schedule a time to visit while children are present. At the site, watch how the children play and interact with one another.

- Contact other parents using the programs. Ask if they are satisfied with the care and if their children are happy and well-cared-for.

- Select the program that best meet your needs. "Trust your feelings and your instincts."

This is a bare-bones approach. Referral centers can supply you with more information. To get you started, we are listing here the names of the infant centers in the four counties.

San Francisco County

San Francisco

Angela's Children's Ctr., 775 7th Ave., (415) 386-0184

Associated Students Children's Ctr., 1650 Holloway Ave., (415) 338-2403

C5 Inf. Ctr., 505 Van Ness Ave., (415) 626-4880

Caheed Inf. DC Prog., 1030 Oakdale Ave., (415) 821-1300

Cecil Williams Glide Comm. House, 333 Taylor St., (415) 771-0633

Children First, 555 California St., (415) 392-7531

Children's Village CDCtr., 250 10th St., (415) 865-2610

Child's Time Too, 3099 San Bruno Ave., (415) 468-6286

Clara House Children's Ctr., 111 Page St., (415) 863-0681

EOC-Oscaryne Williams Ctr. of Hope, 85 Turner Terr., (415) 647-6970

EOC-Rainbow Inf.Care Ctr., 799 Pacific Ave., (415) 982-6522

Epiphany Parent-Child Ctr., 100 Masonic Ave., (415) 567-8370

Family Dev. Ctr., 2730 Bryant St., (415) 282-1090

Family Sch., 548 Fillmore St., (415) 554-0425

Family Sch. CDCtr.-Bernal Gateway, 3101 Mission St., (415) 550-4178

Florence Crittenton Inf. DCCtr., 836 Broderick St., (415) 567-2357

Florence Crittenton Srvcs., 305 Buchanan St., (415) 552-1535

Frandelja Enrichment Ctr., 950 Gilman St., (415) 822-1699

Grace Inf. Care Ctr., 3201 Ulloa St., (415) 681-6606

Healthy Environments CDCtr., 95 Hawthorne St., (415) 744-8754

Helen Hawk CC, 111 Page St., (415) 863-0681

Holy Family Day Home, 675 Minna St., (415) 487-3753

Katherine Michiels Sch., 1335 Guerrero St., (415) 821-1434

Kidango-Treasure Island, 850 Avenue D, (415) 834-0602

Marin Day Sch.-City Hall CCCtr., 1 Carlton B. Goodlett Way, (415) 554-7560

Marin Day Sch.-Fox Plaza Campus, 1390 Market St., (415) 554-3979

Marin Day Sch.-Hills Plaza Campus, 2 Harrison St., (415) 777-9696

Marin Day Sch.-Spear St. Campus, 220 Spear St., (415) 777-2081

Marin Day Sch.-UCSF Laurel Heights, 3333 California St., (415) 775-2111

Mary Lane Inf.-Toddlr Ctr., One Webster St., (415) 921-7019

Montessori Sch. of the Bay Area, 1550 Eddy St., (415) 292-7970

Pacific Gas & Electric Children's Ctr., 77 Beale St., (415) 972-5535

Parkview Place CDC, 3401 Mission St., (415) 641-4072

SFUSD-Presidio CDCtr., Main Post Bldg. 387, (415) 561-5822

St. Nicholas DC, 5200 Diamond Heights Blvd., (415) 550-1536

Tenderloin CCCtr., 144 Leavenworth St., (415) 776-4010

Tiny Giants, 1748 Clay St., (415) 359-9499

Visitacion Valley Heritage Homes CDCtr., 245 Rey St., (415) 586-8700

Visitacion Valley-John King CDCtr., 500 Raymond Ave., (415) 333-1375

Wu Yee CDCtr.-Chinatown, 831 Broadway St., (415) 391-4721

Wu Yee CDCtr.-Golden Gate, 220 Golden Gate Ave., (415) 864-8396

Wu Yee CDCtr.-Sunnydale, 700 Velasco Ave., (415) 391-4721

Yerba Buena Gardens CDCtr., 790 Folsom St., (415) 820-3500

San Mateo County

Atherton

Menlo Sch. Inf. Care Ctr., 50 Valparaiso Ave., (650) 330-2000

Sacred Heart Inf./Todd. Ctr., 150 Valparaiso Ave., (650) 473-4055

Burlingame

Palcare CCCtr., 945 California Dr., (650) 340-1289

Papillon Presch., 700 Peninsula Ave., (650) 340-7241

Daly City

Bayshore CC Srvcs., 45 Midway Dr., (650) 330-1717

Bayshore CC Svcs-Mission., 7222 Mission St., (650) 330-1725

Foster City
Hoover Children's Ctr., 280 92nd St., (650) 746-8356
KinderCare,1006 Metro Center Blvd., (650) 573-6023
Marin Day Schls., 301 Velocity Way., (650) 357-4250

Half Moon Bay
Coastside Inf.-Toddler Ctr., 565 Redondo Beach Rd., (650) 726-7416
Moonridge Inf. Ctr., 2001 Miramontes Point Rd., (650) 712-9687

Millbrae
Peace of Mind, 1 Alp Way, (650) 697-0941

Redwood City
Our Place, SM Co. Employees CCCtr., 403 Winslow St., (650) 363-4939
Redwood CDCtr., 1968 A Old County Rd., (650) 306-1780
Redwood City CD Prog., 2600 Middlefield Rd., (650) 364-6104
Sequoia Children's Ctr., 1234 Brewster Ave., (650) 369-5277

Redwood Shores
Children's Creative Lrng. Ctr., 250 Shoreline Dr., (650) 486-4949
Children's Creative Lrng. Ctr., 1050 Twin Dolphin Dr., (650) 592-0122

San Bruno
Highlands Christian Sch., 1900 Monterey Dr., (650) 873-4090
Hoover Children's Ctr., 2396 Evergreen Dr., (650) 697-4620

San Carlos
Happy Camper's Presch. & DC, 510 Laurel St., (650) 593-2005
Kindercourt Inf.-Toddler Ctr., 1025 Laurel St., (650) 592-7980

San Mateo
FSA Inf.-Toddler Ctr., 225 Tilton Ave., (650) 347-3177
Ganon Inf.-Toddler DC, 1700 Alameda de las Pulgas, (650) 341-7701
Kidz Care Inf. Ctr., 2612 El Camino Real, (650) 212-5439
Kindercourt, 211 S. Delaware, (650) 344-6612
Siebell Children's Ctr., 2207 Bridgepointe Pkwy., (650) 477-7020

South San Francisco
Baden inft. Ctr., 825 Southwood Dr., (650) 737-57489

Building Kids, 600 Grand Ave., (650) 837-9348
Friends to Parents, 2525 Wexford Ave., (650) 588-8212
Gateway CCCtr., 559 Gateway Bl., (650) 650-873-8145
Genentech's 2nd Generation, 850 Gateway Blvd., (650) 225-3666
Kaplan-Grand Inf. Ctr., 600 Grand Ave., (650) 837-9348

Marin County

Corte Madera
Golden Poppy Inf. & Presch. Ctr., 50 El Camino Dr., (415) 924-2828
Kids Place in Corte Madera-Inf., 50 El Camino Dr., (415) 927-0498

Fairfax
Fairfax-San Anselmo Children's Ctr., 199 Porteous Ave., (415) 454-1811

Nicasio
Marin Day Sch.-Big Rock, 3838 Lucas Valley Rd., (415) 662-1746

Novato
All Saints Presch. & Children's Ctr., 2 San Marin, (415) 893-4202
Creekside Village Sch., 1787 Grant Ave., (415) 898-7007
Marin Headstart-Hamilton, 5520 Nave Dr., (415) 883-5318
Miss Sandie's Sch., 2001 Center Rd., (415) 892-2712
North Bay Children's Ctr., 932 C St., (415) 883-6222
Novato Children's Ctr., 5520 Nave Dr., (415) 883-4591
Novato Youth Ctr., 680 Wilson Ave., (415) 892-1643

San Rafael
Marin 5th Ave. Early Head Start, 1510 5th Ave., (415) 457-8222
Marin Day Sch.-San Rafael, 1123 Court St., (415) 453-9822
Marin Day Sch.-St. Vincent's, 1 St. Vincent Dr., (415) 479-0531
Marin Headstart-Pilgrim Hill, 96 Pilgrim Way, (415) 507-9731
Old Gallinas Children's Ctr., 251 N. San Pedro Rd., (415) 479-2771
Osher Marin Jewish Comm. Ctr., 200 N. San Pedro Rd., (415) 444-8042
Santa Margarita CCCtr., 1055 Las Ovejas Ave., (415) 499-1277

Sausalito

Children's Cultural Ctr., 620 Drake Ave., (415) 332-1044

Iniece Bailey Inf./Toddler Ctr., 100 Ebbtide, (415) 332-5698

Sonoma County

Healdsburg

4 Cs-William K. Johnson, 931 University St., (707) 431-0236

Petaluma

Children's Corner, 629 E. D St., (707) 763-6191

Learning Universe, 100 Gnoss Concourse, (707) 778-7230

Learning Universe, 1485 N. McDowell Blvd., (707) 794-0211

Rohnert Park

KinderCare, 6150 State Farm Dr., (707) 584-0124

La Petite Acad., 1301 Medical Center Dr., (707) 585-7588

Learning to Learn, 1300 Medical Center Dr., (707) 584-4224

Sonoma State Univ. Children's Sch., 1801 E. Cotati Ave., (707) 664-2230

Santa Rosa

Bethlehem Children's Ctr., 1300 St. Francis Rd., (707) 538-2266

Children & Family Circle Inf. Ctr., 1260 N. Dutton., (707) 544-4653

La Petite Acad., 2055 Occidental Rd., (707) 573-1623

Merryhill Sch., 4044 Mayette Ave., (707) 575-7660

Santa Rosa Jr. Coll. Inf. Ctr., 1501 Mendocino Ave., (707) 527-4224

Sonoma

Montessori Sch. of Sonoma, 19675 8th St. E., (707) 996-2422

Windsor

Robin's Nest, 9451 Brooks Rd., (707) 838-0549

Chapter 13

Day Care

SEE THE PRECEDING chapter on baby care for more information about how local baby and child care is provided and who provides it.

For insights on how to pick a day-care center or provider, here is some advice offered by a person who runs a day-care center.

- Ask about age restrictions. Many centers and family care providers will not take care of children under age two or not toilet trained. See previous chapter for infant centers.

- Give the center or home a visual check. Is it clean? In good condition or in need of repairs? Is there a plan for repairs when needed?

- Find out if the person in charge is the owner or a hired manager. Nothing wrong with the latter but you should know who is setting policy and who has the final say on matters.

- Ask about the qualifications of the people who will be working directly with your child. How long have they worked in day care? Training? Education? Many community colleges now offer training in early child-hood and after-school care.

- What philosophy or approach does the center use? The Piaget approach believes children move through three stages and by exploring the child will naturally move through them. The job of the teacher is to provide activities appropriate to the right stage. For example, from age 2-7, many children master drawing and language; from 7-11, they begin to think logically. For the younger child art and sorting and language games would be appropriate; multiplication would not.

  Montessori believes that if given the right materials and placed in the right setting, children will learn pretty much by themselves through trial and error. Montessorians employ specific toys for teaching.

  Traditional emphasizes structure and repetition.

  These descriptions are oversimplified and do not do justice to these approaches or others. Our only purpose here is to point out that day-care providers vary in methods and thinking, and in choosing a center, you also choose a distinct philosophy of education.

- For family day-care providers. Some set up a small preschool setting in the home. Often your child will be welcomed into the family as an extended member. Is this what you want?

- Discipline. Johnny throws a snit. How is it handled? Does the provider have a method or a plan? Do you agree with it?

- Tuition. How much? When it is due? Penalty for picking up child late? Penalty for paying late?

- Hours of operation. If you have to be on the road at 5:30 a.m. and the day-care center doesn't open until 6, you may have to look elsewhere or make different arrangements. Some centers limit hours of operation, e.g., 10 hours.

- Holidays. For family providers, when will the family take a vacation or not be available? For the centers, winter breaks? Summer vacations?

- Communication. Ask how you will be kept informed about progress and problems. Regular meetings? Notes? Calls? Newsletters?

- Classes-Tips for parents. Opportunities to socialize with other parents? Activities for whole family?

- Field trips and classes. Outside activities. Your son and daughter play soccer, an activity outside the day-care center. How will they get to practice? What's offered on site? Gymnastics? Dance?

- Siestas. How much sleep will the children get? When do they nap? Does this fit in with your child's schedule?

- Activities. What are they? How much time on them? Goals?

- Diapers, bottles, cribs, formula, extra clothes. Who supplies what?

- Food, lunches. What does the center serve? What snacks are available?

Remember, day-care centers and providers are in business. The people who staff and manage these facilities and homes may have the best intentions toward the children but if they can't make a profit or meet payrolls, they will fail or be unable to provide quality care. Even "nonprofits" must be run in a businesslike way or they won't survive.

Some centers may offer a rich array of services but for fees beyond your budget. You have to decide the trade-offs.

For licensing, the state divides child care into several categories, including infant, licensed family, child-care centers, and school-age centers for older children. The previous chapter lists the infant providers. This chapter will list the large day-care centers, for both preschool and school-age children.

For a list of family-care providers, please call the Children's Council of San Francisco at (415) 276-2900. In San Mateo County, call the Child Care Coordinating Council of San Mateo County, 2121 South El Camino Real, Suite A-100, San Mateo. Ph: (650) 655-6770. Note SFUSD (San Francisco Unified School District) For Marin and Sonoma, see previous chapter.

San Francisco County

San Francisco

1st Place 2 Start, 1252 Sunnydale Ave., (415) 333-2659

3 N 1 Presch., 240 Leland Ave., (415) 584-8555

ABC Presch., 426 33rd Ave., (415) 387-9111

ABC's Unlimited, 6555 Geary Blvd., (415) 752-5533

After Sch. Enrichment Prog., 1025 14th St., (415) 255-4852

After Sch. Pursuits, 2290 14th Ave., (415) 731-5007

Alta Plaza Presch., 2140 Pierce St., (415) 928-6483

Alvarado After Sch., 625 Douglass St., (415) 285-7756

Angelina's Presch., 1851 Noriega St., (415) 242-6295

Ark Christian Presch., 3141 Vicente St., (415) 731-0912

Ark Two, 3155 Vicente St., (415) 564-8313

Associated Students Children's Ctr., 1650 Holloway Ave., (415) 338-2403

Balboa Presch., 521 Balboa St., (415) 668-5877

Before & After Sch. Immersion Care, 1541 12th Ave., (415) 753-1113

Big City Montessori Sch., 240 Industrial St., (415) 648-5777

Buen Dia Family Sch., 589 Guerrero St., (415) 821-1852

Buena Vista CC, 2641 25th St., (415) 285-0221

CCFC-30th Ave., 741 30th Ave., (415) 668-6539

CCFC-31st Ave., 750 31st Ave., (415) 668-7863

CCFC-Eddy, 1672 Eddy St., (415) 567-9126

CCFC-Turk, 259 Turk St., (415) 928-5178

Calvary Presby. Ch. Nursery Sch., 2515 Fillmore St., (415) 346-4715

Candlelight CDCtr., 283 Farallones St., (415) 587-1070

Catholic Youth Activities-Mission DC, 180 Fair Oaks St., (415) 826-6880

Cheryl Andersen-Sorensen CCCtr., 4150 Clement St., (415) 751-8511

Chibi-Chan Presch., 2507 Pine St., (415) 351-0955

Child's Time, 3061-3099 San Bruno Ave., (415) 468-6286

Children First, 555 California St., (415) 392-7531

Children's Day Sch., 333 Dolores St., (415) 861-5432

Children's Village CDCtr., 250 10th St., (415) 865-2610

Chinatown Comm. Children's Ctr., 979 Clay St., (415) 986-2528

Chinese American Int'l. Sch., 150 Oak St., (415) 865-6000

Civic Center CC, 455 Golden State Ave., (415) 703-1277

Clara House Children's Ctr., 111 Page St., (415) 863-0681

Clara Lilienthal After Sch., 3960 Sacramento St., (415) 750-1577

Clara Lilienthal After Sch., 3630 Divisadero St., (415) 928-4560

Compañeros Del Barrio, 474-478 Valencia St., (415) 431-9925

Cornerstone Acad., 1925 Lawton St., (415) 665-9747

Cornerstone Acad., 1943,1947,1955 Lawton St., (415) 661-8810

Cornerstone Acad., 4250 Judah St., (415) 661-2517

Cornerstone Acad., 801 Silver Ave., (415) 665-9747

Cow Hollow Presch., 2325 Union St., (415) 921-2328

Cross Cultural Fam. Ctr., 259 Turk St., (415) 928-5178

Cross Cultural Fam. Ctr., 741 30th Ave., (415) 668-6539

Cross Cultural Fam. Ctr. II, 1672 Eddy St., (415) 567-9126

Cross Cultural Fam. Ctr. III, 1901 O'Farrell, (415) 921-7019

Cross Cultural Fam. Ctr. IV, 750 31st Ave., (415) 668-7863

Discoveryland of S.F., 7777 Geary Blvd., (415) 752-0107

EOC–Busy Bee, 548 Delta St., (415) 467-6960

EOC–Chinatown-N. Beach CCCtr., 715 Chestnut St., (415) 771-4869

EOC-Cleo Wallace CDCtr., 71 Turner Terr., (415) 282-6300

EOC–Martin Luther King CCCtr., 200 Cashmere, (415) 821-7000

EOC–Mission CCCtr., 754 14th St., (415) 863-2228

EDC-OMI CCCtr., 201 Victoria St., (415) 586-5725

EOC–Rainbow Presch., 799 Pacific Ave., (415) 982-6522

EOC-Sojourner Truth CCCtr., 1 Cashmere, (415) 821-7090

EOC-Western Add. CC, 1455 Golden Gate Ave., (415) 929-1580

Eureka Lrng. Ctr., 464 Diamond St., (415) 648-0380

Eureka Lrng. Ctr., 551 Eureka St., (415) 821-3422

Everyday Magic, 220 Middlefield Dr., (415) 681-9168

Fairmount After Sch., 65 Chenery St., (415) 824-1236

Family Connections-Presch. & Sch. Age Ctr., 2565 San Bruno Ave., (415) 715-6746

Family Dev. Ctr., 2730 Bryant St., (415) 282-1090

Family Sch., 548 Fillmore St., (415) 554-0425

Family Sch. CDCtr., 3101 Mission St., (415) 550-4178

Fellowship Presch., 495 Cambridge St., (415) 239-0511

Florence Crittenton Svcs., 305 Buchanan St., (415) 567-2357

Forest Hill Christian Ch. Nursery Sch., 250 Laguna Honda Blvd., (415) 566-3780

Frandelja Enrichment Ctr., 950 Gilman St., (415) 822-1699

French-American Int'l Sch., 150 Oak St., (415) 558-2000

Friends of Potrero Hill Nursery, 1801 Mariposa St., (415) 864-5464

Friends of St. Francis CCCtr., 50 Belcher St., (415) 861-1818

Gates & Bridges Presch., 1601 10th Ave., (415) 664-3005

Glen Park Presch., 647 Chenery Ln., (415) 585-7701

Glenridge Coop. Nursery Sch., Glen Park Canyon, (415) 586-2771

Glide CC & Family Support, 434 Ellis St., (415) 771-6300

Good Samaritan Fam. Resource Ctr., 1294 Potrero Ave., (415) 824-9475

Grace CDCtr., 1551 Newcomb, (415) 550-4393

Grace Fountain DCCtr., 1145 Cabrillo St., (415) 668-0188

Grattan After Sch., 165 Grattan St., (415) 664-3164

Haight Ashbury Coop. Nursery Sch., 1180 Stanyan St., (415) 661-9204

Hamilton Family Presch., 1631 Hayes St., (415) 665-2100

Happy Day Presch., 809 Taraval St., (415) 564-7999

Happy Times Nursery Sch., 1090 Quintara St., (415) 753-3012

Healthy Environments CDCtr., 95 Hawthorne St., (415) 744-8754

Head Start-Cadillac, 316 Leavenworth St., (415) 447-1384

Head Start-Ella Hill Hutch, 1050 McAllister St., (415) 885-6547

Head Start-Hunter's View, 125 West Point Rd., (415) 824-4686

Head Start-OMI, 1111 Junipero Serra Blvd., (415) 337-0220

Head Start-Potrero Hill, 824 Carolina St., (415) 821-6639

Head Start-Southeast Ctr., 1300 Phelps Ave., (415) 821-6005

Head Start-Westside, 2400 Post St., (415) 474-7637

Hebrew Acad., 645 14th Ave., (415) 752-9583

Helen Hawk Children's Ctr., 111 Page St., (415) 863-0681

Holy Family Day Home, 299 Dolores St., (415) 861-5361

JCCSF-Rosenberg Early Childhood Ctr., 325 Arguello Blvd., (415) 386-4999

Jewish Comm. Ctr. Presch., 655 Brotherwood Way, (415) 406-1002

Jewish Comm. Ctr. Helen Diller Family Presch., 3200 California St., (415) 292-1291

Jewish Comm. Ctr. Havura Youth Ctr. & Presch., 1808 Wedemeyer St., (415) 292-1250

Jewish Family Presch., 318 15th Ave., (415) 221-8736

Kai Ming Head Start-Clay, 1600 Clay St., (415) 771-3340

Kai Ming Head Start-Geary, 6221 Geary Blvd., (415) 387-3133

K.E.E.P., 1570 31st Ave., (415) 681-0930

K.E.E.P., 2051 34th Ave., (415) 564-2741

Kathy Michiels Sch., 1335 Guerrero St., (415) 821-1434

Kidango-Treasure Island Ctr. Presch., 850 Avenue D, (415) 834-0602

Kiddieland Play Nursery, 637 Peralta Ave., (415) 824-7061

Kids Kollege Presch. & DC, 3939 Lawton St., (415) 753-1869

Kids R First Presch., 1655 46th Ave., (415) 664-5437

Krouzian-Zekarian Elem. Sch. of St. Gregory, 825 Brotherhood Way, (415) 586-8686

Lakeside Presby. Nursery Sch., 201 Eucalyptus Dr., (415) 564-5044

Laurel Hill Nursery Sch., 401 Euclid Ave., (415) 751-8784

Learning Bridge Presch., 1050 Kirkham St., (415) 753-1802

Little Angels Japanese Presch., 1457 9th Ave., (415) 564-6123

Little Bear Sch., 3726 Cesar Chavez St., (415) 282-2224

Little Children's Dev. Ctr., 1223 Webster St., (415) 921-5329

Little Gators, 3149 Steiner, (415) 346-8608

Little People Presch., 420 29th Ave., (415) 751-1006

Little School, 1520 Lyon St., (415) 567-0430

Little Star, 2540 Taraval St., (415) 731-7933

Little Star Presch., Too, 1105 Quintera St., (415) 731-7933

Lone Mountain Children's Ctr., 1806 Belle St., (415) 561-2333

Louise & Claude Rosenberg ECCtr., 325 Arguello Blvd., (415) 386-4999

Love & Learn Nursery Sch., 1419 Howard St., (415) 863-4059

Lutheran Church of Our Savior, 1011 Garfield St., (415) 587-1424

Lycee Francais Int'l. La Perouse, 755/765 Ashbury St., (415) 668-1833

Maria Montessori Sch. of the Golden Gate, 62 Lenox Way, (415) 731-8188

Maria Montessori Sch. of the Golden Gate, 678 Portola Dr., (415) 731-8188

Marin Day Sch.-City Hall Presch., 1 Carlton B. Goodlett Way, (415) 554-7560

Marin Day Sch.-Fremont Campus Presch., 342 Howard St., (415) 836-0102

Marin Day Sch.-Hills Plaza Campus, 2 Harrison St., (415) 777-9696

Marin Day Sch.-SF Campus, 2266 California St., (415) 775-2211

Marin Day Sch.-Spear St. Campus, 220 Spear St., (415) 777-2081

Marin Day Sch.-UCSF Laurel Heights, 3333 California St., (415) 775-2111

Marina Children, 3219-A Laguna St., (415) 931-0833

Mio Presch., 4377 Mission St., (415) 587-2922

Miraloma Nursery, 443 Foerster St., (415) 585-6789

Miraloma School, 175 Omar Way, (415) 584-7080

Mission CC Consortium, 4750 Mission St., (415) 586-6139

Mission Head Start-101 Valencia, 1330 Stevenson, (415) 252-7008

Mission Head Start-Bernal CCCtr., 3141 26th St., (415) 826-1653

Mission Head Start-Capp Ctr., 362 Capp St., (415) 206-7752

Mission Head Start-Jean Jacobs Ctr., 459 Vienna St., (415) 469-2162

Mission Head Start-Mission Bay CDCtr., 152 Berry St., (415) 856-0650

Mission Head Start-Regina Chiong Ctr., 3013 24th St., (415) 285-9662

Mission Head Start-Valencia Ctr., 675 Valencia St., (415) 863-6647

Mission Head Start-Womens Bldg. Ctr., 3543 18th St., (415) 701-1995

Mission YMCA at Sunnyside Elem., 250 Foerster St., (415) 586-6900

Mission YMCA at Paul Revere Elem., 555 Tompkins St., (415) 970-9020

Montessori Children's Ctr., 81 Bautista Cir., (415) 333-4410

Montessori Children's House, 25 Lake St., (415) 922-9235

Montessori House of Children, 1187 Franklin St., (415) 441-7691

Montessori Sch. of the Bay Area, 1550 Eddy St., (415) 292-7970

Mother Goose Sch., 334 28th Ave., (415) 221-6133

Multicultural Presch., 3300 Balboa St., (415) 668-3300

Nihonmachi Little Friends, 2031 Bush St., (415) 922-8898

Nihonmachi Little Friends, 1830 Sutter St., (415) 922-4060

Noe Valley Nursery, 1021 Sanchez St., (415) 647-2278

One Fifty Parker Ave. Nursery Sch., 150 Parker Ave., (415) 221-0294

Pacific Gas & Electric Children's Ctr., 77 Beale St., (415) 972-5535

Pacific Primary, 1500 Grove St., (415) 346-0906

Parkside Presch. & K, 2425 19th Ave., (415) 668-5815

Parkview Place, 3401 Mission St., (415) 225-3196

Peter's Place Nursery Sch., 227 Balboa St., (415) 752-1444

Phoebe A. Hearst Presch., 1315 Ellis St., (415) 931-1018

Playmates Coop. Nursery Sch., 2340 42nd Ave., (415) 681-2025

Preschool, The, 102 San Jose Ave., (415) 285-5327

Rainbow Montessori, 2358 24th Ave., (415) 661-9100

Rocky Mountain Participation Nursery, 2475 15th St., (415) 552-2929

Salvation Army Harbor House CCCtr., 407 9th St., (415) 508-3032

San Francisco Sch., 300 Gaven St., (415) 239-5065

Second Comm. CCCtr., 500 Clarendon Ave., (415) 759-1897

SFCCD-Bernal Heights Presch., 500 Cortland Ave., (415) 285-6215

SFCCD-Campus Children's Ctr., 50 Phelan Ave., (415) 239-3462

SFCCD-Grace CDCtr., 1551 Newcomb, (415) 550-4393

SFCCD-Mission Comm. College, 90 Bartlett St., (415) 282-0204

SFCCD-Orfalea Family Ctr., 1860 Hayes St., (415) 561-1959

SFCCD-Oceanview, 105 Aptos Ave., (415) 561-1920

SFCCD-Sunnydale, 1652 Sunnydale Ave., (415) 239-3966

SFSU-Ella Hill Hutch Head Start, 1050 McAllister St., (415) 885-6547

SFUSD-21st Century Acad., 2055 Silver Ave., (415) 695-5400

SFUSD-Argonne CDCtr. Presch., 750 16th Ave., (415) 950-8500

SFUSD-Bessie Carmichael, 55 Sherman St., (415) 241-6294

SFUSD-Bret Harte CDCtr., 950 Hollister Ave., (415) 822-4892

SFUSD-Bryant CDCtr., 1060 York St., (415) 695-5784

SFUSD-Buena Vista ECIA PreK, 2641 25th St., (415) 695-5838

SFUSD-Burnett CDCtr., 1520 Oakdale Ave., (415) 648-5663

SFUSD-Cesar Chavez Pre-K, 825 Shotwell St., (415) 695-5946

SFUSD-Commodore Stockton CDCtr., 954 Washington St., (415) 291-7932

SFUSD-Dr. Charles S. Drew CDCtr., 50 Pomona St., (415) 330-1546

SFUSD-Dr. William Cobb CDCtr., 2725 California St., (415) 922-3050

SFUSD-E.R. Taylor State Presch., 423 Burrows, (415) 467-3445

SFUSD-Excelsior CDCtr., 859 Prague St., (415) 469-4753

SFUSD-Fairmount Elem., 65 Chenery St., (415) 695-5669

SFUSD-F.E.C. CDCtr., 824 Harrison St., (415) 291-7983

SFUSD-Golden Gate ECIA PreK, 1601 Turk St., (415) 749-3552

SFUSD-Gordon Lau PreK, 954 Washington St., (415) 291-7932

SFUSD-Grattan CDCtr., 165 Grattan St., (415) 664-1421

SFUSD-Jefferson CDCtr., 1325 18th Ave., (415) 759-2795

SFUSD-Jefferson CDCtr., 1350 25th Ave., (415) 731-4513

SFUSD-John McLaren CDCtr., 2055 Sunnydale Ave., (415) 469-4519

SFUSD-John Muir ECIA PreK, 380 Webster St., (415) 241-6339

SFUSD-Junipero Serra CDCtr., 155 Appleton St., (415) 920-5138

SFUSD-Kate Kennedy CDCtr., 1670 Noe St., (415) 695-5873

SFUSD-Las Americas CDCtr., 801 Treat Ave., (415) 695-5746

SFUSD-Mission CDCtr., 421 Bartlett St., (415) 824-9330

SFUSD-Mission Main CDCtr., 2950 Mission St., (415) 647-7748

SFUSD-Noriega CDCtr., 1775 44th Ave., (415) 681-9550

SFUSD-Presidio CDCtr., Main Post Bldg. 387, (415) 561-5822

SFUSD-Raphael Weil CDCtr., 1501 O'Farrelll St., (415) 749-3548

SFUSD-Redding CDCtr., 1421 Pine St., (415) 885-5846

SFUSD-San Miguel CDCtr., 300 Seneca Ave., (415) 469-4756

SFUSD-Sanchez ECIA PreK, 325 Sanchez St., (415) 241-6387

SFUSD-Sarah B. Cooper CDCtr., 940 Filbert St., (415) 749-3550

SFUSD-Starr King PreK, 1215 Carolina St., (415) 695-5570

SFUSD-Sutro CDCtr., 235 12th Ave., (415) 751-2247

SFUSD-Tenderloin Comm. CDCtr., 627 Turk St., (415) 614-3000

SFUSD-Theresa S. Mahler CDCtr., 990 Church St., (415) 695-5871

SFUSD-Tule Elk Park CDCtr., 2110 Greenwich St., (415) 749-3551

SFUSD-Yoey at Bessie L. Smith CDCtr., 95 Gough St., (415) 241-6313

Shalom Sch., 862 28th Ave., (415) 831-8399

Sonshine Presch., 3535 Balboa St., (415) 668-0233

South of Market CCCtr., 366 Clementina St., (415) 391-0389

St. James Episcopal Ch. Nursery Sch., 4620 California St., (415) 752-8258

St. Luke's Parish Sch., 1755 Clay St., (415) 474-9489

St. Nicholas DC & Presch., 5200 Diamond Heights Blvd., (415) 550-1536

St. Paul's Ch. Littlest Angel Presch., 221 Valley St., (415) 824-5437

Sts. Peter & Paul CCCtr., 1757 Stockton St., (415) 391-8264

Sts. Peter & Paul-Laura Vicuna Prep., 666 Filbert St., (415) 296-8549

Star Light Christian Presch., 750 26th Ave., (415) 221-8005

Stepping Stones Presch., 1329 7th Ave., (415) 759-1107

Sunrise Presch., 3635 Lawton St., (415) 665-5551

Sunset Nursery Sch., 4245 Lawton St., (415) 681-7659

Teaching Tots Presch., 939 Irving St., (415) 731-9705

Telegraph Hill Coop. Nursery Sch., 555 Chestnut St., (415) 421-3313

Telegraph Hill Nursery & Sch. Age, 660 Lombard St., (415) 421-6444

Temple Emanu-el Presch., 2 Lake St., (415) 751-2535

Tenderloin CCCtr. Presch., 144 Leavenworth St., (415) 776-4010

Tenderloin CCCtr., 351 Turk St., (415) 776-4010

Teremok, 2460 Sutter St., (415) 441-3866

Tiny Giants, 1748 Clay St., (415) 359-9499

Trevor Martin Montessori, 300 Moultrie St., (415) 550-6865

True Sunshine Presch., 777 Stockton St., (415) 956-4207

Turk Sch. Age Ctr., 259 Turk St., (415) 928-5178

UCSF Marilyn Reed Lucia CCCtr., 610 Parnassus Ave., (415) 476-1616

Ulloa Children's Ctr., 2650 42nd Ave., (415) 759-8854

Visitacion Valley Heritage Homes CDCtr., 245 Rey St., (415) 586-8700

Visitacion Valley Child & Fam. Dev. Ctr., 103 Tucker Ave., (415) 467-6300

Visitacion Valley Comm. Ctr., 50 Raymond Ave., (415) 467-6400

Visitacion Valley Family Sch., 325 Leland Ave., (415) 467-6400

Wah Mei School, 1400 Judah St., (415) 665-4212

West Portal C.A.R.E., 5 Lenox Way, (415) 242-8641

Whitney Young CDCtr., 100 Whitney Young Cir., (415) 821-7550

Whitney Young West-Laguna, 1025 Laguna St., (415) 292-6870

Whitney Young West-Masonic, 1101 Masonic Ave., (415) 355-0210

Wind in the Willows, 713 Monterey Blvd., (415) 333-7165

Wu Yee-Children's Svcs. Presch., 177 Golden Gate Ave., (415) 864-8396

Wu Yee-Generations CDCtr., 1010 Montgomery St., (415) 781-7535

Wu Yee-Golden Gate CCCtr., 220 Golden Gate Ave., (415) 391-8993

Wu Yee-Lok Yuen CCCtr., 888 Clay St., (415) 391-4979

Wu Yee-Sunnydale CDCtr., 700 Velasco Ave., (415) 333-6335

Yerba Buena Gardens CDCtr., 790 Folsom St., (415) 820-3500

YMCA-Argonne, 680 18th Ave., (415) 831-4093

YMCA-Bayview, 1601 Lane St., (415) 822-7728

YMCA-Central Branch, 1187 Franklin St., (415) 447-2527

YMCA-Cesar Chavez, 825 Shotwell St., (415) 282-0953

YMCA-Commodore Sloat, 50 Darien Way, (415) 664-9622

YMCA-John O'Connel, 1920 41st Ave., (415) 759-2724

YMCA-Jose Ortega, 400 Sargent St., (415) 584-7328

YMCA-Lafayette, 4545 Anza St., (415) 668-0945

YMCA-Mission Presch., 4080 Mission St., (415) 586-6900

YMCA-New Traditions, 2049 Grove (415) 751-1622

YMCA-Paul Revere, 555 Tompkins, (415) 970-9020

YMCA-Sherman, 1651 Union St., (415) 563-7814

YMCA-St. Francis Presch., 399 San Fernando Way, (415) 242-7100

YMCA-Sunnyside, 250 Foerster St., (415) 586-6900

San Mateo County
Atherton

Children's Creative Lrng. Ctr., 299 Alameda de las Pulgas, (650) 940-0117

Menlo Sch. CCCtr., 50 Valparaiso Ave., (650) 330-2000

Playschool, 150 Watkins Ave., (650) 325-1623

Selby Lane Sch. Age & Presch., 170 Selby Ln., (650) 482-5957

St. Joseph Montessori Presch. & K, 50 Emilie Ave., (650) 473-4061

Belmont

Belmont Comm. Lrng. Ctr., 1835 Belburn, (650) 595-7488

Cipriani After Sch. Care, 2525 Buena Vista Ave., (650) 592-3262

College of Notre Dame Early Lrng. Ctr., 1500 Ralston Ave., (650) 508-3519

Curiosity Corner, 3100 St. James Rd., (650) 592-7664

Holy Cross Presch., 900 Alameda de las Pulgas, (650) 591-4447

Kollage Creative Presch., 500 Biddulph, (650) 620-9003

Merry Moppet Nursery Sch., 2200 Carlmont Dr., (650) 593-6175

Nesbit Club Puma, 500 Biddulph Way, (650) 592-0522

Ralston After-Middle Sch., 2675 Ralston, (650) 610-0813

San Carlos Belmont After Sch., 525 Middle Rd., (650) 593-4229

Serendipity Sch., 2820 Ponce Ave., (650) 596-9100

Burlingame

A Child's Way, 801 Howard Ave., (650) 342-3460

Burlingame Montessori Sch., 525 California Dr., (650) 342-4445

Children's Creative Lrng. Ctr.-Lincoln, 1801 Devereux Dr., (650) 697-7400

First Presby. Ch., 1500 Easton Dr., (650) 342-8326

First Presby. Ch. Nursery Sch., 1500 Easton Dr., (650) 342-8326

Hope Technology-Preschl., 1715 Quesada Wy., (650) 652-9760

Morning Glory Montessori Sch., 2750 Adeline Dr., (650) 343-9627

Our Lady of Angels Presch., 1341 Cortez Ave., (650) 343-3115

Palcare CCCtr., 945 California Dr., (650) 340-1289

Papillon Presch., 700 Peninsula Ave., (650) 340-7241

Peninsula Temple Sholom Presch., 1655 Sebastian Dr., (650) 697-2279

St. Paul's Nursery Sch., 405 El Camino Real, (650) 344-5409

Stepping Stone, 1421 Palm Dr., (650) 343-3362

United Meth. Ch. Coop. Nursery Sch., 1443 Howard, (650) 343-1082

Daly City

Bayshore CC Services-87th St., 377 87th St., (415) 330-1715

Bayshore CC Services-Midway, 45 Midway Dr., (415) 330-1717

Bayshore CC Svcs.-Mission Ctr Prsch., 7222 Mission St., (650) 758-0740

Bayshore CC Services-S. Parkview, 221 S. Parkview Ave., (415) 330-1714

Early Lrng. Acad., 474 San Diego, (650) 755-8440

Hoover Children's Ctr., 280 92nd St., (650) 746-8356

Hope Lutheran Day Sch., 55 San Fernando Way, (650) 755-5020

JSD State Presch., 631 Hanover St., (650) 991-1258

Latchkey Alternative Ctr., 1200 Skyline Dr., (650) 755-8574

Serramonte Head Start, 699 Serramonte Bl., (650) 266-8843

Noah's Ark Presch. & DCCtr., 1595 Edgeworth Ave., (650) 991-9222

Precious Moments Presch., 1020 Sullivan, (650) 756-5233

Serramonte Head Start, 699 Serramonte Blvd., (650) 992-6027

Southgate Presch., 1474 Southgate Ave., (650) 755-8472

Village Nursery Sch., 474 N. Parkview Ave., (650) 992-4350

Young World Lrng. Ctr., 699 Serramonte Blvd., (650) 994-6599

East Palo Alto

Creative Montessori Lrng. Ctr., 1421 Bay Rd., (650) 325-9543

East Palo Alto-Head Start Ctr., 1385 Bay Rd., (650) 326-9498

Laurel Head Start, 1019 Laurel Ave., (650) 330-1595

Little University-A Special Place, 2201 E. University, (650) 326-6741

OICW CDCtr., 1070 Beech St., (650) 322-2129

Ravenswood CDCtr., 2450 Ralmar St., (650) 329-2840

El Granada

Coastside Children's Prog., El Granada School, (650) 712-7415

Picasso Presch., 480 Avenue Alhambra, (650) 726-2017

Wilkinson Early Childhood Ctr., 130 Santa Anna St., (650) 726-8830

Foster City

All Are Friends Montessori, 1130 Balclutha Dr., (650) 286-0400

Foster City Presch. DCCtr., 1064-F Shell Blvd., (650) 341-2041

Kids Connection, 1970 Beach Park Blvd., (650) 578-9696

KinderCare, 1006 Metro Center Blvd., (650) 573-6023

Marin Day Sch., 301 Velocity Way, (650) 357-4250

Newton Learning Cen., 1157 Chess Dr., (650) 345-4043

Peninsula Jewish Comm. Ctr., 499 Boothbay Ave., (650) 349-2816

Peninsula Jewish Comm. Ctr., 800 Foster City Blvd., (650) 357-7733

Sea Breeze Sch., 900 Edgewater Blvd., (650) 574-5437

Half Moon Bay

Coastside Children's Prog., 494 Miramontes St., (650) 726-7412

Coastside Children's Prog., 777 Miramontes Ave., (650) 726-3273

Coastside Parents Nursery Sch., 613 Grandview, (650) 726-2397

Half Moon Bay Head Start Ctr., 900 N. Cabrillo Hwy., (650) 871-2690

Holy Family Children's Ctr., 1590 S. Cabrillo Hwy., (650) 726-0506

Los Niños Nursery Sch., 20 Kelly Ave., (650) 726-6264

Montessori Children's Sch., 315 Clemencia, (650) 726-4065

Moonridge CDCtr., 2001 Miramontes Point Rd., (650) 712-8729

Hillsborough

N. Hillsborough Presch., 545 Eucalyptus Ave., (650) 342-1478

Nueva Sch., 6565 Skyline Blvd., (650) 348-2272

S. Hillsborough Presch., 300 El Cerrito Ave., (650) 344-0303

W. Hillsborough Presch., 376 Barbara Way, (650) 344-9870

La Honda

La Honda Presch., Sears Ranch Rd., (650) 747-0051

Menlo Park

Applebee Presch., 107 Clover Ln., (650) 366-9127

Fair Oaks Head Start Ctr., 3502 Middlefield Rd., (650) 368-0869

Footsteps Presch., 490 Willow Rd., (650) 324-3668

Garfield Early Lrng. Ctr., 3600 Middlefield Rd., (650) 568-3820

German-American Presch. & K, 275 Elliott Dr., (650) 324-8617

Haven CDCtr., 260 Van Buren Ave., (650) 325-8719

Kirk House Presch., 1148 Johnson St., (650) 323-8667

Ladera Comm. Church Presch., 3300 Alpine Rd., (650) 854-0295

Littlest Angels, 1075 Cloud Ave., (650) 854-4973

Menlo Park Children's Ctr. & Aft. Sch., 700 Alma, (650) 323-0678

Menlo Park Head Start, 419 6th Ave., (650) 369-7970

New Beginnings Presch., 1100 Middle Ave., (650) 325-2190

Peninsula Sch., 920 Peninsula Way, (650) 325-1584

Phillips Brooks Nursery Sch., 2245 Avy Ave., (650) 854-4545

Roberts Sch., 641 Coleman Ave., (650) 322-3535

Trinity Presch., 330 Ravenswood Ave., (650) 854-0288

University Hts. Children's Ctr., 2066 Avy Ave., (650) 854-6993

Valda Britschgi CDCtr., 1200 O'Brien Dr., (650) 322-8431

YMCA Kid's Place, 1445 Hudson Ave., (650) 562-0961

Millbrae

A Child's Way II, 817 Murchison Dr., (650) 697-4760

Calvary Lutheran Day Nursery, Santa Lucia & Cypress Aves., (650) 588-2840

Club Happy Hall, 401 Ludeman Ln., (650) 872-2582

Club Happy Hall-Meadows, 1101 Helen Dr., (650) 872-2585

Community Prsch., 450 Chadbourne Ave., (650) 266-8843

Glen Oaks Montessori Sch., 797 Santa Margarita, (650) 872-1112

Hoover Children's Ctr., 1 Alp Way, (650) 697-9444

Millbrae Comm. Presch., 450 Chadbourn Ave., (650) 652-4504

Millbrae Montessori Sch., 797 Santa Margarita Ave., (650) 588-2229

Millbrae Nursery Sch., 86 Center St., (650) 589-3028

Mills Montessori Sch., 1 Alp Way, (650) 697-5561

Peace of Mind Presch., 1 Alp Way, (650) 697-2229

Montara

Coastside Children's Prog., Le Conte & Kanoff Aves., (650) 728-7419

Pacifica

Babe's Presch., 1496 Adobe Dr., (650) 359-2089

Building Kidz, 1152 Peralta Rd., (650) 557-1256

Cabrillo Ext. Care, 601 Crespi Dr., (650) 738-7381

City of Pacifica-Oceanshore CCCtr., 431 Edgemar, (650) 726-7464

City of Pacifica-Sunset Ridge CCCtr., 340 Inverness, (650) 738-7465

City of Pacifica-Vallemar CCCtr., 377 Reina del Mar, (650) 738-7466

City of Pacifica-Vallemar Children's Ctr., 375 Reina Del Mar Ave., (650) 738-7381

City of Pacifica-Sunset Ridge., 340 Inverness, (650) 738-7465

Montessori Sch. of Linda Mar, 1666 Higgins, (650) 355-7272

Pacifica Nursery Sch., Carmel Ave. & Canyon Dr., (650) 355-4465

Pacifica Playschool, 630 Hickey Blvd., (650) 359-5673

Sandcastle Academy, 1922 Palmetto Ave., (650) 359-7364

Temporary Tot Tending, 340 Inverness, (650) 355-7377

Temporary Tot Tending, 411 Oceana Blvd., (650) 738-1737

Temporary Tot Tending, 930 Oddstad, (650) 359-3776

Temporary Tot Tending, 830 Rosita, (650) 355-5026

Temporary Tot Tending, 1283 Terra Nova Bl., (650) 355-5026

Terra Nova Christian DCCtr., 1125 Terra Nova Blvd., (650) 355-2962

Pescadero

La Honda Pescadero USD, 620 North St., (650) 879-0286

Portola Valley

Ladera Comm. Ch. Presch., 3300 Alpine Rd., (650) 854-0295

New Horizon Sch. Age Ctr., 200 Shawnee Pass, (650) 851-5671

Trinity Sch., 815 Portola Rd., (650) 854-0288

Windmill Sch., 4141 Alpine Rd., (650) 851-0771

Woodland Sch., 360 La Cuesta, (650) 854-9065

Redwood City

Adelante Elem., 3150 Granger Way, (650) 733-3689

Beginnings: A Children's Lrng. Ctr., 3430 Michael Dr., (650) 363-1229

Beresford Montessori Sch., 178 Clinton St., (650) 367-5027

Children's Creative Lrng Ctr., 797 Redwood Shores Pkwy., (650) 780-7322

Children's Creative Lrng. Ctr., 250 Shoreline Dr., (650) 486-4949

Children's Creative Lrng. Ctr., 1050 Twin Dolphin Dr., (650) 592-0122

Child Dev. Ctr.-John Gill, 555 Avenue Del Ora, (650) 364-1178

Comm. Ed. Ctr., 631 Charter St., (650) 365-1407

Comm. Ed. Ctr.-Taft Sch., 903 10th Ave., (650) 780-7260

Fair Oaks CDCtr., 2950 Fair Oaks Ave., (650) 482-5939

Garfield Children's Ctr., Middlefield & Semi-Circular Rd., (650) 482-5943

Henry Ford CDCtr., 2498 Massachusetts Ave., (650) 368-1138

Hoover CDCtr., 701 Charter St., (650) 482-5953

Hoover CDCtr., 303 Twin Dolphin Dr., (650) 593-6824

John Gill State Presch., 555 Avenue del Ora, (650) 364-1178

John Gill Sch. Age CDCtr., 555 Avenue del Ora., (650) 371-9900

Montessori Comm. Sch., 2323 Euclid Ave., (650) 366-4932

Neighborhood Kids' Corner, 225 Clifford Ave., (650) 367-7034

Neighborhood Kids' Corner, 3790 Red Oak Way, (650) 365-6117

Noah's Ark Presch. & DCCtr., 401 Hudson St., (650) 366-1414

North Star Acad., 400 Duane St., (650) 368-2981

Open Gate Nursery Sch., 2124 Brewster Ave., (650) 369-6833

Our Lady of Mount Carmel Ch., 601 Katherine St., (650) 366-6587

Our Place, SM Co. Employees CCCtr., 403 Winslow St., (650) 363-4939

Marin Day School-Our Place, 403 Winslow St., (650) 363-4939

Peninsula Christian Sch., 1305 Middlefield Rd., (650) 366-3842

Peninsula Covenant Presch. & After Care, 3560 Farm Hill Blvd., (650) 365-8094

Playschool, 1835-B Valota Rd., (650) 369-4151

Plaza CDCtr., 950 Main St., (650) 369-0527

Rainbow Presch. & DC, 2223 Vera Ave., (650) 365-3510

Red Morton Ctr., 1120 Roosevelt Ave., (650) 780-7311

Redwood Children's Ctr., 1445 Hudson St., (650) 367-7374

Redwood City CD Prog., 2600 Middlefield Rd., (650) 364-6112

Redwoods Int'l. Montessori, 2000 Woodside Rd., (650) 366-9859

Roosevelt Primary Education Ctr., 2434 McGarvey Way, (650) 366-6819

Sequoia Children's Ctr., 1234 Brewster Ave., (650) 369-5277

Sequoia Children's Ctr., 179 Clinton St., (650) 369-5277

Sequoia Presch., 2323 Euclid Ave., (650) 367-0180

St. Matthias DCCtr., 533 Canyon Rd., (650) 367-1320

Taft CDCtr., 903 10th Ave., (650) 482-5992

Temple Beth Jacob Presch., 1550 Alameda de las Pulgas, (650) 366-8481

Thumbelina Nursery Sch., 20 Horgan Ave., (650) 364-5165

West Bay Christian Acad., 901 Madison Ave., (650) 366-8205

Redwood Shores

Children's Creative Lrng. Ctrs., 797 Redwood Shores Pkwy., (650) 780-7322

Children's Creative Lrng. Ctrs., 250 Shoreline Dr., (650) 486-4949

Hoover Children's Ctr., 303 Twin Dolphin Dr., (650) 593-6824

San Bruno

Belle Air Presch., 450 3rd Ave., (650) 624-3155

Bright Star Presch., 498 Cunningham Way, (650) 871-6649

California Montessori Sch., 480 San Anselmo Ave., (650) 589-2237

Champions at John Muir, 130 Cambridge Ln., (650) 876-1023

Champions at Portola, 300 Amador Ave., (650) 952-6298

Crayon College, 300 Piedmont Ave., (650) 588-4197

Happy Hall Sch., 233 Santa Inez Ave., (650) 583-7370

Highlands Presch., 1900 Monterey Dr., (650) 873-4090

Hoover Children's Ctr., 2396 Evergreen Dr., (650) 871-5044

Monte Verde After Sch., 2551 St. Cloud Dr., (650) 742-0613

PARCA Project Reach-Crestmoor, 2322 Crestmoor Dr., (650) 871-8402

S. San Francisco Before & After Sch., 2551 Saint Cloud Dr., (650) 589-5683

Skyline Coll. Children's Ctr., 3300 College Dr., (650) 359-8637

St. Andrew's Presch., 1600 Santa Lucia Ave., (650) 583-1930

San Carlos

Children's Place, 1336 Arroyo Ave., (650) 595-1910

Club Central, 828 Chestnut St., (650) 508-7350

Edison Montessori Sch., 750 Dartmouth, (650) 592-4828

Happy Campers Presch. & DC, 510 Laurel St., (650) 593-2005

Kindercourt Acad., 1225 Greenwood, (650) 591-4882

Kindercourt, 1025 Laurel St., (650) 592-7980

Little Learners Presch., 785 Walnut St., (650) 593-8081

San Carlos After Sch.-Arundel, Arundel and Phelps Rd., (650) 593-0707

San Carlos After Sch.-Brittan Acres, Belle and Tamarack, (650) 591-4599

San Carlos After Sch.-Heather, 2757 Melendy, (650) 591-8039

San Carlos After Sch.-White Oaks, Cedar and White Oak Way, (650) 591-3515

Trinity Presby. Presch., 1106 Alameda de las Pulgas, (650) 593-0770

Wonder Years, 2851 San Carlos Ave., (650) 591-2669

San Mateo

Baywood Elem., 600 Alameda de las Pulgas, (650) 312-7511

Beresford Elem., 300 28th Ave., (650) 345-4043

Beresford Kids Club, 2720 Alameda de las Pulgas, (650) 522-7522

Bright Beginnings Presch., 30 Hobart Ave., (650) 571-0343

Bunker Hill Parent Part. Nursery Sch., 2145 Bunker Hill Dr., (650) 349-1581

Carey Sch., 2101 Alameda de las Pulgas, (650) 345-8205

Children's Sch.- Hillsdale United Meth. Ch., 303 W. 36th Ave., (650) 570-6196

Crystal Springs Early Childhood Ctr., 2145 Bunker Hill Dr., (650) 572-1110

Early Bird Presch., 120 Lindbergh St., (650) 344-8295

FSA Toddler Ctr., 225 Tilton Ave., (650) 347-3177

First Step CDC, 325 Villa Terrace, (650) 340-8814

Ganon Ctr.-Peninsula Temple Beth El, 1700 Alameda de las Pulgas, (650) 349-4911

Gazelle Dev. Sch., 770 N. El Camino Real, (650) 347-8411

Highland Montessori, 614 Highland Ave., (650) 347-6450

Highlands Rec. Ctr., 1851 Lexington Ave., (650) 341-4251

Hoover Children's Ctr., 1717 Gum St., (650) 341-6811

Hope Lutheran Presch., 600 W. 42nd Ave., (650) 345-8438

Intercommunal Survival Sch., 713 2nd Ave., (650) 347-0463

Kidz Care Presch., 2612 S. El Camino Real, (650) 212-5439

Kinder Acad. Montessori, 300 Santa Inez, (650) 340-8819

KinderCare, 1350 Wayne Way, (650) 577-0257

Kindercourt #2, 211 S. Delaware, (650) 344-6612

Mary Meta Lazarus Children's Ctr., 1700 W. Hillsdale Blvd., (650) 574-6279

Montessori Children's House, 315 Tulane Rd., (650) 342-0447

Neighborhood Montessori Sch., 27 10th Ave., (650) 343-8482

Pacific Rim Int'l. Sch., 454 Peninsula Ave., (650) 685-1881

Parkside Elem., 1685 Eisenhower St., (650) 312-7575

Petite Sorbonne Presch., 319 E. Santa Inez Ave., (650) 347-8510

San Mateo ECE, 65 Tower Rd., (650) 573-4010

San Mateo Head Start, 715 Indian Way, (650) 871-2690

San Mateo Montessori, 15 14th Ave., (650) 571-5095

San Mateo Parent's Nursery Sch., 1732 Mt. Diablo, (650) 347-1955

Serendipity Sch., 3172 Clearview Way, (650) 574-7400

Siebell Children's Ctr.-Bridgepointe Presch., 2207 Bridgepointe Pkwy., (650) 477-7020

SM-FC-Fiesta Gardens, 1001 Bermuda Dr., (650) 312-7737

SM-FC-George Hall, 130 San Miguel, (650) 312-7533

SM-FC-Horrall, 949 Ocean View, (650) 312-7550

SM-FC-North Shoreview, 1301 Cypress Ave., (650) 312-7588

St. Matthew's Episcopal Day Sch., 16 Baldwin Ave., (650) 342-5436(650)

Stella Piccolo, 65 Tower Rd., (650) 804-5923

Temporary Tot Tending, 39 E. 39th Ave., (650) 871-5790

Transfiguration Nursery, 3900 Alameda de las Pulgas, (650) 341-7878

Turnbull Children's Ctr., 715 Indian Ave., (650) 312-7766

Under the Weather Emergency Back-up Care, 2612 El Camino Real, (650) 212-5439

South San Francisco

Building Kids Prsch., 600 Grand Ave., (650) 837-9348

Early Years, 371 Allerton Ave., (650) 588-7525

Friends to Parents, 2525 Wexford Ave., (650) 588-8212

Genentech's 2nd Generation, 850 Gateway Blvd., (650) 225-3666

Hillside Nursery Sch., 1415 Hillside Blvd., (650) 583-6854

Leo J. Ryan CDCtr., 1200 Miller Ave., (650) 952-6848

Little Hugs Prsch., 740-A Del M:onte Ave., (650) 869-4847

Martin After Sch. Rec. Prog., 35 School St., (650) 873-0953

Ponderosa After Sch. Rec. Prog., 295 Ponderosa Rd., (650) 873-1096

R.W. Drake Presch. Ctr., 609 Southwood Dr., (650) 871-6833

Siebecker Ctr., 510 Elm Ct., (650) 875-6979

S. San Francisco Head Start, 825 Southwood Dr., (650) 871-2690

Spruce After Sch. Rec. Prog., 501 Spruce Ave., (650) 873-0924

SSFUSD Children's Ctr.-Presch., 530 Tamarack Ln., (650) 877-8826

SSFUSD-Martin CDCtr., 35 School St., (650) 877-8836

Temporary Tot Tending #3, 350 Dolores Way, (650) 588-0128

Westborough Presch., 2380 Galway, (650) 875-6980

Woodside

Woodside Elem. Presch., 3195 Woodside Rd., (650) 529-1917

Woodside Parents Coop. Nursery Sch., 3154 Woodside Rd., (650) 851-7112

Marin County

Belvedere

Belvedere Nursery Sch., 15 Cove Road Pl., (415) 435-1661

Bolinas

Bolinas Children's Center, 270 Elm Rd., (415) 868-2550

Corte Madera

Corte Madera Montessori, 50 El Camino Dr., (415) 927-0919

Golden Poppy Presch., 50 El Camino Dr., (415) 924-2828

Kids on the Hill, 5461 Paradise Dr., (415) 924-3033

Kids Place, 50 El Camino Dr., (415) 927-0498

Lycee Francais, 330 Golden Hinde Passage, (415) 924-1737

Marin Lutheran Children's Ctr., 649 Meadowsweet Dr., (415) 924-3792

Marin Montessori Sch., 5200 Paradise Dr., (415) 924-5388

Mountain Sch., 50 El Camino Dr., (415) 924-4661

Twin Cities CCC–Neil Cummins, 58 Mohawk Ave., (415) 924-6622

Twin Cities Co-op. Nursery Sch., 56 Mohawk Ave., (415) 924-3150

Twin Cities Presch., 58 Mohawk Ave., (415) 924-6630

Fairfax

Day Caring Presch., 2398 Sir Francis Drake, (415) 459-6291

Fairfax-San Anselmo Children's Ctr., 199 Porteous Ave., (415) 454-1811

First Friends Montessori, 86 Mono Ave., (415) 459-7028

Marin YMCA-Manor Sch., 150 Oak Manor Dr., (415) 456-5349

Kentfield

College of Marin Children's Ctr., Arcade Building, (415) 485-9468

Marin Enrichment, 25 McAllister Ave., (415) 461-4395

Marin Enrichment, 250 Stadium Way, (415) 454-5994

Ross Valley Nursery Sch., 689 Sir Francis Drake Blvd., (415) 461-5150

Larkspur

Children's Cottage Co-op., 2900 Larkspur Landing, (415) 461-0822

Marin Primary, 20 Magnolia Ave., (415) 924-2608

Marin City

Head Start-Marin City, 620 Drake Ave., (415) 332-2337

Manzanita CDCtr., 620 Drake Ave., (415) 332-3460

Marin Early Head Start-Manzanita, 620 Drake Ave., (415) 339-9322

Marin Lrng. Ctr., 100 Phillips Dr., (415) 339-2834

Mill Valley

Extd. Day Svcs.-Edna McGuire Sch., 80 Lomita Ave., (415) 381-2231

Extd. Day Svcs.-Tam Valley Sch., 350 Bell Ln. (415) 388-8304

Extd. Day Svcs.-Strawberry Point., 117 E. Strawberry Dr. (415) 383-6204

Golden Gate Baptist Theo. Sem. Presch. Ctr., 201 E. Seminary Dr., (415) 380-1400

Kumara Day School, 540 Marin Ave., (415) 388-5437

Little Sch., 285 Miller Ave., (415) 383-9696

Marin Day Sch.-Cottage, 322 Throckmorton, (415) 381-4206

Marin Day Sch.-Hillside Presch., 80 Lomita Dr., (415) 381-3120

Marin Day Sch.-Mill Valley, 10 Old Mill Rd., (415) 381-4206

Marin Day Sch.-Old Mill Sch., 352 Throckmorton, (415) 383-1308

Marin Day Sch.-Park Sch., 360 E. Blithedale Ave., (415) 388-1458

Marin Horizon Sch., 305 Montford Ave., (415) 388-8408

Mill Valley Co-op. Nursery Sch., 51 Shell Rd., (415) 388-9174

Robin's Nest-Mill Valley, 70 Lomita Dr., (415) 388-5999

Ross Acad. Montessori Sch., 7 Thomas Dr., (415) 383-5777

Tamalpais Presch., 410 Sycamore Ave., (415) 388-4286

Nicasio

Marin Day Sch.-Big Rock, 3800 Lucas Valley Rd., (415) 662-1746

Novato

All Saints Presch. & Children's Ctr., 2 San Marin Dr., (415) 893-4202

Creekside Village Sch., 1787 Grant Ave., (415) 898-7007

Good Shepherd Lutheran Sch., 1180 Lynwood Dr., (415) 897-2510

Hamilton CDCtr., 531 Hamilton Pkwy., (415) 883-4313

Head Start - Hamilton Site, 5520 Nave Dr., (415) 883-5315

Heidi's Kinderhaus, 799 Plaza Linda, (415) 899-0029

Indian Valley College CCtr., 1800 Ignacio Blvd., (415) 883-2211

Little Village Sch., 84 Martin Dr., (415) 382-9022

Marin YMCA-Loma Verde, 399 Alameda De La Loma, (415) 883-2663

Marin YMCA–Rancho, 1430 Johnson St., (415) 898-6061

Marin YMCA-San Ramon, 45 San Ramon Way, (415) 982-4849

Miss Sandie's Sch., 2001 Center Rd., (415) 892-2712

Montessori Sch., 1466 S. Novato Blvd., (415) 892-2228

Noah's Ark Presch., 1370 S. Novato Blvd., (415) 892-8498

North Bay Children's Ctr., 932 C St., (415) 883-6222

North Bay Childrn's Ctr., 22 Tinker Wy., (415) 883-6222

Novato Charter Sch. Ext. Day, 940 C St., (415) 883-4254

Novato Children's Ctr., 5520 Nave Dr., (415) 883-4385

Novato Enrichment Care, 749 Sutro Ave., (415) 893-0271

Novato Parents Nursery Sch., 1473 S. Novato Blvd., (415) 897-4498

Novato State Presch. & Enrichment Care, 601-A Bolling Dr., (415) 382-7919

Novato Youth Ctr. & Presch., 680 Wilson Ave., (415) 892-1643

Quality Care for Kids-Lynwood, 1320 Novato Blvd., (415) 892-6223

Quality Care for Kids-Olive, 629 Plum St., (415) 892-4111

Robin's Nest-Novato, 1990 Novato Blvd., (415) 897-1990

St. Francis Presch., 967 5th St., (415) 892-2597

Sunrise Montessori Sch., 1915 Novato Blvd., (415) 898-7111

TLC Presch., 288 San Marin Dr., (415) 892-8002

Pt. Reyes Station

Papermill Creek Children's Corner, 503 B St., (415) 663-9114

Ross

Ross Rec., 14 Lagunitas Rd., (415) 459-2704

San Anselmo

ABC Acad. Presch., 176 Tunstead Ave., (415) 459-7611

Creekside Aftersch. Ctr., 116 Butterfield Rd., (415) 459-6745

Little Arrows, 1543 Sir Francis Drake Blvd., (415) 482-0800

Parkside Presch., 1000 Sir Francis Drake Blvd., (415) 258-4644

Robin's Nest-San Anselmo, 100 Shaw Dr., (415) 459-5355

San Anselmo Co-op. Nursery Sch., 24 Myrtle Ln., (415) 454-5308

San Anselmo Montessori Sch., 100 Shaw Dr., (415) 457-3428

San Anselmo Presch., 121 Ross Ave., (415) 453-3181

San Domenico Early Ed. Prog., 1500 Butterfield Rd., (415) 258-1946

SFTS Children's Ctr., 100 Mariposa Ave., (415) 258-6660

Sleepy Hollow Nursery Sch., 1317 Butterfield Rd., (415) 453-1462

San Geronimo

San Geronimo Cultural Ctr. CC, Sir Francis Drake & Sch. Rd., (415) 488-8888

San Geronimo Valley DCCtr., 5501 Sir Francis Drake Blvd., (415) 488-9344

San Geronimo Presch. & CCCtr., 6001 Sir Francis Drake Blvd., (415) 488-4655

After Sch. DC, 6350 Sir Francis Drake Blvd., (415) 488-9344

San Rafael

Abbey Montessori Sch., 138 N. San Pedro Rd., (415) 479-8865

Canal CCCtr.-Presch. & Sch. Age, 215 Mission Ave., (415) 457-1444

Canal Comm. Alliance After Sch. Prog., 125 Bahia Way, (415) 258-0809

City of SR-Coleman, 140 Rafael Dr., (415) 485-3121

City of SR-Dixie, 1175 Idyleberry, (415) 485-3189

City of SR-Gallinas Children Ctr., 177 N. San Pedro Rd., (415) 485-3105

City of SR-Glenwood, 25 W. Castlewood, (415) 485-3102

City of SR-Mary Silveria, 375 Blackstone, (415) 485-3190

City of SR-Parkside, 51 Albert Ln., (415) 485-3386

City of SR-Pickleweed, 40 Canal St., (415) 485-3101

City of SR-Vallecito, 50 Nova Albion, (415) 485-3103

Gan Israel Nursery Sch., 1055 Las Ovejas Ave., (415) 507-0460

Head Start-Bahia Vista, 125 Bahia Way, (415) 883-3791

Head Start-Family Village, 21 Front St., (415) 485-1489

Head Start-Greenfield, 199 Greenfield, (415) 454-1243

Head Start-San Pedro, 8 N. San Pedro Rd., (415) 491-1419

Ice Cream & Shoe Presch. & K, 1055 Las Ovejas Ave., (415) 492-0550

Lollipops & Letters, 360 Nova Albion Way, (415) 479-8980

Marin Day Sch.-San Rafael, 1123 Court St., (415) 453-9822

Marin Day Sch.-St. Vincent's Presch., 1 St. Vincent Dr., (415) 479-0531

Marin Formative, 2000 Las Gallinas Ave., (415) 479-4140

Marin Waldorf Sch., 755 Idylberry Rd., (415) 479-8190

Merry Times Presch. Acad., 159 Merrydale Rd., (415) 472-4777

Montessori De Terra Linda, 620 Del Ganado Rd., (415) 479-7373

Montessori in Motion, 3 Wellbrock Hts., (415) 472-5622

Montessori Sch. of Central Marin, 317 Auburn, (415) 456-1748

Morning Star Presch., 50 Los Ranchitos Rd., (415) 499-8663

Oakview Sch., 70 Skyview Terr., (415) 479-6026

Old Gallinas Children's Ctr., 251 N. San Pedro Rd., (415) 479-2771

Osher Marin Jewish Comm. Ctr. Presch., 200 N. San Pedro Rd., (415) 444-8042

Parkside Children's Ctr., 51 Albert Park Ln., (415) 485-3387

Redeemer Presch. & DC, 123 Knight Dr., (415) 457-9500

Santa Margarita CCCtr., 1055 Las Ovejas Ave., (415) 499-1277

Trinity Presch., 333 Woodland Ave., (415) 453-4526

Sausalito

Children's Cultural Ctr., 620 Drake Ave., (415) 332-1044

Sausalito Nursery Sch., 625 Main St., (415) 332-0174

Sparrow Creek Sch., 304 Caledonia St., (415) 332-9595

Stinson Beach

Stinson Beach Montessori, BSUSD-Hwy 1, (415) 868-0949

Tiburon

Belvedere Tiburon CCCtr., 1185 Tiburon Blvd., (415) 435-4366

Belvedere Tiburon CCCtr.-Bel Aire, 277 Karen Way, (415) 381-2243

Hawthorne Nursery Sch., 145 Rock Hill Dr., (415) 435-9757

Little School, 11 Shepherd Way, (415) 435-3521

Ring Mountain Day Sch., 215-A Blackfield Dr., (415) 381-8181

Strawberry Presch., 240 Tiburon Blvd., (415) 388-4437

Tomales

Shoreline Acres Presch. & Sch. Age, 40 John St., (707) 878-9442

Woodacre

West Marin Montessori Sch., 1 Garden Way, (415) 488-4500

Sonoma County

Boyes Hot Springs

Head Start-Sonoma Valley, 17600 Sonoma Hwy., (707) 996-5464

Cloverdale

Cloverdale Presch. Coop., 315 North St., (707) 894-4328

Head Start-Cloverdale, 322 Washington St., (707) 894-9072

Imagination Station DCCtr., 530 N. Cloverdale Blvd., (707) 894-2371

Little Friends Presch. & CCCtr., 1 Citrus Fair Dr., (707) 894-9050

Cotati

4 Cs-Child's Play, 768 E. Cotati Ave., (707) 792-2614

Cotati-Rohnert Park Coop., 150 W. Sierra Ave., (707) 795-4846

Rainbow Bridge Montessori, 21 William St., (707) 795-6666

Rainbow Bridge Montessori #2, 70 William St., (707) 795-6666

Small Miracles Presch., 45 Henry St., (707) 792-9256

Training Wheels Presch., 65 W. Cotati, (707) 795-3527

YMCA Sunshine-Thomas Page, 1075 Madrone, (707) 792-4474

Geyserville
Comm. Children's Ctr., 21465 Geyserville Ave., (707) 857-3214

Glen Ellen
YMCA Sunshine-Dunbar, 11700 Dunbar Rd., (707) 996-9220

Guerneville
River Area Head Start, 14520 Armstrong Woods Rd., (707) 869-2261

YMCA Sunshine-Guerneville Elem., 14630 Armstrong Woods Rd., (707) 869-0422

Healdsburg
4 Cs-Healdsburg CDCtr., 555 North St., (707) 433-2556

Fitch Mountain State Presch., 565 Sanns Ln., (707) 431-3470

Good Beginnings Nursery & DC, 1043 Felta Rd., (707) 433-6855

Healdsburg Comm. Nursery Sch., 444 1st St., (707) 433-1817

Healdsburg Elem. State Presch., 400 1st St., (707) 431-3480

Healdsburg Head Start, 3200 Rio Lindo Ave., (707) 431-1213

Healdsburg Montessori, 500 Grove St., (707) 431-1727

Live Oak Presch., 75 W. Matheson, (707) 433-1543

Pine Tree Sch., 20 Adeline Way, (707) 433-8447

St. John the Baptist Sch., 217 Fitch St., (707) 433-2758

Kenwood
Kenwood Presch., 230 Randolph Ave., (707) 833-6551

Monte Rio
Monte Rio Presch., 20700 Foothill Dr., (707) 865-0223

Penngrove
Building Blocks Presch., 228 Adobe Rd., (707) 792-2280

Redwood Montessori Sch., 11201 Main St., (707) 665-9830

YMCA Sunshine-Penngrove Sch., 365 Adobe Rd., (707) 794-9831

Petaluma
4 Cs-Old Elm CDCtr., 305 W. Payran St., (707) 782-0408

4 Cs-Petaluma CDCtr., 401 S. McDowell, (707) 763-4990

Adobe Christian Presch., 2875 Adobe Rd., (707) 762-7713

Children's Corner, 629 East D St., (707) 763-6191

Children's Haven, 1500-B Petaluma Blvd. S., (707) 765-6530

Children's Workshop, Arts & Crafts Bldg., Fairgd., (707) 763-1083

Gan Israel Presch., 740 Western Ave., (707) 763-5136

Happy Day Presby. Presch., 939 B St., (707) 762-8671

Head Start-Petaluma, 110 Ellis St., (707) 778-3896

Learning to Learn Presch. & CCCtr., 391 Maria Dr., (707) 762-8607

Learning Universe, 100 Gnoss Concourse, (707) 778-7230

Learning Universe DCCtr., 1485 N. McDowell Blvd., (707) 794-0211

Little Oaks Presch. & CC, 715 Petaluma Blvd. N., (707) 763-3235

Little Shepherd Luth. Presch., 220 Stanley St., (707) 769-0462

Montessori Sch., 825 Middlefield Dr., (707) 763-9222

Old Adobe Christian Presch., 2875 Old Adobe Rd., (707) 763-0646

Old Adobe Union Sch. Dist.-Presch., 1010 St. Francis Dr., (707) 765-4376

Petaluma Enrichment Care & Presch., 1001-A Cherry St., (707) 762-7337

Petaluma Enrichment Care & Presch., 405 S. McDowell Blvd., (707) 769-8891

Play & Learn Presch., 100 Gnoss Concourse, (707) 769-9714

St. John Lutheran Presch., 455 McNear Ave., (707) 762-8520

W.H. Pepper Presch., 627 F St., (707) 762-8151

Willow Tree Sch., 137 Payran St., (707) 763-2546

YMCA Sunshine-Grant, 200 Grant Ave., (707) 763-1723

YMCA Sunshine-McNear, 605 Sunnyslope Ave., (707) 782-0734

You & Me Children's Ctr., 450 Hayes Ln., (707) 762-8998

Rohnert Park

Cross & Crown Luth. Presch., 5474 Snyder Ln., (707) 795-7853

Head Start-Rohnert Park, 1290 Southwest Blvd., (707) 544-6911

KinderCare, 6150 State Farm Dr., (707) 584-0124

La Petite Acad., 1301 Medical Center Dr., (707) 585-7588

Learning to Learn, 1300 Medical Center Dr., (707) 584-4224

Little Ones Backyard Club, 399 College View Dr., (707) 792-1620

Mt. Taylor Children's Ctr. Too, 190 Arlen Dr., (707) 793-9020

Redwood Country Day, 1300 Medical Center Dr., (707) 586-0675

Sonoma State Univ. Children's Sch., 1801 E. Cotati Ave., (707) 664-2230

YMCA Sunshine-Evergreen, 1125 Emily Ave., (707) 584-8229

YMCA Sunshine-Gold Ridge, 1455 Golf Course Dr., (707) 586-1622

YMCA Sunshine-Mauguerite Hahn, 825 Hudis, (707) 584-8294

YMCA Sunshine-Monte Vista, 1400 Magnolia Ave., (707) 794-7318

Santa Rosa

4 Cs-Luther Burbank CDCtr., 315 South A St., (707) 542-7570

4 Cs-Florence Kirby CDCtr., 1931 Biwana Dr., (707) 542-6181

4 Cs-Monroe State Presch., 2567 Marlow Rd., (707) 570-2607

A Special Place, 1128 Edwards Ave., (707) 523-2337

Apples and Bananas Presch., 1931 Biwana Dr., (707) 545-0100

Apples and Bananas Presch., 950 Sebastopol Rd., (707) 545-4541

Bennett Valley Montessori Presch., 2810 Summerfield Rd., (707) 537-8889

Bethel Children's Ctr., 1577 Guerneville Rd., (707) 527-0332

Bethlehem Children's Ctr., 1300 St. Francis Rd., (707) 538-2266

Bridge School, The, 1625 Franklin Ave., (707) 538-1140

Brush Creek Family Svcs., 4657 Badger Rd., (707) 539-1612

Brush Creek Montessori , 1569 Brush Creek Rd., (707) 539-7980

CCS Presch., 1315 Pacific Ave., (707) 528-0940

Casa for Kids Nursery Sch., 2260 W. Steele Ln., (707) 526-6892

Childkind Presch., 2200 Laguna Rd., (707) 823-6993

Children's Discovery Ctr.-Discoveries West, 28 Maxwell Ct., (707) 523-0454

Children's Discovery Ctr. - Rincon, 6170 Montecito Blvd., (707) 539-3638

Children's Lrng. Ctr. Presch., 1213 W. Steele Ln., (707) 575-7486

Christ Meth. Nursery Sch., 1717 Yulupa Ave., (707) 526-0204

College Oak Montessori Sch., 1925 W. College Ave., (707) 579-5510

Countryside Presch., 1592 Fulton Rd., (707) 526-3789

Faith Luth. Presch., 4930 Newanga Ave., (707) 538-3068

Franklin Park Presch., 2095 Franklin Ave., (707) 546-7330

FUMC Presch. CCCtr., 1551 Montgomery Dr., (707) 546-7012

Happy Time DCCtr., 1135 Farmers Ln., (707) 527-9135

Head Start-Doyle Park, 1620 Sonoma Ave., (707) 544-6911

Head Start–Grace Reese Ctr., 1931 Biwana Rd., (707) 528-9149

Head Start-Lincoln Ctr., 604 Simpson St., (707) 546-2825

Head Start-Luther Burbank, 203 S. A St., (707) 528-6122

Head Start-Roseland, 1931 Biwana Rd., (707) 528-3008

Head Start-South Park, 1330 Temple St., (707) 544-6318

Jewish Comm. Ctr. Nursery Sch., 4676 Mayette Ave., (707) 578-3338

J.X. Wilson CCCtr., 246 Brittain Ln., (707) 575-6988

Kids Ctr., 2250 Mesquite Dr., (707) 546-5328

Kiwi Presch., 573 Summerfield Rd., (707) 539-6232

La Petite Acad., 2055 Occidental Rd., (707) 573-1623

Lattice Educational Svcs., 3273 Airway Dr., (707) 571-1234

Little Angels Children's Ctr. 3, 1363 Fulton Rd., (707) 528-2933

Little Angels Children's Ctr. 1, 4305 Hoen Ave., (707) 579-4305

Little Ones Ctr.-West, 301 Fulton Rd., (707) 578-8363
Little People's Playhouse, 1561 Herbert St., (707) 544-0951
Mark West Ext. CC, 4600 Lavelle Rd., (707) 524-2990
Merryhill Country Sch., 4044 Mayette Ave., (707) 575-7660
Mt. Taylor Children's Ctr., 1451 Slater St., (707) 576-0773
Multicultural CDCtr., 1650 W. 3rd St., (707) 544-0104
My Circle of Friends CCCtr., 1611 Dutton Ave., (707) 576-1929
New Directions Adolescent Svcs., 3641 Stony Point Rd., (707) 585-3700
Nueva Vista Early Head Start, 2232 Lomitos Ave., (707) 522-3291
Presby. Presch., 1550 Pacific Ave., (707) 542-7396
R.L. Stevens Ext. CC, 2345 Giffen Ave., (707) 544-6911
Redwood Christian Presch., 385 Mark West Springs Rd., (707) 545-1697
Rhio's Casa Dei Bambini, 2427 Professional Dr., (707) 528-0889
Riebli Ext. CC, 305 Mark West Springs Rd., (707) 545-2897
Rincon Valley Christian PreK, 4585 Badger Rd., (707) 538-2753
Roseland Ext. CC, 950 Sebastopol Rd., (707) 545-0100
San Miguel Ext. CC, 5350 Faught Rd., (707) 546-0667
Santa Rosa Jewish Comm. Ctr. CDCtr., 4676 Mayette Ave., (707) 578-3338
Santa Rosa Jr. Coll. Children's Ctr., 1501 Mendocino Ave., (707) 527-4224
Sonoma County Kid's Ctr., 2250 Mesquite Rd., (707) 546-5328
Sonshine Kids Sch., 3595 Sonoma Ave., (707) 544-1620
St. Eugene's Cathedral Presch., 360 Farmers Ln., (707) 528-9133
St. Luke Luth. Presch., 905 Mendocino Ave., (707) 545-0512
St. Rose Presch., 400 Angela Dr., (707) 526-9844
Stepping Stones Presch., 4295 Montgomery Dr., (707) 538-5437
Summerfield Waldorf Sch., 655 Willowside Rd., (707) 575-7194
Tiny Treasures, 180 Wikiup Dr., (707) 544-8469

Willow Creek Children's Ctr., 2536 Marlow Rd., (707) 528-2813
Woodside West Sch., 2577 Guerneville Rd., (707) 528-6666
Wright Ext. CC, 4389 Price Ave., (707) 527-6724
YMCA Sunshine-Olivet, 1825 Willowside Rd., (707) 544-3309
YMCA Sunshine-Piner Presch. & Sch. Age, 2590 Piner Rd., (707) 544-1820
YMCA Sunshine-Schaefer, 1370 San Miguel Rd., (707) 579-9558
YMCA Sunshine-Steele Lane, 301 Steele Ln., (707) 544-9817
YMCA Sunshine-Strawberry, 2311 Horseshoe, (707) 527-6224
YMCA Sunshine-Yulupa, 2250 Mesquite Dr., (707) 575-5219
YWCA-A Children's Place, 2614 Paulin Dr., (707) 523-4646
Sebastopol
4 Cs Taylor Mountain CDCtr., 1606 Gravenstein Hwy. S., (707) 824-4383
Alphabet Soup Presch. & DC, 4411 Gravenstein Hwy. N., (707) 829-9460
Castle Prschl., 7601 Huntley St., (707) 829-4577
Childkind Schools-Oak Grove, 8760 Bower Rd., (707) 823-4930
Cricket House, 955 Gravenstein Hwy. S., (707) 829-0378
Happy Days Comm. Church, 1000 Gravenstein Hwy. N., (707) 829-2814
Head Start-Oak Grove, 8760 Bower Rd., (707) 824-1761
Montessori Children's House, 500 N. Main St., (707) 823-1110
Mt. Olive Luth. Nursery Sch., 460 Murphy Ave., (707) 823-6316
Pleasant Hill Casa Dei Bambini, 789 Pleasant Hill Rd., (707) 823-6003
Sunflower Presch., 2804 Thorn Rd., (707) 829-1210
Taylor Childrn's Prschl, 546 N. Main St., (707) 823-1110
Tiny Tots-Sebastopol Comm. Ctr., 7985 Valentine Ave., (707) 823-0355
Sonoma
4 Cs Sonoma CDCtr., 620 5th St., (707) 996-3494
Blue Sky Presch., 18345 Railroad Ave., (707) 935-0999
Crescent Montessori, 276 E. Napa St., (707) 996-2456

Faith Luth. Presch., 19355 Arnold Dr., (707) 938-9464

Gingerbread House, 504 Calle Del Monte, (707) 938-1102

Little School, 991 Broadway, (707) 935-3922

Little Shepherd Presch., 18980 Arnold Dr., (707) 938-4199

Montessori Sch., 19675 8th St. E., (707) 996-2422

Old Adobe Sch., 252 W. Spain St., (707) 938-4510

Sunshine Nursery Sch., 109 Patten St., (707) 996-2702

Valley of the Moon Nursery Sch., 136 Mission Terr., (707) 938-4265

YMCA Sunshine-Prestwood, 343 E. MacArthur, (707) 935-1793

Windsor

Brooks Ext. CC, 750 Natalie Dr., (707) 838-3540

Cali Calmecac Ext. CC, 9491 Starr Rd., (707) 838-3859

Little Sch. House Presch. & Sch. Age, 270 Mark West Station Rd., (707) 527-8116

Mattie Washburn Ext. CC, 75 Pleasant Ave., (707) 838-9025

Robin's Nest-Windsor, 9451 Brooks Rd., (707) 838-0549

Windsor Christian Acad., 10285 Starr Rd., (707) 838-3757

Windsor Christian Acad.-Presch., 10151 Starr Rd., (707) 838-3084

Windsor Co-op. Nursery Sch., 9161 Starr Rd., (707) 838-9306

Windsor Creek Ext. CC, 8955 Conde Ln., (707) 838-6801

Windsor Head Start, 9491 Starr Rd., (707) 837-0437

Population by Age Groups in San Mateo County

City or Area	Under 5	5-19	20-34	35-54	55+
Atherton	371	1,540	714	2,170	2,399
Belmont	1,512	3,821	5,365	8,559	5,866
Brisbane	161	531	699	1,555	651
Burlingame	1,574	4,240	6,255	9,339	6,750
Colma	62	254	246	356	273
Daly City	6,246	19,816	25,086	30,634	21,839
East Palo Alto	2,943	8,485	8,331	6,713	3,034
El Granada	393	1,265	839	2,382	845
Foster City	1,685	4,846	6,109	9,980	6,183
Half Moon Bay	699	2,200	2,267	4,292	2,384
Hillsborough	551	2,338	944	3,473	3,519
Menlo Park	2,030	5,178	6,770	9,444	7,363
Millbrae	955	3,689	3,316	6,339	6,419
Montara	191	610	361	1,235	553
Moss Beach	94	410	272	854	323
Pacifica	2,170	7,541	7,653	13,701	7,325
Portola Valley	223	852	315	1,471	1,601
Redwood City	5,679	13,373	18,991	23,916	13,443
San Bruno	2,440	7,658	9,035	13,098	7,934
San Carlos	1,951	4,544	4,553	9,973	6,697
San Mateo	5,631	14,892	21,394	28,760	21,805
South San Francisco	3,914	12,309	13,352	18,112	12,865
Woodside	325	995	492	1,968	1,572
County Total	45,374	131,912	153,019	225,258	151,598

Source: 2000 Census.

Chapter **14**

Hospitals & Health Care

GOOD HEALTH CARE. You want it. Where, how, do you get it? The question is particularly puzzling these days because so many changes are taking place in medicine and medical insurance.

The operations of a few years ago are the procedures of today, done in the office, not the surgery, completed in minutes, not hours, requiring home care, not hospitalization.

Large insurance companies, through their health maintenance plans, are setting limits on what doctors and hospitals can charge, and — critics contend — interfering with the ability of doctors to prescribe what they see fit. The companies strongly deny this, arguing they are bringing reforms to a profession long in need of reforming.

Many hospitals are merging, the better to avoid unnecessary duplication and to save money by purchasing supplies and medicine in larger amounts.

Universal health insurance having failed to clear congress, about 45 million Americans are not covered by any medical plan. Unable to afford medical bills, many ignore ailments and illnesses.

The state legislature has passed a law that makes it easier for patients to sue Health Maintenance Organizations and insurers.

This chapter will give you an overview of Northern California health care and although it won't answer all your questions — too complex a business for that — we hope that it will point you in the right directions.

For most people, health care is twined with insurance, in systems that are called "managed care." But many individuals, for a variety of reasons, do not have insurance. This is a good place to start: with nothing, all options open. Let's use as our seeker for the best of all health-care worlds — on a tight budget — a young woman, married, one child. Her choices:

No Insurance — Cash Care

The woman is self-employed or works at a small business that does not offer health benefits. She comes down with the flu. When she goes into the doctor's office, she will be asked by the receptionist, how do you intend to pay? With no insurance, she pays cash (or credit card), usually right there. She takes her prescription, goes to the pharmacy and pays full cost.

If her child or husband gets sick and needs to see a doctor, the same procedure holds. Also, the same for treatment of a serious illness, to secure X-rays or hospitalization. It's a cash system.

Medi-Cal

If an illness strikes that impoverishes the family or if the woman, through job loss or simply low wages, cannot afford cash care, the county-state health system will step in.

The woman fills out papers to qualify for Medi-Cal, the name of the system (it's known elsewhere as Medicaid), and tries to find a doctor that will treat Medi-Cal patients. If unable to find an acceptable doctor, the woman could turn to a county hospital or clinic. There she will be treated free or at very low cost.

Drawbacks-Pluses of Medi-Cal

County hospitals and clinics have competent doctors and medical personnel. If you keep appointments promptly, often you will be seen with little wait. If you want immediate treatment for, say, a cold, you register and you wait until an urgent-care doctor is free.

If you need a specialist, often the county facility will have one on staff or will be able to find one at a teaching hospital or other facility. You don't choose the specialist; the county physician does.

County facilities are underfunded and, often, inconveniently located — a major drawback. Some counties, lacking clinics and hospitals, contract with adjoining counties that are equipped. You have to drive some distance for treatment. The paperwork can be demanding.

County hospitals and clinics are not 100 percent free. If you have money or an adequate income, you will be billed for service. Some county hospitals run medical plans designed for people who can pay. These people can ask for a "family" doctor and receive a higher (usually more convenient) level of care.

Let's say the woman lacks money but doesn't want to hassle with a long drive and, possibly, a long wait for treatment of a minor ailment. She can sign up for Medi-Cal to cover treatment of serious illnesses, and for the colds, etc., go to a private doctor for treatment and pay in cash, ignoring Medi-Cal.

There are many ways to skin the cat and much depends on circumstances. For the poor and low-income, Medi-Cal is meant to be a system of last resort.

Medicare— Veterans Hospital

If our woman were disabled or elderly, she would be eligible for Medicare, the federal insurance system, which covers 80 percent, with limitations, of medical costs or allowable charges. Many people purchase supplemental insurance to bring coverage up to 100 percent (long-term illnesses requiring hospitalization may exhaust some benefits.)

If the woman were a military veteran with a service-related illness, she could seek care at a Veteran's Administration clinic or hospital.

Indemnity Care

Usually the most expensive kind of insurance, this approach allows complete freedom of choice. The woman picks the doctor she wants. If her regular doctor recommends a specialist, she can decide which one, and if she needs hospital treatment, she can pick the institution. In reality, the choice of hospital and specialist will often be strongly influenced by her regular doctor but the patient retains control. Many indemnity plans have deductibles and some may limit how much they pay out in a year or lifetime.

Managed Care

This divides into three systems, Preferred Provider Organizations (PPO), and Health Maintenance Organizations (HMO) and a spin-off of HMOs, Point of Service (POS). All are popular in California and if your employer provides health insurance, chances are almost 100 percent you will be pointed toward, or given a choice of, one of the three.

PPOs and HMOs differ among themselves. It is beyond the scope of this book to detail the differences but you should ask if coverage can be revoked or rates increased in the event of serious illness. Also, what is covered, what is not. Cosmetic surgery might not be covered. Psychiatric visits or care might be limited. Ask about drug costs and how emergency or immediate care is provided.

Preferred Provider

The insurance company approaches certain doctors, clinics, medical facilities and hospitals and tells them: We will send patients to you but you must agree to our prices — a method of controlling costs — and our rules. The young woman chooses her doctor from the list, often extensive, provided by the PPO.

The physician will have practicing privileges at certain local hospitals. The young woman's child contracts pneumonia and must be hospitalized. Dr. X is affiliated with XYZ hospital, which is also signed up with the PPO plan. The child is treated at XYZ hospital.

If the woman used an "outside" doctor or hospital, she would pay extra — the amount depending on the nature of the plan. It is important to know the doctor's affiliations because you may want your hospital care at a certain institution.

Hospitals differ. A children's hospital, for instance, will specialize in children's illnesses and load up on children's medical equipment. A general hospital will have a more rounded program. For convenience, you may want the hospital closest to your home.

If you need specialized treatment, you must, to avoid extra costs, use the PPO-affiliated specialists. The doctor will often guide your choice.

Complaints are surfacing from people who started out with a general physician, who was affiliated with their PPO, then moved on to a specialist who was not affiliated with the PPO. When the second doctor submits a bill, people are shocked. Each time you see a doctor you should ask if he or she is affiliated with your PPO.

Besides the basic cost for the policy, PPO insurance might charge fees, co-payments or deductibles. A fee might be $15 or $20 a visit. With co-payments, the bill, say, comes to $100. Insurance pays $80, the woman pays $20.

Deductible example: The woman pays the first $250 or the first $2,000 of any medical costs within a year, and the insurer pays bills above $250 or $2,000. With deductibles, the higher the deductible the lower the cost of the policy. The $2,000 deductible is really a form of catastrophic insurance.

Conversely, the higher the premium the more the policy covers. Some policies cover everything. (Dental care is usually provided through a separate insurer.) The same for prescription medicines. You may pay for all, part, or nothing, depending on the type plan.

The PPO doctor functions as your personal physician. Often the doctor will have his or her own practice and office, conveniently located. If you need to squeeze in an appointment, the doctor usually will try to be accommodating.

Drawback: PPOs restrict choice.

Health Maintenance Organization (HMO)

Very big in California because Kaiser Permanente, one of the most popular medical-hospital groups, is run as an HMO. The insurance company and medical provider are one and the same. All or almost all medical care is given by the HMO. The woman catches the flu. She sees the HMO doctor at the HMO clinic or hospital. If she becomes pregnant, she sees an HMO obstetrician at the HMO hospital or clinic and delivers her baby there.

With HMOs you pay the complete bill if you go outside the system (with obvious exceptions; e.g., special treatments or emergency care).

HMOs encourage you to pick a personal physician. The young woman wants a woman doctor; she picks one from the staff. She wants a pediatrician as her child's personal doctor; the HMO, usually, can provide a choice.

HMO clinics and hospitals bring many specialists and services together under one roof. You can get your eyes examined, your hearing tested, your prescriptions filled, your X-rays taken within a HMO facility (this varies), and much more.

If you need an operation or treatment beyond the capability of your immediate HMO hospital, the surgery will be done at another HMO hospital within the system or at a hospital under contract with the HMO. Kaiser recently started contracting with other facilities to provide some of the services that it used to do in its own hospitals or clinics.

HMO payment plans vary but many HMO clients pay a monthly fee and a small per visit fee. Often the plan includes low- or reduced-cost or free prescriptions and prevention or health programs — quitting tabacco, losing weight, eating healthy, dealing with diabetes or mental-health problems, and so on.

Drawback: Freedom of choice limited. If HMO facility is not close, the woman will have to drive to another town.

Point of Service (POS)

Essentially, an HMO with the flexibility to use outside doctors and facilities for an extra fee or a higher deductible. POS systems seem to be popular with people who don't feel comfortable limiting themselves to an HMO.

They pay extra but possibly not as much as other alternatives.

Choices, more information

If you are receiving medical insurance through your employer, you will be limited to the choices offered. In large groups, unions often have a say in what providers are chosen. Some individuals will base their choice on price, some on convenience of facilities, others on what's covered, and so on.

Many private hospitals offer Physician Referral Services. You call the hospital, ask for the service and get a list of doctors to choose from. The doctors will be affiliated with the hospital providing the referral. Hospitals and doctors will also tell you what insurance plans they accept for payment and will send you brochures describing the services the hospital offers.

For Kaiser and other HMOs, call the local hospital or clinic.

A PPO will give you a list of its member doctors and facilities.

Ask plenty of questions. Shop carefully.

Common Questions

The young woman is injured in a car accident and is unconscious. Where will she be taken?

Generally, she will be taken to the closest emergency room or trauma center, where her condition will be stabilized. Her doctor will then have her admitted into a hospital. Or she will be transferred to her HMO hospital or, if indigent, to a county facility.

If her injuries are severe, she most likely will be rushed to a regional trauma center. Trauma centers have specialists and special equipment to treat serious injuries. Both PPOs and HMOs offer urgent care and emergency care.

The young woman breaks her leg. Her personal doctor is an internist and does not set fractures. What happens?

The personal doctor refers the case to a specialist. Insurance pays the specialist's fee.

In PPO, the woman would generally see a specialist affiliated with the PPO. In an HMO, the specialist would be employed by the HMO.

The young woman signs up for an HMO then contracts a rare disease or suffers an injury that requires treatment beyond the capability of the HMO. Will she be treated?

Often yes, but it pays to read the fine print. The HMO will contract treatment out to a facility that specializes in the needed treatment.

The young woman becomes despondent and takes to drink. Will insurance pay for her rehabilitation?

Depends on her insurance. And often her employer. Some may have drug and alcohol rehab plans. Some plans cover psychiatry.

The woman becomes pregnant. Her doctor, who has delivered many babies, wants her to deliver at X hospital. All the woman's friends say, Y Hospital is much better, nicer, etc. The doctor is not cleared to practice at Y Hospital. Is the woman out of luck?

With a PPO, the woman must deliver at a hospital affiliated with the PPO — or pay the extra cost. If her doctor is not affiliated with that hospital, sometimes a doctor may be given courtesy practicing privileges at a hospital where he or she does not have staff membership. Check with the doctor.

With HMOs, the woman must deliver within the HMO system.

The young woman goes in for minor surgery, which turns into major surgery when the doctor forgets to remove a sponge before sewing up. Upon reviving, she does what?

Some plans require clients to submit complaints to arbitrators, who decide damages, if any. The courts are chipping away at this requirement.

The woman's child reaches age 18. Is she covered by the family insurance?

All depends on the insurance. Some policies will cover the children while they attend college. (But attendance may be defined in a certain way, full-time as opposed to part-time.) To protect your coverage, you should read the plan thoroughly.

At work, the woman gets her hand caught in a revolving door and is told she will need six months of therapy during which she can't work. Who pays?

Insurance will usually pay for the medical costs. Workers Compensation, a state plan that includes many but not all people, may compensate the woman for time lost off the job and may pay for medical costs. If you injure yourself on the job, your employer must file a report with Workers Comp.

The woman wakes up at 3 a.m. with a sore throat and headache. She feels bad but not bad enough to drive to a hospital or emergency room. She should:

Many hospitals and medical plans offer 24-hour advice lines. This is something you should check on when you sign up for a plan.

The woman wins a vacation to Switzerland where she falls off an Alp, breaks a leg, and spends three days in a Swiss hospital. Her HMO or PPO is 7,000 miles away. Who pays?

Usually the insurance company, but it is wise to check out how to obtain medical services before going on vacation. The woman may have to pay out-of-pocket and then file for reimbursement on her return home.

While working in her kitchen, the woman slips, bangs her head against the stove, gets a nasty cut and becomes woozy. She should:

Call 9-1-1, which will send an ambulance. 9-1-1 is managed by police dispatch. It's the fastest way to get an ambulance — with one possible exception.

If you are on the road and in need of emergency help and you don't have a cell phone or can't get through, try one of the emergency call boxes.

What's the difference between a hospital, a clinic, an urgent-care center and a doctor's office?

The hospital has the most services and equipment. The center or clinic has several services and a fair amount of equipment. The office, usually, has the fewest services and the smallest amount of equipment but in some places "clinic-office" means about the same.

Hospitals have beds. If a person must have a serious operation, she goes to a hospital. Hospitals have coronary-care and intensive-care units, emergency care and other specialized, costly treatment units. Many hospitals also run clinics for minor ailments and provide the same services as medical centers. Some hospitals offer programs outside the typical doctor-patient relationships. For example, wellness plans — how control stress or quit smoking.

Urgent care or medical centers are sometimes located in neighborhoods, which makes them more convenient for some people. The doctors treat the minor, and often not-so-minor, ailments of patients and send them to hospitals for major surgery and serious sicknesses.

Some doctors form themselves into groups to offer the public a variety of services. Some hospitals have opened neighborhood clinics or centers to attract patients. Kaiser has hospitals in some towns and clinic-offices in other towns.

The doctor in his or her office treats patients for minor ailments and uses the hospital for surgeries, major illnesses. Many illnesses that required hospitalization years ago are now treated in the office or clinic.

Major Hospitals In San Francisco

California Pacific Medical Center, California Campus, 3700 California St., San Francisco, 94118. Ph: (415) 387-8700. Pacific Campus, 2333 Buchanan St., San Francisco, 94115. Ph: (415) 563-4321. Breast health center, cancer care programs, cardiovascular services, critical care (includes cardiopulmonary unit, CCU, ICUS, NICUS, pediatric ICUs), coming home hospice, diabetes services, emergency services, GI (includes inflammatory bowel disease center), home health care, immunotherapy and infectious diseases including HIV/AIDS, internal medicine, OB (includes high-risk neonatology and perinatology), GYN, occupational health, ophthalmology, organ transplantation, orthopaedics, outpatient clinics, pediatrics, perinatal education and lactation center, physician referral, plastic surgery, primary care, psychiatric services, rehabilitation medicine, geriatric program, skilled nursing, surgical services.

California Pacific Medical Center Davies Campus, Castro & Duboce, San Francisco, 94114. Ph: (415) 600-6000. ICU, CCU, emergency care, HIV/AIDS, geriatric psychiatry, workers' compensation, orthopaedics, nutrition/metabolism clinic, vocational services, physical therapy, skilled nursing, radiology, home health care, cancer treatment, microvascular surgery, plastic surgery, hemodialysis, rehabilitation, sports medicine, fitness evaluation, occupational medicine. California Pacific is affiliated with Sutter Health.

Chinese Hospital, 845 Jackson St., San Francisco, 94133. Ph: (415) 982-2400. ICU, GYN, physical therapy, CCU, physician referral, radiology, emergency care, ambulatory surgery, community services, ophthalmology, health education, breast health center, med-surgical unit, pharmacy, cardiopulmonary services and cancer treatment.

Kaiser Permanente Medical Center—San Francisco, Geary Campus: 2425 Geary Blvd., San Francisco, 94115; French Campus: 4131 Geary Blvd., San Francisco, 94118. Ph. (415) 833-2000. Services include emergency, acute and intensive care, cardiology and cardiovascular surgery, high risk OB and neonatal, home health, hospice, HIV research. Outpatient care includes internal medicine, OB, GYN, pediatrics, teen clinic, psychiatry and chemical dependency recovery, health education.

Saint Francis Memorial Hospital, 900 Hyde St., San Francisco, 94109. Ph: (415) 353-6000. ICU, CCU, adult impatient psychiatric care, physical therapy, skilled nursing, home health care, physicians referral, radiology, MRI, geriatric services, emergency care, cancer treatment, sports medicine, clinical research for HIV, Bothin Burn Center, San Francisco Spine Center, Total Joint Center. 359 beds.

San Francisco General Hospital Medical Center, 1001 Potrero Ave., San Francisco, 94110. Ph: (415) 206-8000. ICU, CCU, GYN, OB, psychiatric care, physical therapy, trauma center, chemical dependency, radiology, geriatric services, emergency care, pediatric services, cancer treatment. 582 beds.

St. Luke's Hospital, 3555 Cesar Chavez St., San Francisco, 94110. Ph: (415) 647-8600. ICU, CCU, GYN, OB, pediatrics with a level II nursery, psychiatric care, physical therapy, skilled nursing, subacute unit, industrial and occupational medicine, sports medicine, emergency department, PromptCare with 24-hour pediatrician, hospitalist, radiology, geriatric services, cancer treatment, diabetes education, and asthma education, free physician referral (415) 821-DOCS. **St. Luke's Health Care Centers**, a parallel organization with 8 health care centers specializing in women's health, pediatric care and family health. St. Luke's is affiliated with Sutter Health.www.stlukes-sf.org.

St. Mary's Medical Center, 450 Stanyan St., San Francisco, 94117-1079. Ph: (415) 668-1000. Cardiovascular Services, State-of-the-Art Cardiac Cath Lab, Adolescent Behavioral Health Services, Cardiology, Cardiac Rehabilitation, HIU Services, ICU/CCU, MRI, ophthalmology, physical therapy, occupational therapy, acute & outpatient rehabilitation, radiology, spine center, emergency services, home care, physician referral, senior services, skilled nursing and come and go surgical services.

UCSF Medical Center (University of California, San Francisco): Moffit-Long Hospitals, 505 Parnassus Ave., San Francisco, 94143. Ph: (415) 476-1000. ICU, CCU, OB/GYN, primary care, family-oriented birth center for normal and high risk OB, emergency care, physician referral service. Ph. (415) 885-7777 or 1-800-888-8664. multi-speciality ambulatory care center, cardiovascular services, neurological and neurosurgical services, orthopedics, organ transplantation, general and specialty pediatric care, cancer referral service for diagnosis and treatment.

UCSF/Mount Zion Medical Center: Integrated with the UCSF Medical Center in 1990. 1600 Divisadero St., San Francisco, 94115. Ph: (415) 567-6600. Physician referral service, Ph: (800) 444-2559. Urgent care, sleep center, dermatology, ambulatory surgery center, outpatient primary care, breast care, cancer diagnosis and treatment, cardiology, urology, home health program.

Veterans Affairs Medical Center, 4150 Clement St., San Francisco, 94121. Ph: (415) 221-4810. ICU, CCU, GYN, emergency and psychiatric care, physical therapy chemical dependency, alcohol treatment, skilled nursing, radiology, eating disorders, home health care, geriatric services, cancer treatment, dentistry, special programs include treatment of posttraumatic stress disorder, prosthetic treatment center, MRS/MRI. Medical and surgical services in virtually all specialties except obstetrics and pediatrics.

Major Hospitals In or Near San Mateo County

Kaiser Permanente Medical Center Redwood City, 1150 Veterans Blvd., Redwood City, 94603. Ph. (650) 299-2000. Inpatient/outpatient services including neurosurgery, physical and occupational therapy, emergency services, hospice, home health care, substance abuse program, baby club, maternal/child services, teen clinic, ICU/CCU, OB, GYN, internal medicine, neurology, psychiatry, inpatient and ambulatory care surgery, diabetes clinic, health education department. 202 beds.

Kaiser Permanente Medical Center, 1200 El Camino Real, South San Francisco, 94080. Ph. (650) 742-2000. Alcohol and drug abuse program, allergy, AIDS/HIV Services, EEG/EMG, EKG/ECHO/Treadmill/doppler, diagnostic imaging (nuclear medicine, ultrasound, CAT scan, MRI, mammography, radiology), emergency medicine, employee assistance, health plan member services, geriatric evaluation & management, gynecology, health appraisal program, health education, hospice, internal medicine, neurology, nutritional services, ophthalmology, orthopedics, otolaryngology, patient assistance, pediatrics, pharmacy, physical therapy, psychiatry (adult), respiratory care, social services, surgery, and urology. 127 beds.

Mills-Peninsula Health Services — Mills Health Center, 100 S. San Mateo Dr., San Mateo, 94401. Ph. (650) 696-4400. Outpatient services including Institute for Health and Healing, surgery center, arthritis and rehabilitation center, breast center, cancer center, diabetes research institute, renal dialysis, occupational health services, physical therapy, pediatric rehabilitation, cardiac diagnostic and rehabilitation services, cancer center, diabetes research institute, health education resource center,rehabilitation program. 24-hour standby urgent care-emergency department for limited emergency care. Affiliated with Sutter Health.

Mills-Peninsula Health Services — Peninsula Medical Center, 1783 El Camino Real, Burlingame, 94010. Ph. (650) 696-5400. ICU, CCU, TCU, 24-hour emergency department, occupational health and industrial rehabilitation, physical therapy, family birth center, surgery center, cardiac services, mental health and chemical dependency programs, renal dialysis, fitness center, senior focus. Affiliated with Sutter Health.

San Mateo County General Hospital, 222 W 39th Ave., San Mateo, 94403. Ph. (650) 573-2222. ICU, GYN, emergency care, pediatrics, psychiatry, physical rehabilitation & skilled nursing affiliated with Crystal Springs Rehabilitation Center of San Mateo.

Sequoia Hospital, 170 Alameda de las Pulgas, Redwood City, 94062. (650) 369-5811. ICU, CCU, OB, GYN, cardiovascular care, chest pain center, emergency care, mental health, physician referral, physical, occupational and speech therapy, acute rehabilitation, subacute (extended) care, maternity & family services, radiology, pain treatment center, cardiopulmonary rehabilitation, wound treatment center, infusion center, seniors services, social services, MRI/radiation therapy, nuclear medicine, cancer treatment, sleep center, health & wellness, orthopedic and sports medicine services, pulmonary services, diabetes treatment, weight management, occupational health and community education.

Seton Medical Center, 1900 Sullivan Ave., Daly City, 94015. Ph. (650) 992-4000. ICU, CCU, OB, GYN, emergency care, physician referral, physical rehabilitation, skilled nursing, radiology, home health care, cancer treatment, wound care center, community outreach and education programs, level II NICU, outpatient surgery and services, GI lab, orthopedic & spine care services, San Francisco Heart Institute, health education, pulmonary and cardiac rehabilitation, physical & occupational therapy, breast health center.

Seton Medical Center, Coastside, 600 Marine Blvd., Moss Beach, 94038. Ph. (650) 728-5521. Radiology, senior services, emergency care, physical rehabilitation, skilled nursing, home care, medical/surgical, physician referral, outpatient services includes radiology, physical therapy, and health education programs.

Stanford University Hospital, 300 Pasteur Dr., Stanford, 94305. Ph: (650) 723-4000. ICU, CCU, OB, GYN, emergency care & prompt care, trauma center, cardiovascular, stroke center, epilepsy, bone marrow transplantation, psychiatric care, physician referral, radiology, home health care, cancer treatment, ambulatory surgery center, multi-organ transplant center, comprehensive rehabilitation center, helicopter transportation.

Department of Veterans Affairs Medical Center, 3801 Miranda Ave., Palo Alto, 94304. Ph: (650) 493-5000. ICU, GYN, alcohol & chemical dependency, physical rehab, skilled nursing care, wellness program, home care, urgent care, psychiatry.

Major Hospitals In Marin County

Kaiser Permanente Medical Center-San Rafael, 99 Montecillo Rd., San Rafael, 94903. Phone: (415) 444-2000. ICU, CCU, obstetrics, GYN (outpatient), emergency care, psychiatric care (outpatient), physicians referral, pediatric services, physical therapy, chemical dependency, alcohol treatment (outpatient), radiology, home health care.

Kaiser Permanente Medical Offices-Novato, 97 San Marin Dr., Novato, 94945. Phone: (415) 899-7400. Allergy injection, health education, internal medicine, laboratory, materiel services, obstetrics/gynecology, optical services, optometry, pediatrics, pharmacy, radiology, home health.

Kentfield Rehabilitation Hospital & Outpatient Center, 1125 Sir Francis Drake Blvd., Kentfield, 94904. Phone: (415) 456-9680. LTAC and acute rehabilitation services, occupational medicine and comprehensive outpatient services. Physical, occupational, speech and repiratory therapies. Neuropsychology services. Specialty hospital for brain injury, spinal cord injury, pulmonary/ventilator weaning and complex medical conditions. General rehabilitation services for other neurological disorders, orthopedic and oncology services

Marin General Hospital, 250 Bon Air Rd., Greenbrae, 94904. Phone: (415) 925-7000. ICU, CCU, obstetrics, Family Birth Center, lactation services GYN, emergency care, psychiatric care, physicians referral, pediatric services, physical therapy, cardiac surgery, radiology, home health care, cancer treatment, cardiac catheterization, angioplasty, cardiac surgery, ambulatory surgery, women's health programs, home care, mammography, outpatient cancer care center. Also, acute care, nuclear medicine, respiratory care, hearing & speech services, physical therapy, laboratory and electrophysiology.

Novato Community Hospital, 180 Rowland Way, Novato, 94947. Phone: (415) 209-1300. ICU/CCU, Emergency care, physical therapy, respirator therapy, inpatient & outpatient radiology services, same day surgery available.

Major Hospitals In Sonoma County

Healdsburg District Hospital, 1375 University, Healdsburg, 95448. Phone: (707) 431-6500. 24-Hour emergency care, industrial medicine, medical/surgical unit, transitional care center, same-day surgery center, physician referral service, diagnostic imaging (X-ray, ultrasound), infusion services, CAT scan, home health care, outpatient geriatric psychiatric center, laboratory, mammography center, physical therapy.

Kaiser Permanente Medical Center-Santa Rosa, 401 Bicentennial Way, Santa Rosa, 95403. Phone: (707) 571-4000. ICU, CCU, obstetrics, GYN, emergency care, psychiatric care, physicians referral, pediatric services, intensive care nursery, physical therapy, chemical dependency (outpatient), alcohol treatment, skilled nursing, radiology including mammography, home health care, geriatric services, cancer treatment, health education programs, industrial medicine clinic, gastroenterology, cancer care and orthopedics.

Kaiser Permanente Medical Offices-Petaluma, 3900 Lakeville Highway, Petaluma, 94954. Phone: (707) 765-3900. Allergy injection, health education, internal medicine, laboratory, material services, obstetrics, GYN, optical services, optometry, pediatrics, pharmacy, radiology.

Kaiser Permanente Medical Offices-Rohnert Park. Kaiser is opening clinic and offices in Rohnert Park. For information, call (707) 765-3900.

Palm Drive Hospital, 501 Petaluma Ave., Sebastopol 95472. Phone (707) 823-8511. 7 days/24-hour emergency room. Acute care, intensive care unit, physician referral, physical & occupational therapy, skilled nursing, radiology, laboratory, mammography, bone density testing center, infusion services, medical/surgical, colonoscopy and endoscopy & same-day surgery center, helipad, orthopedics, spine surgery center. Conveniently located near North Bay Breast Medical Center. Advanced Open View MRI, and Sebastopol Eye Center.

Petaluma Valley Hospital, 400 N. McDowell Blvd., Petaluma, 94954. Phone: (707) 778-1111. ICU, CCU, obstetrics, GYN, emergency care, physicians referral, pediatric services, physical therapy, skilled nursing, radiology, home health care, hospice, industrial medicine and clinical laboratory, cancer treatment, med-surgical department, prenatal child care and immunization clinics, outpatient surgery pavilion, community health library, health education, occupational health services, mammography, same-day surgery, birthing center.

Santa Rosa Memorial Hospital, 1165 Montgomery Dr., Santa Rosa, 95405. Phone: (707) 546-3210. Emergency & trauma services, Heart Alert Center, helipad; ICU/CCU; Regional Heart Center including cardiac catheterization, angioplasty, electrophysiology lab and open heart surgery; Comprehensive Cancer Center including infusion therapy, radiation therapy, research and cancer library; Northern California Kidney Transplant Center, McDermott Family Birth Center including comprehensive perinatal services and education; newborn intensive care; pediatrics; internal medicine including cardiology, neurology, endocrinology and gastroenterology; surgery services including general and vascular surgery, neurosurgery, orthopedics, endoscopy and same-day surgery; physical

& speech therapy; clinical lab; pharmacy; pastoral care; diagnostic imaging including radiology, ultrasound, nuclear medicine, CAT scan, mammography and MRI transitional care; outreach services including Rohnert Park Healthcare Center, mobile health clinic, dental clinic, home health care; Hospice, home infusion; "Senior Class" including health screenings, insurance counseling and wellness education classes for persons over 50 years of age.

Sonoma Valley Hospital, 347 Andrieux St., Sonoma, 95476. Phone: (707) 935-5000. ICU/CCU, obstetrics, GYN, 24-hour emergency dept., physicians referral, physical therapy, skilled nursing, medical imaging, home health care, mammography, geriatric services, cardiac rehab, same-day surgery, birthing center, industrial health, laboratory.

Sutter Medical Center, 3325 Chanate Rd., Santa Rosa, 95404. Phone: (707) 576-4000. Neuro-trauma and emergency trauma department with heliport; high-risk maternity and community-rated neonatal ICU; pediatric intensive care unit and child-life program; ICU, CCU, medical surgical unit and a transitional care unit, diagnostic imaging, MRI, CT, nuclear medicine, cardiac catheterization, mammography, full-service laboratory; pulmonary function and respiratory rehabilitation center; physical therapy, occupational therapy, two occupational health centers; adult psychiatric care hospital; university consultation service and UCSF family practice residency program; NorthCoast Faculty Medical Group accepting most health plans; surgery services including same-day surgery and outpatient infusion center; family practice center with urgent care center and pediatric walk-in clinic; Visiting Nurses Association and Home Hospital of Northern California; Sutter/CHS Health Resource Center including an advice-nurse line, maternity education, women's health network, sixty-plus senior programs, 24-hour access to taped health information service, physician referral services, referral to self-help support groups.

Sutter Warrack Hospital, 2449 Summerfield Rd., Santa Rosa, 95405. Phone: (707) 542-9030. ICU, CCU, GYN, emergency care, physicians referral, physical therapy; diagnostic imaging including radiology, ultrasound, nuclear medicine, CAT scan, and mammography; geriatric services, cancer treatment, pediatric services, same-day surgery, diabetes education program, coronary disease program, home health care. Senior Program for persons over 55 years. Program is free and provides education seminars, health screenings, insurance counseling and discharge planning services.

Key: ICU, intensive care unit; CCU, coronary care unit; OB, obstetrics; GYN gynecology; CAT, computerized axial tomography; MRI, magnetic resonance imaging.

Chapter 15

Fun & Games

SAN FRANCISO, SAN MATEO, MARIN AND SONOMA offer lots in the way of fun and recreation — San Francisco with its fine restaurants, museums, theaters and tourist attractions. San Mateo, excelling in nature's delights: beaches, trails, forests, vistas, parks. Marin is famous for its redwoods, Sonoma for its wineries.

All counties do quite well in the hometown diversions: baseball, softball, soccer, basketball, bowling, clubs, personal enrichment classes.

In addition to Fisherman's Wharf and other attractions in San Francisco, a partial list of activities in the City and San Mateo would include sunbathing or fishing at ocean and Bay beaches, deep-sea fishing (cod, salmon), camping under the redwoods in state and county parks, ice skating, boating, recreational auto racing, whale watching, elephant seal watching or just taking a drive.

Classes, Clubs, Shopping, Too

What the public sector lacks, the private sector provides — racquetball, golf, bowling, tennis, plays, concerts, movies, activity classes. Also, shopping, an unsung, often-maligned pursuit but one that brings pleasure to thousands.

San Francisco's Union Square is the hub of big-city shopping with Macys and specialty stores. A couple blocks south, Nordstrom anchors San Francisco Center and its glitzy array of shops.

San Mateo County, too, has some delightful shopping centers: Serramonte Center and Westlake Shopping Center in Daly City, Tanforan Shopping Center in San Bruno and Hillsdale Mall in San Mateo.

In Sonoma, downtown Santa Rosa. In Marin, downtown San Rafael and the stores of Corte Madera.

City Parks, Recreation, the Arts

Regional parks tend to get most of the attention but city parks can be counted in the dozens and draw many people. Bicycle and jogging trails wind their way throughout the four counties. Children's activities include soccer, swimming, ice skating, football, basketball, baseball, gymnastics, tennis, golf, surfing, dancing.

Where to Look

One flaw mars this happy picture of abundance: There is so much to do that it is sometimes hard to know where to start. Here are suggestions that will help with the sorting out.

- Find out who is organizing activities in your neighborhood or town and in nearby towns. Usually this can be accomplished by calling or visiting the chambers of commerce, the city recreation departments and the school districts.

- Get on the mailing or e-mail lists. Adult schools and recreation departments change their classes about every three months. Theaters and orchestras issue calendars every season.

- Find out the rules. Some cities provide minimal support for certain activities. You may have to sign up the players on your softball team and collect the fees and meet application deadlines.

- Baseball and soccer leagues usually guarantee the younger children, no matter what their skill, two innings or two quarters of play. But other sports (football) often go by skill. Ask about playing time.

- Disregard city boundaries. If you live in Pacifica and want to take a class in San Mateo, go ahead. A person with a Foster City job might want to tackle an aerobics class in that city before hitting the freeway.

- The San Mateo Convention and Visitors' Bureau puts out maps, brochures. Write 111 Anza Blvd., Suite 410, Burlingame, 94010, or phone (650) 348-7600.

- Subscribe to a local newspaper. Almost all of them will have calendars of events, lists of local attractions and hours of operation.

Major Offerings

These counties offers so much to do that we have space only for a few highlights. Buy yourself a map or a tourist guide. Check the Sunday Chronicle's Datebook for detailed listing on specific events.

All four counties have many public beaches. Take care. The tides are often treacherous and the water is quite cold.

Museums

- **Asian Art Museum**. Art works from Asia over the centuries. 200 Larkin Street. Phone (415) 581-3500.

- **Cable Car Museum**. In addition to photographs and memorabilia of the city's long love affair with its cable cars, there is an underground viewing room to watch the cables at work, 1201 Mason St. Phone (415) 474-1887.

- **California Academy of Sciences,** 875 Howard St. Temporary quarters while new academy is built; completion 2008. Phone (415) 750-7145.

- **DeYoung Memorial Museum**. Perhaps the most popular museum in San Francisco. Overhauled, redesigned and reopened in 2005. Golden Gate Park. Phone (415) 863-3330.

- **Museum of the African Diaspora.** San Francisco's newest major museum. Mission and Third streets, (415) 358-7200.

- **National Maritime Museum Assoc**. San Francisco. Near Fishermen's Wharf. Liberty ship, schooners, models and nautical history displays, bookstore, museum open daily.

- **Palace of the Legion of Honor.** Rodin sculptures and medieval to post-impressionist European art in permanent collections. Clement Street and Legion of Honor Drive, Lincoln Park. Phone (415) 750-3600.

- **San Francisco Museum of Modern Art.** Touring and permanent collections of art and photography. 151 Third St. Phone (415) 357-4000.

- **Turpen Aviation Library and Museum**. Located in the new international terminal at SFO. Artifacts from history of aviation. Library.

Highlights

- **Alcatraz**. Former prison, now a park. Ferries leave from San Francisco's Fisherman's Wharf. Jackets, comfortable shoes. Phone (415) 705-5555.

- **Angel Island**. near Tiburon. Cycling, hiking and picnicking all on a San Francisco Bay island. Phone Park information (415) 435-3522, ferry info (415) 435-2131.

- **Año Nuevo State Reserve.** 1,192 acres. 27 miles south of Half Moon Bay on Highway 1. Visitor center open 9 a.m. to 3 p.m. plus guided tours daily Dec. 1 to April 1 during the elephant seal season. Fishing, nature and hiking trails, exhibits. Phone (650) 879-2025.

- **Armstrong Redwoods.** Grove of giants. Located outside Guerneville. Take Armstrong Woods Road from Hwy. 116. Info. (707) 869-2015.

- **Bay Meadows Racetrack.** Adjacent to San Mateo County Fairgrounds. Between Highway 101 on the east, El Camino Real on the west, 25th Avenue on the north and Hillsdale Boulevard on the south. 100 live racing days per year. Thoroughbreds, Labor Day through January. Satellite wagering the rest of the year. Phone (650) 574-RACE or 573-4516.

- **Charles Shultz Museum, Santa Rosa.** An interactive memorial to "Peanuts" creator Charles Schultz, features displays of Snoopy, Charlie Brown and the gang, as well as classes for cartoonists. (707) 579-4452.

- **Cow Palace.** Daly City, one mile from Highway 101. Home of Grand National and Junior Grand National Livestock Exposition, world-class wrestling matches, and other sporting and music events and national exhibits and conventions. Rock music.

- **Coyote Point Beach Park & Museum.** San Mateo County. Take Peninsula Avenue exit off Highway 101 in Burlingame and head east. Exhibits on humans' ties with nature. Also, an aquarium, computer games, films, giant mural, bee tube. Phone (650) 342-7755.

- **Golden Gate Bridge.** You can't walk across the Bay Bridge or the San Rafael. You can the Golden Gate. It's worth it. Parking lots, view points on both sides of the bridge.

- **Golden Gate Park.** Large park located on the west side of San Francisco. Home to DeYoung Museum, Japanese Tea Garden, Strybing Arboretum and other ornaments of the City. Playing fields, hiking, biking, roller blading, boating.

- **Exploratorium.** Science museum. Many of its 650 exhibits are interactive and hands-on. Palace of Fine Arts, Lyon Street and Marina Boulevard, San Francisco. Phone (415) 561-0399.

- **Filoli House & Garden.** On Cañada Road in Woodside, south of the Highway 92-Interstate 280 intersection. Tours of modified Georgian-style mansion and 17 acres of formal gardens. Phone (650) 364-2880.

- **Fisherman's Wharf.** Former center of San Francisco's commercial fishing industry, now collection of restaurants and shops. Open daily. Good place for stroll.

- **Fort Ross, Sonoma County.** What Russians built when they lived in California. A detailed restoration. Interesting. Just off Highway 1, above Jenner. State park. Info. (707) 847-3286.

- **Haas-Lilienthal House.** Elaborate gables and Queen Anne-style circular tower adorn this 19th century mansion. 2007 Franklin St., San Francisco. Phone (415) 441-3000.

- **Hiller Aviation Museum.** Exhibit displaying the time line of aviation history. Over 40 planes, restoration shop, gift shop. 601 Skyway Rd., San Carlos. Phone (650) 654-0200.

- **Jack London State Historic Park.** Where Jack London, California's favorite son, wrote and lived. Ruins of London mansion, the Wolf House. Above City of Sonoma, off Highway 12, in Sonoma Valley wine country. Jack London State Historic Park. (707) 938-5216.

- **Luther Burbank Home and Gardens.** Perhaps the most famous green thumb in the history of California, Burbank made everything grow. Santa Rosa and Sonoma avenues in downtown Santa Rosa. (707) 524-5445.

- **Marin Civic Center, San Rafael.** What Marin County inspired in Frank Lloyd Wright. Public building. Drop in any time. Take Civic Center Drive or San Pedro Road off Highway 101. Tours available. Call first. (415) 499-6646.

- **Marin Headlands,** the land just west of the bridge. Spectacular vistas of San Francisco, the Golden Gate, the Pacific. Formerly used to place artillery; fortifications still there. To reach, take Sausalito exit closest to bridge, pick up Bunker Road. Information (415) 331-1540.

- **Mission Dolores.** Founded in 1776, built in 1791, the city's oldest building includes museum and cemetery garden, 16th and Dolores streets, San Francisco. Phone (415) 621-8203.

- **Mount Tamalpais.** Highest point in Marin County. See Farallones, Sierra, Richmond, Oakland, San Fran. Many trails to top. Pick up Panoramic Highway off Route 1. Info at Pan Toll ranger station. (415) 388-2070..

- **Monterey Bay Aquarium**. 886 Cannery Row, Monterey. In historic Cannery Row, features 1-million-gallon indoor ocean aquarium, jellyfish exhibit, sea otter grove, kelp forest pedestrian tunnel through aquarium and more. (831) 644-7548.

- **Muir Woods.** Giant redwoods a short drive from San Francisco. In Marin County. Take Highway 1 off of Highway 101, go west and follow signs.

- **Petaluma.** Good collection of Victorians, some with iron fronts, an effort at fireproofing and prefabrication. Start on Petaluma Boulevard north. Many activities that attract visitors year round. For information (707) 762-2785.

- **Pigeon Point Lighthouse. San Mateo County.** Quarter mile west of Highway 1 on Pigeon Point Road. About 30 miles north of Santa Cruz. Views of ocean.

- **River Rock Casino.** Opened in 2002 near Geyserville. Highway 101 to Geyserville Road, east to Highway 128, cross Russian River, keep right, drive three miles, you will see entrance to casino. Slots and Las Vegas games. Call for hours of operation. (707) 857-2777.

- **San Francisco Zoo**. Penguins, gorillas, monkeys, elephants, etc. Remodeled. Sloat Boulevard at 45th Avenue, San Francisco. Phone (415) 753-7080.

- **Sears Point International Raceway.** Sports car, drag, motorcycle racing. NASCAR racing. Some events draw over 100,000. Raceway has expanded, added more parking. Car shows. School for how to race like the pros. Highway 37 to Highway 121 near Novato. (707) 938-8448.

- **Sonoma Coast.** Highway 1. Start at Bodega Bay or Jenner. Rugged. Great views. For good view of seals, stroll beach at Goat Rock near Jenner. Restaurants, resorts along route.

- **Sonoma Mission.** Small, plain and interesting. The last mission built on El Camino Real, the King's Highway. Nicely restored. Also restored barracks. Downtown City of Sonoma. (707) 938-9560.

- **Sports, professional.** Baseball: The Giants play in San Francisco and the Athletics in Oakland. Football: Forty Niners in San Francisco, Raiders in Oakland. Basketball: Warriors in Oakland. Hockey: Sharks in San Jose. Also top-drawer college teams, including UC Berkeley, Stanford, University of San Francisco.

- **Strybing Arboretum.** Enormous greenhouse; home to more than 6,000 plant and tree species. Ninth Avenue at Lincoln Way, San Francisco. Phone (415) 661-1316.

- **Whale watching.** Migration off California coast from December through March. Whales visible from many places along coast, but best place to view is from boat. Several tours embark from Pillar Point Harbor in Half Moon Bay. Capt. John's Fishing Trips, Phone (650) 728-3377. Can also be seen from Bodega Head State Park, Salt Point State Park, and bluffs of state beach along Sonoma coast. (707) 847-3221.

- **Wine Country.** For the quick tour, drive Highway 12 or Highway 29 south to north, or travel the Redwood Highway north of Santa Rosa. Wineries are all along both routes. Also in Alexander and Dry Creek valleys, along Westside Road near Healdsburg, and the Russian River area.

- **Yerba Buena Center.** Next to Moscone Convention Center, short walk from Powell BART station. Center for the Arts. Exhibits, performances, film and video screenings, gallery tours, educational events, carousel. 701 Mission St. Phone (415) 978-2787.

Chapter 16

Newcomer's Guide

FOR NEWCOMERS, here are some answers to frequently asked questions.

Voter Registration

You must be 18 years and a citizen. Go to the nearest post office and ask for a voter registration postcard. Fill it out and pop it into the mail box. Or register in person at most county offices, or political party headquarters, which are listed in the phone book.

For more information on voting, call the elections office in San Mateo County at (650) 312-5222, San Francisco at (415) 554-4375, Marin County at (415) 499-6456, or Sonoma County at (707) 565-6800.Before every election, the county will mail you a sample ballot with the address of your polling place.

Change of Address — Mail

The change-of-address form can also be picked up at the post office but to assure continuity of service, fill out this form 30 days before you move.

Dog (and Cat) Licensing-Spaying

For licensing, in San Francisco, (415) 554-6364. In San Mateo, (650) 363-4220.

In Sonoma County, these chores are spread over several groups. Call local or nearest city hall for phone numbers.

For Marin, for licensing and general information, phone (415) 883-4621, for spaying-neutering, (415) 883-3383, for training, (415) 506-6281

In San Mateo County, Peninsula Humane Society rescues wild animals in trouble, rounds up wild dogs and cats, and performs other services. Phone (650) 340-8200.

Driving

California has the most stringent smog requirements in the country. If your car is a few years old, you may have to spend a couple of hundred dollars to bring it up to code. You have 20 days from the time you enter the state to register your vehicles. After that you pay an added penalty and risk a ticket-fine.

For registration, go to any office of the Department of Motor Vehicles. Bring your smog certificate, your registration card, your license plates and proof of insurance. In some cases, registration can be handled on-line.

If you move and are a California resident, all you need to do is complete a change-of-address form, which can be obtained by calling the Department of Motor Vehicles at (800) 777-0133.

Driving Rules, Requirements and Tests

To obtain a driver's license, you must be 16, pass a state-certified Driver's Education (classroom) and Driver's Training (behind-the-wheel) course, and at Dept. of Motor Vehicles a vision test and written and driving tests.

Once you pass the test, your license is usually renewed by mail. Retesting is rare, unless you have a restricted license or your driving record is poor. High schools have all but dropped driver's education. Private driving schools have moved in to fill the gap, at a cost of $100 to $200.

Teenagers older than 15 1/2 years who have completed driver's training can be issued a permit. New law restricts driving hours for young teens to daylight hours and, unless supervised, forbids them for six months to drive other teens. Law also requires more parental training and extends time of provisional license. Purpose is to reduce accidents.

If no driver's education program has been completed, you must be at least 18 years old to apply for a driver's license.

Out-of-state applicants must supply proof of "legal presence," which could be a certified copy of a birth certificate.

If going for a driver's license, ask to have the booklet mailed to you or pick it up. Study it. All the questions will be taken from the booklet.

Turning Rules. If signs don't say no, you can turn right on a red light (after making a full stop) and make a U-turn at an intersection.

Stop for pedestrians. Stop for discharging school buses, even if on opposite side of road. Insurance. Must have it to drive.

Earthquakes

They're fun and great topics of conversation, until a big one strikes. Then they are anything but funny. At the beginning of your phone book is some advice about what to do before, during and after a temblor. Worth reading.

Garbage Service

The garbage fellows come once a week. Rates vary by city but figure $15 to $20 a month for one-can weekly service.

Besides the cans, many homes will receive recycling bins for plastics, glass and cans. Pickup weekly, usually the same day as garbage. The garbage firms have switched to wheeled carts that can be picked up by mechanical arms attached to the garbage truck.

Grocery Prices

Item	Store one	Store two	Average.
Apple Juice, 1 gal. store brand	4.79	3.96	4.38
Almonds, whole, 2.25 oz.	2.49	2.17	2.33
American Cheese, Kraft, 1 lb.	5.19	5.19	5.19
Apple Pie, Sara Lee	6.49	5.99	6.24
Apples, Red Delicious, 1 lb.	1.99	1.00	1.50
Aspirin, cheapest, 250 count	4.49	4.99	4.74
Baby Shampoo, Johnson's, 15 fluid oz.	4.39	4.19	4.29
Bacon, Farmer John Sliced, 1 lb.	4.99	5.79	5.39
Bagels, store brand, half doz.	2.99	3.08	3.04
Bananas, 1 lb.	.79	.79	.79
Beef, round tip boneless roast, 1 lb.	4.59	4.49	4.54
Beef, ground round, 1 lb.	4.49	2.49	3.49
Beer, O'Douls 6-pack bottles	5.99	5.99	5.99
Beer, Coors, 12-pack, cans	10.99	10.69	10.84
Bisquick batter, 2 lbs. 8 oz.	2.99	2.99	2.99
Bleach, Clorox, 96 oz.	2.69	2.59	2.64
Bok Choy, 1lb.	.99	.99	.99
Bread, sourdough, Colombo, 1.5 lb.	3.89	3.87	3.88
Bread, wheat, cheapest 1.5 lb.	.99	.99	.99
Broccoli, 1 lb.	1.99	1.00	1.50
Butter, Challenge, 1 lb.	5.49	5.49	5.49
Cabbage, 1 lb.	.99	.69	.84
Cantaloupe, 1 lb.	.99	1.29	1.14
Carrots, fresh, 1 lb.	.59	.69	.64
Cat Food, store brand, small can	.49	.55	.52
Cereal, Grapenuts, 18 oz.	4.89	4.99	4.94
Cereal, Wheaties, 18 oz.	4.99	4.89	4.94
Charcoal, Kingsford, 10 lbs.	4.99	4.99	4.99
Cheese, Cream, Philadelphia, 8 oz.	2.89	2.59	2.74
Cheese, Mild Cheddar, 1 lb.	4.99	3.69	4.34
Chicken breasts, Foster Farms bone/skinless, 1 lb.	5.99	5.99	5.99
Chicken, Foster Farms, whole, 1 lb.	1.59	1.29	1.44
Chili, Stagg, with beans, 15 oz. box	2.29	2.29	2.29
Cigarettes, Marlboro Lights, carton	48.99	48.99	48.99
Coca Cola, 12-pack, 12 oz. cans	4.99	5.29	5.14
Coffee, Folgers Instant Coffee, 6 oz.	5.99	5.99	5.99
Cafe latte, Starbucks, 1 cup	2.30	2.30	2.30
Coffee, Starbucks, 1 cup	1.35	1.35	1.35
Cookies, Oreo, 18 oz. pkg.	3.99	3.99	3.99
Diapers, Huggies, size 2, (42-pack)	16.99	9.99	13.49
Dishwashing Liquid, Dawn, 25 oz.	3.99	3.69	3.84
Dog Food, Pedigree, 22-oz. can	1.39	1.54	1.47
Eggs, large, Grade AA, 1 doz.	3.19	2.69	2.64
Flour, Gold Medal, 5 lbs.	2.39	2.39	2.39
Flowers, mixed	4.99	4.99	4.99
Frozen Dinners, Marie Callendar's	4.59	4.59	4.59
Frozen Yogurt, Dreyer's, half gallon	5.99	5.99	5.99
Gatorade, 64 oz.	3.29	2.99	3.14
Gerber's baby food, fruit or veg., 4 oz.	.57	.50	.54
Gerber's baby food, meat, 2.5 oz.	.79	.79	.79
Gerber's baby food, cereal, 8 oz.	1.69	2.08	1.89
Gin, Gilbeys, 1.75 Ltrs.	18.99	18.99	18.99
Ginger Root, 1 lb.	2.99	1.99	2.49
Granola Bars, 10-bar box	3.99	3.79	3.89
Grapes, Red Seedless, 1 lb.	2.99	2.99	2.99

Grocery Prices

Item	Store one	Store two	Average
Ham, Dubuque, 5 lb., canned	14.39	13.99	14.19
Ice Cream, Dreyers, half gal.	$5.99	$5.99	$5.99
Ice Cream, Haagen Daaz, 1 pint	3.99	3.99	3.99
Jam, Mary Ellen, strawberry, 18 oz.	4.99	3.86	4.43
Ketchup, Del Monte, 36 oz.	2.99	3.11	3.05
Kleenex, 144-count box	2.59	2.53	2.56
Laundry Detergent, Tide, 87 oz.	9.29	8.99	9.14
Lettuce, Romaine, head	1.29	1.49	1.39
Macaroni & Cheese, Kraft, 14.5 oz	2.25	2.29	2.27
Margarine, tub, Brummel & Brown	2.39	2.39	2.39
Mayonnaise, Best Foods, 1 qt.	3.99	3.49	3.74
Milk, 1% fat, half gal.	1.29	1.29	1.29
Milk, soy, half gal.	2.99	2.39	2.69
M&M Candies, plain, 2 oz.	.65	.65	.65
Mushrooms, 8 oz. package	2.29	2.29	2.29
Olive Oil, cheapest, 17 oz.	6.39	5.99	6.19
Onions, yellow, 1 lb.	.99	1.69	1.34
Oranges, Navel, 1 lb.	.69	.99	.84
Orange Juice, Tropicana, 64-oz., Original Style	4.59	4.79	4.69
Paper Towels, single pack	.99	1.18	1.09
Peanuts, cocktail, Planter's, 12 oz.	4.19	4.19	4.19
Peas, frozen, 16 oz.	2.39	3.00	2.70
Peanut Butter, Jiff, 18 oz.	3.19	3.29	3.24
Pizza, Frozen, Di Giorno, 1 lb. 13 oz.	7.59	6.29	6.94
Popcorn, Orville Reddenbacher, 3-pack	3.49	3.55	3.52
Pork chops, center cut, 1 lb.	4.99	3.99	4.49
Potato Chips, Lays, 12 oz.	2.99	2.99	2.99
Potatoes, Russet, 10 lbs.	2.99	2.99	2.99
Raisins, 2 lbs.	4.99	3.99	3.49
Reese's Mini-Peanut Butter Cups, 13 oz.	3.99	3.29	3.39
Rice, cheapest, 5 lbs.	3.69	3.39	3.54
Salmon, fresh, 1 lb.	4.49	5.99	5.24
Seven-Up, 6-pack, cans	2.99	2.99	2.99
Soap, bar, Zest, 3-pack	2.89	2.89	2.89
Soup, Campbell, chicken noodle, 10-oz. can	.99	1.85	1.42
Soup, Top Ramen	.25	.37	.31
Soy Sauce, Kikkoman, 10 oz.	2.29	2.19	2.24
Spaghetti, Golden Grain, 2 lbs.	2.79	2.79	2.79
Spaghetti Sauce, Prego, 12 oz.	1.99	1.99	1.99
Sugar, cheapest, 5 lbs.	1.99	1.99	1.99
Tea, Lipton's, 48-bag box	2.99	4.21	4.10
Toilet Tissue, 4-roll pack, cheapest	1.79	3.29	2.54
Tomatoes, on the vine, 1 lb.	3.69	3.49	3.59
Toothpaste, Colgate 6.4 oz	2.99	2.99	2.99
Tortillas, flour, cheapest, 10-count pack	2.59	1.99	2.29
Tuna, Starkist, Chunk Light, 6 oz.	1.99	.99	1.49
Vegetable Oil, store brand, 64 oz.	3.79	4.41	4.10
Vegetables, mixed, frozen, 1 lb.	2.39	2.50	2.45
Vinegar, 1 gallon	3.39	3.83	3.61
Water, 1 gallon	1.49	1.29	1.39
Whiskey, Seagrams 7 Crown, 750ml.	13.49	13.49	13.49
Wine, Cabernet, Glen Ellen	9.99	9.99	9.99
Yogurt, Frozen, Dreyers, half gal.	5.99	5.99	5.99
Yogurt, Yoplait Original, single	.99	.85	.92o

To get rid of car batteries and used motor oils and water-soluble paints, call your local garbage firm and ask about disposal sites. Or call city hall. Don't burn garbage in the fireplace or outside. Don't burn leaves. Against the law.

Property Taxes

The average property tax rate in California is 1.25 percent. If you buy a $600,000 home, your property tax will be $7,500. Once the basic tax is established, it goes up about 2 percent annually in following years.

"Average" needs to be emphasized. Many jurisdictions have tacked costs on to the property tax to pay for bonds or special services. Some school districts, in recent years, have won approval of annual parcel taxes.

Property taxes are paid in two installments, due by April 10 and December 10. They are generally collected automatically through impound accounts set up when you purchase a home, but check your sale documents carefully. Sometimes homeowners are billed directly.

Sales Tax

In San Francisco, it is 8.5 percent, in San Mateo, 8.25 percent, in Marin, 7.75%, in Sonoma, 7.75% and 8%. Food, except when eaten in restaurants, is not taxed.

State Income Taxes

See chart next page.

Disclosure Laws

California requires homes sellers to give detailed reports on their offerings, including house flaws and information on flood, fire and earthquake zones.

Cigarette-Tobacco Tax

Special taxes imposed by state. Adds 87 cents to a pack of cigarettes. Many Californians load up on cigarettes in Nevada or Mexico or order over Internet.

Cable TV Service-High speed modems.

Almost all Bay Area homes can get cable TV. Rates vary according to channels accessed but a basic rate plus some extra tiers runs $75 a month. Installation is extra.

High speed cable-modem service throughout the Bay Area. Check with phone company or other firms.

Phones

SBC charges $34.75 to run a line to your house. It charges extra for jack installation. If you're handy, you can do the jack wiring and installation yourself. Many homes will have the jacks in place.

California Tax Rates 2005

Single Filing Separate Returns

Taxable Income		Basic Tax	Plus
Over	But Not Over		
$0	$6,147	$0.00 +	1% over $0.00
$6,147	$14,571	$61 +	2% over $6,147
$14,571	$22,997	$230 +	4% over $14,571
$22,997	$31,925	$567 +	6% over $22,997
$31,925	$40,346	$1,103 +	8% over $31,925
$40,346	And Over	$1,776 +	9.3% over $40,346

Married Filing Jointly & Qualified Widow(er)s

Taxable Income		Basic Tax	Plus
Over	But Not Over		
$0	$12,294	$0.00 +	1% over $0.00
$12,294	$29,142	$123 +	2% over $12,294
$29,142	$45,994	$460 +	4% over $29,142
$45,994	$63,850	$1,134 +	6% over $45,994
$63,850	$80,692	$2,205 +	8% over $63,850
$80,692	And Over	$3,553 +	9.3% over $80,692

Heads of Households

Taxable Income		Basic Tax	Plus
Over	But Not Over		
$0	$12,300	$0.00 +	1% over $0.00
$12,300	$29,143	$123 +	2% over $12,300
$29,143	$37,567	$460 +	4% over $29,143
$37,567	$46,494	$797+	6% over $37,567
$46,494	$54,918	$1,332 +	8% over $46,494
$54,918	And Over	$2,006 +	9.3% over $54,918

Example

John and Jackie Anderson have a taxable income of $125,000.

Taxable Income	Basic Tax	Plus
$125,000	$3,553 +	9.3% over $80,692

They subtract the amount at the beginning of their range from their taxable income.

$125,000
-80,692
$44,308

They multiply the result by the percentage for their range.

$ 44,308
x .093
$ 4,121

Total Tax

Basic	$3,553
% +	+4,121
Total	$7,674

Note: Amounts rounded off. This chart is not a substitute for government forms. If you have questions, consult tax authorities or your tax advisor.   '06

Phone companies offer "basic" charges often less than $15 a month. But some tack charges onto the basic charge. Check with phone companies.

Gas and Electricity

Most homes are heated with natural gas. Up until a few years ago, gas averaged $30 a month and electric $60 a month. California has gone through an energy mess. Rates have been increased but structured to reward conservation so it's possible to keep your costs down. Read your utility bill to see how the system works.

Almost never between May and September, and rarely between April and October, will you need to heat your home. The exceptions concern neighborhoods that have summer fog. Often it's cold. West Coast homes do not lay in a supply of heating oil. Air conditioners are used throughout the summer but on many days they're not needed.

Tipping

Tip the newspaper delivery person, cab drivers, waiters and waitresses, and, at the holidays, people who perform regular personal services: yard maintenance, child care, housekeeping.

Don't tip telephone or cable TV installers. Your garbage collector will usually be a Teamster. No beer. No money. Maybe a little cake or box of candy at Christmas. State has liquor law that can put one in violation for as little as one drink. If garbage collector gets nailed for drunken driving, it will probably cost him his job. Some people give the mailman or mail lady a little holiday gift; many don't.

Smoking

In 1998 a state law took effect forbidding smoking in saloons, public buildings and most work places. Bars in restaurants comply. Saloons sporadically enforce but many people refrain from smoking and those that do, often hide the cigarette under the table. Even this practice is disappearing.

If visiting socially, you are expected to light up outside. Some cities have passed laws restricting smoking in public places and on beaches. Within the state, feelings against smoking seem to grow more intense by the year and this has translated into higher taxes on tabacco and more restrictions on where people can smoke.

Ages

You must be 18 to vote and smoke and 21 to drink alcohol. Watch the booze. California has a drunken-driving law so stringent that even a drink or two can put you in violation. Clerks are supposed to ask you for ID if you look under 27 for smokes and under 30 for booze.

Chapter 17

Rental Housing

AFTER YEARS OF INCREASES, rents fell then seem to stabilize but as we enter 2006 the picture is murky.

Rents are influenced by home sales. When home sales are brisk and monthly home payments come close to monthly rents, this tends to drive down rents. It also encourages kindlier attitudes toward pets, shorter leases and lower security deposits.

Conversely, when monthly home payments are high or rising quickly, this depresses home sales and pushes more people into renting — which favors rent increases. And less understanding attitudes toward pets, leases and deposits.

The local housing market, inflated for several years by low interest rates, may be returning to normal. Or it may hit a real slow down. The predictions are many and contradictory.

Many people coming to the Bay Area are shocked by the rents. You often pay a lot for a little.

San Francisco has the toughest and most complex rent control laws in California. Many occupants of the controlled units have stayed put. Their rents are sometimes $300 to $1,000 or more below what the market is charging. Why move? This has taken some or many apartments — depending on who you talk to — out of circulation.

If you plan to rent in San Francisco, it is worth your while to find out more about rent control and what apartments are covered. This goes for anyone thinking about buying a flat or condo in the City. Your resale rights may be restricted. For information, call (415) 252-4600. This will take you to an automated line that will fax you an overview of rent policies and, if you want, detailed reports on the policies.

Many people in the City share apartments, one way to beat the game. Others are moving to places like downtown Oakland, where rents are lower. For rentals, read the classified, use an agency or use the web. Or put out the word through friends and coworkers.

(Continued on page 357)

SAN FRANCISCO

Balboa Terrace
•Apt., 1BR/1BA, remod., $1,200

Bayview/Hunters Point
•Apt., 1BR/1BA, $1,000
•Home, 4BR/2BA, $1,595

Bernal Heights
•Apt., 1BR/1.5BA, den, $1,450
•Home, 2BR/2BA, $1,750

Castro
•Apt., 2BR/1BA, $1,700

Civic Center
•Apt., 1BR/1BA, $2,500
•Apt., 2BR/1BA, $2,900

Diamond Heights
•Apt., 1BR/1BA, $1,475
•Home, 3BR/2BA, $2,000

Excelsior
•Studio, $1,050
•Home, 2BR/1BA, $2,075

Financial District
•Apt., 1BR/1BA, $2,250
•Townhouse, 3BR/2BA, $4,795

Forest Hill/West Portal
•Apt., 1BR/1BA, garden, $1,600
•Home, 3BR/2BA, $3,000

Glen Park
•Apt., 2BR/1BA, $1,400
•Home, 3BR/2BA, $3,250

Haight-Ashbury
•Apt., 2BR/1BA, $1,795

Ingleside Terrace
•Home, 3BR/2.5BA, $3,025

Inner Sunset
•Apt., 1BR/1BA, $1,400
•Apt., 2BR/2BA, $1,995

Marina
•Apt., 3BR/2BA, $5,000

Mission
•Apt., 1BR/1BA, $1,395
•Home, 2BR/1BA, $2,000

Nob Hill
•Apt., 1BR/1BA, $2,100

Noe Valley
•Apt., 1BR/1BA, $1,500
•Home, 2BR/2BA, $3,850

North Beach
•Apt., 1BR/1BA, $2,600

Outer Mission
•Studio, $900
•Home, 3BR/2BA, $2,300

Pacific Heights
•Studio, $845
•Apt., 2BR/2BA, $3,000

Parkside
•Home, 2BR/1BA, $2,000

Portola
•Home, 2BR/1BA, $1,400
•Home, 3BR/2BA, $2,600

Potrero Hill
•Apt., 2BR/2BA, $2,500
•Home, 2BR/1.5BA, $3,100

Presidio Heights
•Apt., 2BR/1BA, $1,950
•Apt., 4BR/2BA, $2,550

Richmond
•Apt., 1BR/1BA, $1,200
•Home, 2BR/1.5BA, $2,375

Russian Hill
•Apt., 2BR/2BA, $5,500
•Apt., 2BR/2BA, $2,900

Sea Cliff
•Apt., 1BR/1BA, patio, $1,645
•Home, 5BR/4.5BA, $9,600

South of Market
•Apt., 3BR/2BA, $2,750
•Home, 2BR/1BA, $2,100

Sunset
•Apt., 2BR/2BA, $1,995
•Home, 3BR/2BA, $2,150

Twin Peaks
•Apt., 1BR/1BA, $1,450
•Home, 3BR/2.5BA, $6,000

Upper Market
•Apt., 1BR/1BA, $1,300

Western Addition/Hayes Valley
•Studio, $900

SAN MATEO COUNTY

Belmont
• Apt., 2BR/1BA, $1,275
• Home, 3BR/2BA, $2,350

Brisbane
• Apt., 1BR/1BA, $975
• Home, 3BR/1BA, $1,800

Burlingame
• Apt., 1BR/1BA, $1,200
• Apt., 4BR/2BA, $1,995

Daly City
• Apt., 1BR/1BA, $875
• Home, 3BR/2BA, $2,000

East Palo Alto
• Home, 4BR/3.5BA, $2,650

Foster City
• Apt., 1BR/1BA, $1,250
• Home, 4BR/2BA, $2,100

Hillsborough
• Home, 4BR/3.5BA, $5,500
• Home, 5BR/3BA, $4,950

Menlo Park
• Apt., 2BR/2BA, $1,750
• Home, 3BR/2BA, $3,000

Millbrae
• Apt., 2BR/1BA, $1,600
• Home, 3BR/1.5BA, $2,200

Pacifica
• Apt., 1BR/1BA, $915
• Home, 3BR/2BA, $2,200

Redwood City
• Condo, 3BR/2.5BA, $2,150
• Home, 3BR/3BA, $2,400

San Bruno
• Apt., 2BR/2BA, $1,495
• Home, 3BR/2BA, $2,300

San Carlos
• Apt., 2BR/1BA, $1,150
• Home, 3BR/2BA, $2,850

San Mateo
• Apt., 1BR/1BA, $1,050
• Home, 2BR/1BA, $2,300

South San Francisco
• Apt., 1BR/1BA, $1,050
• Home, 3BR/1BA, $2,300

Average Rent Sampler for Selected Cities

San Mateo County

City	Average Rents
Belmont	$1,130
Daly City	1,255
East Palo Alto	988
Foster City	1,596
Pacifica	1,393
Redwood City	1,515
San Mateo	1,475
South San Francisco	1,286

Marin County

City	Average Rents
Novato	$1,242
San Rafael	1,409

Sonoma County

City	Average Rents
Petaluma	$1,279
Rohnert Park	1,028
Santa Rosa	1,067

Source: REALFACTS Novato, California. As of December 2004. Key: NA - not available.

Rent Sampler from Classified Ads

MARIN COUNTY

Corte Madera
- Apt., 1BR/1BA, $1,050
- Home, 3BR/2BA, pano. view, $3,200

Fairfax
- Apt., 2BR/1BA, patio, $1,300

Greenbrae
- Apt., 1BR/1BA, cath. ceil., $1,795
- Home, 3BR/2BA, pool, $3,500

Kentfield
- Apt., 2BR/1BA, deck, $1,200
- Home, 3BR/1.5BA, hrdwd. flrs., $2,850

Larkspur
- Condo, 2BR/2BA, $2,300
- Home, 2BR/1BA, yard, $2,450

Mill Valley
- Apt., 2BR/2BA, nr. shops, $2,200
- Home, 4BR/2.5BA, views, $5,500

Novato
- Apt., 2BR/1BA, lower, $1,195
- Home, 4BR/2BA, hot tub, $2,250

San Anselmo
- Apt., 2BR/1BA, grdn. setting, $1,500
- Home, 3BR/1.5BA, skylights, $2,300

San Rafael
- Apt., 2BR/1BA, storage, $1,400
- Home, 3BR/2BA, remod., $3,500

Sausalito
- Apt., 2BR/2BA, frplc., $2,500
- Home, 3BR/2BA, new appl., $2,700

Tiburon
- Apt., 1BR/1BA, gym, $1,520
- Home, 3BR/2BA, office, $2,900

Woodacre
- Apt., 1BR/1BA, sunny, $1,400

SONOMA COUNTY

Cloverdale
- Apt., 2BR/1BA, $850
- Home, 3BR/2BA, cul-de-sac, $1,395

Cotati
- Apt., 2BR/1BA, nr. schs., $995
- Home, 4BR/3BA, Med. style, $3,600

Healdsburg
- Studio, loft, $700
- Home, 3BR/2BA, hillside, $2,300

Penngrove (near Rohn. Park)
- Apt., 2BR/2BA, newer, $1,200
- Cottage, 1BR/1BA, $1,000

Petaluma
- Apt., 2BR/2BA, huge, $999
- Home, 4BR/2BA, gazebo, $1,825

Rohnert Park
- Apt., 2BR/1BA, remod., $925
- Home, 4BR/3BA, corner lot, $2,000

Santa Rosa
- Apt., 2BR/2BA, $950
- Home, 4BR/3.5BA, formal DR, $2,400

Sebastopol
- Studio, wooded, $725
- Home, 3BR/2BA, fresh pnt., $1,500

Sonoma
- Condo, 2BR/1.5BA, $1,350
- Home, 3BR/2.5BA, custom, $2,800

Windsor
- Apt., 1BR/1BA, quiet, $1,150
- Home, 3BR/2BA, lrg. yrd., $1,475

(Continued from page 353)

For those new to the region and shopping for homes, a hotel might do the trick — short term. The major chains have built large and small hotels in the suburbs, many of them near freeway exits and a few smack in the middle of residential neighborhoods.

Residency hotels offer a slightly different experience. They combine the conveniences of a hotel — maid service, continental breakfast, airport shuttle — with the pleasures of home: a fully-equipped kitchen and a laundry room (coin-operated). They may also have a pool, a spa, a sportscourt, a workout room. Some offer free grocery shopping and on evenings a social hour.

In the Bay Area, apartments come in all sizes and settings. If you're strapped for funds, you can find in the suburbs single bedrooms and studios for under $800 a month. No pool, no spa, no extras. But the closer to the City, the newer and nicer the apartment, the more you will pay.

Renters pay for cable service, electricity or gas and phone (in some instances, deposits may be required to start service.)

You will be asked for a security deposit and for the first month's rent up front. State law limits deposits to a maximum two months rent for an unfurnished apartment and three months for a furnished (this includes the last month's rent.) If you agree to a lease, you might get an extra month free. If you move out before the lease is up, you pay a penalty. To protect themselves, landlords will ask you to fill out a credit report and to list references.

Some apartments forbid pets, some will accept only cats, some cats and small dogs. Many will ask for a pet deposit (to cover possible damage.)

The Fair Housing laws will apply: no discrimination based on race, sex, family status and so on. But some complexes will be designed to welcome one or several kinds of renters. A complex that wants families, for example, might include a tot lot. One that prefers singles or childless couples might throw Friday night parties or feature a large pool and a workout room but no kiddie facilities. Some large complexes will offer furnished and unfurnished apartments or corporate setups, a variation of the residency hotel.

If hotels or apartments are not your cup of tea, you might take a look at renting a home or townhouse. Many owners turn the maintenance and renting over to a professional property manager. In older towns, many of the cottages and smaller homes in the older sections will often be rentals. If you see a "For Sale" sign in front of a home that interests you, inquire whether the place is for rent. Rents will vary by town.

Finally, there are shared rentals. They are most popular around colleges and universities. Many people looking to share post rentals on bulletin boards or the internet. Newspapers routinely carry ads from people looking to share a rental. Preferences are stated: no smokers, women only, no pets, etc.

If you don't want to buy furniture, you can rent it. Check the Yellow Pages under furniture rental. For cheap furniture, check out the garage sales.

When you're out scouting for a rental, check out the neighborhood and think about what you really value and enjoy. If you want the convenient commute without the hassle of a car, pick a place near a BART line or bus stop. If it's the active life, scout out the parks, trails and such things as bars and restaurants and community colleges.

For parents, your address will usually determine what public school your child attends (San Francisco is the main exception. See Chapter on How Public Schools Work.) If you want a high-scoring school, see the scores in this book before making a decision. Always call the school before making a renting decision. You may not be able to get your child into the "neighborhood" school.

The same advice applies to day care. Make sure that it is available nearby before signing a lease.

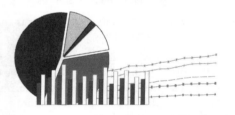

Chapter 18

New Housing

SHOPPING FOR A NEW HOME? This chapter gives a sampling of new housing under way in the Bay Area and nearby counties. If you know where you want to live, drive that town or ask the local planning department, what's new in housing.

Prices change. Incidentals such as landscaping fees may not be included. In the 1980s, to pay for services, cities increased fees on home construction. Usually, these fees are included in the home prices but in what is known as Mello-Roos districts, the fees are often assessed like tax payments (in addition to house payments).

Nothing secret. By law, developers are required to disclose all fees and in fact California has some of the toughest disclosure laws in the country. But the prices listed may not include some fees.

Many people working in one county and live in another, where prices are cheaper. Some people commute 200 miles round trip a day.

This information covers what's available at time of publication. For latest information, call the developers for brochures.

If you have never shopped for a new home, you probably will enjoy the experience. In the larger developments, the builders will decorate models showing the housing styles and sizes offered.

You enter through one home, pick up the sales literature, then move to the other homes or condos. Every room is usually tastefully and imaginatively decorated — and enticing.

An agent or agents will be on hand to answer questions or discuss financing or any other aspect you're interested in. Generally, all this is done low-key. On Saturdays and Sundays thousands of people can be found visiting developments around the Bay Area and Northern California.

Developers call attention to their models by flags. When you pass what appears to be a new development and flags are flying, it generally means that units are available for sale.

Extraordinary living environments throughout Northern California.

PRIVATE RESERVE
Livermore
Stunning wine country homes on large homesites.
From the Low $1,000,000's
925-373-3440

STATION SQUARE
Livermore
Townhome-style condominiums in a historic downtown.
From the $500,000's
925-245-0760

CEDARWOOD
Brentwood
Distinctive 3- to 5-bedroom single-family homes.
From the $600,000's
925-513-1057

HARBORWALK
Oakland
Condominium homes one block from the Estuary.
From the $500,000's
510-532-8843

THE ESTUARY
Oakland
Final Waterfront Homes!
Contemporary townhomes on the Estuary.
From the high $700,000's
510-535-0120

CLAREMONT
Rocklin
Spacious homes and homesites in Stanford Ranch.
From the high $600,000's
916-434-7787

GARIN CORNERS
Brentwood
3- to 5-bedroom courtyard homes in Garin Ranch.

BRODERICK PLACE
San Francisco
Stylish condominium homes near Golden Gate Park.

235 BERRY
San Francisco
New waterfront condominium homes in the heart of Mission Bay.

288 THIRD
Oakland
Condominium homes near Jack London Square.

ANCHOR COVE AT MARINA BAY
Richmond
Contemporary townhomes one block from the marina.

CITRUS GROVE AT SORRENTO
Lincoln
Spacious single family homes in a master-planned setting.

FIDDYMENT
Roseville
Distinctive new neighborhoods in a master-planned setting.

Signature PROPERTIES
A Tradition in Homebuilding

EQUAL HOUSING OPPORTUNITY

Visit www.sigprop.com for the latest information about all of our new home communities.

MARIN COUNTY

San Rafael

The Forest at Redwood Village, Signature Properties, 36 Apricot Ct., (415) 479-8808, townhomes, 2-3 bedrooms, from high $500,000.

ALAMEDA COUNTY

Livermore

Cresta Blanca, Signature Properties, 2394 Peregrine St., (925) 960-9220, single family homes, 3-6 bedrooms, from high $800,000.

Station Square, Signature Properties, 1832 Railroad Ave., (925) 245-0760, townhomes, 2-3 bedrooms, from low $500,000.

Private Reserve, Signature Properties, 5436 Stockton Loop, (925) 373-3440, single family homes, 4-5 bedrooms, from low $1 million.

Oakland

Harborwalk, Signature Properties, 3090 Glascock St., (510) 532-8843, townhomes, 1-3 bedrooms, from high $400,000.

The Estuary, Signature Properties, 2909 Glascock St., (510) 535-0120, townhomes, 2-3 bedrooms, from low $600,000.

CONTRA COSTA COUNTY

Brentwood

Cedarwood, Signature Properties, 502 Richdale Ct., (925) 513-1057, single family homes, 3-5 bedrooms, from low $600,000.

Garin Landing, Signature Properties, 570 Almanor St., (925) 240-1585, single family homes, 3-4 bedrooms, from mid $500,000.

San Pablo

Abella Villas, Signature Properties, 102 Carmel St., (510) 236-8215, condominiums, 2-3 bedrooms, from mid $400,000.

SOLANO COUNTY

Fairfield

Andalucia, Standard Pacific, 3001 Pebble Beach Cir., (707) 422-3199, single family homes, 2-4.5 bedrooms, from $700,000.

Vacaville

Lantana at Alamo Place, Standard Pacific, call for address, (707) 450-0178, single family homes, 4-6 bedrooms, from lower $600,000.

SHE'S NOT JUST COMING FOR A LITTLE STAY

Life is really full of surprises. But we don't think home buying should be. So we do all we can to ease you through every step of buying your new home. From selecting your floor plan through closing escrow. Even after move in. Which shouldn't be surprising, considering we've spent over 39 years doing our best to make home buying as easy as possible.

STANDARD PACIFIC HOMES
Making You Right At Home™

1-877-STNDPAC (786-3722)
www.standardpacifichomes.com

HomeAid America. *Home Loans Provided by FAMILY LENDING* Prices, terms, and specifications subject to change without notice. Models do not reflect racial preferences.

SAN JOAQUIN COUNTY

Stockton

Fox Hollow, Morrison Homes, 2352 Etcheverry Dr., (209) 954-1305, single family homes, 3-4 bedrooms, from high $300,000.

Tracy

Redbridge, Standard Pacific, 2624 Redbridge Rd., (209) 833-7000, single family homes, 3-4 bedrooms, from mid $500,000.

PLACER COUNTY

Lincoln

Traditions, Morrison Homes, 1603 Allenwood Cir., (916) 434-6927, single family homes, 4-5 bedrooms, from high $400,000.

Woodbury Glen, Standard Pacific, call for location, (916) 826-7129, single family homes, 3-5 bedrooms, from $400,000.

Rocklin

Claremont, Signature Properties, 2103 Wyckford Blvd., (916) 434-7787, single family homes, 4-5 bedrooms, from mid $600,000.

Roseville

Willow Creek, Standard Pacific, call for location, 1 (877) STNDPAC, single family homes, 4-6 bedrooms, from mid $400,000.

STANISLAUS COUNTY

Patterson

Bella Flora at Patterson Gardens, Morrison Homes, 1256 Fawn Lily Dr., (209) 895-4034, single family homes, 4-5 bedrooms, from mid $400,000.

Turlock

Ventana, Morrison Homes, 4077 Enclave Dr., (209) 632-0025, single family homes, 3-4 bedrooms, from high $300,000.

MERCED COUNTY

Merced

University Park, Morrison Homes, 1339 Irvine Ct., (209) 388-0611, single family homes, 3-4 bedrooms, from mid $300,000.

SACRAMENTO COUNTY

Rancho Cordova

Anatolia, Morrison Homes, 4008 Kalamata Way, (916) 869-5779, single family homes, 3-4 bedrooms, from high $300,000.

Sacramento

Silver Hollow, Morrison Homes, 8151 Stallion Way, (916) 525-3945, single family homes, 4-5 bedrooms, from high $800,000.

Chapter **19**

Colleges & Job Training

IF YOU ARE LOOKING for a job but need training or additional education, local colleges, public adult schools and private institutions have put together a variety of programs, ranging from word processing to MBA degrees.

Many institutions have devised programs for working adults or parents who must attend the duties of school and child rearing.

In many instances jobs and careers are mixed in with personal enrichment. At some colleges, you can take word processing, economics and music.

This chapter lists the major local educational and training institutes. All will send you literature (some may charge a small fee), all welcome inquiries.

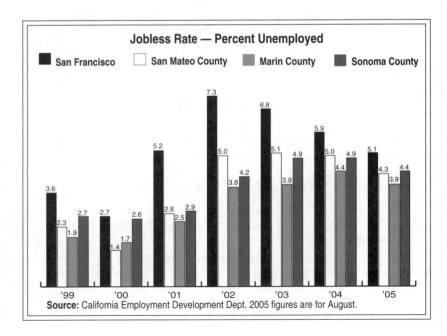

Jobless Rate — Percent Unemployed

■ San Francisco　□ San Mateo County　▨ Marin County　■ Sonoma County

Source: California Employment Development Dept. 2005 figures are for August.

Adult Schools

Although rarely in the headlines, adult schools serve thousands in the four counties. Upholstery, microwave cooking, ballroom dancing, computers, cardiopulmonary resuscitation, aerobics, investing in stocks, art, music, Quicken, how to raise children — all these and more are offered in adult schools.

These schools and programs are run by school districts and by cities. Many schools also run adult sports programs, basketball, volleyball, tennis. Call your local school or city for a catalog.

Older Students

Many colleges offer evening and weekend programs, especially in business degrees and business-related subjects. Some programs — an MBA — can take years, some classes only a day. The Bay Area is loaded with educational opportunities. Here is a partial list of local colleges. As with any venture, the student should investigate before enrolling or paying a fee.

San Francisco Colleges

- Academy of Art College, 540 Powell St., San Francisco, 94108. Day and evening classes. Phone (415) 274-2200.

- City College of San Francisco, 50 Phelan Ave., San Francisco, 94112. Liberal arts. Phone (415) 239-3000. City College has numerous branches about the city. Call the main number for information.

- Golden Gate University, 536 Mission St., San Francisco, 94105. Business and law. Phone (415) 442-7000.

- John Adams Community College Center, 1860 Hayes St., San Francisco, 94117. Remedial instruction. Phone (415) 561-1900.

- New College of California, 766 Valencia St., San Francisco, 94110. Humanities and public interest law. Phone (415) 437-3460 .

- San Francisco State University-Downtown Center, 814 Mission St., San Francisco, 94103. Day, evening, extended education. Phone (415) 338-1111.

- San Francisco State University, 1600 Holloway Ave., San Francisco, 94132. Phone (415) 338-1111.

- University of San Francicso, (415) 422-5555, 2130 Fulton St. Catholic university. Runs traditional academic programs and many programs aimed at general public.

- University of California-Berkeley Extension. Many enrichment and business classes. Phone (510) 642-4111.

San Francisco's community college system has several campuses devoted to teaching English as a second language. They include:

- Alemany Center, 750 Eddy St., Phone (415) 561-1875.

- Chinatown-North Beach Center, 940 Filbert St. (415) 561-1850.

- Downtown Community College Center, 800 Mission. (415) 267-6500.

- Southeast Community College Center, 1800 Oakdale Ave. (415) 550-4300.

San Mateo County Colleges

- Cañada College. 4200 Farm Hill Blvd., Redwood City, 94601. Community college. Phone (650) 364-1212.

- College of San Mateo. 1700 West Hillsdale Blvd., San Mateo, 94402. Community college. Phone: (650) 574-6161.

- College of Notre Dame. 1500 Ralston Ave., Belmont, 94002. Catholic. Private, co-ed. Undergrad and grad, including MBA. (650) 593-1601.

- Menlo School and College. 1000 El Camino Real, Atherton. Private.

  Business admin., humanities, mass communication. Phone (650) 543-3723.

- Skyline Comm. Col. 3300 College Dr., San Bruno. (650) 355-7000.

- Stanford University. Located in Palo Alto. One of the great universities of the planet. Worth a visit just to see place. Concerts, lectures and events are open to the public. Continuing ed. (650) 723-2300.

Marin & Sonoma Colleges and Universities

- College of Marin: Kentfield campus, College Avenue, (415) 457-8811; Indian Valley campus, 1800 Ignacio Blvd., Novato. (415) 883-2211.

- Santa Rosa Junior College, 1501 Mendocino Ave., Santa Rosa. (707) 527-4011. Also run by Santa Rosa City College: a facility in Petaluma.

- Sonoma State University, Rohnert Park. Bachelor's and master's, teaching credentials. Day, evening classes. Phone (707) 664-2880.

- Dominican University, 1520 Grand Ave., San Rafael. Private university, emphasis international studies but variety of programs.. (415) 485-3255.

- San Francisco Theological Seminary, 2 Kensington Rd., San Anselmo. (415) 451-2800.

- University of San Francisco, North Bay Campus, Santa Rosa. (707) 527-9612.

Chapter *20*

Commuting

COMPLAINTS ARE MANY BUT San Francisco and San Mateo County have to be considered good commutes — compared to other counties.

The same for most of Marin. If commuting from Sonoma to San Francisco, it's a long and tiring haul.

San Francisco

Before the 1989 earthquake, freeways frequently jammed during peak hours. The quake made matters worse: The Embarcadero freeway, badly damaged, was demolished, wiping out a main road to Chinatown, North Beach, Fisherman's Wharf and a good portion of the financial district. In 1996, Caltrans demolished the upper deck of the Central Freeway, which moved a lot of the traffic going to the west part of the City. In 1997, however, bowing to complaints from residents in the Richmond and Sunset districts, Caltrans opened what remained of the Central Freeway. Voters, by a slim margin, later confirmed that they wanted the Central Freeway rebuilt, then in another vote, said, don't rebuild. The result: what is now called the Octavia-Market corridor, a new boulevard. See Hayes Valley in the San Francisco profiles.

Over the last 15 years, San Francisco went through a boom in office construction, opened a baseball stadium and started work on the giant Mission Bay project. More high-rise residential buildings are being erected in and near the downtown. But, deliberately, San Francisco has skimped on parking for the stadium and the new buildings. The City's attitude: take public transit.

With so much kaput, why is San Francisco still a good commute? Because it's a small city that has an extensive bus-street car system, the MUNI.

Because BART (rail transit) picked up some of the load. In 2003, BART extended its line to San Francisco International Airport and opened three stations in San Mateo County, at South San Francisco, San Bruno and Millbrae.

Because the old Southern Pacific line, now Caltrain, still runs passenger trains (from Gilroy to downtown San Francisco, stopping at the Giants stadium). In 2004, Caltrain started a bullet train service between Gilroy and downtown San Francisco.

Driving Miles to Bay Bridge

City	Hwy 101	I-280
Atherton	31	31
Belmont	22	25
Brisbane	7	N.A.
Burlingame	15	18
Colma	N.A.	11
Daly City	N.A.	7
East Palo Alto	31	N.A.
Foster City	21	N.A.
Half Moon Bay	N.A.	N.A.
Hillsborough	N.A.	21
Menlo Park	30	36
Millbrae	14	17
Pacifica	N.A.	10
Portola Valley	N.A.	36
Redwood City	25	31
San Bruno	11	14
San Carlos	24	29
San Mateo	18	25
South San Francisco	9	11
Woodside	27	33

Note: These are approximate distances from the west end of the Bay Bridge near downtown San Francisco to the first available exit to each city. Highway 101 and Interstate 280 merge in San Francisco and share a common route to the bridge. **Key**: NA, not applicable. Either exits were not available or the freeway was judged to be too distant for a reasonable estimate.

Because little "big" improvements help push traffic along. These include FasTrak tolls (electronic billing) on the Golden Gate Bridge and the other bridges.

MUNI, which carries over 700,000 riders daily, catches a lot of flak but matters have improved. The City hired a professional manager to run the system. More cars were purchased, the computer system overhauled and the oversight body made more efficient. In 2005, the manager moved on, replaced by another professional.

If San Franciscans were bereft of buses, cabs, street cars and cable cars, if they were reduced to bicycles, skates and shoe leather, chances are that the great majority would arrive home before most of the suburban commuters. This is one benefit of living in a small city — roughly eight miles by eight miles.

In 2006, the Third Street line (light rail) is scheduled to open. Will help commuters on the Bay side.

The San Mateo Advantages

San Mateo residents, many of whom work in San Francisco, have it tougher but again, compared to other Bay Area counties, they come off OK.

The northern towns are within a few minutes drive or bus or train ride to downtown San Francisco. No bridges — the great bottlenecks for commuters from the East and North Bays — separate San Mateo cities from San Francisco. Highway 101 and Interstate 280 feeds straight into the downtown.

The new BART stations at South San Francisco, San Bruno and Millbrae should prove a great help to people who work at the airport or in San Francisco. BART, which runs to San Francisco and East Bay cities, also has stations at Colma and Daly City.

Caltrain runs about 40 trains a day in each direction up and down the Peninsula from Gilroy, in southern Santa Clara County, to downtown San Fran, stopping blocks from the financial district. Funding has been secured to repair and upgrade equipment. In 2004, Caltrain started bullet train service that speeds passengers from San Jose to the City in 50 minutes.

SamTrans, the public bus agency serving San Mateo County, makes connections with MUNI (the San Francisco bus system) and runs express buses into the downtown. In the works is a transit center in downtown San Francisco which will make for smoother switching between train, bus and streetcar.

The International Airport, one of the largest employers in the region, is located in San Mateo County, a short drive for most residents. The same for the hundreds of firms that feed into the airport's economy, the hotels, the office complexes, the warehouses, the shippers.

Southern San Mateo County is oriented toward Silicon Valley (roughly Palo Alto to Cupertino and including parts of San Jose). Santa Clara County has traffic jams but it also has many freeways, and the great bulk of industry is located within a half-hour drive of Redwood City.

One more big job done, a second span to the San Mateo Bridge. The work was completed in 2002 and makes commuting to the East Bay much easier.

In 2004, San Mateo voters agreed to continue a half-cent sales tax that will be used to fund road and transit improvements throughout the county.

North Bay

AFTER YEARS OF VOTING DOWN transit taxes and enduring traffic jams, Marin and Sonoma County in late 2004, to the shock of many, each passed an increase in the sales tax to improve the roads and local transportation.

The Marin tax was for a half-cent, the Sonoma tax for a quarter-cent.

Not surprisingly, Marin had a catch. For decades, transit planners have been trying to widen what is called the Novato Narrows, a stretch of Highway 101 from San Rafael up to about Petaluma. This widening would unclog traffic from Sonoma County and allow it to flow more quickly to the Golden Gate. It would have also benefitted Novato, which is located in North Marin.

But it would not have benefitted South Marin, where most Marinites live. And many residents thought the widening would encourage development.

The half-cent increase will not help the widen the Narrows. Rather the money will be spent on extending a car-pool lane on Highway 101 through San Rafael, providing more buses for the elderly and the disabled and improving roads, paths, sidewalks and bike lanes and transit safety around schools.

The Sonoma increase will be used to widen Highway 101 in that county and make general road and transit improvements.

And a portion will be used to study reviving a rail line between Cloverdale and San Rafael, with the hope of taking thousands off the road and sticking them on buses and ferries.

Next up, another effort to get Marin to support a tax that would pay for its share of the rail revival. An attempt may be made in 2006.

Toward the end of 2005, Congress passed a transit bill that includes money to widen the Novato Narrows.

Timesaving Strategies

- Buy a good map book and keep it in the car. The editors favor Thomas Guides. Sooner than later you will find yourself jammed on the freeway and in desperate need of an alternate route. They're out there. Many

downtown streets in San Francisco are one-way and for obscure historical reasons many streets— east and west, north and south — take a sharp turn at Market Street, confusing everything. If you travel the downtown frequently, a map is a necessity.

- El Camino Real runs the length of San Mateo County. When freeways jam, take El Camino Real.

- Listen to traffic reports on the radio. Helicopters and planes give immediate news of jams. Avoid trouble before you get on the road.

- Buy SamTrans and MUNI (bus) passes and $45 BART tickets. They save delays and fumbling for the right change when you're in a hurry.

- Join a car pool. RIDES will help you find people to share a ride — free. RIDES works with thousands of commuters each month and sets up pools going everywhere in the Bay Area. If you want to start a van pool, RIDES will help you find passengers, lease a van. Call 511.

- Avoid peak hours. If you can leave for work — it gets earlier every year — about 6:30 a.m. and hit the freeway home before 4 p.m., your kids might not greet you, "Hey, stranger."

- Take public transportation. Yes, the car is flexible, so handy, so private. But if other, easier, cheaper ways of commuting are at hand, why ignore them?

Bus, Train, Light Rail, Street Car and Cable

- BART. In 2004, BART completed a $1.2 billion system renovation including upgrading car interiors and overhauling fare gates, ticket machines, escalators and elevators. Coupled with opening of the SFO BART station, and expansion in Contra Costa, Alameda and San Mateo counties, the improvements have upped both system efficiency and customer satisfaction. Ridership on BART now averages close to three million passenger trips every month. In addition to connecting to the East Bay via the Transbay Tube, BART runs from downtown San Francisco, through the Mission District, then takes a dogleg west to Daly City, Colma, South San Francisco, San Bruno and Millbrae. BART riders at Millbrae can connect with Caltrain, extending into San Mateo and Santa Clara counties. For BART info, schedules, (415) 989-2278. BART also serves Alameda and Contra Costa counties.

- SamTrans. The bus system serving San Mateo County and the Peninsula. Also connects with BART, Caltrain, MUNI, Santa Clara County Transit and AC Transit. SamTrans serves the major shopping centers and civic centers. Express buses to San Francisco. For information, call (800) 660-4BUS.

- San Francisco Municipal Railway (The MUNI). Runs almost all the street public transit in San Francisco, diesel buses, electric buses, cable cars.

Express buses along popular routes. Beefed-up service during commute hours. For information, schedules, discount passes, (415) 673-MUNI.

- Caltrain. Runs from San Francisco down the peninsula through San Mateo County to Santa Clara County. "Baby Bullet" train zips from Downtown San Francisco (at Giants ball park) to San Jose in just under an hour, with stops in Millbrae, San Mateo, Palo Alto and Mountain View. Caltrain also offers local service between San Francisco and Gilroy. In addition to above stations, these trains stop at South San Francisco, San Bruno, Burlingame, Belmont, San Carlos, Redwood City, Menlo Park, Sunnyvale, Santa Clara and Morgan Hill. Weekend service at Atherton station. Buses to stations. Rails have upgrades, stations overhauled. Phone (800) 660-4287.

Other Transit Systems.

- AC Transit. Serves Alameda County and parts of Contra Costa. Express buses to San Francisco. (510) 839-2882.

- Alameda-Oakland Ferry. East Bay ferry service. (510) 522-3300.

- Golden Gate Transit. Buses to Marin and Sonoma counties. Ferries to Sausalito and Larkspur in Marin County. (415) 923-2000.

- Universal number for information. Effort to make it simple: 511.

Miscellaneous

- San Francisco gives its residents preferred parking on 40 percent of its streets. Applicants must show proof of residence (driver's license, utility bill, rental agreement) and vehicle registration. Call (415) 554-5000.

- On the comeback: ferries. Before the bridges, they were the commute workhorses of the Bay Area. In recent years, Vallejo and Oakland-Alameda have started ferry service to San Francisco. Marin has never stopped running ferries to San Francisco.

- In 2003, the Calif. Dept. of Motor Vehicles counted in San Francisco 447,585 vehicles and 525,639 licensed drivers.

  San Mateo: 647,783 vehicles and 506,735 licensed drivers.

  Marin: 218,583 vehicles, 189,576 licensed drivers.

  Sonoma: 413,453 vehicles, 334,512 licensed drivers.

- Devil's Slide. Just south of Pacifica Highway 1 travels over an unstable, steep and winding stretch of coastal slopes known as Devil's Slide. When rain erosion or simply gravity takes over, the road collapses and forces many residents into long detours. Two tunnels are under construction to fix the problem. Work could be completed by 2010.

Chapter 21

Weather

SAN MATEO AND SAN FRANCISCO weather can be described as delightful — with one big exception. In spring and summer, fog often envelops the ocean towns and neighborhoods and, in some places, penetrates to the Bay.

If you like fog and brisk air ... no problem. If you don't, you may find balmy winters a fair swap but the bottom line is that some people just plain don't like the fog.

Other than that, summers are rarely excessively hot, rarely humid, and winters are rarely cold. Rain confines itself to the winter months, and winds blow pollution elsewhere.

Although erratic, the weather follows broad patterns, easily understood, and worthwhile understanding. It will help you decide when to hold picnics, when to eat in, when to visit the coast.

Five actors star in the weather extravaganza: the sun, the Pacific, the Golden Gate, the Central Valley and the Mountains.

The Sun

In the spring and summer, the sun moves north bringing a mass of air called the Pacific High. The Pacific High blocks storms from the California coast and dispatches winds to the coast.

In the fall, the sun moves south, taking the Pacific High with it. The winds slough off for a while, then in bluster the storms. Toward spring, the storms abate as the Pacific High settles in.

When should you have a picnic? Rarely will the summer disappoint you with rain, and if it does, the rain will be minuscule. But in some neighborhoods and towns the fog may seem like rain.

The Pacific

Speeding across the Pacific, the spring and summer winds pick up moisture and, approaching the coast at an angle, strip the warm water from the surface and brings the frigid to the top.

Average Daily Temperature

Location	Ja	Fb	Mr	Ap	My	Ju	Jy	Au	Sp	Oc	No	Dc
Half Mn. Bay	51	52	52	53	55	57	58	59	60	57	54	51
Redwd. City	48	52	54	57	61	66	68	68	66	61	53	58
S.F. Airport	50	53	54	56	59	62	63	64	65	62	55	53
San Jose	50	54	55	58	63	67	70	69	69	63	55	50
San Fran.	51	55	55	55	57	59	60	61	63	62	60	53

Source: Figures derived from 1971-2000 records, National Climatic Center, Asheville, North Carolina.

Cold water exposed to warm wet air makes a wonderfully thick fog. In summer, the Sunset and Richmond districts in San Francisco, Monterey, Half Moon Bay and Pacifica, among others, often look like they are buried in mountains of cotton.

The Golden Gate and the Mountains

This fog would love to scoot inland to the Bay neighborhoods — Bayview, Potrero Hill, Mission, Noe Valley and others — and Bay towns such as San Mateo, Redwood City, Burlingame and Foster City.

But the coastal hills and mountains stop or greatly impede its progress — except where there are openings. Of the half dozen or so major gaps, the biggest is that marvelous work of nature, the Golden Gate.

The fog shoots through the Golden Gate in the spring and summer, visually delighting motorists on the Bay Bridge, banging into the East Bay hills, and easing down toward San Jose, where it takes the edge off the summer temperatures.

For most of San Mateo County, the Santa Cruz Mountains hold back the fog — one major reason why the weather delights. The fog takes the edge off the summer heat yet leaves the Bay towns basking in the sun.

Where the mountains or hills dip or flatten out, the fog penetrates. The Golden Gate Park, flat, ushers fog into Haight Ashbury and parts of the downtown. The Alemany Gap, near Lake Merced, allows some fog into Hunters Point.

In San Mateo County, the hills dip at Daly City and just north of Daly City. In July and August, it's not unusual for residents of Daly City, Colma and South San Francisco to bundle up in sweaters and jackets.

The hills dip to a lesser extent about the middle of Crystal Springs, near the City of San Mateo, which will get some of the cooler ocean air. South San Francisco and Brisbane are located side by side. Brisbane is tucked behind San Bruno Mountain. South San Francisco is more exposed to ocean winds so it will get more fog.

Temperatures for Selected Cities
Number of Days Greater than 90 Degrees in a Typical Year

City	Ja	Fb	Mr	Ap	My	Ju	Jy	Au	Sp	Oc	No	Dc
San Francisco	0	0	0	0	0	0	0	1	0	0	0	0
Half Moon Bay	0	0	0	0	0	0	0	0	0	0	0	0
Redwood City	0	0	0	0	0	4	5	9	2	0	0	0

Source: National Weather Service.

Temperatures for Selected Cities
Number of Days 32 Degrees or Less in a Typical Year

City	Ja	Fb	Mr	Ap	My	Ju	Jy	Au	Sp	Oc	No	Dc
San Francisco	0	0	0	0	0	0	0	0	0	0	0	4
Half Moon Bay	0	0	0	0	0	0	0	0	0	0	0	3
Redwood City	0	0	0	0	0	0	0	0	0	0	0	7

Source: National Weather Service.

The sun dances in here. On many days it burns the fog away by 2 or 3 in the afternoon. But come night, the cold and the fog often assert themselves.

By day, the radio tower atop Mt. Sutro appeals visually to no one. At night, the hills for a few hours will hold back the fog, and all of a sudden, surrender. Great clouds will billow around the tower and down into the valleys, and the upper antennas, with their guy wires, will seem like the masts of a sailing ship making its way across the heavens.

The Central Valley

Also known as the San Joaquin Valley. Located about 75 miles inland, the Central Valley is influenced more by continental weather than coastal. In the summer, this means heat.

Hot air rises, pulling in cold air like a vacuum. The Central Valley sucks in the coastal air through the Golden Gate and openings in the East Bay hills, until the Valley cools. Then the Valley says to the coast: no more cool air.

With the suction gone, the inland pull on the ocean fog drops off, often breaking down the fog-producing apparatus and clearing San Francisco and the coastline. Coast residents enjoy days of sunshine. Meanwhile, lacking the cooling air, the Valley heats up again, creating the vacuum that pulls in the fog.

This cha-cha between coast and inland valley gave rise to the Bay Region's boast of "natural air conditioning." In hot weather, nature works to bring in cool air; in cool weather, she works to bring in heat.

The Mountains and Pacific Again

In the winter, great banks of tule fog often form in the Central Valley and chill the air. The Pacific in the winter holds the heat better than the land and,

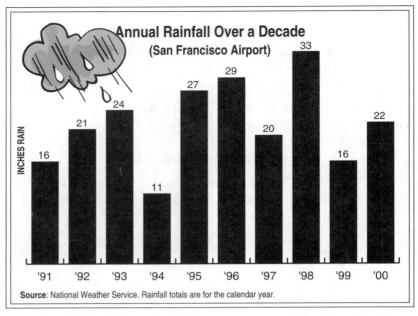

Annual Rainfall Over a Decade
(San Francisco Airport)

INCHES RAIN

| '91 | '92 | '93 | '94 | '95 | '96 | '97 | '98 | '99 | '00 |
| 16 | 21 | 24 | 11 | 27 | 29 | 20 | 33 | 16 | 22 |

Source: National Weather Service. Rainfall totals are for the calendar year.

when not raining, often settles balmy weather along coast and Bay cities — another major reason why San Francisco and San Mateo enjoy a mild climate.

Recall that cold moves toward heat, much as if heat were a suction vacuum. The Central Valley fog would like to move into the Bay but is blocked by the mountain range running up the East Bay. Occasionally, however, Central Valley fog will penetrate through its openings, foremost the Carquinez Strait near Vallejo, and work down into the Bay — a perilous time for shipping.

Coastal fog often forms well above the Pacific and, pushed by the wind, generally moves at a good clip. In thick coastal fog, you will have to slow down but you can see the tail lights of a car 50 to 75 yards ahead. In valley or tule fog, you sometimes can barely make out your hood ornament. This winter fog blossoms at shoe level when cold air pulls moisture from the earth. When you read of 50- and 75-car pileups in the Central Valley, tule fog is to blame. Dust storms are another culprit in the Valley.

Within the Bay, tule fog, before radar, was often responsible for shipping accidents, including the 1901 sinking of the liner, Rio de Janeiro, 130 lives lost.

On rare days, tule fog will settle over San Francisco Airport, making takeoffs and landings risky. On the ocean side of the county, Half Moon Bay Airport will be basking in the sun. In late 1995, a patch of fog settled over the runway at San Francisco Airport and grounded flights; the control tower and terminals were fog free.

Mountains and Rain

Besides blocking the fog, the hills also greatly decide how much rain falls in a particular location. Many storms travel south to north, so a valley that opens to the south (San Lorenzo-Santa Cruz) will receive more rain than one that opens to the North (Santa Clara-San Jose.)

When storm clouds rise to pass over a hill, they cool and drop much of their rain. Some towns in the Bay Region will be deluged during a storm, while a few miles away another town will escape with showers.

That basically is how the weather works in the Bay Area but, unfortunately for regularity's sake, the actors often forget their lines or are upstaged by minor stars.

Weather Tidbits: The 'Stick

Why the Giants moved. Candlestick Park lies at the junction of two wind streams that shoot through the Alemany Gap in the hills. The result: eddies and vacuums that did circus tricks with fly balls. The new stadium, sheltered better by the hills, does a better job of keeping out the fog. As for the Forty Niners, they play in fall and winter, by which time the summer fog and winds are long gone from Candlestick Park, the sun back in fine form.

Swimming

September and October are the best months to swim in the Pacific. The upwelling of the cold water has stopped. Often the fog has departed. Sunshine glows upon the water and the coast. Almost every year the summer ends with hot spells in September and October. Be careful of the ocean coast; treacherous rip tides.

Sunshine

Like sunshine? You're in the right place. Records show that during daylight hours the sun shines in New York City 60 percent of the time; in Boston, 57 percent; in Detroit 53 percent; and in Seattle, 43 percent.

Atop Mt. Tamalpais (in Marin County) the sun shines 73 percent of the year. San Jose averages 63 percent. San Mateo and San Francisco ... well, it depends on where you're located. But 60 percent plus is a realistic figure.

Humidity

When hot spells arrive, the air usually has little moisture — dry heat. When the air is moist (the fog), the temperatures drop.

Redwood Drizzle

If you are planning a redwoods excursion to Big Basin or Muir Woods in the summer, bring a jacket and an umbrella. Redwoods are creatures of the fog, need it to thrive. Where you find a good redwood stand, you will, in summer, often find cold thick fog.

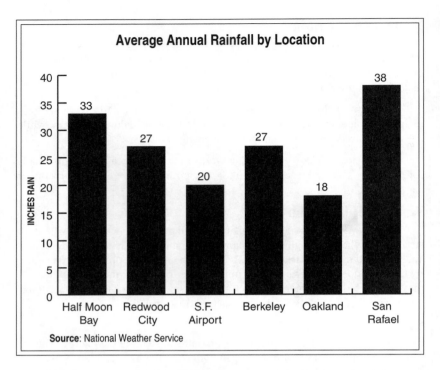

Average Annual Rainfall by Location

INCHES RAIN

Location	Inches
Half Moon Bay	33
Redwood City	27
S.F. Airport	20
Berkeley	27
Oakland	18
San Rafael	38

Source: National Weather Service

When fog passes through a redwood grove, the trees strip the moisture right out of the air. In some parts of the Bay Region redwood-fog drip has been measured at 10 inches annually.

One of the editors recalls attending a summer picnic in a redwood grove. We arrived about 11 a.m. to find the air cold and the drip heavy enough to soak our clothes. Parents bundled up children, plastic tablecloths were used as rain jackets. Two hours later, we were playing softball under a hot sun.

Average Monthly Temperatures

City	Ja	Fb	Mr	Ap	My	Ju	Jy	Au	Sp	Oc	No	Dc
Kentfield	49	52	55	58	62	67	69	69	67	63	54	49
San Rafael	49	53	55	58	61	65	68	68	67	63	55	49
Fort Ross	49	50	51	51	53	56	57	58	58	56	53	49
Petaluma	48	52	54	57	61	64	67	68	66	62	54	48
San Francisco	49	53	54	56	58	62	63	64	63	61	55	50

Source: Figures derived from 1971-2000 records, National Climatic Center, Asheville, North Carolina.

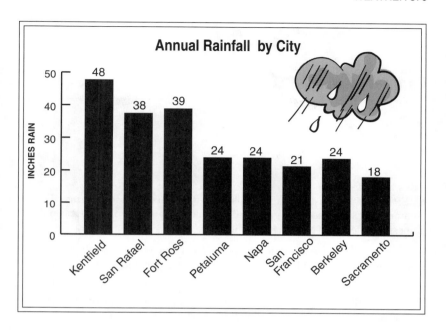

Annual Rainfall by City

Temperatures for Selected Cities

Number of Days Greater than 90 Degrees in a Typical Year

City	Ja	Fb	Mr	Ap	My	Ju	Jy	Au	Sp	Oc	No	Dc
Kentfield	0	0	0	0	0	4	6	11	8	0	0	0
San Rafael	0	0	0	0	0	4	5	11	6	0	0	0
Napa	0	0	0	0	0	4	5	12	10	0	0	0
Petaluma	0	0	0	0	0	4	5	5	6	0	0	0
Sonoma	0	0	0	0	0	4	13	13	11	0	0	0

Source: National Weather Service.

Temperatures for Selected Cities

Number of Days 32 Degrees or Less in a Typical Year

City	Ja	Fb	Mr	Ap	My	Ju	Jy	Au	Sp	Oc	No	Dc
Kentfield	4	3	0	0	1	0	0	0	0	0	0	10
San Rafael	1	0	0	0	0	0	0	0	0	0	0	5
Napa	13	5	0	2	0	0	0	0	0	0	0	11
Petaluma	5	6	0	0	0	0	0	0	0	0	0	10
Sonoma	14	5	3	1	0	0	0	0	0	0	0	14

Source: National Weather Service.

Chapter 22

Crime

EVERY neighborhood and city in this country suffers from some crime. Even communities surrounded by gates and patrolled by guards will on occasion see domestic violence or pilfering by visitors.

So the question to ask when shopping for a home or apartment is not: Is this neighborhood safe? But rather, how safe is it compared to other places?

In California, crime often follows demographics: High-income neighborhoods generally have low crime, middle-income places middling crime, and low-income towns and neighborhoods high crime.

In many instances, these patterns mislead. You can take probably every high-crime city in the country and find within it low-crime neighborhoods. New York City, to look at its statistics, seemingly is overrun with felons but the City includes Staten Island, generally suburban and probably low to middle in crime.

The same for Oakland, San Diego and Los Angeles. These are not crime cities; they are cities with certain neighborhoods high in crime.

The demographic connection also can mislead. Many peaceful, law-abiding people live in the "worst" neighborhoods. But these neighborhoods also contain a disproportionate number of the troubled and criminally inclined.

Why does crime correlate with income and demographics? In many countries, it doesn't. Japan, devastated after World War II, did not sink into violence and thievery. Many industrialized nations with about the same or lower standards of living than the U.S. have far fewer murders. In 2000, France, about 54 million people, counted 503 homicides; in 2002, the United Kingdom (England, Wales, Scotland and Northern Ireland), 58 million people, recorded 513 homicides. By contrast, in 2004, the City of Los Angeles, 3.9 million people, tallied 518 homicides (and historically this was low for L.A.). In recent years Europeans have seen more burglaries, robberies, etc. In fact, in some categories, the U.S. is doing better than some Europe nations. The big exception: shootings.

Crime Statistics by City
San Mateo County

City	Population	Violent Crimes*	Homicides
*Atherton***	*7,256*	*26*	*0*
Belmont	25,470	19	0
*Brisbane***	*3,724*	*6*	*0*
Burlingame	28,280	64	0
*Colma***	*1,567*	*5*	*0*
Daly City	104,661	318	3
East Palo Alto	32,202	323	7
Foster City	29,876	34	0
Half Moon Bay	12,688	20	1
Hillsborough	10,983	3	1
Menlo Park	30,648	78	3
Millbrae	20,708	36	1
Pacifica	38,678	61	0
*Portola Valley***	*4,538*	*N.A.*	*0*
Redwood City	75,986	319	1
San Bruno	42,215	115	1
San Carlos	28,190	25	1
San Mateo	94,212	416	4
So. San Francisco	61,661	119	1
*Woodside***	*5,496*	*N.A.*	*0*
County Total	723,453	2,168	26

Crime in San Francisco & Bay Area Cities

City	Population	Violent Crimes*	Homicides
Berkeley	104,727	557	4
Concord	126,539	393	5
Hayward	144,215	588	9
Novato	48,636	68	1
Oakland	407,003	5,151	83
Palo Alto	58,147	89	2
San Francisco	772,065	5,757	88
San Jose	909,890	3,379	24
San Rafael	56,879	197	1
Santa Rosa	155,099	1,002	5
Sunnyvale	131,048	161	2
Walnut Creek	66,031	115	1

Source: Annual reports from FBI, 2004 data. Homicides include murders and non-negligent manslaughter. *Number of violent crimes. N.A. (Not available). ** The FBI does not track communities under 10,000 population but sometimes we are able to obtain these statistics from the state — but at a much later date. To give some idea how the italicized communities shape up, we have included 2003 figures.

Crime Statistics by City

Marin County

City	Population	Violent Crimes	Homicides
Belvedere	*2,132*	*0*	*0*
Fairfax	*7,309*	*7*	*0*
Mill Valley	13,686	14	0
Novato	50,586	68	1
Ross	*2,349*	*0*	*0*
San Anselmo	12,385	17	0
San Rafael	57,224	197	1
Sausalito	*7,374*	*4*	*0*
Tiburon	*8,772*	*2*	*0*
Twin Cities**	21,392	11	0
County total	*252,485*	*554*	*0*

Sonoma County

City	Population	Violent Crimes*	Homicides
Cloverdale	*8,241*	*22*	*0*
Cotati	*7,337*	*35*	*0*
Healdsburg	11,711	28	0
Petaluma	56,632	142	0
Rohnert Park	42,445	177	0
Santa Rosa	156,268	1,002	5
Sebastopol	*7,794*	*34*	*0*
Sonoma	*9,834*	*22*	*0*
Windsor	25,475	65	2
County total	*478,440*	*1,806*	*12*

Source: Annual reports from FBI, 2004 data. Homicides include murders and non-negligent manslaughter. *Number of violent crimes. **Twin Cities includes Corte Madera and Larkspur. The FBI does not break out towns with fewer than 10,000 residents. The state often does but its 2004 figures were not available at the time of publication. For this reason, the italicized cities show figures from 2003.

Demographics and Crime

Sociologists blame the breakdown of morals and the family in the U.S, the pervasive violence in the media, the easy access to guns, and other forces. Any one of these "causes" could be argued into the next century but if you're shopping for a home or an apartment just keep in mind that there is a correlation between demographics and crime. Drive the neighborhood. The signs of trouble are often easily read: men idling around the liquor store, bars on many windows, security doors in wide use.

Should you avoid unsafe or marginal neighborhoods? For some people, the answer depends on trade-offs and personal circumstances. The troubled neighborhoods often carry low prices or rents and are located near job centers. Many towns and sections are in transition; conditions could improve, the investment might be worthwhile. What's intolerable to a parent might be acceptable to a single person.

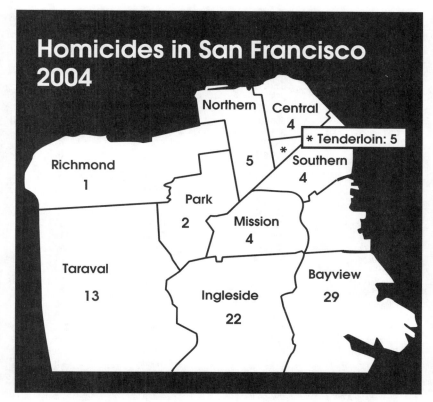

Homicides in San Francisco 2004

This map, courtesy of the San Francisco Police Dept., shows 2004 homicides and non-negligent manslaughter according to police districts. Total for year,88. The map is misleading in the Northern District. The Marina and Pacific Heights are located in this district but are generally low in crime. Most of the homicides show up closer to the southern section of this district. Other large sections, such as Ingleside, Taraval (Sunset) and Bayview, have crime hotspots and places where crime runs low to average.

If you don't have the bucks, often you can still buy safe but you may have to settle for a smaller house or yard. Whatever your neighborhood, don't make it easy for predators. Lock your doors, join the neighborhood watches, school your children in safety, take extra precautions when they are called for.

California Crime

Of the 2,394 homicides in 2004, guns, mostly pistols, accounted 73 percent of the total, knives 12 percent, blunt objects such as clubs 4 percent, hands and feet other personal weapons 6 percent, and unidentified weapons 5.

Megan's Law

For a list of registered sex offenders by town or city, go to www.meganslaw.ca.gov.

Crime in Other Cities Nationwide

City	Population	Violent Crimes*	Homicides
Anchorage	273,714	2,164	15
Atlanta	430,066	7,922	112
Austin	683,298	3,589	27
Birmingham	238,167	3,261	59
Boise	193,864	745	0
Boston	580,087	6,917	61
Chicago	2,882,746	NA	448
Cleveland	462,260	5,983	78
Dallas	1,228,613	16,165	248
Denver	563,688	4,490	87
Hartford, Conn.	125,109	1,514	16
Detroit, MI	914,353	15,913	385
Honolulu	906,589	2,507	26
Houston	2,043,446	23,427	272
Jacksonville, FLA	790,972	6,533	104
Las Vegas	1,239,805	9,783	131
Little Rock	185,870	3,048	40
Milwaukee	590,874	4,637	87
Miami	385,186	6,461	69
New York City	8,101,321	55,688	570
New Orleans	471,057	4,467	264
Oklahoma City	525,094	4,321	39
Philadelphia	1,484,224	20,902	330
Phoenix	1,428,973	9,465	202
Pittsburgh, PA	334,231	3,739	46
Portland, OR	543,838	4,034	29
Reno	201,981	1,480	9
St. Louis, MO	335,143	6,897	113
Salt Lake City	182,768	1,328	15
Scottsdale, AZ	224,357	468	4
Seattle	575,816	3,798	24
Tucson	522,487	4,873	55

Source: Annual 2004 FBI crime report. *Number of violent crimes.
Key: NA (not available).

Pit Bulls

In 2005, a 12-year-old boy was killed at his San Francisco home by the family's two pit bulls. In 2001, also in San Francisco, a young woman was attacked by pit bulls and killed. San Francisco is famous for loving its dogs but pit bulls may be falling out of public favor.

Crime in States

States	Population	Homicides	Violent Crimes	Rate*
Alabama	4,530,182	254	19,324	427
Alaska	655,435	37	4,159	635
Arizona	5,743,834	414	28,952	504
Arkansas	2,752,629	176	13,737	499
California	35,893,799	2,392	198,070	552
Colorado	4,601,403	203	17,185	374
Connecticut	3,503,604	91	10,032	286
Delaware	830,364	17	4,720	568
Florida	17,397,161	946	123,754	711
Georgia	8,829,383	613	40,217	456
Hawaii	1,262,840	33	3,213	254
Idaho	1,393,262	30	3,412	245
Illinois	12,713,634	776	69,026	543
Indiana	6,237,569	316	2,294	325
Iowa	2,954,451	46	8,003	271
Kansas	2,735,502	123	10,245	375
Kentucky	4,145,922	236	10,152	245
Louisiana	4,515,770	574	28,844	639
Maine	1,317,253	18	1,364	104
Maryland	5,558,058	521	38,932	701
Massachusetts	6,416,505	169	29,437	459
Michigan	10,112,260	643	49,577	490
Minnesota	5,100,958	113	13,751	270
Mississippi	2,902,966	227	8,568	295
Missouri	5,754,618	354	28,226	491
Montana	926,865	30	2,723	294
Nebraska	1,747,214	40	5,393	309
Nevada	2,334,771	172	14,379	616
New Hampshire	1,299,500	18	2,170	167
New Jersey	8,698,879	392	30,943	356
New Mexico	1,903,289	169	13,081	687
New York	19,227,088	889	84,914	442
North Carolina	8,541,221	532	38,244	448
North Dakota	634,366	9	504	79
Ohio	11,459,011	517	39,163	342
Oklahoma	3,523,553	186	17,635	501
Oregon	3,594,586	90	10,324	298
Pennsylvania	12,406,292	650	50,998	411
Rhode Island	1,080,632	26	2,673	274
South Carolina	4,198,068	288	32,922	784
South Dakota	770,883	18	1,322	172
Tennessee	5,900,962	351	41,024	695
Texas	22,490,022	1,364	121,554	541
Utah	2,389,039	46	5,639	236
Vermont	621,394	16	696	112
Virginia	7,459,827	391	20,559	276
Washington	6,203,788	190	21,330	344
West Virginia	1,815,35	68	4,924	271
Wisconsin	5,509,026	154	11,548	210
Wyoming	506,929	11	1,163	230
Washington D.C.	553,523	198	7,590	1,371

Source: FBI 2004 Figures.

Crime In Other California Cities

City	Population	Violent Crimes*	Homicides
Anaheim	345,317	1,530	10
Bakersfield	274,162	1,948	23
Fresno	456,663	3,496	53
Huntington Beach	200,763	421	6
Riverside	285,537	1,777	17
Los Angeles	3,864,018	42,785	518
San Diego	1,294,032	6,774	62
Santa Ana	351,697	1,858	25
Santa Barbara	89,269	264	0

Source: Annual reports from FBI, 2004 data. Homicides include murders and non-negligent manslaughter.
*Number of violent crimes.

U.S. Crime

• In 2004, the FBI reports, 16,137 people were murdered in the U.S. Of these, the FBI was able to assemble data on 14,121. The following is based on these 14,121 deaths. Of them, 9,326 or 66 percent were shot, 1,866 stabbed, 663 beaten with a blunt instrument, 933 assaulted with feet, hands or fists, 11 poisoned, 15 drowned, 114 killed by fire and 155 strangled. Narcotics killed 76 and asphyxiation 105. In 856 homicides, weapons were not identified.

• Of total murdered, 10,990 were male, 3,099 female and 32 unknown.

• In murders involving guns, handguns accounted for 7,365 deaths, rifles 393, shotguns 507, and other guns or type unknown 1,161.

• Of the 14,121 murdered in 2004, the FBI said that 3,976 lost their lives in violence stemming from arguments or brawls. Next largest category was robberies, 988 homicides. Romantic triangles led to 97 homicides, narcotic drug laws 554, juvenile gang violence 804, gangland violence 95, rape 36, arson 28, baby-sitter-killing-child 17, burglary 77, prostitution 9, gambling 7.

• In 2004, there were 666 justifiable homicides in the U.S. — 437 by police officers, 229 by private citizens.

• In 1993, the U.S. recorded 24,526 homicides. There then began dramatic decreases. By the year 2000, total homicides numbered 15,586. Among possible reasons for decline: better emergency-trauma care, locking up more people, prosperity, more cops and according to the author of the book, "Freaknomics," abortions.

Subject Index

—A-B—

Academy of Sciences, 342
Agua Caliente, 190
Alcatraz, 342
Alexander Valley School District, 237
Angel Island, 342
Año Nuevo State Reserve, 342
Armstrong Redwoods, 342
Asian Art Museum, 341
Atherton, 74-75
Baby care, directory of, 301-306
Baby names, 29, 66, 140, 188
BART, 8, 367, 371
Bay Meadows Racetrack, 342
Bayshore Elementary School District, 226, 249
Bayview/Hunters Point, 25-26
Bellevue School District, 237, 254
Belmont, 76-77
Belmont-Redwood Shores Elementary School District, 226, 249
Belvedere, 143
Bennett Valley School District, 237, 254
Bernal Heights, 40, 43
Births, 302-303
Bodega Bay, 191
Bolinas, 144
Bolinas-Stinson School District, 234, 252
Boyes Hot Springs, 190
Brisbane, 78-79
Brisbane Elementary School District, 226, 249
Burlingame, 80-81
Burlingame Elementary School District, 226, 249

—C-D—

Cable Car Museum, 341
Cabrillo Unified School District, 226-227, 249
Caltrain, 266, 267
Carpooling, 371
Castro, The, 32
Catholic Schools, 288-289
China Basin, 49
Chinatown, 42-43
Cinnabar School District, 237, 254
Cloverdale, 192-193
Cloverdale School District, 237, 254
College Admissions, 262, 263, 264, 265, 271, 284-285, 287, 290, 291, 292
College Directory, 364-366
Colma, 82
Corte Madera, 145-146
Cotati, 194
Cotati-Rohnert Park School Dist., 237-238, 254
Cow Palace, 343
Coyote Point Beach Park & Museum, 343
Crime, 380-386
Crocker-Amazon, 31
Daly City, 83-85
Day care, directory of, 307-326
DeYoung Museum, 342
Diamond Heights, 56
Dixie Elem. School District, 234, 252
Dog and cat licensing and spaying, 346
Driver's Licensing, 346-347
Dunham Elem. School District, 238, 254

—E-F-G—

Earthquakes, 18, 347
East Palo Alto, 86-87
Education levels, 19, 71, 137, 185
El Granada, 109
El Verano, 190
Eureka Valley, 32
Excelsior-Portola, 34
Exploratorium, 343
Fairfax, 147
Ferry Services,
Fetters Hot Springs, 190
Filoli House & Garden, 343
Fisherman's Wharf, 343
Forest Hill, 35
Forestville, 195
Forestville School District, 238, 254
Fort Ross, 343
Fort Ross School District, 238
Foster City, 88-91
Geyserville, 195
Geyserville School District, 238
Glen Ellen, 196
Glen Park, 41
Golden Gate Bridge, 343
Golden Gate Park, 343
Golden Gate Transit, 372
Gravenstein School District, 238, 254
Greenbrae, 148
Grocery prices, 348-349
Guerneville, 197
Guerneville School District, 238, 254

—H-I-J—

Haas-Lilienthal House, 343
Haight-Ashbury, 36
Half Moon Bay, 92-93
Harmony School District, 238, 254
Hayes Valley, 37
Healdsburg, 198-199
Healdsburg School District, 238-239, 254
Hiller Aviation Museum, 343
Hillsborough, 94-95

Hillsborough City Elementary School District, 227, 249
History, 16-21, 67-72, 135-139, 181-187
Home prices, 48, 79, 89, 146, 169, 202, 210
Homicides, 380-386
Horicon School District, 239
Hospitals, directory of, 334-339
Housing, new, 359-363
Income, household, 16, 63, 184
Ingleside, 44
Inverness, 149
Jack London State Park, 343
Jefferson Elementary School District, 227, 249
Jefferson Union High School District, 228, 249
Jenner, 191
Junipero Serra County Park, 232

—K-L-M—

Kentfield, 150
Kentfield School District, 234, 252
Kenwood, 196
Kenwood School District, 239, 254
Lagunitas School District, 234, 252
La Honda, 96
La Honda-Pescadero Unified School District, 228, 249
Lakeshore, 38
Las Lomitas Elementary School District, 228, 249
Larkspur, 151-153
Larkspur School District, 234, 252
Liberty Elem. School District, 239, 254
Lucas Valley, 155

Luther Burbank Home & Gardens, 344
Marin City, 154
Marin Civic Center, 344
Marin Headlands, 344
Marinwood, 155
Marina, 45
Mark West School District, 239, 254
Menlo Park, 98-100
Menlo Park City Elementary School District, 228, 249-250
Mill Valley, 156-157
Mill Valley School District, 234, 252
Millbrae, 101-103
Millbrae Elementary School District, 228, 250
Mission Bay, 49
Mission District, 39
Mission Dolores, 344
Montara, 104
Monte Rio, 200
Monte Rio School District, 239
Monterey Bay Aquarium, 344
Moss Beach, 104
Mount Tamalpais, 130, 344
Muir Woods, 344
Muni, San Franciso (Municipal Railway), 368, 371-372
Museum of the African Diaspora, 342

—N-O-P—

National Maritime Park, 342
Nicasio, 158
Nicasio Elem. School District, 234
Nob Hill, 40
Noe Valley, 41
North Beach, 42-43
Novato, 159-162
Novato School District, 234-235, 252
Oak Grove School District, 239, 254

Oakland Athletics, 345
Occidental, 200
Ocean View, 44
Old Adobe School District, 239, 254
Olema, 149
Pacific Heights, 45
Pacifica, 105-106
Pacifica Elementary School District, 228-229, 250
Palace of the Legion of Honor, 342
Petaluma, 201-203, 344
Petaluma School Districts, 240, 254-255
Pigeon Point Lighthouse, 344
Piner-Olivet School Dist., 240, 255
Population, 8, 10, 59, 61, 132, 139, 179, 183, 207, 326
Portola Valley, 107-108
Portola Valley Elementary School District, 229, 250
Potrero Hill, 46
Presidential voting, 19, 20, 69, 133, 187
Presidio Heights, 45
Presidio, 47
Princeton, 109
Private Schools Directory, 295-300
Pt. Reyes Station, 149

—Q-R-S—

Rainfall, 376, 378-379
Ravenswood City Elementary School District, 229, 250
Reed School District, 235, 252
Redwood City, 110-114
Redwood City Elementary School District, 229-230, 250
Rents, 353-358
Richmond District, 48

Rincon Valley School Dist., 241, 255
River Rock Casino, 344
Rohnert Park, 204-207
Roseland School Dist., 241, 255
Ross, 163
Ross School District, 235, 252
Ross Valley School Dist., 235, 252
Russian Hill, 40
SamTrans, 371
San Anselmo, 164-165
San Bruno, 115-116
San Bruno Park Elementary School District, 230-231, 250
San Carlos, 117-118
San Carlos Elementary School District, 231, 250-251
San Francisco Forty-Niners, 345
San Francisco Giants, 49, 345
San Francisco Museum of Modern Art, 342
San Francisco Schools, 24-28, 30-34
San Francisco School Scores, 221-225, 245-248, 269-270
San Francisco Zoo, 344
San Geronimo, 166
San Mateo-Foster City Elementary School District, 231-232, 251
San Mateo Union High School District, 231-251
San Mateo, City of, 119-121
San Pedro Valley County Park, 232
San Quentin Prison, 171
San Rafael, 167-171
San Rafael School Districts, 235-236, 252
Santa Clara Valley Transportation Authority, 267

Santa Rosa, 208-211
Santa Rosa School Districts, 241-242, 255
SAT scores, 161, 162, 181-182, 258, 259, 260, 282-283
Sausalito, 172
Sausalito School Dist., 236, 252
School Accountability Report Card, 178, 278
School Districts, list of, 180, 278-281
School Rankings, 220-256
School registration, 170
Sea Ranch, 212
Seacliff, 48
Sears Point Raceway, 345
Sebastopol, 213-214
Sebastopol School District, 242, 255-256
Sequoia Union High School District, 232, 251
Shoreline School District, 236, 252-253
Shultz Museum, 342
Sonoma, City of, 215-216
Sonoma Coast, 345
Sonoma Valley School Dist., 242-243
South of Market, 49
South San Francisco, 122-125
South San Francisco Unified School District, 232-233, 251
St. Francis Wood, 35
Steinhart Aquarium,
Stinson Beach, 173
Strawberry Point, 175
Strybing Arboretum, 345
Sunset District, 52-53
—T-U-V—
Tamalpais School Dist., 236, 253

Taxes, 350-351
Temperatures, 374, 375, 379
Tenderloin, 54
Tiburon, 175-176
Tomales, 177
Treasure Island, 55
Turpen Aviation Library and Museum, 342
Twin Hills School Dist., 243, 256
Twin Peaks, 56
Two Rock School Dist., 243, 256
Unemployment Rates,
Upper Market, 31
Utilities, 352
Vehicle Registration, 346-347, 372
Visitacion Valley, 57
Voter registration, 68, 133, 346
—W-X-Y-Z—
Waugh School Dist., 243, 256
Weather, 373-379
Western Addition, 58
West Portal, 35
West Side School Dist., 243, 256
West Sonoma School Dist., 243-244, 256
Whale watching, 345
Wilmar School Dist., 244, 256
Windsor, 217-219
Windsor School Dist., 244, 256
Wine Country, 345
Woodacre, 166
Woodside, 126-127
Woodside Elementary School District, 233, 251
Wright School Dist., 244, 256
Yerba Buena Center, 345

BUY 10 OR MORE & SAVE!

If you order 10 or more books of any mix, price drops by about 50 percent.
1-800-222-3602. Or fill out form and send with check to:
McCormack's Guides, P.O. Box 190, Martinez, CA 94553. Or fax
order to (925) 228-7223. To order online go to www.mccormacks.com

1-800-222-3602

Next to title, write in number of copies ordered:

No.	McCormack's Guide	Single	Bulk
___	Alameda & Central Valley 2006	$13.95	$6.25
___	Contra Costa & Solano 2006	$13.95	$6.25
___	Orange County 2006	$13.95	$6.25
___	Greater Sacramento 2006	$13.95	$6.25
___	San Diego County 2006.	$13.95	$6.25
___	San Francisco, San Mateo, Marin, Sonoma 2006	$13.95	$6.25
___	Santa Clara & Santa Cruz 2006	$13.95	$6.25
___	How California Schools Work	$15.95	$6.25

Subtotal $ _____

CA sales tax (8.25%) _____

Shipping* _____

Total Amount of Order $ _____

*For orders of 10 or more, shipping is 60 cents per book. For orders of
fewer than 10, shipping is $4.50 for first book, $1.50 per book thereafter.

VISA MasterCard *Circle one: Check/Visa/MC/Am.Exp. or Bill Us*

Card No. _____ *Exp. Date* _____

Name _____

Company _____

Address _____

City _____ *State* _____ *Zip* _____

Phone: (_____) _____ Fax (_____) _____

The following guides are available online at www.mccormacks.com:
Los Angeles County 2006, Riverside County 2006, Ventura County 2006,
San Bernardino County 2006 and Santa Barbara County 2006.

☐ **Check here to receive advertising information**

Advertisers' Index

Developers

Signature Properties 360
Standard Pacific Homes 362

Information Services

DataQuick 97
Real Facts 358

Major Employers

Genencor .... Front Cover, 7

Realtors & Relocation Services

Don Diltz and Elaine Berlin White, Coldwell Banker 5
Mary Kay Yamamoto, Re/Max of Marin .... Inside Front Cover, 9, 131

Transit

SamTrans 370

To advertise in McCormack's Guides, call 1-800-222-3602